# Central America and the Caribbean

## development assistance abroad

# 1983

*A TAICH regional directory of U.S. nonprofit organizations in overseas development assistance*

Wynta Boynes
*Managing Editor*

Florence M. Lowenstein
Roger B. McClanahan
*Editors*

**taich** TECHNICAL ASSISTANCE INFORMATION CLEARING HOUSE
200 PARK AVENUE SOUTH, NEW YORK, NEW YORK 10003
AMERICAN COUNCIL OF VOLUNTARY AGENCIES FOR FOREIGN SERVICE, INC.

**CONTRIBUTING STAFF**

Word Processing:
David Chappel
Laura Hughes
Missault Lherisson
Fred Haight, Systems Manager

Shari Perretti, Editorial Assistant

ISBN 0-932140-03-3
ISSN 0740-0004

## AMERICAN COUNCIL OF VOLUNTARY AGENCIES FOR FOREIGN SERVICE, INC.

The American Council of Voluntary Agencies for Foreign Service was founded in November 1943, and incorporated in June 1944, to provide a professional forum for cooperation, joint planning and the exchange of ideas and information between voluntary agencies, governments and intergovernmental bodies. The Council is organized as a 49 member confederation of voluntary agencies and consortia and is supported by membership fees. Member agencies listed in the directory are identified by +.

The work is carried on primarily through functional committees. For other than purely administrative purposes and in addition to the Board of Directors and the Executive Committee, the Council has three standing committees dealing with areas of concern to the membership: the Committee on Development Assistance, the Committee on Material Resources and the Committee on Migration and Refugee Affairs.

Since 1955 the Council has operated the Technical Assistance Information Clearing House with support from the U.S. Agency for International Development. TAICH serves as an information center specializing in the socio-economic development programs abroad of U.S. voluntary agencies, church missions, foundations, an other nonprofit organizations. It makes available to organizations, government, researchers and others through publications and the maintenance of an inquiry service, current information about development assistance with particular reference to the resources and concerns of the private, nonprofit sector.

# CONTENTS

# INTRODUCTION

This first edition of **Central America and the Caribbean - Development Assistance Abroad** is the successor to a series of TAICH country reports and regional directories on the overseas development assistance programs of U.S. nonprofit organizations dating back to 1966 when TAICH published the first regional book. Over 80 countries have been covered in TAICH country reports. These are being supplanted by a new series of regional directories which provides program data for a variety of countries within a specific region.

A number of U.S. private, nonprofit organizations have been operating programs in Central America and the Caribbean for a long time; a rough average is around 16 years. Many of those which initiated program operations during the last century began with missionary endeavors as they attempted to address the effects of poverty and maldistribution of resources. Other organizations, expecially those which started programs in the last three decades in the region, have frequently done so with the sole purpose of providing specific kinds of development assistance.

More recently, both Central America and the Caribbean have been the focus of economic and political developments which has made the involvement of the private and voluntary community in the region of particular interest and importance. This directory serves as a guide to finding out which agencies provide what kinds of assistance in the 32 countries which make up the region. The format provides basic agency and program data to help facilitate cooperation among agencies and with other organizations, and includes indexes which lead the user directly to the information that he or she seeks.

A total of 267 organizations appears in the directory. These include voluntary agencies, foundations, religious organizations and other nonprofit organizations including affiliates and branches of business, labor and the cooperative sector. A total of 162 organizations are listed as operating programs and 105 as providing program support. It should be noted that the distinction between operating and support is somewhat arbitrary, but needed in indicating those organizations which conduct long-term programs with in-country offices and personnel. This differentiation between organizations is also useful in reviewing the program expenditures of these agencies.

Some 173 organizations reported program expenditures for 26 countries which totalled $130,836,909. This figure can be broken down geographically to show a total of $47,569,741 in program expenditures for the 18 countries in the Caribbean, $81,948,838 for the eight countries in Central America and $1,318,330 for programs carried out on a regional basis. These figures must be seen as the "tip of the iceberg" since many agencies were unable to identify their development program expenditures or break them out by country from their overall program costs.

Questionnaires were sent to organizations listed as providing program assistance in the region in the 1983 TAICH directory - **U.S. Nonprofit Organizations in Development Assistance Abroad**. The information given on each organization is based on the data supplied to us by the organization whether this was specially prepared in response to the questionnaire or derived by the editors from reports and promotional materials which the organization supplied. This information, as corrected and approved by the organization, has been accepted in good faith, without further investigation. Publication of the information does not guarantee accuracy of content or the endorsement of any organization by the American Council or TAICH.

Additional information regarding the organizations and programs included in this directory is available in the TAICH system. TAICH has on file information on specific program details including some data on agencies not appearing in this report for one reason or another but which are involved in providing development assistance in the region.

Appreciation is extended to the entire TAICH team for their assistance and cooperation during the compilation of this directory. The word processing operators who are responsible for the production of this book deserve praise for their patience and thorough work. A special note of thanks goes to all the staff of the agencies included, who gave their full cooperation in providing the requested information.

Wynta Boynes
Managing Editor

Florence M. Lowenstein
Roger B. McClanahan
Editors

First Edition
August 1983

# HOW TO USE THIS DIRECTORY

**PART I - Organization Profiles**

This section is an alphabetical listing of the U.S. nonprofit organizations included in this directory. Entries contain: agency address and telephone number, name and title of the agency executive, name and title of the regional program director, and a list of the countries of assistance. Those organizations which primarily provide support assistance are noted by an (S) for support and their entries in Part I include a general description of their overall program. In cases where an organization has both operating and support programs, a particular country of assistance is listed as operating (o) or support (s). An organization index to Part I appears at the end of the directory.

**PART II - Country Program Information**

This section contains country program data for those organizations which operate programs in the region. At the top right side of each entry is a code name and country code which is used in identifying organizations in the program activity index. Further information on the use of this index along with a list of the terms or types of program activities is found on pages 285-289.

To the extent to which organizations provided the appropriate information, entries include the following data:

1. **Name of organization**

2. **In-country contact name, address and telephone number**

3. **Program of assistance**
   A listing of terms (descriptors) which describe the nature of the assistance in that country.

4. **Personnel**
   Numbers of overseas personnel (U.S., local and international) involved in program of assistance.

5. **Program initiation**
   Date when organization started working in that country.

6. **Expenditures for FY (fiscal year) 1982**
   Program expenditures for development programs.

7. **Cooperating organizations**
   Governments and organizations which assist or cooperate with the program.

Where there is no name and address of contact, it can frequently be presumed that the program is administered from an organization's headquarters in the U.S. (see Part I). Often expenditures could not be broken out for individual countries because they were accounted for on a regional basis.

Each country listing is preceded by a brief summary which gives the total number of U.S. organizations listed in that country, and the expenditures for FY 1982 which were provided by some of the organizations. Support organizations are listed along with their program expenditures (when available) at the end of each set of country program data.

The asterik (*) before the name of an organization indicates that it is registered with the Agency for International Development. Registered organizations are eligible to apply for A.I.D. resources, including grants and participation in the U.S. Government overseas freight reimbursement, Food for Peace and Government-owned excess property programs. For a current list of registered agencies write to the Office of Private and Voluntary Cooperation, Bureau for Food for Peace and Voluntary Assistance, Agency for International Development, Washington, D.C. 20523.

The plus (+) indicates that an organization is a member of the American Council of Voluntary Agencies for Foreign Service, Inc.

### Indexes

The directory includes three basic indexes: a country index that lists all the organizations which provide assistance in a given country, including support organizations which are noted by an (s); a program activity index which uses a comprehensive listing of terms (descriptors) to identify organizations by their areas of assistance; and an organization index which includes the code names of all the organizations with page references to their entries in Part I of the directory.

### Appendix

The country code names which are used along with organization code names to identify programs in specific countries are found in the appendix.

# PART I -

## ORGANIZATION PROFILES

This section contains brief information about the organizations included in this directory.

Organizations are listed alphabetically. Those organizations which primarily provide support assistance are labeled (S) for support and their entries in Part I include a general description of their overall program.

In cases where an organization has both operating and support programs, a particular country of assistance is listed as operating (o) or support (s).

An organization index to Part I appears at the back of the directory.

* Registered with the U.S. Agency for International Development
+ Member of the American Council of Voluntary Agencies for Foreign Service

**A.T. INTERNATIONAL (S)**
1724 Massachusetts Avenue, N.W., Washington, D.C. 20036
(202) 861-2900

AGENCY EXECUTIVE: Ton de Wilde, Executive Director.

REGIONAL DIRECTOR: John G. Smith, Manager, Latin America and Caribbean.

Assists and financially supports indigenous organizations that carry out development projects that directly benefit the poor. These projects adapt technology to local skills and conditions in order to add value to local resources. Provides assistance for project planning, implementation, management and evaluation.

COUNTRIES OF ASSISTANCE: Barbados, Guatemala, Haiti, Jamaica, Nicaragua, regional (Caribbean).


**ACADEMY FOR EDUCATIONAL DEVELOPMENT**
1414 22nd Street, N.W., Washington, D.C. 20037
(202) 862-1900

AGENCY EXECUTIVE: Alvin C. Eurich, President.

REGIONAL DIRECTOR: Stephen F. Moseley, Director of International Division.

COUNTRY OF ASSISTANCE: Honduras.


\* **ACCION INTERNATIONAL/AITEC**
10-C Mount Auburn Street, Cambridge, Massachusetts 02138
(617) 492-4930

AGENCY EXECUTIVE: William W. Burrus, Executive Director.

REGIONAL DIRECTOR: Jeffrey Ashe, Director, PISCES (Program for Investment in the Small Capital Enterprise Sector) Project.

COUNTRIES OF ASSISTANCE: Costa Rica, Dominican Republic, Guatemala (s), Mexico.


**AFL-CIO (AMERICAN FEDERATION OF LABOR AND CONGRESS OF INDUSTRIAL ORGANIZATIONS)**
\* **American Institute for Free Labor Development (AIFLO)**
1015 20th Street, N.W., Washington, D.C. 20036
(202) 659-6300

AGENCY EXECUTIVE: William C. Doherty, Jr., Executive Director.

COUNTRIES OF ASSISTANCE: Barbados, Costa Rica, Dominican Republic, El Salvador, Guatemala, Honduras, Mexico, Panama, regional (Anguilla, Antigua, Bahamas, Barbados, Belize, Bermuda, Dominica, Grenada, Guyana, Haiti, Jamaica, Montserrat, Netherlands Antilles, St. Kitts - Nevis, St. Lucia, St. Vincent and the Grenadines, Suriname, Trinidad and Tobago, Turks and Caicos Islands).

**AFS INTERNATIONAL/INTERCULTURAL PROGRAMS** (S)
313 East 43rd Street, New York, New York  10017
(212) 661-4550

AGENCY EXECUTIVE:  William M. Dyal, Jr., President.

REGIONAL DIRECTOR:  Don Mohanlal, Vice President for Latin America, Canada,
Asia and the Pacific.

Administers intercultural learning program for high school students, teachers
and young workers spending a month to a year living with families and at-
tending school or language training courses in the United States and other
countries.

COUNTRIES OF ASSISTANCE (participating countries in 1981-82):  Barbados, Costa
Rica, Dominican Republic, Honduras, Jamaica, Mexico, Panama.


**SISTERS OF THE CONGREGATION OF ST. AGNES (C.S.A.)**
475 Gillett Street, Fond du Lac, Wisconsin  54935
(414) 923-2121

AGENCY EXECUTIVE:  Sister Judith Schmidt, C.S.A., Superior General.

COUNTRY OF ASSISTANCE:  Nicaragua.


\*   **AGRICULTURAL COOPERATIVE DEVELOPMENT INTERNATIONAL**
1012 14th Street N.W., Suite 201, Washington, D.C.  20005
(202) 638-4661

AGENCY EXECUTIVE:  Bartlett Harvey, Executive Vice President.

REGIONAL DIRECTOR:  Robert C. Flick, Project Officer/Latin America and
Caribbean.

COUNTRIES OF ASSISTANCE:  Guatemala, Guyana, Honduras, Jamaica.


\*   **AGUA DEL PUEBLO**
3421 M Street, N.W.  #333, Washington, D.C.  20007
(202) 483-2448

AGENCY EXECUTIVE:  Stephen B. Cox, Director.

COUNTRIES OF ASSISTANCE:  El Salvador, Guatemala (o), Honduras.


**AID FOR INTERNATIONAL MEDICINE, INC.**  (S)
1828 Wawaset Street, Wilmington, Delaware  19806
(302) 655-8290

AGENCY EXECUTIVE:  Dr. John M. Levinson, M.D., President.

Ships medical supplies and equipment, medical books and periodicals; funds hospitals; maintains volunteer physician program.

COUNTRY OF ASSISTANCE:  St. Lucia.


**AID TO ARTISANS, INC.  (S)**
64 Fairgreen Place, Chestnut Hill, Massachusetts  02167
(617) 277-7220

AGENCY EXECUTIVE:  James S. Plaut, President.

Provides funding and technical assistance to crafts programs in developing countries; assists in marketing crafts in the United States.  Provides small grants to craft producing communities for materials and equipment.  Beginning in 1982, small grants have been made to craft producing communities for the purpose of acquiring needed materials and equipment.

COUNTRIES OF ASSISTANCE:  Guatemala, Honduras, Nicaragua.


**AMERICAN BAPTIST CHURCHES IN THE USA**
**Board of International Ministries**
Valley Forge, Pennsylvania  19481
(215) 768-2000

AGENCY EXECUTIVE:  Rev. Chester J. Jump, Jr., Executive Secretary.

REGIONAL DIRECTOR:  Rev. Victor M. Mercado, Director for Latin America.

COUNTRIES OF ASSISTANCE:  Dominican Republic, El Salvador, Haiti, Mexico, Nicaragua.


\* **AMERICAN DENTISTS FOR FOREIGN SERVICE  (S)**
619 Church Avenue, Brooklyn, New York  11218
(212) 436-8686

AGENCY EXECUTIVE:  Dr. Herman Ivanhoe, President.

Ships used dental equipment to agencies, clinics and hospitals upon request.

COUNTRIES OF ASSISTANCE:  Antigua, Honduras, Mexico, Montserrat.


**AMERICAN FRIENDS OF CHILDREN, INC.**
172 Richard Place, Massapequa Park, New York  11762
(516) 541-8066

AGENCY EXECUTIVE:  Charles W. Coles, Vice President.

COUNTRY OF ASSISTANCE:  Guatemala.

**\*+  AMERICAN FRIENDS SERVICE COMMITTEE**
1501 Cherry Street, Philadelphia, Pennsylvania  19102
(215) 241-7000

REGIONAL DIRECTOR:  Corrine B. Johnson, International Division Secretary.

COUNTRIES OF ASSISTANCE:  Honduras, Mexico, regional.


**\*  AMERICAN LEPROSY MISSIONS, INC.**  (S)
1262 Broad Street, Bloomfield, New Jersey  07003
(201) 338-9197

AGENCY EXECUTIVE:  John R. Sams, Executive Director.

REGIONAL DIRECTOR:  Dr. Felton Ross, Medical Director.

Supports leprosaria and leprosy control programs by providing funds for construction of facilities, outpatient and mobile clinics, medical equipment and supplies, specialized training for medical personnel and rehabilitation.

COUNTRY OF ASSISTANCE:  Guyana.


**AMERICAN LUNG ASSOCIATION  (S)**
1740 Broadway, New York, New York  10019
(212) 245-8000

AGENCY EXECUTIVE:  James A. Swomley, Managing Director.

Provides funds to the International Union Against Tuberculosis for its activities to promote the fight against tuberculosis and respiratory diseases; there are voluntary national associations in 138 countries.

COUNTRIES OF ASSISTANCE:  Costa Rica, Cuba, El Salvador, Guatemala, Haiti, Honduras, Mexico, Nicaragua, Panama, Trinidad and Tobago.


**AMERICAN/MEXICAN MEDICAL FOUNDATION, INC.**
11019 Stanley Road, Minneapolis, Minnesota  55437
(612) 888-1351

AGENCY EXECUTIVE:  Dr. Roger A. Belisle, President and Chairman of Board.

COUNTRY OF ASSISTANCE:  Mexico.


**\*+  AMERICAN ORT FEDERATION, INC.**
817 Broadway, New York, New York  10003
(212) 677-4400

AGENCY EXECUTIVE:  Donald. H. Klein, Executive Vice President.

REGIONAL DIRECTOR:  Arlene B. Lear, Executive Officer of Technical Assistant.

COUNTRIES OF ASSISTANCE: Dominican Republic, Mexico.

**AMERICAN PUBLIC HEALTH ASSOCIATION (S)**
**International Health Programs**
1015 18th Street, N.W., Washington, D.C. 20005
(202) 789-5600

AGENCY EXECUTIVE: Dr. William H. McBeeth, Executive Director.

REGIONAL DIRECTOR: Dr. Susi Kessler, Director, International Health Programs.

Upon request of countries participating in A.I.D. programs provides short-term consultants in all aspects of health, family planning, water supply/sanitation and nutrition; supports the efforts of the University of West Indies and its member governments in training for health system design, planning and management.

COUNTRIES OF ASSISTANCE: Barbados, Costa Rica, Dominican Republic, Guatemala, Honduras, Jamaica, Panama, Trinidad and Tobago, regional (Caribbean).

**AMERICAN RED CROSS (S)**
17th and D Streets, N.W., Washington, D.C. 20006
(202) 737-8300

AGENCY EXECUTIVE: Richard F. Schubert, President.

REGIONAL DIRECTOR: Joseph P. Carniglia, Director, International Services.

Responds, to the extent possible, to appeals for assistance to Red Cross and Red Crescent Societies channeled through the League of Red Cross Societies and the International Committee of the Red Cross, both based in Geneva. Programs include disaster assistance, material aid and medical and social welfare programs.

**AMERICAN WOMEN'S HOSPITALS SERVICE**
**Committee of the American Medical Women's Association**
465 Grand Street, New York, New York 10002
(212) 533-5104

AGENCY EXECUTIVE: Nellys Bard, Administrative Director.

COUNTRY OF ASSISTANCE: Haiti.

**AMERICANS FOR INTERNATIONAL AID AND ADOPTION (S)**
460 North Woodward, Birmingham, Michigan 48011
(312) 645-2211

AGENCY EXECUTIVE: Nancy M. Fox, Executive Director.

Provides supplies and money for child care centers overseas.

COUNTRY OF ASSISTANCE: Guatemala.


**AMERICAS--HAND IN HAND**
P.O. Box 424, Billings, Montana   59103
(406) 245-7426

AGENCY EXECUTIVE:  Robert Hagstrom, Chairman of the Board.

COUNTRY OF ASSISTANCE:  Honduras.


**AMG INTERNATIONAL**
6815 Shallowford Road, Chattanooga, Tennessee   37421
(615) 894-6062

AGENCY EXECUTIVE:  Rev. Spiros Zodhiates, President.

REGIONAL DIRECTOR:  Louise Ebner, Mission Coordinator.

COUNTRIES OF ASSISTANCE:  Guatemala, Haiti, Nicaragua.


\* **AMIGOS DE LAS AMERICAS  (S)**
5618 Star Lane, Houston, Texas   77057
(713) 782-5290

AGENCY EXECUTIVE:  Dr. Richard Miller, Executive Director.

REGIONAL DIRECTOR:  John Sloan, Associate Director.

Sends volunteers who work with community members on public health programs including:  immunization, tuberculosis detection, dental hygiene, vision health, latrine and well construction, as well as animal health.

COUNTRIES OF ASSISTANCE:  Costa Rica, Dominican Republic, Honduras, Mexico, Panama.


**APROVECHO INSTITUTE  (S)**
442 Monroe Street, Eugene, Oregon   97402
(503) 683-2776

AGENCY EXECUTIVE:  Coordinator (position rotated).

Provides assistance to local people to develop fuel efficient cook stoves and other energy-saving devices.

COUNTRIES OF ASSISTANCE:  Guatemala, Mexico.

**ASSOCIATE REFORMED PRESBYTERIAN CHURCH**
**World Witness**
One Cleveland Street, Greenville, South Carolina  29641
(803) 232-8297

AGENCY EXECUTIVE:  John E. Mariner, Executive Secretary.

COUNTRY OF ASSISTANCE:  Mexico.


* **ASSOCIATION FOR VOLUNTARY STERILIZATION,INC.  (S)**
**International Project**
122 East 42nd Street, 18th floor, New York, New York  10168
(212) 573-8350

AGENCY EXECUTIVE:  Hugo Hoogenboom, Executive Director.

REGIONAL DIRECTOR:  Terrence Jezowski, Director of International Programs.

Provides grants for voluntary sterilization services; supports training of
medical personnel.

COUNTRIES OF ASSISTANCE:  Dominican Republic, Guatemala, Haiti, Honduras,
Jamaica, Mexico, Nicaragua, Panama.


**ASSOCIATION INTERNATIONALE DES ETUDIANTS EN SCIENCES ECONOMIQUES ET
COMMERCIALES (AIESEC-UNITED STATES)  (S)**
622 Third Avenue, 31st Floor, New York, New York  10017
(212) 687-1905

AGENCY EXECUTIVE:  Russ D. Gerson, President.

REGIONAL DIRECTOR:  Tom Beck, Director of Exchange.

As part of the International Association, and in cooperation with overseas
affiliates administers a bilateral exchange of student trainees in management,
economics and business at member colleges and universities.  AIESEC affiliates
are located in Mexico, Panama and Costa Rica.

COUNTRIES OF ASSISTANCE:  Costa Rica, Panama.


**BAPTIST MISSIONARY ASSOCIATION OF AMERICA**
721 Main Street, Little Rock, Arkansas  72201
(501) 376-6788

AGENCY EXECUTIVE:  James Schoenrock, Executive Director.

COUNTRIES OF ASSISTANCE:  Honduras, Mexico.


+ **BAPTIST WORLD AID  (S)**
1628 16th Street, N.W., Washington, D.C.  20009
(202) 265-5027

AGENCY EXECUTIVE: A.R. Goldie, Staff Executive.

As the funding agency for relief and development work of the Baptist World Alliance supports food-for-work programs; assists in construction and reha- bilitation of schools and housing; provides aid for schools; makes grants for agricultural projects; provides disaster relief; supports health programs.

COUNTRIES OF ASSISTANCE: El Salvador, Haiti, Nicaragua.


**BENEDICTINE FATHERS (O.S.B.)**
**Swiss-American Federation, Blue Cloud Abbey**
Marvin, South Dakota  57251
(605) 432-5528

AGENCY EXECUTIVE: Rt. Rev. Alan Berndt, O.S.B., Abbot.

COUNTRY OF ASSISTANCE: Guatemala.


**BENEDICTINE MONKS (O.S.B.)**
**Swiss-American Federation, St. Benedict's Abbey**
Benet Lake, Wisconsin  53102
(414) 396-4311

AGENCY EXECUTIVE: Rt. Rev. Robert Schoofs, O.S.B., President.

COUNTRY OF ASSISTANCE: Mexico.


**BEREAN MISSION, INC.**
3536 Russell Boulevard, St. Louis, Missouri  63104
(314) 773-0110

AGENCY EXECUTIVE: Rev. Donald E. Hurlbert, General Director.

COUNTRIES OF ASSISTANCE: Barbados, Dominica.


**BETHANY FELLOWSHIP, INC.**
6820 Auto Club Road, Minneapolis, Minnesota  55438
(612) 944-2121

AGENCY EXECUTIVE: Rev. T.A. Hegre, President.

REGIONAL DIRECTOR: Rev. Loren Garborg, Director, West Indies and Mexico Programs.

COUNTRIES OF ASSISTANCE: Dominican Republic, Mexico.

**BRETHREN IN CHRIST MISSIONS**
(Board for Missions of the Brethren in Christ Church)
P.O. Box 27, Mt. Joy, Pennsylvania  17552 - 0027
(717) 653-8067

AGENCY EXECUTIVE:  Dr. Donald R. Zook, Executive Secretary.

REGIONAL DIRECTOR:  Roy V. Sider, Secretary, Overseas Missions.

COUNTRY OF ASSISTANCE:  Nicaragua.


\* **BROTHER'S BROTHER FOUNDATION  (S)**
P.O. Box 6067, Pittsburgh, Pennsylvania  15211
(412) 431-1600

AGENCY EXECUTIVE:  Luke L. Hingson, Executive Director.

Assists mass immunizations campaigns; sends food and food supplements, seeds and farm tools, medical supplies and equipment, insecticides, teaching materials and books.

COUNTRIES OF ASSISTANCE:  Bahamas, Costa Rica, Dominican Republic, Grenada, Guatemala, Guyana, Haiti, Honduras, Jamaica, Nicaragua, St. Lucia, St. Vincent and the Grenadines.


**LA BUENA FE ASSOCIATION**
P.O. Box #2, Independence, Missouri  64051
(816) 836-4613

AGENCY EXECUTIVE:  James A. Christenson, President.

COUNTRIES OF ASSISTANCE:  Honduras, Mexico.


**CAM INTERNATIONAL**
8625 La Prada Drive, Dallas, Texas  75228

AGENCY EXECUTIVE:  Rev. Malon Collins, Executive Vice President.

COUNTRIES OF ASSISTANCE:  El Salvador, Guatemala, Honduras.


\*+ **CARE**
660 First Avenue, New York, New York  10016
(212) 686-3110

AGENCY EXECUTIVE:  Dr. Philip Johnston, Executive Director.

REGIONAL DIRECTOR:  Ray Rignall, Latin America Director.

COUNTRIES OF ASSISTANCE:  Belize, Costa Rica, Dominican Republic, Guatemala, Haiti, Honduras, Nicaragua, Panama.

\* **CARIBBEANA COUNCIL**
2016 O Street, N.W., Washington, D.C.   20036
(202) 775-1136

AGENCY EXECUTIVE:   Walker A. Williams, Executive Director.

COUNTRIES OF ASSISTANCE:   Regional (Antigua, Barbados, Dominica, Dominican
Republic, Jamaica, St. Lucia).

**CARNEGIE CORPORATION OF NEW YORK   (S)**
437 Madison Avenue, New York, New York   10022
(212) 371-3200

AGENCY EXECUTIVE:   David R. Hood, Director, International Program.

REGIONAL DIRECTOR:   Jill Sheffield, Program Associate.

Provides grants to former Commonwealth countries in the Caribbean.   Grants
include those for development of a national training program for primary
school teachers, university staff recruitment and development, educational
exchange programs, support for educational research reports, management
training and community-level programs for women, and production of a directory
for women in development-related graduate study in the United States.

COUNTRIES OF ASSISTANCE:   Barbados, regional.

**THE CARR FOUNDATION   (S)**
10350 Wyton Drive, Los Angeles, California   90024
(213) 272-1540

AGENCY EXECUTIVE:   Dr. Omar John Fareed, M.D., President and Medical Director.

Supports daily radio and TV broadcasts on a variety of medical and sanitation
related topics; supports medical programs through direct participation in
medical and laboratory work; arranges for shipments of equipment.

COUNTRIES OF ASSISTANCE:   Antigua, Belize, Costa Rica, El Salvador, Grenada,
Guatemala, Honduras, Mexico, Panama, St. Lucia, Trinidad and Tobago.

**CATHOLIC MEDICAL MISSION BOARD, INC.   (S)**
10 West 17th Street, New York, New York   10011

AGENCY EXECUTIVE:   Rev. Joseph J. Walter, S.J., Director.

Sends donated medical supplies and equipment to hospitals and other medical
facilities worldwide.

COUNTRIES OF ASSISTANCE:   Bahamas, Costa Rica, Dominican Republic, Guatemala,
Haiti, Honduras, Jamaica, Mexico, Panama.

**\*+  CATHOLIC RELIEF SERVICES -- UNITED STATES CATHOLIC CONFERENCE**
1011 First Avenue, New York, New York  10022
(212) 838-4700

AGENCY EXECUTIVE:  Lawrence E. Pezzullo, Executive Director.

REGIONAL DIRECTOR:  Dr. William Pruzensky, Director, Central America and Caribbean.

COUNTRIES OF ASSISTANCE:  Costa Rica, Dominican Republic, El Salvador, Guatemala, Haiti, Honduras, Jamaica, Mexico, Nicaragua, Panama, regional (Dominica, St. Lucia, St. Vincent and the Grenadines).


**CENTER FOR HUMAN SERVICES  (S)**
**Primary Care Institute**
5530 Wisconsin Avenue N.W., Chevy Chase, Maryland  20815
(301) 654-8338

AGENCY EXECUTIVE:  Dr. Stanley Scheyer, Director, Primary Care Institute.

Under a Cooperative Agreement with the Agency for International Development, operates Primary Health Care Operations Research project (PRICOR) which solicits, reviews and funds studies designed to help developing countries improve primary health care delivery.

COUNTRIES OF ASSISTANCE:  Dominica, Dominican Republic, Haiti, Honduras, Jamaica, Mexico.


**\*  THE CENTRE FOR DEVELOPMENT AND POPULATION ACTIVITIES  (S)**
1717 Massachusetts Avenue, N.W., Suite 202, Washington, D.C.  20036
(202) 667-1142

AGENCY EXECUTIVE:  Kaval Gulhati, President.

Conducts training programs in the U.S. which offer seminar-workshops on management, supervision and program evaluation for Third World family planning, and development health administrators.

COUNTRIES OF ASSISTANCE:  Costa Rica, Dominica, Dominican Republic, El Salvador, Guatemala, Haiti, Honduras, Jamaica, Mexico, Panama, Trinidad and Tobago.


**CHILDREN, INCORPORATED  (S)**
P.O. Box 5381, Richmond, Virginia  23220
(804) 359-4562

AGENCY EXECUTIVE:  Jeanne Clarke Wood, President and International Director.

REGIONAL DIRECTOR:  Elvia Mamani, Director, Latin America Operations.

Supports sponsorship programs by providing material assistance, food, medical supplies, clothing and educational supplies.

COUNTRIES OF ASSISTANCE: Costa Rica, Dominican Republic, El Salvador, Guatemala, Honduras, Mexico, Nicaragua.

**\*+ CHRISTIAN CHILDREN'S FUND, INC.**
P.O. Box 26511, Richmond, Virginia 23261
(804) 644-4654

AGENCY EXECUTIVE: Dr. James MacCracken, Executive Director.

REGIONAL DIRECTOR: J.C. Hostetler, Field Office Operations Manager.

COUNTRIES OF ASSISTANCE: Guatemala, Honduras, Mexico.

**CHRISTIAN CHURCH (DISCIPLES OF CHRIST), INC.**
**Division of Overseas Ministries**
P.O. Box 1986, Indianapolis, Indiana 46206
(317) 353-1491

AGENCY EXECUTIVE: Robert A. Thomas, President.

REGIONAL DIRECTOR: Judith Ann Douglas, Executive Secretary, Latin America and Caribbean.

COUNTRY OF ASSISTANCE: Mexico.

**CHRISTIAN FOUNDATION FOR CHILDREN**
13001 Wornall Road, Kansas City, Missouri 64145
(816) 941-9100

AGENCY EXECUTIVE: Robert K. Hentzen, President.

REGIONAL DIRECTOR: Jerry E. Tolle, Director, International Programs.

COUNTRIES OF ASSISTANCE: Belize, Dominican Republic, Guatemala, Honduras, Mexico.

**CHRISTIAN MEDICAL SOCIETY**
**Medical Group Missions**
P.O. Box 689, Richardson, Texas 75080
(214) 783-8384

AGENCY EXECUTIVE: Dr. Arden Almquist, General Director.

COUNTRY OF ASSISTANCE: Dominican Republic.

**CHRISTIAN NATIONALS' EVANGELISM COMMISSION, INC.**
P.O. Box 15025, San Jose, California 95115-0025
(408) 298-0965

**ERRATA**

<u>Central America and the Caribbean--Development Assistance Abroad, 1983</u>

P. 21, line 35:  "Eye Care International" should read "Eye Care, Inc."

PP. 289-310:  The program activities of Eye Care, Inc. should be indexed under Haiti by the code name "EYE CARE" <u>not</u> "INTL EYE."

P. 316, line 16:  "Eye Care International" should read "Eye Care, Inc."

AGENCY EXECUTIVE: Rev. Allen Finley, International President.

REGIONAL DIRECTOR: Philip J. Dempster, Vice President, Overseas Ministries.

COUNTRIES OF ASSISTANCE: Guatemala, Mexico.


**CHRISTIAN REFORMED WORLD MISSIONS**
2850 Kalamazoo Avenue, S.E., Grand Rapids, Michigan  49560
(616) 241-6568

AGENCY EXECUTIVE: Rev. Dr. Eugene Rubingh, Executive Secretary.

REGIONAL DIRECTOR: Rev. G. Bernaard Dokter, Latin American Secretary.

COUNTRY OF ASSISTANCE: Dominican Republic.


+ **CHRISTIAN REFORMED WORLD RELIEF COMMITTEE**
2850 Kalamazoo Avenue, S.E., Grand Rapids, Michigan  49560
(616) 241-1691

AGENCY EXECUTIVE: John de Haan, Executive Secretary.

REGIONAL DIRECTOR: Gary Nederveld, Director, Foreign Programs.

COUNTRIES OF ASSISTANCE: Costa Rica, Dominica, Dominican Republic, El Salvador, Guatemala, Haiti, Honduras, Mexico, Nicaragua.


**BROTHERS OF THE CHRISTIAN SCHOOLS (F.S.C.)**
**Christian Brothers Conference (Council on the Overseas Apostolate)**
100 De La Salle Drive, Romeoville, Illinois  60441
(815) 838-8900

AGENCY EXECUTIVE: Bro. Francis Huether, F.S.C., Overseas Executive Secretary.

COUNTRIES OF ASSISTANCE: Guatemala, Jamaica.


**CHURCH OF BIBLE UNDERSTANDING**
P.O. Box 841, Radio City Station, New York, New York  10019
(212) 246-4371

AGENCY EXECUTIVE: Stewart T. Traill, President.

REGIONAL DIRECTOR: Carol A. Tomme, Director, Overseas Programs.

COUNTRY OF ASSISTANCE: Haiti.

**CHURCH OF GOD, INC. (ANDERSON, INDIANA)**
**Missionary Board**
P.O. Box 2498, Anderson, Indiana  46018
(317) 642-0258

AGENCY EXECUTIVE:  Donald D. Johnson, Executive Secretary.

REGIONAL DIRECTOR:  Maurice Caldwell, Associate Secretary of the Missionary Board.

COUNTRIES OF ASSISTANCE:  Costa Rica, Panama.


**CHURCH OF GOD (HOLINESS)**
**Foreign Mission Board**
P.O. Box 4711, Overland Park, Kansas  66204
(913) 432-0303

AGENCY EXECUTIVE:  David H. Mauck, Executive Secretary.

COUNTRIES OF ASSISTANCE:  Haiti, Jamaica.


**CHURCH OF THE BRETHREN GENERAL BOARD  (S)**
**(World Ministries Commission)**
1451 Dundee Avenue, Elgin, Illinois  60120
(312) 742-5100

AGENCY EXECUTIVE:  Robert W. Neff, General Secretary.

REGIONAL DIRECTOR:  Merle Crouse, Latin American Representative.

Provides funding to indigenous organization for meals for street children; sends volunteers who assist refugees.

COUNTRIES OF ASSISTANCE:  Haiti, Honduras.


**CHURCH OF THE NAZARENE**
**Department of World Mission**
6401 The Paseo, Kansas City, Missouri  64131
(816) 333-7000

AGENCY EXECUTIVE:  Dr. L. Guy Nees, Executive Director.

REGIONAL DIRECTOR:  John Smee, Administrative Assistant, World Mission Division.

COUNTRIES OF ASSISTANCE:  Dominican Republic, Haiti.


*+  **CHURCH WORLD SERVICE**
475 Riverside Drive, New York, New York  10115-0050
(212) 870-2257

AGENCY EXECUTIVE:  Dr. Paul F. McCleary, Executive Director.

REGIONAL DIRECTOR:  Oscar Bolioli, Director, Central America, Caribbean, Latin America.

COUNTRIES OF ASSISTANCE:  Barbados, Costa Rica, Dominican Republic, Guatemala, Haiti, Honduras, Nicaragua, regional (Caribbean).


**CHURCHES OF GOD, GENERAL CONFERENCE**
**Commission on World Missions**
700 East Melrose Avenue, Findlay, Ohio   45840
(419) 424-1961

AGENCY EXECUTIVE:  Rev. W.S. Darrah, Chairman.

COUNTRY OF ASSISTANCE:  Haiti.


**CLARETIAN FATHERS (C.M.F.)**
**(Missionary Sons of the Immaculate Heart of Mary)**
**Eastern Province**
221 West Madison Street, Chicago, Illinois   60606
(312) 848-2076

AGENCY EXECUTIVE:  Rev. Martin Kirk, C.M.F., President.

REGIONAL DIRECTOR:  Rev. Richard Todd, C.M.F., Director of Overseas Programs.

COUNTRIES OF ASSISTANCE:  Guatemala (s), Honduras (s), Mexico, Panama.


**COMBONI MISSIONARIES OF THE HEART OF JESUS (M.C.C.J.)**
**(Verona Fathers)**
8108 Beechmont Avenue, Cincinnati, Ohio   45230
(513) 474-4997

AGENCY EXECUTIVE:  Rev. Charles Walter, M.C.C.J., Province Superior.

REGIONAL DIRECTOR:  Rev. Aurelio Cervantes, M.C.C.J., Missions Secretariat Director.

COUNTRIES OF ASSISTANCE:  Costa Rica, Mexico.


**COMBONI MISSIONARY SISTERS (C.M.S.)**
1307 Lakeside Avenue, Richmond, Virginia   23228
(804) 266-2975

AGENCY EXECUTIVE:  Sister M. Bernadette Hilmer, C.M.S., Regional Superior.

COUNTRY OF ASSISTANCE:  Mexico.

**COMPASSION INTERNATIONAL, INC.**
* **COMPASSION RELIEF AND DEVELOPMEMT (S)**
P.O. Box 7000, 3955 Cragwood Drive, Colorado Springs, Colarado  80933
(303) 594-9900

AGENCY EXECUTIVE:  Edward A. Kimball, Overseas Program Director, Compassion International.

REGIONAL DIRECTOR:  Paul Stubbs, North America Regional Director.

Provides assistance for needy children, their families and communities; aids victims of natural disasters.  Sponsors children in orphanges, hostels and family helper plans; assists disabled children.  Provides scholarships for children and medical services to sponsored children and their families; supports community-based health programs, including public health education, provision of basic health services and training of village level health workers; supplies donated medical supplies.

COUNTRIES OF ASSISTANCE:  Belize, Dominican Republic (o), El Salvador, Guatemala, Haiti (o), Honduras, Jamaica, Mexico, Nicaragua.


**CONCERN America**
1818-$\frac{1}{2}$ North Main Street, Santa Ana, California  92706
(714) 541-6119

AGENCY EXECUTIVE:  Marianne Loewe, President.

COUNTRIES OF ASSISTANCE:  Honduras, Mexico.


**CONSERVATIVE BAPTIST FOREIGN MISSION SOCIETY**
P.O. Box 5, Wheaton, Illinois  60189
(312) 665-1200

AGENCY EXECUTIVE:  Dr. Warren W. Webster, General Director.

REGIONAL DIRECTOR:  Arno Enns, Overseas Secretary, Europe and South America.

COUNTRIES OF ASSISTANCE:  Belize, Honduras.


**CONSERVATIVE MENNONITE BOARD OF MISSIONS AND CHARITIES, INC.**
9220 Rosedale-Milford Center Road, Irwin, Ohio  43029
(614) 857-1366

AGENCY EXECUTIVE:  David I. Miller, President.

COUNTRY OF ASSISTANCE:  Costa Rica.

**CONVENTUAL FRANCISCANS (O.F.M. Conv.)**
**Province of Our Lady of Consolation**
**Franciscan Mission Association**
322 West Street, Carey, Ohio  43316
(419) 396-7107

AGENCY EXECUTIVE:  Rev. Juniper Cummings, O.F.M. Conv., Executive Secretary.

COUNTRY OF ASSISTANCE:  Honduras.


\* **COOPERATIVE HOUSING FOUNDATION**
2501 M Street, N.W., Washington, D.C.  20037
(202) 887-0700

AGENCY EXECUTIVE:  Charles Dean, President.

REGIONAL DIRECTOR:  Ted Priftis, Vice President, Latin America and Caribbean.

COUNTRIES OF ASSISTANCE:  Belize, Dominican Republic, Guatemala, Honduras.


\* **THE COOPERATIVE LEAGUE OF THE USA**
**Cooperative League Fund, Inc.**
1828 L Street, N.W., Suite 1100, Washington, D.C.  20036
(202) 872-0550

AGENCY EXECUTIVE:  E. Morgan Williams, President.

COUNTRIES OF ASSISTANCE:  Costa Rica, Haiti, Honduras, Jamaica, Panama.


\*+ **COORDINATION IN DEVELOPMENT, INC. (CODEL)  (S)**
79 Madison Avenue, New York, New York  10016
(212) 685-2030

AGENCY EXECUTIVE:  Rev. Boyd Lowry, Executive Director.

REGIONAL DIRECTOR:  Kenneth Brown, Jr., Area Coordinator for Latin America and the Caribbean.

Serves as an ecumenical clearinghouse for the sharing of resources and techniques, and coordinates efforts of its 40 member agencies; sets up guidelines for ecumenical projects (Protestant and Roman Catholic cooperation imperative) and provides fund-raising assistance for a variety of member and other agency programs in the areas of agriculture, health and nutrition, non-formal education, community development and environmental planning.

COUNTRIES OF ASSISTANCE:  Dominican Republic, Guatemala, Honduras, Jamaica, Mexico, Nicaragua, regional.

\* **COUNCIL OF INTERNATIONAL PROGRAMS FOR YOUTH LEADERS AND SOCIAL WORKERS, INC. (S)**
1001 Huron Road, Room 209, Cleveland, Ohio 44115
(216) 861-5478

AGENCY EXECUTIVE: Dr. Thomas C. Hatcher, Secretary General.

In cooperation with the United States Government supports training program for social service professionals, special education teachers and youth workers between the ages of 23-40 from all parts of the world.

COUNTRIES OF ASSISTANCE (1982 participants): Bahamas, Barbados, Belize, Costa Rica, Dominica, Dominican Republic, El Salvador, Guatemala, Haiti, Jamaica, Martinique, Mexico, Netherlands Antilles, Panama, St. Lucia, St. Vincent and the Grenadines, Suriname, Trinidad and Tobago.


**COVENANT INTERNATIONAL FOUNDATION**
460 West 41st Street, New York, New York 10036
(212) 354-4323

AGENCY EXECUTIVE: Rev. Bruce Ritter, O.F.M., Executive Director.

COUNTRY OF ASSISTANCE: Guatemala.


**CSI MINISTRIES, INC.**
3808 North Locrest Street, Muncie, Indiana 47304
(312) 286-6711

AGENCY EXECUTIVE: Eddy Cline, Executive Director.

COUNTRIES OF ASSISTANCE: Haiti, Jamaica.


**CULTURAL SURVIVAL, INC. (S)**
11 Divinity Avenue, Cambridge, Massachusetts 02138
(617) 495-2562

AGENCY EXECUTIVE: David Maybury-Lewis, President.

Provides consultancy to international agencies and local planners on the ecological and social impact of economic development in areas inhabited by indigeous peoples.

COUNTRIES OF ASSISTANCE: Honduras, Mexico, Nicaragua, Panama.


**DARIEN BOOK AID PLAN, INC. (S)**
1926 Post Road, Darien, Connecticut 06820
(203) 655-2777

AGENCY EXECUTIVE: Mrs. Edward R. Tinsley, President.

Ships donated books and magazines as requested to libraries, colleges, schools, hospitals and other institutions.

COUNTRIES OF ASSISTANCE: Antigua, Bahamas, Barbados, Belize, Cayman Islands, Costa Rica, Dominica, Dominican Republic, El Salvador, Grenada, Guadeloupe, Guatemala, Guyana, Honduras, Jamaica, Martinique, Montserrat, Netherlands Antilles, Nicaragua, Panama, St. Kitts - Nevis, St. Lucia, St. Martin, St. Vincent and the Grenadines, Suriname, Trindad and Tobago, Turks and Caicos Islands.


**GEORGE DETELLIS EVANGELISTIC ASSOCIATION, INC.**
**New England World Missions**
P.O. Box 1126, Worcester, Massachusetts 01613
(617) 753-5817

AGENCY EXECUTIVE: Jeanne M. DeTellis, U.S. Director.

COUNTRY OF ASSISTANCE: Haiti.


* **DIRECT RELIEF INTERNATIONAL (S)**
P.O. Box 30820, Santa Barbara, California 73130
(805) 687-3694

AGENCY EXECUTIVE: Dennis G. Karzag, Executive Director.

Donates contributed medical supplies and equipment to needy health facilities, and for the care of refugees and victims of war and disaster; arranges over-seas assignments for volunteer medical personnel.

COUNTRIES OF ASSISTANCE: Dominica, Dominican Republic, El Salvador, Guate-mala, Haiti, Honduras, Jamaica, Mexico, Montserrat, Nicaragua, St. Lucia.


* **DOCARE INTERNATIONAL, INC.**
1750 N.E. 168th Street, North Miami, Florida 33162
(305) 949-4000

AGENCY EXECUTIVE: Robert Simmons, D.O., President.

COUNTRIES OF ASSISTANCE: Haiti, Mexico.


**DOMINICAN FATHERS (O.P.), ORDER OF PREACHERS**
**Province of the Holy Name of Jesus**
**Western Dominican Province**
**Dominican Mission Foundation**
2506 Pine Street, San Francisco, California 94115
(415) 931-2183

AGENCY EXECUTIVE: Rev. Joseph L. Asturias, O.P., Director.

COUNTRY OF ASSISTANCE: Mexico.

**DOMINICAN SISTERS (O.P.)**
**Congregation of St. Dominic**
Western Highway, Blauvelt, New York   10913
(914) 359-5600

AGENCY EXECUTIVE:  Sister Timothy Cunningham, O.P. Superior General.

COUNTRY OF ASSISTANCE:  Jamaica.


**EASTERN MENNONITE BOARD OF MISSIONS AND CHARITIES**
Oak Lane & Brandt Boulevard, Salunga, Pennsylvania   17538
(717) 898-2251

AGENCY EXECUTIVE:  Leon Stauffer, General Secretary.

REGIONAL DIRECTOR:  Millard Garrett, Associate Secretary, Overseas Ministries.

COUNTRIES OF ASSISTANCE:  Belize, Guatemala, Honduras.


**EDUCATION DEVELOPMENT CENTER  (S)**
55 Chapel Street, Newton, Massachusetts   02160
(617) 969-7100

AGENCY EXECUTIVE:  Malcolm Odell, Director of International Programs.

REGIONAL DIRECTOR:  Ron Israel, Project Manager, International Nutrition
Community Service.

Assists in planning, implementation and evaluation of nutrition programs;
helps strengthen the remedial import of nutrition education or maternal and
infant feeding problems.

COUNTRIES OF ASSISTANCE:  Dominican Republic, Guatemala, Haiti, Honduras,
Jamaica, Panama.


**EISENHOWER EXCHANGE FELLOWSHIPS, INC.  (S)**
256 South 16th Street, Philadelphia, Pennsylvania   19102
(215) 546-1738

AGENCY EXECUTIVE:  William R. Crawford, Executive Director.

Awards fellowships which provide three months of professional consultations,
visits and seminars in the U.S.

COUNTRY OF ASSISTANCE:  Jamaica.


**ENVIRONMENTAL RESEARCH PROJECTS  (S)**
P.O. Box 208, Narragansett, Rhode Island   02882
(401) 789-5133

AGENCY EXECUTIVE: Sandra T. Goodwin, Executive Director.

Designs informative and educational materials to improve marine literacy so as to increase community support and action for sustained use of Caribbean marine resources; designs vocational training programs for artisanal fisherman; conducts workshops on marine resource management techniques; carries out research and pilot/demonstration projects directed toward specific local resource management problems such as artificial reef development and mariculture systems; provides on-site training and short-term technical assistance to governmental agencies on data collection and evaluation.

COUNTRIES OF ASSISTANCE: Regional (Grenada, Montserrat, St. Kitts - Nevis, St. Lucia, St. Vincent and the Grenadines).

\*+ **THE EPISCOPAL CHURCH IN THE U.S.A.**
**The Domestic and Foreign Missionary Society**
**(including + The Presiding Bishop's Fund for World Relief)**
815 Second Avenue, New York, New York 10017
(212) 867-8400

AGENCY EXECUTIVE: Rt. Rev. John M. Allin, Presiding Bishop.

REGIONAL DIRECTOR: Rev. Samir J. Habiby, Executive Director, Presiding Bishop's Fund for World Relief.

COUNTRIES OF ASSISTANCE: Costa Rica, Dominican Republic, El Salvador, Guatemala, Haiti, Honduras, Mexico, Nicaragua, Panama.

**ERIE DIOCESAN MISSION OFFICE**
246 W. 10th Street, Erie, Pennsylvania 16501
(814) 459-3003

AGENCY EXECUTIVE: Sister Mary Sarah Rudy, S.S.J., Mission Program Coordinator.

COUNTRY OF ASSISTANCE: Mexico.

**EVANGELICAL MENNONITE CHURCH, INC.**
**Commission on Overseas Missions**
1420 Kerrway Court, Fort Wayne, Indiana 46805
(219) 423-3649

AGENCY EXECUTIVE: Rev. Gary Gates, President.

REGIONAL DIRECTOR: Rev. Andrew M. Rupp, Director of Overseas Missions.

COUNTRY OF ASSISTANCE: Dominican Republic.

\* **EYE CARE INTERNATIONAL**
523 8th Street S.E., Washington, D.C. 20003
(202) 544-4700

AGENCY EXECUTIVE:  E. Timothy Carroll, Executive Director.

COUNTRY OF ASSISTANCE:  Haiti.


**FAMILY HEALTH INTERNATIONAL  (S)**
Research Triangle Park, North Carolina  27709
(919) 549-0517

AGENCY EXECUTIVE:  Dr. Malcolm Potts, President.

Provides contraceptive research, information, training, technology and demographic research to speed diffusion of latest health care and family planning
techniques.

COUNTRIES OF ASSISTANCE:  Costa Rica, El Salvador, Guatemala, Haiti, Honduras,
Mexico, Panama.


**FAMILY PLANNING INTERNATIONAL ASSISTANCE  (S)**
\* **Planned Parenthood Federation of America, Inc.**
**International Division**
810 Seventh Avenue, New York, New York  10019
(212) 541-7800

AGENCY EXECUTIVE:  Daniel R. Weintraub, Vice President for International
Programs and Chief Operating Officer.

REGIONAL DIRECTOR:  Richard Pomeroy, Coordinator of Management Information.

In cooperation with the International Planned Parenthood Federation and other
groups provides financial support, commodities and technical assistance;
programs include integrated family planning services, income generating projects, production and distribution of educational materials, and training of
field workers.

COUNTRIES OF ASSISTANCE:  Barbados, Dominican Republic, Guatemala, Jamaica,
Mexico, Panama.


**FARALLONES INSTITUTE  (S)**
15290 Coleman Valley Road, Occidental, California  95465
(707) 874-3060

AGENCY EXECUTIVE:  Glen Price, Coordinator, International Programs.

Provides research, education and information on issues of renewable energy
sources, low-cost housing, water and waste recovery, health and nutrition,
food production and land and resource use planning, within the context of
cultural and social acceptability.

COUNTRIES OF ASSISTANCE:  Regional (Belize, Costa Rica, Dominican Republic,
Grenada, Guatemala, Haiti, Honduras, Nicaragua).

**FARM CENTERS INTERNATIONAL**
2375 Twining Road, Ukiah, California  95482
(707) 462-7930

AGENCY EXECUTIVE:  Howard H. Twining, President.

COUNTRY OF ASSISTANCE:  Mexico.

**FARMS INTERNATIONAL, INC.**
123 West 57th Street, New York, New York  10019
(212) 246-9692

AGENCY EXECUTIVE:  Gareth B. Miller, President and Director of Overseas Programs.

COUNTRY OF ASSISTANCE:  Haiti.

* **FOOD FOR THE HUNGRY INTERNATIONAL**
  **International Coordination Center**
  7729 East Greenway Road, Scottsdale, Arizona  85260
  (602) 998-3100

AGENCY EXECUTIVE:  Dr. Tetsunao Yamamori, President.

REGIONAL DIRECTOR:  Bernabe Manon, Area Director.

COUNTRIES OF ASSISTANCE:  Dominican Republic, Guatemala.

**THE FORD FOUNDATION  (S)**
320 East 43rd Street, New York, New York  10017
(212) 573-5000

AGENCY EXECUTIVE:  William D. Carmichael, Vice President, Developing Country Programs.

REGIONAL DIRECTOR:  Jeffrey M. Puryear, Program Officer.

Provides grants, mostly to institutions of higher learning in developing countries, particularly to foster education and research in agriculture, family planning, demography and the social sciences; makes grants to universities, research centers and foreign agencies for development planning and management.

COUNTRIES OF ASSISTANCE:  Barbados, Costa Rica, Cuba, Dominican Republic, Honduras, Jamaica, Mexico, Nicaragua.

* **FOSTER PARENTS PLAN**
  155 Plan Way, Warwick, Rhode Island  02887
  (401) 738-5600

AGENCY EXECUTIVE: George W. Ross, International Executive Director.

REGIONAL DIRECTORS: Alexander Gray, Central America Coordinator; Edward Tureotte, Caribbean Coordinator.

COUNTRIES OF ASSISTANCE: El Salvador, Guatemala, Haiti, Honduras, Nicaragua.

**FOUNDATION FOR HIS MINISTRY (S)**
P.O. Box 675, Garden Grove, California 92642
(714) 542-7223

AGENCY EXECUTIVE: David L. Taylor, Chairman of the Mexican Missions Committee.

Provides supplies for local schools and medical and dental facilities; provides food and clothing for migrant farm workers; operates orphanage which provides food, clothing, education and vocational training for homeless and needy children.

COUNTRY OF ASSISTANCE: Mexico.

**SISTERS OF ST. FRANCIS, CLINTON, IOWA (O.S.F.)**
**General Motherhouse**
**Mount St. Clare Convent**
Bluff & Springfield Drive, Clinton, Iowa 52732
(319) 242-7611

AGENCY EXECUTIVE: Sister Mary Smith, O.S.F., President.

COUNTRY OF ASSISTANCE: Bahamas.

**SCHOOL SISTERS OF ST. FRANCIS (O.S.F.)**
**General Motherhouse**
**St. Joseph Convent**
1501 South Layton Boulevard, Milwaukee, Wisconsin 53215
(414) 384-4105

AGENCY EXECUTIVE: Sister Lauretta Mather, O.S.F., President.

REGIONAL DIRECTOR: Sister Barbara Kraemer, O.S.F., Vice President.

COUNTRY OF ASSISTANCE: Honduras.

**SISTERS OF ST. FRANCIS OF THE PERPETUAL ADORATION (O.S.F.)**
**Province of the Immaculate Heart of Mary**
P.O. Box 766, Mishawaka, Indiana 46544
(219) 259-5427

AGENCY EXECUTIVE: Sister M. Theresa, O.S.F., Provincial.

COUNTRY OF ASSISTANCE: Honduras.


**FRANCISCAN FRIARS (O.F.M.)**
**Province of Santa Barbara, (Franciscan Friars of California)**
1500 34th Avenue, Oakland, California  94601
(415) 536-1266

AGENCY EXECUTIVE:  Very Rev. Louis Vitale, O.F.M., President.

REGIONAL DIRECTOR:  Rev. Cornelius Snyder, O.F.M., Procurator.

COUNTRY OF ASSISTANCE:  Mexico.


**FRANCISCAN FRIARS (O.F.M.)**
**Province of the Immaculate Conception, (Franciscan Missionary Union)**
147 Thompson Street, New York, New York  10012
(212) 674-5490

AGENCY EXECUTIVE:  Very Rev. Alban Montella, O.F.M., Provincial.

REGIONAL DIRECTOR:  Rev. Marion Cascino, O.F.M., Mission Promoter.

COUNTRIES OF ASSISTANCE:  El Salvador, Guatemala, Honduras.


**FRANCISCAN SISTERS OF ALLEGANY, N.Y. (O.S.F.)**
St. Elizabeth's Motherhouse, Allegany, New York  14706
(716) 373-0200

AGENCY EXECUTIVE:  Sister Mary Lourdes Donovan, O.S.F., President.

COUNTRY OF ASSISTANCE:  Jamaica.


**FREE METHODIST CHURCH OF NORTH AMERICA**
**General Missionary Board**
901 College Avenue, Winona Lake, Indiana  46590
(219) 267-6278/7656

AGENCY EXECUTIVE:  Dr. Charles D. Kirkpatrick, General Missionary Secretary.

REGIONAL DIRECTOR:  Elmone L. Clyde, Executive Assistant.

COUNTRIES OF ASSISTANCE:  Dominican Republic, Haiti, Mexico.


**FREEDOM HOUSE, INC.  (S)**
20 West 40th Street, New York, New York  10018
(212) 730-7744

AGENCY EXECUTIVE:  Leonard R. Sussman, Executive Director.

Distributes free books to developing countries in Asia, Africa and Latin America through the cooperation of Peace Corps Volunteers, voluntary agencies and local leaders and teachers within countries.

COUNTRIES OF ASSISTANCE: Antigua, Bahamas, Belize, Costa Rica, Dominica, St. Kitts - Nevis, St. Vincent and the Grenadines, Turks and Caicos Islands.


\* **FRIENDS OF CHILDREN, INC.**
14 Brookside Road, Darien, Connecticut 06820
(203) 655-2218

AGENCY EXECUTIVE: Constance Boll, Executive Director.

COUNTRIES OF ASSISTANCE: Guatemala, Haiti, Honduras.


**FRIENDS OF SOS CHILDREN'S VILLAGES, INC. (S)**
1170 Broadway, New York, New York 10001
(212) 686-0670

AGENCY EXECUTIVE: Arthur B. Dodge, Jr., President.

REGIONAL DIRECTOR: Elizabeth Shuman, Executive Secretary.

As the U.S. fund raising arm of SOS/Kinderdorf International, provides support for the maintenance, construction and enlargement of SOS Children's Villages which provide permanent homes for abandoned children. SOS villages are located in Costa Rica, Dominican Republic, El Salvador, Guatemala, Haiti, Honduras, Jamaica, Mexico, Nicaragua, Panama, Suriname.

COUNTRIES OF ASSISTANCE: Costa Rica, Dominican Republic, El Salvador, Guatemala, Haiti, Honduras, Jamaica, Mexico, Nicaragua, Panama, Suriname.


**FRIENDS OF THE THIRD WORLD, INC. (S)**
611 West Wayne Street, Fort Wayne, Indiana 46802
(212) 422-6821/1650

AGENCY EXECUTIVE: James F. Goetsch, Administration Coordinator.

Provides support for handicraft projects with emphasis on women's projects, cooperatives and community projects.

COUNTRIES OF ASSISTANCE: Guatemala, Haiti, Mexico.


**FRIENDS UNITED MEETING**
**Wider Ministries Commission**
101 Quaker Hill Drive, Richmond, Indiana 47374
(317) 962-7573

AGENCY EXECUTIVE: Kara Cole, General Secretary.

REGIONAL DIRECTOR:  A. Eldon Helm, Associate Secretary, Wider Ministries Commission.

COUNTRIES OF ASSISTANCE:  Belize, Jamaica.


**GENERAL CONFERENCE MENNONITE CHURCH**
**Commission on Overseas Mission**
P.O. Box 347, 722 Main Street, Newton, Kansas   67114
(316) 283-5100

AGENCY EXECUTIVE:  Erwin Rempel, Executive Secretary.

REGIONAL DIRECTOR:  Glendon Klaassen, Secretary for Latin America.

COUNTRY OF ASSISTANCE:  Mexico.


\*   **VICTORIA AND ALBERT GILDRED FOUNDATION FOR LATIN AMERICAN HEALTH AND EDUCATION**
1150 N.W. 14th Street, Suite 706, Miami, Florida   33136
(305) 547-2113

AGENCY EXECUTIVE:  Victoria Gildred, President.

REGIONAL DIRECTOR:  Dr. Edmund R. Ciaglia, Executive Director.

COUNTRY OF ASSISTANCE:  Dominican Republic.


\*   **GLOBAL OUTREACH**
P.O. Box 1, Tupelo,  Mississippi   38801
(601) 842-4615

AGENCY EXECUTIVE:  Sammy Simpson, Executive Director.

COUNTRIES OF ASSISTANCE:  Belize, Haiti, Honduras.


\*+  **GOODWILL INDUSTRIES OF AMERICA, INC.**
9200 Wisconsin Avenue, Bethesda, Maryland   26814
(310) 530-6500

AGENCY EXECUTIVE:  Robert B. Ransom, Director, International Department.

COUNTRIES OF ASSISTANCE:  Costa Rica, Jamaica, Panama.


**GOSPEL MISSIONARY UNION**
10000 North Oak, Kansas City, Missouri   64155
(816) 734-8500

AGENCY EXECUTIVE:  Rev. Dick L. Darr, President and General Director.

REGIONAL DIRECTOR:  Rev. Donald C. Palmer, Director of Field Ministries for Latin America.

COUNTRIES OF ASSISTANCE:  Bahamas, Belize, Panama.


**HABITAT FOR HUMANITY, INC.**
419 West Church Street, Americus, Georgia  31709
(912) 924-6935

AGENCY EXECUTIVE:  Millard Fuller, Executive Director.

REGIONAL DIRECTOR:  Robert W. Stevens, Director of Operations.

COUNTRIES OF ASSISTANCE:  Guatemala, Haiti.


*+  **HEIFER PROJECT INTERNATIONAL, INC.  (S)**
P.O. Box 808, 625 West 3rd Street, Little Rock, Arkansas  72201
(501) 376-6836

AGENCY EXECUTIVE:  Alden R. Hickman, Executive Director.

REGIONAL DIRECTOR:  Jerry Aaker, Program Director for Latin America.

Assists low-income/limited income farmers by providing livestock, poultry, and related agricultural services.  Special emphasis on practical training and local leadership; participants are selected on basis of need and each recipient agrees to return one or more offspring for another family in community. Works through indigenous groups including non-profit development groups, self-help cooperatives, rural church missions and agricultural schools, and when appropriate through government ministries for extension services and cross-breeding programs.

COUNTRIES OF ASSISTANCE:  Belize, Costa Rica, Dominica, Dominican Republic, Guatemala, Haiti, Honduras, Mexico, Panama, St. Vincent and the Grenadines.


*+  **HELEN KELLER INTERNATIONAL**
15 West 16th Street, New York, New York  10011
(212) 620-2100

AGENCY EXECUTIVE:  John H. Costello, Executive Director.

REGIONAL DIRECTOR:  Edward A. Glaeser, Director, Overseas Programs.

COUNTRY OF ASSISTANCE:  Haiti.


**HELP THE AGED  (S)**
1010 Vermont Avenue, Suite 712, Washington, D.C.  20005
(202) 638-5915

AGENCY EXECUTIVE:  Philip Jackson, Executive Director.

Help the Aged is an independent voluntary organization affiliated with Help the Aged organization in Britain, Canada and India (Helpage). Provides grants for self-help projects concerned with the longterm welfare of the elderly and for disaster relief assistance.

COUNTRIES OF ASSISTANCE: Honduras, Nicaragua.


\* **HERMANDAD, INC.**
85 Reid Avenue, Port Washington, New York   11050
(516) 767-2317

AGENCY EXECUTIVE: Christine Garofalo, Executive Director.

COUNTRY OF ASSISTANCE: Honduras.


**THE HESPERIAN FOUNDATION**
Project Piaxtla
P.O. Box 1692, Palo Alto, California   94302
(415) 327-4576

AGENCY EXECUTIVE: David Werner, President and Director.

REGIONAL DIRECTOR: Roberto Fojardo, Mexico Coordinator.

COUNTRY OF ASSISTANCE: Mexico.


\* **HIGH/SCOPE EDUCATIONAL RESEARCH FOUNDATION**
600 North River Street, Ypsilanti, Michigan   48197
(313) 485-2000

AGENCY EXECUTIVE: David D. Fisk, Director, High/Scope International Centers.

COUNTRY OF ASSISTANCE: St. Kitts - Nevis.


**HOGAR INFANTIL (ILLINOIS), INC.**
P.O. Box 18250, 1276 West Third Street, Suite 203, The Marion Building,
Cleveland, Ohio   44113
(216) 861-3756; 932-6967

AGENCY EXECUTIVE: Richard A. Bloomquist, President.

COUNTRY OF ASSISTANCE: Mexico.


**CONGREGATION OF THE SISTERS OF THE HOLY FAMILY (S.S.F.)**
General Motherhouse
6901 Chef Menteur Highway, New Orleans, Louisiana   70126
(504) 242-8315; 241-5400

AGENCY EXECUTIVE:  Mother M. Tekakwitha Vega, S.S.F., Superior General.

COUNTRY OF ASSISTANCE:  Belize.


* **HOLY LAND CHRISTIAN MISSION INTERNATIONAL**
**American Headquarters**
2000 East Red Bridge Road, Kansas City, Missouri  64131
(816) 942-2000

AGENCY EXECUTIVE:  R. Joseph Gripkey, President.

REGIONAL DIRECTOR:  Ted Smith, Vice President for International Operations.

COUNTRIES OF ASSISTANCE:  Dominican Republic, Guatemala, Honduras.


* **INSA**
**(International Nursing Services Association)**
P.O. Box 15086, 1712 Clifton Road, N.E., Atlanta, Georgia  30329
(404) 634-5748

AGENCY EXECUTIVE:  James A. Brinks, Administrative Director.

REGIONAL DIRECTOR:  Robin C. Haines, R.N., M.M., Director of Program
Development.

COUNTRY OF ASSISTANCE:  Haiti.


* **INSTITUTE FOR INTERNATIONAL DEVELOPMENT, INC.**
360 Maple Avenue, West, Suite F, Vienna, Virginia  22180
(703) 281-5040

AGENCY EXECUTIVE:  Barry C. Harper, Executive Director.

COUNTRIES OF ASSISTANCE:  Costa Rica, Dominican Republic, Honduras.


* **INSTITUTE OF CULTURAL AFFAIRS**
4750 North Sheridan Road, Chicago, Illinois  60640
(312) 769-5635

AGENCY EXECUTIVE:  Frank F. Hillard, Management Director.

COUNTRIES OF ASSISTANCE:  Guatemala, Jamaica.


* **INSTITUTE OF INTERNATIONAL EDUCATION**
809 United Nations Plaza, New York, New York  10017
(212) 883-8200

AGENCY EXECUTIVE:  Wallace B. Edgerton, President.

REGIONAL DIRECTOR: Edwin Battle, Executive Assistant to the President.

COUNTRY OF ASSISTANCE: Mexico.


**INTER-AID INC. (S)**
P.O. Box 250, Camarillo, California 93011
(805) 987-8888

AGENCY EXECUTIVE: Rev. L. Joseph Bass, President.

REGIONAL DIRECTOR: Moises Medina, Central American Coordinator.

Provides medical supplies, clothing and other material assistance to refugees and displaced persons.

COUNTRIES OF ASSISTANCE: El Salvador, Guatemala, Honduras.


\* **INTER-AMERICAN DEVELOPMENT INSTITUTE (S)**
1789 Columbia Road, N.W., Washington, D.C. 20009
(202) 483-0491

AGENCY EXECUTIVE: Marina Fanning-Firfer, Executive Director.

Supports, designs and implements multi-purpose programs in literacy, health, nutrition, santitation, agriculture, leadership training, family life education, and crafts and basic skills training.

COUNTRIES OF ASSISTANCE: Regional program (Costa Rica, Mexico, Panama).


**INTERCHURCH MEDICAL ASSISTANCE, INC. (S)**
P.O. Box 429, New Windsor, Maryland 21776
(301) 635-6474

AGENCY EXECUTIVE: Dr. William Eugene Grubbs, Executive Director.

Collects and distributes medical supplies for the overseas programs of U.S. Protestant churches; provides disaster relief.

COUNTRIES OF ASSISTANCE: Belize, Dominican Republic, El Salvador, Guatemala, Guyana, Haiti, Honduras, Jamaica, Nicaragua, Panama.


**INTERMEDIA**
**Division of Overseas Ministries**
**National Council of Churches of Christ**
**in the U.S.A.**
475 Riverside Drive, Suite 670, New York, New York 10015
(212) 870-2376

AGENCY EXECUTIVE: Rev. David Bridell, Director

COUNTRIES OF ASSISTANCE: Costa Rica, Haiti, Mexico.


**INTERNATIONAL ADOPTIONS, INC.** (S)
218 Walnut Street, Newton, Massachusetts  02160
(617) 965-2320

AGENCY EXECUTIVE: Phyllis Loewenstein, Executive Director.

Sends donated money, clothing, medical equipment and medicines for orphans; arranges intercountry adoptions.

COUNTRIES OF ASSISTANCE: Dominican Republic, Guatemala.


**INTERNATIONAL AGRICULTURAL DEVELOPMENT SERVICE** (S)
1611 N. Kent Street, Arlington, Virginia  22209
(703) 525-9430

AGENCY EXECUTIVE: Dr. A. Colin McClung, Executive Officer.

REGIONAL DIRECTOR: Dr. Jerome H. Maner, Program Officer for Latin America
   and Caribbean.

Provides services which developing countries request to achieve increased agricultural productivity and rural prosperity; to establish local institutions and train the personnel required for sustained progress; and provide a range of agricultural planning, research, training, and implementing and logistical services, to assist countries in achieving self-sufficiency in agricultural production to the greatest extent possible.

COUNTRIES OF ASSISTANCE: Belize, Dominican Republic, Honduras, Jamaica.


**INTERNATIONAL BOOK PROJECT, INC.** (S)
17 Mentelle Park, Lexington, Kentucky  40502
(606) 266-1407

AGENCY EXECUTIVE: Harriet D. Van Meter, Executive Director.

Sends books, textbooks, professional journals and audiovisual materials to schools, libraries and other institutions. Half of this program is person to person.

COUNTRIES OF ASSISTANCE: Antigua, Belize, Costa Rica, Dominica, Haiti, Jamaica, Mexico, Montserrat.


**INTERNATIONAL CENTER FOR RESEARCH ON WOMEN** (S)
1010 16th Street, N.W., 3rd Floor, Washington, D.C.  20036
(202) 293-3154

AGENCY EXECUTIVE: Mayra Buvinic, Director.

Provides technical assistance in the design and evaluation of projects which incorporate women into the development process; organizes work shops, seminars and supports an international fellows program.

COUNTRY OF ASSISTANCE: Panama.


**INTERNATIONAL CHILD CARE (USA), INC.**
P.O. Box 2645, Toledo, Ohio  43606
(419) 472-7470

AGENCY EXECUTIVE:  Harold F. Detweiler, President.

COUNTRY OF ASSISTANCE:  Haiti.


**INTERNATIONAL COMMUNITY FOR THE RELIEF OF STARVATION AND SUFFERING (ICROSS)**
P.O. Box 1649, Southampton, New York  11768
(516) 283-2430

AGENCY EXECUTIVE:  Kenneth B. Cairns, M.D., Director.

COUNTRY OF ASSISTANCE:  Jamaica


\*  **INTERNATIONAL EXECUTIVE SERVICE CORPS  (S)**
P.O. Box 10005, 8 Stamford Forum, Stamford, Connecticut  06904-2005
(203) 967-6000

AGENCY EXECUTIVE:  Thomas S. Carroll, President.

Recruits experienced executives (often retired) for short-term assignments abroad as volunteer advisors to locally-owned firms that request managerial or technical assistance.

COUNTRIES OF ASSISTANCE:  Barbados, Belize, Costa Rica, Dominica, Dominica Republic, El Salvador, Guatemala, Haiti, Honduras, Jamaica, Mexico, Nicaragua, Panama, St. Lucia, Trinidad and Tobago.


\*  **INTERNATIONAL EYE FOUNDATION**
7801 Norfolk Avenue, Bethesda, Maryland  20814
(301) 986-1830

AGENCY EXECUTIVE:  Robert H. Meaders, M.D., Medical Director.

COUNTRIES OF ASSISTANCE:  Barbados, Dominican Republic, Honduras, Montserrat, St. Lucia,  regional (Caribbean).


\*  **INTERNATIONAL INSTITUTE OF RURAL RECONSTRUCTION**
1775 Broadway, New York, New York  10019
(212) 245-2680

AGENCY EXECUTIVE: Ping-sheng Chin, Vice President.

COUNTRY OF ASSISTANCE: Guatemala.


**INTERNATIONAL LIAISON, INC.** **(S)**
**U.S. Catholic Coordinating Center for Lay Volunteer Ministries**
1234 Massachusetts Avenue, N.W., Washington, D.C.  20005
(202) 638-4197

AGENCY EXECUTIVE: David J. Suley, Executive Director.

Fills requests from overseas missions and agencies for lay personnel who have expertise in development.

COUNTRIES OF ASSISTANCE:  Bahamas, Dominican Republic, Guatemala, Haiti, Jamaica, Trinidad and Tobago.


**INTERNATIONAL LIFELINE, INC.**
P.O. Box 32714, 4520 36th Street, N.W., Oklahoma City, Oklahoma
(405) 728-2828

AGENCY EXECUTIVE: Dr. Robert E. Watkins, Executive Director.

COUNTRY OF ASSISTANCE: Haiti.


**INTERNATIONAL PROJECTS ASSISTANCE SERVICES** **(S)**
P.O. Box 100, Carrboro, North Carolina  27510
(919) 967-7052

AGENCY EXECUTIVE: Edward N. Meldahl, Executive Director.

REGIONAL DIRECTOR: Elra Gaza-Hazel, Program Coordinator for Latin America.

Provides technical assistance, loan funds and equipment for abortion and sterilization services; trains medical personnel in surgical family planning techniques.

COUNTRIES OF ASSISTANCE: Honduras, Mexico.


**INTERNATIONAL ROAD FEDERATION** **(S)**
525 School Street, S.W., Washington, D.C.  20024
(202) 554-2106

AGENCY EXECUTIVE: W.G. Wilson, President.

Promotes international exchange of engineering and technical knowledge in the highway field through its research and development program; acts as consultant to private enterprises, governments and intergovernmental organizations;

publishes and distributes information on benefits of good roads; establishes training schools for operators and mechanics of construction equipment; provides scholarships for graduate study for engineers in the United States.

COUNTRIES OF ASSISTANCE:  El Salvador, Jamaica, Mexico.


\* **INTERNATIONAL VOLUNTARY SERVICES, INC.**
1424 16th Street, N.W., Suite 504, Washington, D.C.   20036
(202) 387-5533

AGENCY EXECUTIVE:  Nan Borton, Executive Director.

REGIONAL DIRECTOR:  Heather Clark, Latin America Program Officer.

COUNTRY OF ASSISTANCE:  Honduras.


**INTERPLAST, INC.  (S)**
378-J Cambridge Avenue, Palo Alto, California  94306
(415) 329-0670

AGENCY EXECUTIVE:  Mary Cottrell, Executive Director.

Sends teams of volunteer surgeons, anesthesiologists, pediatricians and nurses to developing countries to provide reconstructive surgery for severe burns, congenital defects and other crippling injuries; helps train host country professionals.   Children requiring multiple surgeries are brought to the U.S. for treatment.

COUNTRIES OF ASSISTANCE:  Honduras, Jamaica, Mexico.


**IRI RESEARCH INSTITUTE, INC.**
One Rockefeller Plaza, Room 1401, New York, New York   10020
(212) 581-1942

AGENCY EXECUTIVE:  Jerome F. Harrington, President.

COUNTRY OF ASSISTANCE:  Guyana.


**ISLAND RESOURCES FOUNDATION  (S)**
P.O. Box 33, Red Hook Center, U.S. Virgin Islands   00802
(809) 775-3225

AGENCY EXECUTIVE:  Edward L. Towle, President and Executive Director.

Assists small island communities in finding appropriate development strategies which combine low-level technology, limited existing resources and traditional skills into workable development plans involving community participation in definition of goals.

COUNTRIES OF ASSISTANCE: Regional (Anguilla, Antigua, Barbados, Cayman Islands, Dominica, Dominican Republic, Grenada, Jamaica, Montserrat, Netherlands Antilles, St. Kitts - Nevis, St. Lucia, St. Vincent and the Grenadines, Trinidad and Tobago, Turks and Caicos Islands.


**JESUIT FATHERS AND BROTHERS (S.J.)**
**(Society of Jesus) Jesuit Missions, Inc.**
1717 Massachusetts Avenue, N.W. #402, Washington, D.C.   20036
(202) 387-3720

AGENCY EXECUTIVE: Rev. Simon E. Smith, S.J., Executive Secretary, Jesuit Missions.

COUNTRY OF ASSISTANCE: Jamaica.


**SISTERS OF ST. JOSEPH (C.S.J.)**
**Rockville Centre Diocese**
St. Joseph Convent, Brentwood, New York   11717
(516) 273-4531

AGENCY EXECUTIVE: Sister John Raymond, C.S.J., General Superior.

COUNTRY OF ASSISTANCE: Dominican Republic.


**SISTERS OF ST. JOSEPH (C.S.J.)**
**Salina Diocese, Nazareth Motherhouse and Novitiate**
13th and Washington, Concordia, Kansas   66901
(913) 243-2113

AGENCY EXECUTIVE: Sister Bette Moslander, C.S.J., President.

REGIONAL DIRECTOR: Sister Margarida Boucher, C.S.J., Director of Mission Development.

COUNTRY OF ASSISTANCE: Mexico.


**ST. JUDE EXPRESS, INC.**
P.O. Box 5333, 1320 Truman, Albuquerque, New Mexico   87108
(505) 268-5051

AGENCY EXECUTIVE: Gregory W. Donohue, President.

COUNTRY OF ASSISTANCE: Mexico.


**W. K. KELLOGG FOUNDATION  (S)**
400 North Avenue, Battle Creek, Michigan   49016
(616) 968-1611

AGENCY EXECUTIVE: Robert D. Sparks, Chairman of the Board and Chief
Programming Officer.

REGIONAL DIRECTOR: Dr. Marion M. Chaves, Latin America Program Director.

Provides seed money for pilot demonstrations in the areas of agriculture,
education and, especially, health. Helps develop comprehensive health education, including graduate study.

COUNTRIES OF ASSISTANCE: Bermuda, Costa Rica, Dominican Republic, Guatemala,
Jamaica, Mexico, Panama, St. Lucia.

* **LAUBACH LITERACY INTERNATIONAL**
P.O. Box 131, 1320 Jamesville Avenue, Syracuse, New York  13210
(315) 422-9121

AGENCY EXECUTIVE: Robert F. Caswell, President.

COUNTRIES OF ASSISTANCE: Mexico, Panama.

**LEAGUE FOR INTERNATIONAL FOOD EDUCATION  (S)**
915 15th Street, N.W., Room 915, Washington, D.C.  20005
(202) 331-1658

AGENCY EXECUTIVE: Dr. Mahlon A. Burnette, III, Executive Director.

Under contract to the U.S. Agency for International Development provides
volunteer technical advisers who provide information on food, including processing and marketing, and nutrition; sponsors workshops and conferences on
food and nutrition.  Provides these services throughout Central America and
the Caribbean.

COUNTRIES OF ASSISTANCE: Regional.

* **LA LECHE LEAGUE INTERNATIONAL**
9616 Minneapolis Avenue, Franklin Park, Illinois  60131
(312) 455-7730

AGENCY EXECUTIVE: Betty Wagner, Chief Executive Officer.

REGIONAL DIRECTOR: Norma Jane Bumgarner, Regional Administrator, Latin
America and Caribbean.

COUNTRIES OF ASSISTANCE: Bahamas, Barbados, Cayman Islands, Costa Rica, El
Salvador, Guatemala, Haiti, Honduras, Mexico, Panama.

**LIONS CLUBS INTERNATIONAL  (S)**
**International Association of Lions Clubs**
300 22nd Street, Oak Brook, Illinois  60570
(312) 986-1700

David Livingston Missionary Foundation, Inc.--**Part I**

AGENCY EXECUTIVE: Roy Schaetzel, Executive Administrator.

REGIONAL DIRECTOR: Robert Cywinski, Manager, Program Development.

Provides disaster assistance and vocational training; supports medical and rehabilitation programs; funds agricultural programs and cottage industries.

COUNTRIES OF ASSISTANCE: Antigua, Bahamas, Barbados, Belize, Bermuda, Cayman Islands, Costa Rica, Dominica, Dominican Republic, El Salvador, Grenada, Guadeloupe, Guatemala, Guyana, Haiti, Honduras, Jamaica, Martinique, Mexico, Netherlands Antilles, Nicaragua, Panama, St. Lucia, St. Vincent and the Grenadines, Suriname, Trinidad and Tobago, Turks and Caicos Islands.


**DAVID LIVINGSTONE MISSIONARY FOUNDATION, INC.** (S)
P.O. Box 232, 5115 South Utica, Tulsa, Oklahoma  74105
(918) 749-9902

AGENCY EXECUTIVE: Lonnie Rex, President.

Provides food, clothing, shelter, medical supplies and other material assistance to orphanges and emergency/disaster areas.

COUNTRIES OF ASSISTANCE: Haiti, Mexico, Suriname.


**LUTHERAN CHURCH IN AMERICA** (S)
**Division for World Mission and Ecumenism**
231 Madison Avenue, New York, New York  10016
(212) 696-6700

AGENCY EXECUTIVE: Dr. Gerald E. Currens, Executive Director.

REGIONAL DIRECTOR: Rev. James Henneberger, Director, Latin America and Caribbean

Assists rural and urban self-help and leadership training programs, schools, colleges and universities, and scholarship and exchange programs, teacher training and basic education; assists agricultural programs; funds public health programs and a variety of medical institutions, and training for medical personnel.

COUNTRY OF ASSISTANCE: Guyana.


**THE LUTHERAN CHURCH-MISSOURI SYNOD** (S)
**Board for Social Ministry Services**
1333 South Kirkwood Road, St. Louis, Missouri  63122
(314) 965-9000

AGENCY EXECUTIVE: Rev. Melvin E. Witt, Secretary, World Relief.

Provides grants through indigenous churches for ongoing relief, rehabilitation, reconstruction, health care, clothing and self-help development projects administered by parallel relief agencies.

COUNTRIES OF ASSISTANCE:  El Salvador, Jamaica.


**\*+  LUTHERAN WORLD RELIEF, INC.**
360 Park Avenue South, New York, New York  10010
(212) 532-6350

AGENCY EXECUTIVE:  Norman E. Barth, Executive Director.

REGIONAL DIRECTOR:  Dr. J. Robert Busche, Assistant Executive Director.

COUNTRIES OF ASSISTANCE:  Costa Rica, Guatemala, Honduras, Nicaragua.


**MANAGEMENT SCIENCES FOR HEALTH  (S)**
141 Tremont Street, Boston, Massachusetts  02111
(617) 482-9450

AGENCY EXECUTIVE:  Dr. Ronald O'Connor, President.


Provides technical consultancy services for rural health programs on a short
and long-term basis in the following areas:  planning and evaluation; training
and manpower development; and management support for program operations,
including information systems, financial management, logistics and supervisory
systems.  Has undertaken applied research on topics including rehydration,
development of logical flow charts to guide paramedical decision-making, solar
energy technology, pharmaceutical procurement and utilization processes, and
village health services, expenditures and epidemiology.

COUNTRIES OF ASSISTANCE:  Barbados, Dominica, Dominican Republic, Guatemala,
Haiti (o), Honduras (o), Jamaica, Mexico, St. Kitts - Nevis, St. Lucia, St.
Vincent and the Grenadines.


**\*+  MAP INTERNATIONAL  (S)**
P.O. Box 50, 327 Gunderson Drive, Carol Stream, Illinois  60187
(312) 653-6010

AGENCY EXECUTIVE:  Larry Dixon, President.

REGIONAL DIRECTOR:  Calvin S. Williams, Director of Program.

Distributes medical supplies and equipment to Christian medical installations;
provides disaster relief; grants fellowships for medical students to work in
mission hospitals; assists in design and evaluation of community development
projects.

COUNTRIES OF ASSISTANCE:  Belize, Costa Rica, Dominican Republic, Guatemala,
Haiti, Honduras, Jamaica, Mexico, Panama.

**MARIST MISSIONARY SISTERS**
**(MISSIONARY SISTERS OF THE SOCIETY OF MARY, INC.)**
**(S.M.S.M.)**
357 Grove Street, Waltham, Massachusetts  02154
(617) 893-0149

AGENCY EXECUTIVE:  Sister M. Elizabeth Bonia, S.M.S.M., Provincial.

COUNTRY OF ASSISTANCE:  Jamaica.


**SOCIETY OF MARY (S.M.)**
**(Marianists--Brothers of Mary), Province of St. Louis**
P.O. Box 23130, 4538 Maryland Avenue, St. Louis, Missouri   63108
(314) 367-0390

AGENCY EXECUTIVE:  Rev. David Fleming, S.M., Provinical Superior.

COUNTRY OF ASSISTANCE:  Mexico.


**MARYKNOLL FATHERS AND BROTHERS (M.M.)**
Maryknoll, New York   10545
(914) 941-7590

AGENCY EXECUTIVE:  Rev. James P. Noonan, M.M., Superior General.

COUNTRIES OF ASSISTANCE:  Guatemala, Honduras, Mexico, Nicaragua.


**MARYKNOLL SISTERS OF ST. DOMINIC (M.M.)**
Maryknoll Sisters Center, Maryknoll, New York   10545
(914) 941-7575

AGENCY EXECUTIVE:  Sister Melinda Roper, M.M., Community President.

COUNTRIES OF ASSISTANCE:  Guatemala, Mexico, Panama.


*+  **MEALS FOR MILLIONS/FREEDOM FROM HUNGER FOUNDATION**
P.O. Box 2000, 1644 De Vinci Court, Davis, Callifornia   95616
(916) 758-6200

AGENCY EXECUTIVE:  Peter J. Davis, President.

REGIONAL DIRECTOR:  Louis Ziskind, Regional Director, Caribbean/Latin America.

COUNTRIES OF ASSISTANCE:  Antigua, Honduras.


**MEDICAL BENEVOLENCE FOUNDATION  (S)**
P.O. Box 310, Route 1, Woodville, Texas   75979
(713) 283-3775

AGENCY EXECUTIVE: Keith McCaffety, Executive Director.

Supports the overseas medical work of the Presbyterian Church in the United States with grants and donated equipment and supplies.

COUNTRY OF ASSISTANCE: Haiti.


**MEDICAL MISSION SISTERS (S.C.M.M.)**
**(Society of Catholic Medical Missionaries, Inc.)**
8400 Pine Road, Philadelphia, Pennsylvania  19111
(215) 742-6100

AGENCY EXECUTIVE:  Sister Janet Gottschalk, S.C.M.M., North American Sector Superior.

REGIONAL DIRECTOR:  Sister Sarah Summers, Sector Superior for Latin America.

COUNTRY OF ASSISTANCE:  Nicaragua.


**THE MEDICAL RELIEF OF HAITI, INC.  (S)**
1760 Gold Street, Redding, California  96001
(916) 243-1331

AGENCY EXECUTIVE:  Dr. Edward D. Ryan, M.D., President.

Collects and ships medical supplies, books, food and eyeglasses.

COUNTRY OF ASSISTANCE:  Haiti.


**MENNONITE BRETHREN MISSIONS/SERVICES**
315 South Lincoln Street, Hillsboro, Kansas  67063
(316) 947-3151

AGENCY EXECUTIVE:  Victor Adrian, General Secretary.

REGIONAL DIRECTOR:  John Wall, Secretary for Latin America.

COUNTRY OF ASSISTANCE:  Panama.


*+ **MENNONITE CENTRAL COMMITTEE**
P.O. Box M, Akron, Pennsylvania  17501
(717) 859-1151

AGENCY EXECUTIVE:  Reginald Toews, Executive Secretary.

REGIONAL DIRECTOR:  Herman Bontrager, Secretary for Latin America.

COUNTRIES OF ASSISTANCE:  Belize, El Salvador, Guatemala, Haiti, Honduras, Jamaica, Nicaragua.

**MENNONITE ECONOMIC DEVELOPMENT ASSOCIATES, INC.**
P.O. Box M, 21 South 12th Street, Akron, Pennsylvania  17501
(717) 738-3715

AGENCY EXECUTIVE:  Neil Janzen, President.

REGIONAL DIRECTOR:  Paul Derstine, Vice President, International Programs.

COUNTRIES OF ASSISTANCE:  Belize, Costa Rica (s), Dominican Republic, Haiti,
Jamaica, St. Kitts - Nevis.


**SISTERS OF MERCY OF THE UNION IN THE U.S.A.  (R.S.M.)**
**National Office**
1320 Fenwick Lane, Suite 500, Silver Spring, Maryland  20910
(301) 587-6310

AGENCY EXECUTIVE:  Sister M. Theresa Kane, R.S.M., Administrator General.

COUNTRIES OF ASSISTANCE:  Guyana, Honduras, Jamaica.


**MEXICAN MEDICAL INCORPORATED**
P.O. Box 80396, 4122 Avocado Boulevard, La Mesa, California  92041
(619) 464-0404

AGENCY EXECUTIVE:  Gaylord I. Bowman, President.

COUNTRIES OF ASSISTANCE:  Mexico.


**MIDWEST MEDICAL MISSION, INC.  (S)**
5707 Darr Street, Toledo, Ohio  43615
(419) 874-4244

AGENCY EXECUTIVE:  James G. Diller, M.D., President.

Provides short-term surgical care with emphasis on outpatient surgery including provision of volunteer medical teams and supplies and equipment.
Facilitates donation of equipment and assists U.S. voluntary organizations in
placement of refurbished equipment.  Assists biomedical technicians in repair
of equipment in recipient country and provides prosthetic services to poor
people.

COUNTRY OF ASSISTANCE:  Haiti.


**MISSION AVIATION FELLOWSHIP**
P.O. Box 202, 1849 Wabash Avenue, Redlands, California  92373
(714) 525-8206

AGENCY EXECUTIVE:  Charles T. Bennett, President.

REGIONAL DIRECTOR:  Jack Walter, Area Vice President for Latin America.

COUNTRIES OF ASSISTANCE:  Guatemala, Honduras, Mexico, Suriname.


**MISSIONARY CHURCH, INC.**
3901 South Wayne Avenue, Fort Wayne, Indiana   46807
(219) 456-4502

AGENCY EXECUTIVE:  Dr. Leonard W. DeWitt, President.

REGIONAL DIRECTOR:  Rev. Steve Zureher.

COUNTRIES OF ASSISTANCE:  Dominican Republic, Haiti.


**MISSIONS HEALTH FOUNDATION, INC.**
P.O. Box 89, 201 West Lexington, Suite 215, Independence, Missouri   64056
(816) 254-6205

AGENCY EXECUTIVE:  Jack W. Maybee, Director of Community Development.

COUNTRIES OF ASSISTANCE:  Dominican Republic, Haiti.


**MONTFORT MISSIONARIES (S.M.M.)**
**(Missionaries of the Company of Mary), United States Province**
101-18 104th Street, Ozone Park, New York   11416
(212) 849-5885

AGENCY EXECUTIVE:  Rev. George Werner, S.M.M., President.

COUNTRIES OF ASSISTANCE:  Haiti, Nicaragua.


**THE MORAVIAN CHURCH IN AMERICA, INC.  (S)**
**Board of World Mission of The Moravian Church**
P.O. Box 1245, 69 West Church Street, Bethlehem, Pennsylvania   18018
(215) 868-1732

AGENCY EXECUTIVE:  Graham H. Rights, Executive Director.

Helps support national church programs involving community development activities, such as agriculture, and literacy and vocational education.

COUNTRY OF ASSISTANCE:   Antigua, Barbados, Costa Rica, Dominican Republic,
Guyana, Honduras (o), St. Kitts-Nevis, Trinidad and Tobago.


**NATIONAL BAPTIST CONVENTION, U.S.A., INC.**
**Foreign Mission Board**
701 South 19th Street, Philadelphia, Pennsylvania   19146
(215) 735-7868

AGENCY EXECUTIVE:  Charles Walker, Chairman.

REGIONAL DIRECTOR: William J. Harvey, III, Corresponding Secretary.

COUNTRY OF ASSISTANCE: Nicaragua.

---

\* **NATIONAL COUNCIL FOR INTERNATIONAL HEALTH, INC. (S)**
2100 Pennsylvania Avenue N.W., Suite 740, Washington, D.C. 20037
(202) 466-4740

AGENCY EXECUTIVE: Dr. Russell E. Morgan, Jr., Executive Director.

REGIONAL DIRECTOR: Dr. S. Curtiss Swezy, Program Manager.

Assists the Caribbean Community (CARICOM) Secretariat to improve and expand its health manpower development capabilities. Helps member countries recruit and place needed personnel, as well as develop their own plans for permanent regionally-based primary health care training activities.

COUNTRIES OF ASSISTANCE: regional (Caribbean).

---

**NATIONAL COUNCIL OF CATHOLIC WOMEN (S)**
1312 Massachusetts Avenue, N.W., Washington, D. C. 20005
(202) 638-6050

AGENCY EXECUTIVE: Winifred Coleman, Executive Director.

In cooperation with Catholic Relief Services supports women's groups, day care centers and orphanages, vocational training programs, and the purchase of books and equipment.

COUNTRIES OF ASSISTANCE: Costa Rica, El Salvador, Haiti, Honduras, Panama, St. Vincent and the Grenadines.

---

\* **NATIONAL 4-H COUNCIL (S)**
7100 Connecticut Avenue, N.W., Chevy Chase, Maryland 20815
(301) 656-9000

AGENCY EXECUTIVE: Grant A. Shrum, President and Chief Executive Officer.

REGIONAL DIRECTOR: Melvin J. Thompson, Coordinator, International Relations.

Provides study and training opportunities for youth program professionals; sponsors International Youth Development Project through which U.S. participants assist developing countries in building and expanding programs similar to 4-H; sponsors two-way exchange which provides opportunities for young people and professionals to exchange ideas with 4-H type organizations in other countries.

COUNTRIES OF ASSISTANCE: Antigua, Barbados, Belize, Costa Rica, Dominica, Grenada, Jamaica, St. Kitts - Nevis, St. Lucia, St. Vincent and the Grenadines, Trinidad and Tobago.

\* **NATIONAL OFFICE FOR SOCIAL RESPONSIBILITY IN THE PRIVATE SECTOR, INC.**
**Social Responsibility International**
208 North Washington Street, Alexandria, Virginia  22314
(703) 549-5305

AGENCY EXECUTIVE:  Robert Gemignani, President.

COUNTRY OF ASSISTANCE:  St. Lucia.


**NATIONAL SAVINGS AND LOAN LEAGUE  (S)**
1101--15th Street, N.W., Suite 400, Washington, D.C.  20005
(202) 331-0270

AGENCY EXECUTIVE:  Jonathan Lindley, Executive Vice President.

Assists in development of shelter finance institutions under contract with
U.S. Agency for International Development.  Services include economic and
financial analysis, financial oversight and loan servicing, urban planning,
project design and implementation, socioeconomic surveys and analysis, and
social service delivery programing.

COUNTRIES OF ASSISTANCE:  Barbados, Costa Rica, El Salvador, Guatemala, Honduras, Jamaica, Panama.


**THE NATURE CONSERVANCY  (S)**
1785 Massachusetts Avenue, N.W., Washington, D.C.  20031
(202) 483-0231

AGENCY EXECUTIVE:  Spencer B. Beebe, Director, International Program.

Helps set up natural parks and other reserves; operates conservation fellowship programs to share its experience in preserving natural diversities, and
to select and train land conservation professionals from Latin America.

COUNTRIES OF ASSISTANCE:  Costa Rica, Dominica, Mexico, Netherlands Antilles,
Panama.


**LOS NINOS**
930 East Gutierrez Street, Santa Barbara, California  93103
(805) 962-9587

AGENCY EXECUTIVE:  Paul Weiss, Director.

COUNTRY OF ASSISTANCE:  Mexico.


**SCHOOL SISTERS OF NOTRE DAME (S.S.N.D.)**
**Southern Province**
320 East Ripa Avenue, St. Louis, Missouri  63125
(314) 544-0455

AGENCY EXECUTIVE: Sister Miriam Victor Jansen, S.S.N.D., Provincial Superior.

COUNTRY OF ASSISTANCE: Honduras.


**OBLATES OF MARY IMMACULATE (O.M.I.)**
**Province of St. John the Baptist**
46 Mount Washington Street, Lowell, Massachusetts 01854
(617) 458-4380

AGENCY EXECUTIVE: Very Rev. Maurice Laliberte, O.M.I., Provincial.

REGIONAL DIRECTOR: Rev. Charles H. Dozois, O.M.I., Director of Overseas Programs.

COUNTRY OF ASSISTANCE: Haiti.


**OMS INTERNATIONAL, INC.**
P.O. Box A, 941 Fry Road, Greenwood, Indiana 46142
(317) 881-6751

AGENCY EXECUTIVE: Dr. Everett N. Hunt, President.

REGIONAL DIRECTOR: Dave Graffenberger, Vice President, Field Ministries.

COUNTRY OF ASSISTANCE: Haiti.


**OPERATION CALIFORNIA, INC. (S)**
336 Foothill Road, Suite 1, Beverly Hills, California 90210
(213) 858-8184

AGENCY EXECUTIVE: Richard Walden, Executive Director and President.

Collects, ships and delivers relief supplies and equipment.

COUNTRIES OF ASSISTANCE: Honduras, Nicaragua.


**OPERATION CROSSROADS AFRICA, INC. (S)**
150 Fifth Avenue, New York, New York 10011
(212) 242-8550

AGENCY EXECUTIVE: Jerome M. Vogel, Executive Director.

REGIONAL DIRECTOR: Judy Manning, Director, Caribbean Program.

Arranges for college and high school students to engage in summer work camp projects in Africa and the Caribbean. Students work with local youth counterparts and professionals in constructing needed community facilities such as a school, youth center or medical clinic. In addition, there are special programs where volunteers with experience in such fields as medicine, public health, anthropology, archaeology and photography are assigned to work with the local ministry in development of such projects.

COUNTRIES OF ASSISTANCE: Anguilla, Antigua, Belize, Cayman Islands, Dominica, Haiti, Jamaica, Montserrat, Netherlands Antilles, St. Kitts - Nevis, St. Lucia, St. Vincent and the Grenadines.


**ORTHOPAEDICS OVERSEAS, INC. (S)**
c/o National Council for International Health, 2100 Pennsylvania Avenue, N.W., Washington, D.C. 20037
(202) 466-6106

AGENCY EXECUTIVE: Paul Spray, M.D., Chairman, (Oak Ridge Orthopaedic Clinic, 145 Yance Road, Oak Ridge, Tennessee 37830).

Provides lectures and demonstrations on the treatment of scoliosis; provides general orthopaedic education; gives treatment and rehabilitation therapy for poliomyelitis; supports visiting professor program for continuing education in plastic surgery and orthopaedic surgery; assists in organization of new departments of orthopaedic surgery in medical colleges and hospitals; provides volunteer orthopaedic surgeons.

COUNTRIES OF ASSISTANCE: Dominican Republic, Honduras, Jamaica.


**OUTREACH INTERNATIONAL (S)**
P.O. Box 223, 221 Lexington, Independence, Missouri 64051
(816) 833-0883

AGENCY EXECUTIVE: Cameron Stuart, Executive Director.

Serves as a fund raising, fund disbursing and coordinating entity for a variety of community development and self-help programs operated by U.S. and local development agencies.

COUNTRIES OF ASSISTANCE: Dominican Republic, Haiti, Honduras, Mexico.


\* **OVERSEAS EDUCATION FUND**
2101 L Street, N.W., Suite 916, Washington, D.C. 20037
(202) 466-3430

AGENCY EXECUTIVE: Elise F. Smith, Executive Director.

REGIONAL DIRECTOR: Carolyn Rose Avile, Director, Program Planning - Latin America/Asia.

COUNTRIES OF ASSISTANCE: El Salvador, Honduras, Panama.


**OXFAM AMERICA (S)**
115 Broadway, Boston, Massachusetts 02116
(617) 247-3304

AGENCY EXECUTIVE:  Dr. Joseph Short, Executive Director.

REGIONAL DIRECTOR:  Michael Scott, Director, Overseas Programs.

Working through a network of 30 field representatives shared with other Oxfam organizations provides grants for emergency aid and for a variety of long-term development projects including agricultural education cooperatives, medical programs, irrigation, leadership training, vehicles, mass communications, educational materials, and refugee programs.

COUNTRIES OF ASSISTANCE:  Antigua, Dominica, El Salvador, Grenada, Guatemala, Honduras, Nicaragua, St. Vincent and the Grenadines.


\*  **PAN AMERICAN DEVELOPMENT FOUNDATION**
   1889 F Street, N.W., Washington, D.C.   20006
   (202) 789-3969

AGENCY EXECUTIVE:  Ed Marasciulo, Chief Operating Officer.

COUNTRIES OF ASSISTANCE:  Antigua (s), Bahamas, Barbados, Belize, Costa Rica (s), Dominica, Dominican Republic, El Salvador (s), Grenada (s), Guatemala (s), Haiti, Honduras, Jamaica, Mexico (s), Nicaragua (s), Panama (s), St. Kitts - Nevis (s), St. Lucia, St. Vincent and the Grenadines (s), Trinidad and Tobago.


\*  **PARTNERS OF THE AMERICAS**
   **(National Association of the Partners of the Alliance, Inc.)**
   1424 K Street, N.W., Washington, D.C.   20005
   (202) 628-3300

AGENCY EXECUTIVE:  Alan A. Rubin, President.

REGIONAL DIRECTOR:  E. David Luria, Director of Administration.

COUNTRIES OF ASSISTANCE:   Antigua, Barbados, Belize, Costa Rica, Dominica, Dominican Republic, El Salvador, Guatemala, Haiti, Honduras, Jamaica, Mexico, Montserrat, Nicaragua, Panama, St. Kitts - Nevis, St. Lucia, St. Vincent and the Grenadines, Trindad and Tobago.


\*  **PARTNERSHIP FOR PRODUCTIVITY INTERNATIONAL, INC.**
   2441 18th Street, N.W., Washington, D.C.   20009
   (202) 483-0067

AGENCY EXECUTIVE:  Andrew H. Oerke, President.

REGIONAL DIRECTOR:  James Hochschwender, Director, Overseas Programs.

COUNTRIES OF ASSISTANCE:   Barbados (s), Costa Rica (s), Dominica, Haiti, Honduras, Jamaica, Panama (s).

\* **THE PATHFINDER FUND (S)**
1330 Boylston Street, Chestnut Hill, Massachusetts 02167
(617) 731-1700

AGENCY EXECUTIVE: Richard B. Gamble, President.

REGIONAL DIRECTOR: David A. Wood, Latin America Regional Director.

Supports urban and rural family planning services; encourages women's projects; funds contraceptive supplies and sterilization equipment; promotes establishment of information centers and family planning clinics; supports midwife training projects.

COUNTRIES OF ASSISTANCE: Costa Rica, Dominica, Dominican Republic, El Salvador, Guatemala, Haiti, Honduras, Jamaica, Mexico, Montserrat, Nicaragua, Panama, St. Kitts - Nevis, Trinidad and Tobago, regional (Caribbean).


**ST. PATRICK'S MISSIONARY SOCIETY (S.P.S.)**
**(St. Patrick Fathers)**
70 Edgewater Road, Cliffside Park, New Jersey 07010
(201) 943-6575; (212) 222-7373

AGENCY EXECUTIVE: Very Rev. Liam Doyle, S.P.S., Local Superior for the U.S.

REGIONAL DIRECTOR: Rev. Derrick Byrne, S.P.S., Administrator.

COUNTRY OF ASSISTANCE: Grenada.


\* **THE PEOPLE-TO-PEOPLE HEALTH FOUNDATION, INC.**
**Project HOPE**
Health Sciences Education Center, Millwood, Virginia 22646
(703) 837-2100

AGENCY EXECUTIVE: Dr. William B. Walsh, President and Medical Director.

REGIONAL DIRECTOR: Dr. E. Croft Long, Vice President International Division.

COUNTRIES OF ASSISTANCE: Antigua, Belize, Guatemala, Honduras, Jamaica, St. Lucia.


**PLENTY**
International Headquarters: The Farm, 156 Drakes Lane, Summertown, Tennessee 38483
Washington, D.C. office: 3309 16th Street, N.W., Washington, D.C. 20010
(615) 964-3574/3992/2334

AGENCY EXECUTIVE: Stephen Gaskin, Chairman and Founder.

REGIONAL DIRECTOR: David Purviance, Program Director.

COUNTRIES OF ASSISTANCE: Dominica, Jamaica, St. Lucia.

\* **THE POPULATION COUNCIL (S)**
One Dag Hammarskjold Plaza, New York, New York 10017
(212) 644-1300

AGENCY EXECUTIVE: George Zeidenskin, President.

REGIONAL DIRECTOR: Dr. George F. Brown, Vice President, International Programs.

The Council carries out a program of research in the social sciences aimed at a deeper understanding of the relationships between demographic change and social and economic development, especially as related to the design of population policies; seeks improvement of technologies for birth planning and monitors safety and health effects of methods now in use through a wide network of clinical studies and laboratory research; publishes and disseminates scientific population information to professionals and to a broader audience of policymakers and nonspecialists; enters into working partnerships with developing country colleagues in key population-related activties; provides a collaborative mechanism through which program initiatives are decentralized for the assistance of local, national and regional institutions in design, implementation and evaluation of research and action programs; awards advanced level fellowships in the biomedical and social sciences.

COUNTRIES OF ASSISTANCE: Barbados, Dominica, Dominican Republic, Guatemala, Guyana, Honduras, Jamaica, Mexico, St. Lucia.

**POPULATION CRISIS COMMITTEE/DRAPER FUND (S)**
1120 19th Street, N.W.,Suite 550, Washington, D.C. 20036
(202) 659-1833

AGENCY EXECUTIVE: Fred O. Pinkham, President.

REGIONAL DIRECTOR: Sharon L. Camp, Vice President.

Funds projects which are implemented by local leaders and monitored by PCC; assistance includes support for family planning clinics, communication programs, and provision of supplies and training.

COUNTRY OF ASSISTANCE: Mexico.

**THE POPULATION INSTITUTE (S)**
110 Maryland Avenue, N.E., Washington, D.C. 20002
(202) 544-3300
Regional office: 777 United Nations Plaza, New York, New York 10017
(212) 687-3366

AGENCY EXECUTIVE: Werner Fornos, President.

REGIONAL DIRECTOR: David O. Poindexter, Communications Center (NY).

Provides population program planning assistance; operates international network of information related to population and relevant areas; runs workshops.

COUNTRY OF ASSISTANCE: Mexico.

**POPULATION REFERENCE BUREAU, INC. (S)**
1337 Connecticut Avenue, N.W., Washington, D.C.   20036
(202) 785-4664

AGENCY EXECUTIVE:   Robert P. Worrall, President.

Conducts professional development training programs in population communication and education, documentation and specialized publication projects at the
request of developing country officials; produces and distributes both English
and Spanish language publications in the region, including INTERCOM, the
International Population News Magazine.

COUNTRIES OF ASSISTANCE:   Regional program.

**PRIMITIVE METHODIST CHURCH IN THE U.S.A.**
**International Mission Board**
30 Linda Lane, Lebanon, Pennsylvania   17042
(717) 273-5951

AGENCY EXECUTIVE:   Rev. Harold J. Barrett, General Director.

COUNTRY OF ASSISTANCE:   Guatemala.

**\*+   PRIVATE AGENCIES COLLABORATING TOGETHER, INC. (PACT) (S)**
777 United Nations Plaza, Suite 6B, New York, New York   10017
(212) 697-6222

AGENCY EXECUTIVE:   Robert F. O'Brien, Executive Director.

REGIONAL DIRECTOR:   Carlos Costello, Latin American Program Oficer.

As an international consortium of private agencies it assists its members by
providing grants for a variety of projects including community programs,
loans, small enterprise development, nonformal educational programs and crop
improvement.

COUNTRIES OF ASSISTANCE:    Guatemala, Honduras, Mexico, Panama, region
(Caribbean).

**PROGRAM FOR APPROPRIATE TECHNOLOGY IN HEALTH (PATH) (S)**
Canal Place, 130 Nickerson Street, Seattle, Washington   98109
(206) 285-4599

AGENCY EXECUTIVE:   Gordon W. Perkin, M.D., Agency Executive.

Identifies appropriate health technologies, provides technical support, and
mobilizes financial assistance for their development; develops instructional
materials, package labiling; provides technical assistance to product
adaptation, design of quality control procedures, and procurement and supply
management.

COUNTRY OF ASSISTANCE:   Mexico.

**\*    PROGRAM FOR THE INTRODUCTION AND ADAPTATION OF CONTRACEPTIVE TECHNOLOGY**
**(PIACT)**
Canal Place, 130 Nickerson Street, Seattle, Washington   98109
(206) 285-3500

AGENCY EXECUTIVE: Dr. Gordon W. Perkin, Executive Director.

REGIONAL DIRECTOR: Manuel Ylanan, Associate Director.

COUNTRY OF ASSISTANCE: Mexico.


\* **PROJECT CONCERN INTERNATIONAL**
P.O. Box 8533, 3550 Afton Road, San Diego, California, 72123
(714) 279-9690

AGENCY EXECUTIVE: Henry Sjaardema, Executive Director.

COUNTRIES OF ASSISTANCE: Belize, Guatemala, Mexico.


**PROMISE, INC.**
P.O. Box 1221, ISU Station, Ames, Iowa, 50010
(515) 233-2702

AGENCY EXECUTIVE: Leland Smithson, Executive Director.

COUNTRY OF ASSISTANCE: Mexico.


**PUBLIC WELFARE FOUNDATION (S)**
2600 Virginia Avenue, N.W., Washington, D.C. 20037
(202) 965-1800

AGENCY EXECUTIVE: Charles Glenn Ihrig, Executive Director.

Provides grants for education, medical services, child welfare and youth
agencies, and self-help projects, primarily in Latin America.

COUNTRIES OF ASSISTANCE: Guatemala, Haiti, Honduras, Jamaica.


**REDEMPTORIST FATHERS (C.SS.R.)**
**(Congregation of the Most Holy Redeemer), Province of Baltimore**
7509 Shore Road, Brooklyn, New York 11209
(212) 833-1900

AGENCY EXECUTIVE: Very Rev. Joseph T. Hurley, C.SS.R., Provincial.

REGIONAL DIRECTOR: Rev. Raymond P. McCarthy, C.SS.R., Mission Provincial.

COUNTRY OF ASSISTANCE: Dominican Republic.


**REORGANIZED CHURCH OF JESUS CHRIST OF LATTER DAY SAINTS**
P.O. Box 1059, The Auditorium, Independence, Missouri 64051
(816) 833-1000

AGENCY EXECUTIVE:  Wallace B. Smith, President.

REGIONAL DIRECTOR:  Otto H. Elser, M.D., Commissioner of Health Ministries.

COUNTRIES OF ASSISTANCE:  Haiti, Honduras.


**RHEMA INTERNATIONAL, INC.**
P.O. Box 34805, 7616 Nevada Avenue East, Detroit, Michigan  48230
(313) 365-7144

AGENCY EXECUTIVES:  J. Peter and Patricia Beall Gruits, Executive Directors.

COUNTRY OF ASSISTANCE:  Haiti.


**THE ROCKEFELLER FOUNDATION  (S)**
1133 Avenue of the Americas, New York, New York  10036
(212) 869-8500

AGENCY EXECUTIVE:  Richard W. Lyman, President.

Provides grants and fellowships for research in food production and agriculture, including support of the international agricultural institutes network;
funds research programs on diseases of the developing world and in the field
of population and family services.

COUNTRIES OF ASSISTANCE:  Costa Rica, El Salvador, Guatemala, Mexico.


**ROTARY INTERNATIONAL**
1600 Ridge Avenue, Evanston, Illinois  60201
(312) 328-0100

AGENCY EXECUTIVE:  Herbert A. Pigman, General Secretary.

REGIONAL DIRECTOR:  John Stucky, Manager, Health, Hunger and Humanity 3-H
Program.

COUNTRIES OF ASSISTANCE:  Belize, Dominican Republic, Guatemala, Haiti, Honduras, Jamaica, Mexico.


**SOCIETY OF THE SACRED HEART (R.S.C.J.)**
**U.S. Province**
4389 West Pine Boulevard, St. Louis, Missouri  63108
(314) 652-1500

AGENCY EXECUTIVE:  Sister Mary McKay, R.S.C.J., Coordinator, Interprovincial
Board.

COUNTRY OF ASSISTANCE:  Nicaragua.

\* **SALESIAN SOCIETY, INC.**
**Salesians of St. John Bosco (S.D.B.)**
148 Main Street, New Rochelle, New York  10802
(914) 633-8344

AGENCY EXECUTIVE:  Very Rev. Dominic DeBlase, S.D.B., Provincial.

REGIONAL DIRECTOR:  Rev. Edward J. Cappelletti, S.D.B., Mission Director.

COUNTRIES OF ASSISTANCE:  Bahamas, Costa Rica, Dominican Republic, El Salvador, Guatemala, Haiti, Honduras, Mexico, Netherlands Antilles, Nicaragua, Panama.


+ **THE SALVATION ARMY**
National Headquarters:
799 Bloomfield Avenue, Verona, New Jersey  07044
(201) 239-0606
\* **World Service Office (SAWSO):**
1025 Vermont Avenue, N.W., Suite 350, Washington, D.C.  20005
(202) 833-5646

AGENCY EXECUTIVE:  Commissioner Norman Marshall, National Commander.

REGIONAL DIRECTOR:  John W. Wiggins, Director, Salvation Army, World Service Office.

COUNTRIES OF ASSISTANCE:  Antigua, Bahamas, Barbados, Belize, Bermuda, Costa Rica, Cuba, Grenada, Guatemala, Guiana, Guyana, Haiti, Jamaica, Mexico, Panama, St. Kitts - Nevis, St. Vincent and the Grenadines, Suriname, Trinidad and Tobago.


**MARGARET SANGER CENTER  (S)**
\* **Planned Parenthood of New York City, Inc.**
380 Second Avenue, New York, New York  10010
(212) 677-6474

AGENCY EXECUTIVE:  L. Richard Kugelman, Executive Director.

REGIONAL DIRECTOR:  George Marshall Worthington, Special Projects Coordinator.

Provides training in family planning and child care to family health practitioners who will function as trainers and clinicians; offers advisory services and material assistance for local family and health training centers.

COUNTRY OF ASSISTANCE: Jamaica.


\*+ **SAVE THE CHILDREN FEDERATION, INC.**
54 Wilton Road, Westport, Connecticut  06880
(203) 226-7271

AGENCY EXECUTIVE:  David L. Guyer, President.

REGIONAL DIRECTOR: John Putnam Grant, Director, Latin America/Caribbean Region.

COUNTRIES OF ASSISTANCE: Dominica, Dominican Republic, El Salvador, Guatemala, Haiti, Honduras, Mexico, Nicaragua.


**SELF HELP FOUNDATION**
P.O. Box 88, Waverly, Iowa   50677
(319) 352-4040

AGENCY EXECUTIVE: Ray C. Howland, Executive Director.

COUNTRY OF ASSISTANCE: Mexico.


**\*+   SEVENTH-DAY ADVENTIST WORLD SERVICE, INC.  (S)**
6840 Eastern Avenue, N.W., Washington, D.C.   20012
(202) 722-6770
P.O. Box 60808, Washington, D.C.   20039

AGENCY EXECUTIVE: Richard W. O'Ffill, Executive Director.

REGIONAL DIRECTOR: Sergio Moctezuma, (P.O. Box 340760, Coral Gables, Florida   33134)

Provides donations of food, clothing, equipment, and medical and disaster relief supplies; supports medical institutions and orphanages, construction activities, cooperatives, agricultural programs and women's groups; conducts adult education programs.

COUNTRIES OF ASSISTANCE: El Salvador, Guatemala, Guyana, Haiti, Honduras, Mexico, Nicaragua, St. Lucia.


**SISTER CITIES INTERNATIONAL  (S)**
**\*   Town Affiliation Association of the U.S., Inc.**
1625 Eye Street, N.W. Suite 424-26, Washington, D.C.   20005
(202) 293-5504

AGENCY EXECUTIVE: Thomas W. Gittins, Executive Vice President.

REGIONAL DIRECTOR: Jim Ekstrom, Technical Assistance Programs.

Through its Sister Cities Technical Assistance Program provides small grants for collaborative efforts including municipal, professional, educational, community service and technical activities, covering such areas as housing, employment generation, sanitation and public health.

COUNTRIES OF ASSISTANCE: Belize, Costa Rica, Dominican Republic, El Salvador, Guatemala, Haiti, Honduras, Jamaica, Mexico, Nicaragua, St. Vincent and the Grenadines.

**SISTERS OF SOCIAL SERVICE OF LOS ANGELES, INC. (S.S.S.)**
1120 Westchester Place, Los Angeles, California 90019
(213) 731-2117

AGENCY EXECUTIVE: Sister Petra Keller, S.S.S., President.

COUNTRY OF ASSISTANCE: Mexico.


**SISTERS OF THE SORROWFUL MOTHER
(THIRD ORDER OF ST. FRANCIS) (S.S.M.)**
Milwaukee Province, Mother of Sorrows Convent, 6618 North Teutonia Avenue,
Broken Arrow, Oklahoma 53209
(414) 35201340

AGENCY EXECUTIVE: Sister M. Jeanine Retzer, S.S.M., Milwaukee Provincial
Superior.

REGIONAL DIRECTOR: Sister Lois, Bush, S.S.M., Assistant Provincial.

COUNTRIES OF ASSISTANCE: Barbados, St. Lucia.


**SOUTHERN BAPTIST CONVENTION (S)**
**Foreign Mission Board**
P.O. Box 6767, 3805 Monument Avenue, Richmond, Virginia 23230
(804) 353-0151

AGENCY EXECUTIVE: R. Keith Parks, President.

REGIONAL DIRECTOR: Don Kammerdiener, Area Director, Central America and the
Caribbean.

Projects are administered by missionaries or national leaders as a holistic
(physical and spiritual) response to needs perceived by community, government
and the mission.

COUNTRIES OF ASSISTANCE: Belize, Costa Rica, El Salvador, Guatemala, Haiti,
Honduras, Mexico, Nicaragua.


**STELIOS M. STELSON FOUNDATION, INC. (S)**
P.O. Box 15663, Columbus, Ohio 43215
(614) 228-6531

AGENCY EXECUTIVE: Stelios M. Stelson, Executive Director.

Ships books, technical, scientific and medical journals, medical and school
supplies, and clothing.

COUNTRY OF ASSISTANCE: Dominica.

\* **SUMMER INSTITUTE OF LINGUISTICS, INC.**
7500 West Camp Wisdom Road, Dallas, Texas 75236
(214) 298-3331

AGENCY EXECUTIVE: Kenneth J. Gregerson, President.

REGIONAL DIRECTOR: John Alsop, Area Director, Latin America.

COUNTRIES OF ASSISTANCE: Guatemala, Honduras, Mexico, Suriname.


**SURGICAL EYE EXPEDITIONS INTERNATIONAL (S)**
**(S.E.E. International)**
P.O. Box 30282, 1216 State Street, Suite 310, Santa Barbara, California 93101
(805) 963-3303

AGENCY EXECUTIVE: Ester Laver, Administrator.

Provides volunteer surgical eye teams including U.S. and local clinical opthalmologists, nurses and technicians; developed and field-tested self-contained mobile, portable ophthalmic medical/surgical unit utilizing specially designed equipment, standardized presterilized sugical packs, volunteer ophthalmic technician course and pilot certification program; provides surgical equipment and supplies and corrective eyeglasses to S.E.E. Chapters requesting them.

COUNTRIES OF ASSISTANCE: Jamaica, Mexico.


\* **TECHNOSERVE, INC.**
11 Belden Avenue, Norwalk, Connecticut 06852
(203) 846-3231

AGENCY EXECUTIVE: Edward P. Bullard, IV, President.

REGIONAL DIRECTOR: Gerald L. Schmaedick, Vice President, Latin America.

COUNTRIES OF ASSISTANCE: Costa Rica, El Salvador, Nicaragua, Panama.


**TRICKLE UP PROGRAM (S)**
54 Riverside Drive, PHE, New York, New York 10024
(212) 362-7958

AGENCY EXECUTIVES: Glen Leet and Mildred Robbins Leet, Co-Directors.

Through local coordinatiors with development experience, provides project grants of $100 each to groups of five or more people who wish to initiate profit-making small enterprises they plan and manage themselves.

COUNTRIES OF ASSISTANCE: Antigua, Barbados, Belize, Costa Rica, Dominica, Grenada, Guadeloupe, Guyana, Haiti, Jamaica, Martinique, Montserrat, Nicaragua, Panama, St. Kitts - Nevis, St. Lucia, St. Vincent and the Grenadines.

**UFM INTERNATIONAL, INC.**
P.O. Box 306, Bala-Cynwyd, Pennsylvania  19004
(215) 667-7660

AGENCY EXECUTIVE:  Rev. Alfred Larson, General Director.

COUNTRIES OF ASSISTANCE:  Dominican Republic, Haiti.


* **UNITARIAN UNIVERSALIST SERVICE COMMITTEE  (S)**
78 Beacon Street, Boston, Massachusetts  02108
(617) 742-2120

AGENCY EXECUTIVE:  Dr. Richard S. Scobie, Executive Director.

REGIONAL  DIRECTORS:    John  McAward,  Director  of  Human  Rights  Education
(Central   America); Elizabeth Coit, Associate Director, International
  Projects (Caribbean).

Sends fact-finding missions; operates networking and training programs for
grassroots leadership; supports income generation, health and family planning
programs.

COUNTRIES OF ASSISTANCE:  Costa Rica, Guatemala, Haiti, Honduras, Nicaragua,
St. Kitts-Nevis.


**UNITED CHURCH BOARD FOR WORLD MINISTRIES  (S)**
**United Church of Christ, Divisions of World Missions and World Service**
475 Riverside Drive, New York, New York  10115
(212) 870-2637

AGENCY EXECUTIVE:  Rev. Alfred C. Bartholomew, General Secretary, Service
Division.

REGIONAL  DIRECTOR:    Pat  Rumer,  Director,  Latin  America/Caribbean/Oceania
Programs.

In partnership with and under the direction of overseas partner churches and
ecumenical ministries supports a variety of development assistance programs
including community development, education, medicine, small enterprise and
public health development and food production and agriculture.

COUNTRIES OF ASSISTANCE:  Service Division - Belize, Honduras, Mexico, Nicaragua.


**THE UNITED METHODIST CHURCH  (S)**
**World Division of the Board of Global Ministries**
475 Riverside Drive, New York, New York  10115
(212) 870-3600

AGENCY EXECUTIVE:  Bishop W. Ralph Ward, Jr., Associate General Secretary.

REGIONAL DIRECTOR:  Dr. Joseph Perez, Executive Secretary, Latin America and
Caribbean.

Provides support to the Methodist Church of the Caribbean and Central America (MCCA) which operates programs throughout the Caribbean region from its head-quarters in St. John, Antigua. Support is also provided to national methodist churches in a number of Central American countries.

COUNTRIES OF ASSISTANCE: Antigua, Belize, Costa Rica, Cuba, Mexico, Panama, regional (Caribbean).


**UNITED METHODIST COMMITTEE ON RELIEF (S)**
475 Riverside Drive, New York, New York 10115
(212) 870-3600

AGENCY EXECUTIVE: Dr. J. Harry Haines, Associate General Secretary.

Provides funds for overseas relief, rehabilitation, refugee services and development programs, with special emphasis on community development and agricultural production projects.

COUNTRIES OF ASSISTANCE: Antigua, Belize, Costa Rica, Dominica, Dominican Republic, El Salvador, Guatemala, Haiti, Honduras, Jamaica, Mexico, Nicaragua, Panama, Trinidad and Tobago, regional.


**UNITED STATES YOUTH COUNCIL (S)**
1522 K Street, N.W., Suite 620, Washington, D.C. 20005
(202) 289-4230

AGENCY EXECUTIVE: Robert E. Lovelace II, Executive Director.

Conducts bilateral educational exchanges with counterpart youth organizations in other countries.

COUNTRIES OF ASSISTANCE: Barbados, Costa Rica, Jamaica, Trinidad and Tobago.


* **VOLUNTEER DEVELOPMENT CORPS (S)**
1629 K Street, N.W., Washington, D.C. 20006
(202) 223-2072

AGENCY EXECUTIVE: David W. Angevine, President.

Provides short-term (90-day maximum), technical help to cooperatives and government agencies responsible for cooperative development at their request throughout the Third World.

COUNTRIES OF ASSISTANCE: Costa Rica, Panama.


**VOLUNTEER OPTOMETRIC SERVICES TO HUMANITY (VOSH INTERNATIONAL) (S)**
243 North Lindbergh Bloulevard, St. Louis, Missouri 63141
(314) 364-1773

AGENCY EXECUTIVE: Dr. Vernon E. Falkenhain, President.

Volunteers in International Service and Awareness (VIISA)--**Part I**

Provides volunteer eye health care professionals who give eye examinations and provide other optometric services.

COUNTRIES OF ASSISTANCE: Belize, Costa Rica, El Salvador, Guatemala, Haiti, Honduras, Jamaica, Mexico, Nicaragua, Panama.


**VOLUNTEERS IN INTERNATIONAL SERVICE AND AWARENESS (VIISA)**
125 West 4th Street, Los Angeles, California  90013
(213) 680-4611

AGENCY EXECUTIVE:  T.J. Grosser, D.D., President.

REGIONAL DIRECTOR:  William McDougal, Executive Vice President.

COUNTRY OF ASSISTANCE:  Dominican Republic.


* **VOLUNTEERS IN TECHNICAL ASSISTANCE, INC. (VITA)  (S)**
P.O. Box 12438, 1815 North Lynn Street, Suite 200, Arlington, Virginia  22209
(703) 276-1800

AGENCY EXECUTIVE:  Henry Norman, Executive Director.

REGIONAL DIRECTOR:  Richard J. Fera, Director, Latin America and Caribbean Region.

Provides small grants, on-site technical assistance and by-mail responses on technical subjects.  Main areas of assistance are in appropriate technology, agriculture and renewable energy (wind, solar, biomass, micro-hydro, charcoal, kilns, improved cookstoves).

COUNTRIES OF ASSISTANCE:  Antigua, Bahamas, Barbados, Costa Rica, Dominica, Dominican Republic, El Salvador, Haiti, Honduras (o), Jamaica, Mexico (o), Montserrat (o), Nicaragua, Panama, St. Lucia, St. Vincent and the Grenadines, Trinidad and Tobago, Turks and Caicos Islands.


**THE WESLEYAN CHURCH**
**The General Department of World Missions**
P.O. Box 2000, 1900 West, 300 South, Marion, Indiana  46952
(317) 674-3301

AGENCY EXECUTIVE:  Dr. Robert N. Lytle, General Secretary, General Department of World Missions.

REGIONAL DIRECTOR:  Rev. Wayne W. Wright, Assistant General Secretary.

COUNTRIES OF ASSISTANCE:  Guyana, Haiti.


* **WINROCK INTERNATIONAL**
Petit Jean Mountain, Route  3, Morrilton, Arkansas  72110
(501) 727-5435

AGENCY EXECUTIVE:  Richard O. Wheeler, Ph.D., President.

REGIONAL DIRECTOR:  H.A. Fitzhugh, Latin America Program Officer.

COUNTRIES OF ASSISTANCE:  Belize, Costa Rica, Haiti, Honduras, Jamaica, Trinidad and Tobago, regional.


**\*+  WORLD CONCERN  (S)**
P.O. Box 33000, 1930 Fremont Avenue North, Seattle, Washington  98133
(206) 546-7201

AGENCY EXECUTIVE:  Dr. Clarence Reimer, President.

REGIONAL DIRECTOR:  Anne K. Sorley, Latin America Director.

Works as a funding and resource agency in the areas of relief, rehabilitation and development.  Assists integrated community development projects including food production and agriculture, small enterprise development, water and sanitation, rural health care and nutrition.

COUNTRIES OF ASSISTANCE:  Costa Rica (o), Dominican Republic, Guatemala, Haiti (o), Honduras, Mexico, Panama, regional (Caribbean).


**\*  WORLD EDUCATION, INC.**
210 Lincoln Street, Boston, Massachusetts  02111
(617) 482-9485

AGENCY EXECUTIVE:  Joel Lamstein, President.

REGIONAL DIRECTOR:  Melinda Dodson, Program Administrator.

COUNTRIES OF ASSISTANCE:  St. Lucia, St. Vincent and the Grenadines.


**WORLD GOSPEL MISSION**
3783 State Road 18, E., Marion, Indiana  46952
(917) 664-7331

AGENCY EXECUTIVE:  Dr. Thomas Hermiz, President.

REGIONAL DIRECTOR:  Burnie H. Bushong, Vice President, Field Ministries.

COUNTRIES OF ASSISTANCE:  Haiti, Honduras.


**WORLD MEDICAL RELIEF, INC.  (S)**
11745 Twelfth Street, Detroit, Michigan  48206
(313) 866-5322

AGENCY EXECUTIVE:  Irene M. Auberlin, President.

Collects and distributes donated medical supplies and equipment; ships relief supplies, particularly food supplements.

COUNTRIES OF ASSISTANCE:  Haiti, Mexico, regional (Caribbean).


**WORLD NEIGHBORS, INC.**
5116 North Portland Avenue, Oklahoma City, Oklahoma  73112
(405) 946-3333

AGENCY EXECUTIVE:  James O. Morgan, President.

REGIONAL DIRECTOR:  Oramel Greene, Regional Director for Latin America.

COUNTRIES OF ASSISTANCE:  Guatemala, Haiti, Honduras, Mexico, Nicaragua.


**WORLD OPPORTUNITIES INTERNATIONAL  (S)**
1415 North Cahuenga Boulevard, Hollywood, California  90028
(213) 466-7187

AGENCY EXECUTIVE:  Dr. Roy B. McKeown, President.

Sends small amounts of medical supplies to a hospital.

COUNTRY OF ASSISTANCE:  Honduras.


**THE WORLD RADIO MISSIONARY FELLOWSHIP, INC.**
P.O. Box 3000, 20201 N.W. 37th Avenue, Opa-Locka, Florida  33055
(305) 624-4252

AGENCY EXECUTIVE:  Dr. Ronald A. Cline, President.

COUNTRY OF ASSISTANCE:  Panama.


**\*+  WORLD RELIEF CORPORATION**
P.O. Box WRC, Wheaton, Illinois  60187
(312) 665-0235

AGENCY EXECUTIVE:  Jerry P. Ballard, Executive Director.

REGIONAL DIRECTOR:  Dr. David E. Kornfield.

COUNTRIES OF ASSISTANCE:  Dominican Republic (s), Guatemala (s), Haiti, Honduras.


**\*+  WORLD VISION RELIEF ORGANIZATION, INC.**
919 West Huntington Drive, Monrovia, California  91016
(213) 357-7979

AGENCY EXECUTIVE: Robert L. Ainsworth, Director.

COUNTRIES OF ASSISTANCE: Belize, Costa Rica, Dominican Republic, El Salvador, Guatemala, Haiti, Honduras, Mexico, Nicaragua, Panama.

**XAVERIAN MISSIONARY FATHERS (S.X.)**
**St. Francis Xavier Foreign Mission Society, Inc.**
12 Helene Court, Wayne, New Jersey  07470
(201) 942-2975

AGENCY EXECUTIVE: Rev. Edward Zannoni, S.X., Vice President-Treasurer, Coordinator for Mission Assistance.

COUNTRY OF ASSISTANCE: Mexico.

\*+ **YOUNG MEN'S CHRISTIAN ASSOCIATIONS OF THE UNITED STATES**
**International Division of the National Board**
101 North Wacker Drive, Chicago, Illinois  60606
(312) 977-0031

AGENCY EXECUTIVE: John O'Melia, Director, International Division.

COUNTRIES OF ASSISTANCE: Costa Rica, Dominican Republic, Guatemala, Mexico.

\*+ **YOUNG WOMEN'S CHRISTIAN ASSOCIATION OF THE U.S.A.**
**World Relations Unit of the National Board**
135 West 50 Street, New York, New York  10020
(212) 621-5115

AGENCY EXECUTIVE: Betty Jo Swayze, Executive, World Relations Unit.

COUNTRIES OF ASSISTANCE: Guyana, Jamaica, Mexico.

# PART II –

## COUNTRY PROGRAM INFORMATION

This section contains country program data for those organizations which operate programs in the region. Operating programs appear first under each country followed by a listing of support organizations with program expenditures of each organization.

A country index and a program activity index for both operating and support organizations appear at the back of the directory.

* Registered with the U.S. Agency for International Development
+ Member of the American Council of Voluntary Agencies for Foreign Service

---

## ANGUILLA

---

### ANGUILLA - PROGRAM SUPPORT

Operation Crossroads Africa

---

## ANTIGUA

---

Of the 20 U.S. organizations listed in Antigua,
7 were able to provide TAICH with financial data
indicating program expenditures for FY 1982
totaling $89,236.

MM/FFHF/ATG

**\*+ MEALS FOR MILLIONS/FREEDOM FROM HUNGER FOUNDATION**
Contact:  Ruth Spencer, Program Director
Mutual Building
High Street
P.O. Box 846
St. Johns, Antigua

PROGRAM OF ASSISTANCE:  Agricultural training - Beekeeping - Gardens - Solar energy - Credit/loans - Income generation - Cooperatives - Mother/child programs - Nutrition education.

PERSONNEL: 5 local.

PROGRAM INITIATION:  1982          EXPENDITURES FOR FY 1982:  $53,000

COOPERATING ORGANIZATIONS:  Christian Action for Development in the Caribbean (CADEC); Government of Antigua, Ministries of Agriculture, Education and Health, U.S. Peace Corps.

. . . . . . . . . .

PARTNERS/ATG

**\* PARTNERS OF THE AMERICAS**
Contact:  Gwendolyn Tonge
Ministry of Education, Culture,
Youth Affairs and Sports
St. Johns, Antigua
Tel.  (809) 462-3990

PROGRAM OF ASSISTANCE: Educational exchange - Sanitation - Women - Crafts - Medical education - Food/food products.

PERSONNEL: U.S. and local volunteers.

PROGRAM INITIATION: 1981

. . . . . . . . . .

HOPE/ATG

* **THE PEOPLE-TO-PEOPLE HEALTH FOUNDATION, INC.**
**Project HOPE**
Contact:  Agatha Lowe, Nurse Educator
          Project HOPE
          P.O. Box 1076
          St. Johns, Antigua
          Tel.  (809) 462-1014

PROGRAM OF ASSISTANCE:  Medical education - Nurses - Sanitation.

PERSONNEL: 9 U.S., 5 local.

PROGRAM INITIATION:  1980

COOPERATING ORGANIZATIONS:  Government of Antigua, Ministry of Health, U.S. Agency for International Development.

. . . . . . . . . .

SALVA/ATG

*+ **THE SALVATION ARMY**
Contact:  Major Joshua Pyle
          P.O. Box 2
          36 Long Street
          St. Johns, Antigua
          Tel.  20-115

Assists programs operated by the international organization.

PROGRAM OF ASSISTANCE:  Counseling - Preschool programs - Community centers.

PROGRAM INITIATION:  1903

. . . . . . . . . .

**ANTIGUA - PROGRAM SUPPORT**

| | |
|---|---|
| * American Dentists for Foreign Service | $ 1,000 |
| Carr Foundation | ----- |
| Darien Book Aid Plan, Inc. | ----- |
| Freedom House, Inc. | 60 |
| International Book Project, Inc. | 1,976 |

|                                                      |        |
|------------------------------------------------------|--------|
| International Book Project, Inc.                      | 1,976  |
| International Liaison, Inc.                           | -----  |
| Lions Clubs International                            | -----  |
| Moravian Church in America, Inc.                     | -----  |
| * National 4-H Council                               | -----  |
| Operation Crossroads Africa, Inc.                    | -----  |
| Oxfam America                                        | 24,600 |
| * Pan American Development Foundation                | -----  |
| Trickle Up Program                                   | 1,100  |
| United Methodist Church                              | -----  |
| United Methodist Committee on Relief                 | 7,500  |
| * Volunteers in Technical Assistance, Inc. (VITA)    | -----  |

---

## BAHAMAS

---

Of the 14 U.S. organizations listed in the Bahamas,
3 were able to provide TAICH with financial data
indicating program expenditures for FY 1982
totaling $122,963.


OSF CLINTON/BHS

**SISTERS OF ST. FRANCIS (CLINTON, IOWA) (O.S.F.)**
Contact:  Sister Pauline Logsdon (O.S.F.)
          P.O. Box 2418
          Freeport, Bahamas
          Tel.  (809) 373-1242

PROGRAM OF ASSISTANCE:  Elementary schools.

PERSONNEL:  2 U.S.


. . . . . . . . . .


GMU/BHS

**GOSPEL MISSIONARY UNION**

Contact:  Bud Couts
          P.O. Box 14
          Tarpum Bay
          Eleuthera, Bahamas

PROGRAM OF ASSISTANCE:  High schools - Adult education - Youth.

PERSONNEL:  15 U.S., 2 local, 1 international.

PROGRAM INITIATION:  1960

COOPERATING ORGANIZATION:  Brethren Church.
. . . . . . . . . .

* **LA LECHE LEAGUE INTERNATIONAL**
Contact:  Huguette Rassin
          La Leche League of the Bahamas
          P.O. Box 972
          Nassau, Bahamas
          Tel.  (809) 3232319

PROGRAM OF ASSISTANCE:  Self-help programs - Women's education - Breast-feeding - Mother/child programs.

PERSONNEL:  1 international.

PROGRAM INITIATION:  1981

..........

PADF/BHS
* **PAN AMERICAN DEVELOPMENT FOUNDATION**
Contact:  Andrew Edwards
          Executive Director
          Development Foundation of the Bahamas
          P.O. Box N 7693
          Nassau, Bahamas
          Tel. 809-325-3311

PROGRAM OF ASSISTANCE:  Credit/loans - Income generation - Management training - Small enterprises - Self-help - Institution building.

PROGRAM INITIATION:  1981

COOPERATING ORGANIZATION:  Private Agencies Collaborating Together, Inc. (PACT).

..........

SALESIAN FR/BHS
* **SALESIAN SOCIETY, INC.**
**Salesians of St. John Bosco (S.D.B)**
Contact:  Rev. Robert Grant, S.D.B.
          P.O. Box F 633
          Hunter, Grand Bahama, Bahamas

PROGRAM OF ASSISTANCE:  Elementary schools - High schools - Youth.

PERSONNEL:  5 U.S.

PROGRAM INITIATION:  1970

..........

SALVA/BHS

**\*+  THE SALVATION ARMY**
Contact:  Major Neil Saunders
P.O. Box N 205
Nassau, Bahamas
Tel. (809) 325-2445

Assists programs operated by the internatinal organization.

PROGRAM OF ASSISTANCE:  Counseling - Rehabilitation - Community centers.

PROGRAM INITIATION:  1931

..........

**BAHAMAS - PROGRAM SUPPORT**

| | | |
|---|---|---|
| \* | Brother's Brother Foundation | $99,000 |
| | Catholic Medical Mission Board, Inc. | 21,463 |
| \* | Council of International Programs for Youth Leaders and Social Workers, Inc. | 2,500 |
| | Darien Book Aid Plan, Inc. | ----- |
| | Freedom House, Inc. | ----- |
| | International Liaison, Inc. | ----- |
| | Lions Clubs International | ----- |
| \* | Volunteers in Technical Assistance (VITA) | ----- |

---

**BARBADOS**

---

Of the 27 U.S. organizations listed in Barbados,
12 were able to provide TAICH with financial data
indicating program expenditures for FY 1982
totaling $614,553.

BEREAN/BRB

**BEREAN MISSION, INC.**
Contact:  Rev. Mark Haeck
P.O. Box 712C
Bridgetown, Barbados
Tel. (809) 424-2252

PROGRAM OF ASSISTANCE:  Education - Literacy education - Courses - Conferences
- Seminars.

PERSONNEL:  4 U.S., 4 local.

PROGRAM INITIATION:  1957

..........

\* **INTERNATIONAL EYE FOUNDATION**
Contact:  A.M.S. Connell, Director
          Inter-Island Eye Services
          Consultant Ophthalmic Surgeon
          Golf Club Road
          Rockley, Barbados

PROGRAM OF ASSISTANCE:  Medical education - Medical equipment - Medical supplies - Air transportation - Consultants.

PERSONNEL:  1 international.

PROGRAM INITIATION:  1983          EXPENDITURES FOR FY 1982:  $6,000

COOPERATING ORGANIZATIONS:  Alcon, Inc., Chibret International, Ethicon, Inc., Inter-island Eye Services, Merck and Co., Inc., Pan American Health Organization, Royal Commonwealth Society for the Blind.

..........

\* **LA LECHE LEAGUE INTERNATIONAL**
Contact:  Ann Harrison
          La Leche League of Barbados
          Enterprise Coast Road
          Christ Church, Barbados
          Tel.  87331

PROGRAM OF ASSISTANCE:  Self-help programs - Women's education - Breast-feeding - Mother/child programs.

PERSONNEL:  1 international.

PROGRAM INITIATION:  1979

..........

\* **PAN AMERICAN DEVELOPMENT FOUNDATION**
Contact:  National Development Foundation of Barbados
          c/o Rev. E. Wason
          Noranda House, Collymore Rock
          St. Michael, Barbados

          Ministry of Education
          Jemmott's Lane
          Bridgetown, Barbados

PROGRAM OF ASSISTANCE:  Credit/loans - Income generation - Management training - Small enterprises - Self help programs - Institution building - Vocational education - Tools.

PROGRAM INITITATION:  1981

TAICH Regional                    72

COOPERATING ORGANIZATIONS:   U.S. Agency for International Development; U.S. manufacturers of tools related to vocational training.

.........

\* **PARTNERS OF THE AMERICAS**
Contact:  Ms. Jacqueline Griffith Banfield
          Richmond, Welches
          St. Michael 16, Barbados
          Tel.  (809) 426-5129

PROGRAM OF ASSISTANCE:   Leadership training - Educational exchange - Agricultural training - Women - Crafts - Vocational education - Rehabilitation - Small enterprises - Nutrition education - Youth - Radio.

PERSONNEL:  U.S. and local volunteers.

PROGRAM INITIATION:  1978

COOPERATING ORGANIZATIONS:   Caribbean Agricultural Research and Development Institute (CARDI), Caribbean Institute for Mental Retardation, University of the West Indies, YMCA.

.........

\*+ **THE SALVATION ARMY**
Contact:  Captain Eugene Anderson
          P.O. Box 57
          Reed Street
          Bridgetown, Barbados
          Tel.  62467

Assists programs operated by the international organization.

PROGRAM OF ASSISTANCE:   Community centers - Preschool programs - Hostels - Food distribution centers.

PROGRAM INITIATION:  1898

.........

**SISTERS OF THE SORROWFUL MOTHER (THIRD ORDER OF ST. FRANCIS) (S.S.M.)**
Contact:  Sister Christine Henry (S.S.M.)
          Villa Maria Convent
          Ashton Hall, St. Peter
          Barbados

PROGRAM OF ASSISTANCE:  Hospitals.
PERSONNEL:  1 U.S.

PERSONNEL:  1 U.S.

PROGRAM INITIATION:  1969          EXPENDITURES FOR FY 1982:  $40,000

. . . . . . . . . .

**BARBADOS - PROGRAM SUPPORT**

|  |  |  |
|---|---|---|
| | A.T. International | $ 10,000 |
| * | AFL-CIO - American Institute for Free labor Development | (see regional listing) |
| | AFS International/Intercultural Programs | 3,000 |
| | American Public Health Association | 17,297 |
| * | Caribbeana Council | (see regional listing) |
| | Carnegie Corporation of New York | 50,000 |
| *+ | Church World Service | (see regional listing) |
| * | Council of International Programs for Youth Leaders and Social Workers, Inc. | 1,000 |
| | Darien Book Aid Plan, Inc. | ----- |
| * | Family Planning International Assistance | 680 |
| | Ford Foundation | 258,500 |
| * | International Executive Service Corps | ----- |
| | Lions Clubs International | ----- |
| | Management Sciences for Health | ----- |
| | Moravian Church in America, Inc. | ----- |
| * | National 4-H Council | ----- |
| | National Savings and Loan League | ----- |
| * | Partnership for Productivity International | ----- |
| * | Population Council | 23,050 |
| | Trickle Up Program | 100 |
| | United States Youth Council | ----- |
| * | Volunteers in Technical Assistance, Inc. (VITA) | ----- |

---

## BELIZE

---

Of the 40 U.S. organizations listed in Belize,
23 were able to provide TAICH with financial data
indicating program expenditures for FY 1982
totaling $1,003,089 (includes 3-year
grant of $341,600).

CARE/BLZ

**\*+  CARE**
    Contact:  Harold Sillcox, Country Director
              No. 60, New Road Pickstock Street
              Belize City, Belize
              Tel.  44384, 44868

PROGRAM OF ASSISTANCE: Schools - Teacher training - Beekeeping - Tools - Nutrition education - Fishing - Cooperatives - Vocational education - Consultants.

PERSONNEL: 1 U.S., 6 local.

PROGRAM INITIATION: 1962          EXPENDITURES FOR FY 1982: $294,943

COOPERATING ORGANIZATIONS: Government of Belize, Ministries of Health, and Education, NORFARM Cooperatives, Rotary Clubs, U.S. Peace Corps.

. . . . . . . . . .

CFC/BLZ

**CHRISTIAN FOUNDATION FOR CHILDREN**
Contact:    Rev. John Waters, S.J.
            Catholic Mission
            P.O. Box 37
            Belmopan, Belize

PROGRAM OF ASSISTANCE: Children - Refugees - Elementary schools - Books.

PERSONNEL: 1 U.S.

PROGRAM INITIATION: 1982          EXPENDITURES FOR FY 1982: $1000

COOPERATING ORGANIZATIONS: Catholic Mission (Belmopan), UN High Commission for Refugees.

. . . . . . . . . .

CONS BAPT/BLZ

**CONSERVATIVE BAPTIST FOREIGN MISSION SOCIETY**
Contact:    Rev. N.T. Dellinger
            P.O. Box 131
            Belize City, Belize
            Tel.  011-501-44047

PROGRAM OF ASSISTANCE: Elementary schools - Educational funding - Extension courses - Teaching materials.

PERSONNEL: 1 U.S., 1 local.

PROGRAM INITIATION: 1960          EXPENDITURES FOR FY 1982: $7,000

COOPERATING ORGANIZATIONS: Government of Belize, Department of Education; World Vision International.

. . . . . . . . . .

CHF/BLZ

\* **COOPERATIVE HOUSING FOUNDATION**
Contact:  Mahlon Barash
         Cooperative Housing Foundation
         P.O. Box 609
         Belize City, Belize
         Tel.  501-2510

PROGRAM OF ASSISTANCE:  Housing - Construction - Cooperatives - Credit/loans -
Consultants.

PERSONNEL:  5 U.S. (includes short-term), 1 local, 3 international.

PROGRAM INITIATION:  1982

COOPERATING ORGANIZATIONS:  Credit Union League of Belize, U.S. Agency for
International Development.

. . . . . . . . . .

EAST MEN/BLZ

**EASTERN MENNONITE BOARD OF MISSIONS AND CHARITIES**
Contact:  Henry Buckwalter, Chairman
         Belize Mennonite Mission
         P.O. Box 461
         Belize City, Belize
         Tel.  2419

PROGRAM OF ASSISTANCE:  Resettlement - Agricultural cooperatives.

PERSONNEL:  2 U.S.

PROGRAM INITIATION:  1960          EXPENDITURES FOR FY 1982:  $18,000

COOPERATING  ORGANIZATIONS:   Government  of  Belize;  High  Commission  for
Refugees;  Mennonite  Central  Committee;  Mennonite  Economic  Development
Associates.

. . . . . . . . . .

FUM/BLZ

**FRIENDS UNITED MEETING**
Contact:  Sadie Vernon
         c/o Belize Christian Council
         P.O. Box 508
         Belize City, Belize

PROGRAM OF ASSISTANCE:  Youth - Social welfare.

PERSONNEL:  1 U.S., 1 local.

PROGRAM INITIATION:  1982          EXPENDITURES FOR FY 1982:  $8,000

. . . . . . . . . .

GLOBAL/BLZ

**GLOBAL OUTREACH**
Contact:  Harold Loewer
          33 Mahogany Street
          Belmopan, Belize

PROGRAM OF ASSISTANCE:  Integrated rural development - Vocational education.

PERSONNEL:  2 U.S.

PROGRAM INITIATION:  1982          EXPENDITURES FOR FY 1982:  $99,702

COOPERATING ORGANIZATION:  Government of Belize.

..........

GMU/BLZ

**GOSPEL MISSIONARY UNION**
Contact:  Phil Stamm
          P.O. Box 290
          Belize City, Belize

PROGRAM OF ASSISTANCE:  Elementary schools - High schools - Seminars - Mass media - Youth - Nutrition education.

PERSONNEL:  8 U.S., 12 local, 3 international.

PROGRAM INITIATION:  1954

COOPERATING ORGANIZATION:  Government of Belize, Department of Education.

..........

HOLY FAM SR/BLZ

**CONGREGATION OF THE SISTERS OF THE HOLY FAMILY (S.S.F.)**
Contact:  Sister Margaret King (S.S.F.)
          Sisters of the Holy Family
          Zangriga, Belize
          Tel.  05-2018

PROGRAM OF ASSISTANCE:  Elementary schools - High schools.

PERSONNEL:  5 U.S.

EXPENDITURES FOR FY 1982:  $1,000 (not including personnel)

..........

MCC/BLZ

**\*+ MENNONITE CENTRAL COMMITTEE, INC.**
Contact: Nelson Weber
P.O. Box 77
Belmopan, Belize
Tel. 08-24581

PROGRAM OF ASSISTANCE: Land tenure - Resettlement - Agricultural extension - Credit/loans - Health education - Clinics.

PERSONNEL: 4 U.S., 3 local.

PROGRAM INITIATION: 1981            EXPENDITURES FOR FY 1982: $20,000
(plus $250,000 in UNHCR funds)

COOPERATING ORGANIZATIONS: Government of Belize, Ministry of Home Affairs; Spanish Lookout Mennonite Colony; U.N. High Commission for Refugees.

. . . . . . . . . .

MEDA/BLZ

**MENNONITE ECONOMIC DEVELOPMENT ASSOCIATES, INC.**
Contact: William Houser
c/o Mennonite Central Committee
P.O. Box 77
Belmopan, Belize

PROGRAM OF ASSISTANCE: Crop improvement - Farm machinery - Storage - Economic research - Cooperatives.

PERSONNEL: 1 U.S.

PROGRAM INITIATION: 1970            EXPENDITURES FOR FY 1982: $3,800

COOPERATING ORGANIZATIONS: Canadian International Development Agency, Government of Belize, Ministry of Natural Resources.

. . . . . . . . . .

PADF/BLZ

**\* PAN AMERICAN DEVELOPMENT FOUNDATION**
Contact: National Development Foundation of Belize
c/o Victor L. Bryant & Co., Ltd.
P.O. Box 36
Belize City, Belize

PROGRAM OF ASSISTANCE: Credit/loans - Grants - Income generation - Management training - Small enterprises - Self-help programs - Institution building - Medical equipment.

PROGRAM INITIATION: 1981

COOPERATION ORGANIZATIONS: U.S. Agency for International Development; U.S. health care institutions, hospitals, and manufacturers of medical equipment.

\* **PARTNERS OF THE AMERICAS**
Contact:   Robert Mahler, President
P.O. Box 703
Belize, Belize
Tel.  7202

PROGRAM OF ASSISTANCE:   Dentistry - Nutrition education - Agricultural
extension - Income generation - Educational exchange - Women.

PERSONNEL:   U.S. and local volunteers.

PROGRAM INITIATION:   1966

COOPERATING ORGANIZATIONS:   CARE; Government of Belize, Ministry of Social
Welfare; Heifer Project International; Save the Children.

. . . . . . . . . .

\* **PEOPLE-TO-PEOPLE HEALTH FOUNDATION, INC.**
**Project HOPE**
Contact:   Dr. Peter Fields
P.O. Box 636
Belize City, Belize

PROGRAM OF ASSISTANCE:   Medical education - Schools - Research/field studies -
Evaluation - Needs assessment - Sanitation - Potable water - Policy and
planning - Disease treatment.

PERSONNEL:   1 U.S.

PROGRAM INITIATION:   1983

COOPERATING ORGANIZATION:   Government of Belize, Ministry of Health.

. . . . . . . . . .

\* **PROJECT CONCERN INTERNATIONAL**
Contact:   Daniel Domizio
Project Concern Belize
Medical Department
P.O. Box 15
Punta Gorda,. Belize

PROGRAM OF ASSISTANCE:   Disease treatment - Medical auxiliaries - Medical
education - Potable water - Preventive medicine - Public health education -
Sanitation - Toilet facilities - Viral bacterial/diseases - Family planning -
Mother/child programs.

PERSONNEL:   1 U.S.

PROGRAM INITIATION:   1982          EXPENDITURES FOR FY 1982:   $35,000

TAICH Regional                    79

COOPERATING ORGANIZATIONS: Government of Belize, Ministry of Health, Housing, and Cooperatives; Toledo District Health Service; local government.

.........

ROTARY/BLZ

**ROTARY INTERNATIONAL**
Contact:  Leslie Sharp
          c/o Belize Sugar Board
          Libertad, Corozal District
          Belize

PROGRAM OF ASSISTANCE:  Agricultural extension.

PROGRAM INITIATION:  1982          EXPENDITURES FOR FY 1982:  $341,600
                                                              (3 year grant)

COOPERATING ORGANIZATIONS:  Government of Belize, Ministry of Education, Agriculture, Social Services; Heifer Project International; U.S. Peace Corps.

.........

SALVA/BLZ

**\*+   THE SALVATION ARMY**
Contact:  Capt. Keith Graham
          P.O. Box 64
          9 Glynn Street
          Belize City, Belize

Assists programs operated by the international organization.

PROGRAM OF ASSISTANCE:  Community centers - Preschool programs - Hostels.

PROGRAM INITIATION:  1915

.........

SBC/BLZ

**SOUTHERN BAPTIST CONVENTION**

Works through local national churches.

PROGRAM OF ASSISTANCE:  Agricultural training - Land reclamation - Appropriate technology.

PROGRAM INITIATION:  1977          EXPENDITURES FOR FY 1982:  $148,400

.........

* **WINROCK INTERNATIONAL**
  Contact:   The Honorable Florencio Marin
             Ministry of Natural Resources
             Belmopan, Belize

PROGRAM OF ASSISTANCE:  Appropriate technology - Integrated rural development
- Research/field studies - Consultants - Crop improvement - Range animals -
Income generation - Marketing - Food/food products - Evaluation - Animal feed.

PERSONNEL:  3 U.S.

PROGRAM INITIATION:  1982          EXPENDITURES FOR FY 1982:  $40,660

COOPERATING ORGANIZATION:  U.S. Agency for International Development.

............

*+ **WORLD VISION RELIEF ORGANIZATION, INC.**
   Contact:   Paul Petersen
              Associate Director, Field Projects
              World Vision International
              Curridabat Apartado 133
              San Jose, Costa Rica

PROGRAM OF ASSISTANCE:  Sponsorships.

PROGRAM INITIATION:  1973          EXPENDITURES FOR FY 1982:  $38,256

COOPERATING ORGANIZATIONS:  Local churches and municipal institutions.

**BELIZE - PROGRAM SUPPORT**

|  |  |  |
|---|---|---|
|  | Carr Foundation | ----- |
| * | Compassion Relief and Development | ----- |
|  | Council of International Programs | |
|  |    for Youth Leaders and Social Workers, Inc. | $ 1,000 |
|  | Darien Book Aid Plan, Inc. | ----- |
|  | Farallones Institute | ----- |
|  | Freedom House, Inc. | 150 |
| *+ | Heifer Project International, Inc. | 38,473 |
|  | Interchurch Medical Assistance, Inc. | 25,153 |
|  | International Agricultural Development Service | 6,500 |
|  | International Book Project, Inc. | 1,926 |
| * | International Executive Service Corps | ----- |
|  | Lions Clubs International | ----- |
| *+ | MAP International | 2,326 |
| * | National 4-H Council | ----- |
|  | Operation Crossroads Africa, Inc. | ----- |
| * | Sister Cities International | ----- |
|  | Trickle Up Program | 500 |
|  | United Church Board for World Ministries (Service | |
|  |    Division) | 10,500 |

TAICH Regional                    81

United Methodist Church                                          -----
United Methodist Committee on Relief                           7,600
Volunteer Optometric Services to Humanity
  (VOSH International)                                           -----

---

## BERMUDA

---

Of the 3 U.S. organizations listed in Bermuda,
1 was able to provide TAICH with financial data
indicating program expenditures for FY 1982
totaling $353,120.

SALVA/BER

**\*+    THE SALVATION ARMY**
Contact:   Major William Ratcliffe
           P.O. Box 412
           Reid Street
           Hamilton 5, Bermuda
           Tel. (809) 292-0601

Assists programs operated by the international organization.

PROGRAM OF ASSISTANCE:   Community centers - Orphanages - Counseling.

PROGRAM INITIATION:   1896

..........

**BERMUDA - PROGRAM SUPPORT**

W.K. Kellogg Foundation                                      $353,120
Lions Clubs International                                       -----

---

## CAYMAN ISLANDS

---

There are 4 U.S. organizations listed in Cayman Islands.

LECHE/CYM

**\*    LA LECHE LEAGUE INTERNATIONAL**
Contact:   Hyacinth G. Rose
           La Leche League of the British West Indies
           P.O. Box 302
           Grand Cayman, Cayman Islands
           Tel. 72370

PROGRAM OF ASSISTANCE: Breastfeeding - Mother/child programs - Self-help programs - Women's education.

PERSONNEL: 1 international.

PROGRAM INITIATION: 1982

. . . . . . . . . .

**CAYMAN ISLANDS - PROGRAM SUPPORT**

Darien Book Aid Plan, Inc. -----
Lions Clubs International -----
Operation Crossroads Africa, Inc. -----

---

## COSTA RICA

---

Of the 67 U.S. organizations listed in Costa Rica,
33 were able to provide TAICH with financial data
indicating program expenditures for FY 1982
totaling $5,113,447.

AFL-CIO/CRI

* **AFL-CIO - American Institute of Free Labor Development**
Contact: Roberto Cazares, Country Program Director
Apartado 4788
San Jose, Costa Rica

PROGRAM OF ASSISTANCE: Unions - Seminars - Adult education - Educational exchange.

PERSONNEL: 1 U.S.

PROGRAM INITIATION: 1965

COOPERATING ORGANIZATIONS: U.S. Agency for International Development.

. . . . . . . . . .

AITEC/CRI

* **ACCION INTERNATIONAL/AITEC**
Contact: Henry Karczynski
ACCION International/AITEC
Apartado Postal 5860
San Jose, Costa Rica

PROGRAM OF ASSISTANCE: Agricultural cooperatives - Agricultural training - Animal feed - Beekeeping - Biogas/methane - Cash crops - Conservation - Crop improvement and processing - Dairies - Demonstration projects - Farm machinery - Fruits - Grains - Intensive farming - Irrigation - Nurseries - Orchards - Reforestation - Solar energy - Vegetables.

PERSONNEL: 1 U.S., 1 local.

PROGRAM INITIATION: 1976          EXPENDITURES FOR FY1982: $79,871

COOPERATING ORGANIZATIONS: Government of Costa Rica, Ministry of Agriculture; Inter-American Foundation; Private Agencies Collaborationg Together (PACT); U.S. Agency For International Development.

. . . . . . . . . .

CARE/CRI

**\*+  CARE**
Contact:   George Menegay, Country Director
           Apartado 3571
           San Jose, Costa Rica
           Tel. 21-19-78, 22-04-49

PROGRAM OF ASSISTANCE: Food/food products - Food supply programs - Food-for-work - PL 480 - Mother/child health - Construction - Agricultural training - Crop improvement - Credit/loans - Seeds - Fertilizers - Potable water - Water - Self-help programs - Management training - Community centers.

PERSONNEL: 1 U.S., 15 local.

PROGRAM INITIATION: 1957          EXPENDITURES FOR FY 1982: $2,860,157

COOPERATING ORGANIZATIONS: Central Agricola de Cartago S.A. (CACSA); Government of Costa Rica, Ministries of Health and Agriculture, Social Assistance Institute, National Insurance Institute; Seed Research Center (CIGRAS).

CRS/CRI

**\*+  CATHOLIC RELIEF SERVICES - UNITED STATES CATHOLIC CONFERENCE**
Contact:   Mark D. Moriarty, Program Director
           Apartado 5483
           San Jose, Costa Rica
           Tel.  32-63-61

PROGRAM OF ASSISTANCE: Needs assessment - Funding - Seminars - Adult education - Cooperatives - Research/field studies - Clothing - Small enterprises - Demonstration projects - Agricultural training - Nutrition education - Public health education - Vocational education - Legal services - Cooperatives - Clinics - Cottage industries - Income generation - Refugees - Food distribution centers.

PERSONNEL: 2 U.S., 5 local.

PROGRAM INITIATION: 1963          EXPENDITURES FOR FY 1982: $75,855

COOPERATING ORGANIZATIONS: Caritas-Costa Rica, Caritas Denmark, European Economic Community, FECOPA (Federation of Agricultural Cooperatives), Government of Costa Rica, Koch Foundation, O'Neil Foundation, U.S. Peace Corps.

. . . . . . . . . .

CRWRC/CRI

+ **CHRISTIAN REFORMED WORLD RELIEF COMMITTEE**
Contact:   Jim Boldenow
           Apartado 225
           San Francisco de Dos Rios
           San Jose, Costa Rica
           Tel.  275397

PROGRAM OF ASSISTANCE: Adult education - Agricultural training - Consultants - Integrated rural development - Management training - Self-help programs - Translation programs.

PERSONNEL: 3 U.S.                   EXPENDITURES FOR FY 1982:  $175,000.

COOPERATING ORGANIZATIONS: Alfalit International, Cavanes, Christian Reformed World Missions.

. . . . . . . . . .

CG ANDER/CRI

**CHURCH OF GOD, INC. (ANDERSON, INDIANA)**
Contact:   Rev. Keith L. Plank
           Apartado 6048
           San Jose, Costa Rica
           Tel.  24-02-57

PROGRAM OF ASSISTANCE:  Community centers - Vocational education - Women - Youth.

PERSONNEL:  2 U.S.

PROGRAM INITIATION:  1977

. . . . . . . . . .

CWS/CRI

*+ **CHURCH WORLD SERVICE**
Contact:   Kenneth Vargas
           c/o Asociacion Caravanas de Buena Voluntad
           Apartado 10250
           San Jose, Costa Rica
           Tel.  26-63-50, 26-35-71

Provides funds and materiel.

TAICH Regional                     85

PROGRAM OF ASSISTANCE: Clothing - Food/food products - Seeds - Medical supplies.

PERSONNEL: Local.

PROGRAM INITIATION: 1974          EXPENDITURES FOR 1982: $86,895

. . . . . . . . . .

COMBONI FR/CRI

**COMBONI MISSIONARIES OF THE HEART OF JESUS, INC. (M.C.C.J.)**
Contact:   Rev. Fr. Juan Pedro Pini, (M.C.C.J.), Father Provincial
               representative
           Apartado 8-3480
           1000 San Jose, Costa Rica
           Tel.  272753/213932

U.S. Comboni Missionaries cooperate with the International Missioneros Combonianos to support the programs listed below.

PROGRAM OF ASSISTANCE: Educational funding - Material assistance.

PERSONNEL: 6 international.

PROGRAM INITIATION: 1979

. . . . . . . . . .

CONS MEN/CRI

**CONSERVATIVE MENNONITE BOARD OF MISSIONS AND CHARITIES, INC.**
Contact:   Nelson Martin, Field Director
           Servicio Voluntario Menonita
           Apartado 4520
           San Jose, Costa Rica

PROGRAM OF ASSISTANCE: Wells - Social welfare - Women's education.

PERSONNEL: 3 U.S.

PROGRAM INITIATION: 1962          EXPENDITURES FOR FY 1982: $4,084

. . . . . . . . . .

EPISCO/CRI

\*  **THE EPISCOPAL CHURCH IN THE U.S.A.**
   **The Domestic and Foreign Mission Society**
   **(including + PRESIDING BISHOP'S FUND FOR WORLD RELIEF)**
   Contact:   The Rt. Rev. C.J. Wilson
              Bishop of Costa Rica
              Apartado 2773
              San Jose, Costa Rica

Provides funding.

PROGRAM OF ASSISTANCE: Hostels - Youth - Counseling - Family planning - Community centers - Preschool programs - Rehabilitation - Disabled.

PERSONNEL: 1 U.S.

PROGRAM INITIATION: 1963

..........

GOODWILL/CRI

**\*+ GOODWILL INDUSTRIES OF AMERICA, INC.**
Contact: Lic. Pablo A.F. Vinocur W., Executive Director
c/o Industrias de Buena Voluntad
Apartado Aereo 6004
San Jose, Costa Rica
Tel. 37-61-43

PROGRAM OF ASSISTANCE: Vocational education - Rehabilitation - Disabled - Consultants.

PERSONNEL: 16 U.S.

PROGRAM INITIATION: 1970

COOPERATING ORGANIZATIONS: Interchurch Coordinating Organization (Netherlands), Government of Costa Rica.

..........

IIDI/CRI

**\* INSTITUTE FOR INTERNATIONAL DEVELOPMENT, INC.**
Contact: Herman Fernandez
ADAPTE
Apartado 20
1001 Plaza Gonzalez Viquez
San Jose, Costa Rica
Tel. 26-17-76

PROGRAM OF ASSISTANCE: Credit/loans - Income generation - Management training - Small enterprises.

PERSNNEL: 1 U.S., 3 local

PROGRAM INITIATION: 1982          EXPENDITURES FOR FY 1982: $75,000

COOPERATING ORGANIZATION: U.S. Agency For International Development.

..........

**INTERMEDIA**
Contact:   Rev. Gilberto Bernal Cepeda
           Apartado 292
           Alajuela, Costa Rica
           Tel.   41- 55-26

PROGRAM OF ASSISTANCE:   Funding - Libraries - Literacy education - Teaching
materials - Mass media - Teacher training.

PROGRAM INITIATION:   1962          EXPENDITURES FOR FY 1982:   $17,500

. . . . . . . . . .

\*   **LA  LECHE  LEAGUE  INTERNATIONAL**
     Contact:   Nancy Sabean
                La Leche League of Costa Rica
                Apartado 10250
                1000 San Jose, Costa Rica
                Tel.   28-49-01

PROGRAM OF ASSISTANCE:   Breast feeding - Mother/child programs - Self-help
programs - Women's education.

PERSONNEL:   1 U.S.

PROGRAM INITIATION:   1979

. . . . . . . . . .

\*+  **LUTHERAN WORLD RELIEF, INC.**
     Contact:   R. Kenneth Vargas, Executive Director
                Goodwill Caravans Association
                Apartado 10 - 250
                San Jose, Costa Rica
                Tel.   26-63-50/26-35-71

PROGRAM OF ASSISTANCE:   Agricultural cooperatives - Agricultural training -
Animal husbandry - Community centers - Construction - Crop improvement -
Family planning - Literacy education - Nutrition education - Orchards -
Potable water - Preventive medicine - Sanitation - Toilet facilities.

PROGRAM INITIATION:   1976          EXPENDITURES FOR FY 1982:   $75,000

COOPERATING ORGANIZATIONS:   Christian Reformed World Relief Committee, Church
World Service.

. . . . . . . . . .

**\*+ MENNONITE CENTRAL COMMITTEE**
Contact: Willard Heatwole, Field Director
c/o Servicio Voluntario Menonita
Apartado 4520
San Jose, Costa Rica

PROGRAM OF ASSISTANCE: Wells.

PROGRAM INITIATION: 1976

..........

**\* PARTNERS OF THE AMERICAS**
Contact: Dr. Sherman Thomas, President
c/o University of Costa Rica
San Jose, Costa Rica

PROGRAM OF ASSISTANCE: Educational exchange - Vocational education - Women's education - Rabbits - Dentistry - Rehabilitation - Disabled.

PERSONNEL: Local and U.S. volunteers.

PROGRAM INITIATION: 1965

..........

**\* SALESIAN SOCIETY, INC.**
**Salesians of St. John Bosco (S.D.B.)**
Contact: Rev. Jorge Miranda, S.D.B.
Apartado 1447
San Jose, Costa Rica
Tel. 21-50-13, 21-37-48

Supports programs of the International Salesian Society.

PROGRAM OF ASSISTANCE: Counseling - Elementary schools - High schools - Vocational education - Youth.

PERSONNEL: 25 local and international.

PROGRAM INITIATION: 1933

..........

**\*+  THE SALVATION ARMY**
Contact:   Major Bernard Smith, Divisional Officer
           Avenida 5, Entre 6 y 8
           Apartado Postal 6227
           San Jose, Costa Rica
           Tel.  22-26-81

Assists programs operated by the international organization.

PROGRAM OF ASSISTANCE:  Counseling - Crafts - Marketing - Preschool programs - Resettlement -  Social welfare - Rehabilitation.

PERSONNEL:  6 U.S., 15 local

PROGRAM INITIATION:  1907

COOPERATING ORGANIZATIONS  Canadian International Development Agency (CIDA), Tear Fund (U.K.), U.S. Agency for International Development.

..........

**SOUTHERN BAPTIST CONVENTION**

Works through local national churches.

PROGRAM OF ASSISTANCE:  Food distribution centers - Refugees.

PROGRAM INITIATION:  1975          EXPENDITURES FOR FY 1982:  $80,000

COOPERATION ORGANIZATIONS:  CESAD (a consortium of evangelical denominations organized to carry out relief efforts).

..........

**\*  WINROCK INTERNATIONAL**
Contact:  Dr. Gilberto Paez, Director
          Centro Agronomico Tropical de Investigacion y Ensenanza (CATIE)
          Turrialba, Costa Rica
          Tel.  5066431

PROGRAM OF ASSISTANCE:  Agricultural experimental centers - Research/field studies - Institution building - Agricultural training - Animal feed - Animal husbandry - Dairy animals - Swine - Poultry.

PERSNNEL:  4 U.S., 2 local

PROGRAM INITIATION:  1981          EXPENDITURES FOR FY 1982:  $17,600

COOPERATING ORGANIZATIONS:  Centro Agronomico Tropical de Investigacion y Ensenanza (CATIE), U.S. Agency for International Development, World Bank.

**\*+ WORLD CONCERN**
Contact:   Kenneth Vargas, Director
           Caravana de Buena Voluntad
           Apartado 258
           San Jose, Costa Rica
           Tel.  (507) 26-35-71

PROGRAM OF ASSISTANCE:  Agricultural training - Animal husbandry -  Clothing -
Gardens - Seeds - Veterinary services.

PERSONNEL:  10 U.S.

PROGRAM INITIATION:  1975          EXPENDITURES FOR FY 1982:  $31,129

COOPERATING ORGANIZATIONS:  Caravanas de Buena Voluntad, Government of Costa
Rica, Department of Public Health.

. . . . . . . . . .

**\*+ WORLD VISION RELIEF ORGANIZATION, INC.**
Contact:   Paul Petersen
           Associate Director, Field Projects

           World Vision International
           Curridabat Apartado 133
           San Jose, Costa Rica

PROGRAM OF ASSISTANCE:  Disaster relief - Sponsorships - Rehabilitation.

PROGRAM INITIATION:  1964          EXPENDITURES FOR FY 1982:  $50,000

COOPERATING ORGANIZATIONS:  Local churches and municipal institutions.

. . . . . . . . . .

**\*+ YOUNG MEN'S CHRISTIAN ASSOCIATION OF THE UNITED STATES**
Contact:   Jerry Shaw, General Secretary
           Apartado 70190
           San Jose, Costa Rica

PROGRAM OF ASSISTANCE:   Adult education - Audio-visual materials - Fish -
Institution building -  Integrated rural development - Research/field studies
- Self-help programs.

**COSTA RICA - PROGRAM SUPPORT**

| | |
|---|---|
| AFS International/Intercultural Programs | $ 50,000 |
| American Lung Association | ----- |
| American Public Health Association | 6,808 |
| \* Amigos de las Americas | 10,000 |

TAICH Regional                    91

|  | | |
|---|---|---:|
| | Association Internationale des Etudiants en Sciences Economiques et Commerciales (AIESEC-United States) | 1,000 |
| * | Brother's Brother Foundation | 153,000 |
| | Carr Foundation | ----- |
| | Catholic Medical Mission Board, Inc. | 757,943 |
| * | Centre for Development and Population Activities National Council of Catholic Women | 3,000 |
| | Children, Incorporated | 4,428 |
| * | Cooperative League of the U.S.A. | ----- |
| * | Council of International Programs for Youth Leaders and Social Workers, Inc. | 1,200 |
| | Darien Book Aid Plan, Inc. | ----- |
| | Family Health International | ----- |
| | Farallones Institute | ----- |
| | Ford Foundation | 355,975 |
| | Freedom House, Inc. | 180 |
| | Friends of SOS Children's Villages, Inc. | 900 |
| *+ | Heifer Project International, Inc. | 6,226 |
| | International Book Project, Inc. | 850 |
| * | International Executive Service Corps | ----- |
| | W.K. Kellogg Foundation | 45,000 |
| | Lions Club International | ----- |
| *+ | MAP International | 13,803 |
| | Mennonite Economic Development Associates, Inc. | ----- |
| | Moravian Church in America, Inc. | ----- |
| | National Council of Catholic Women, Inc. | 3,000 |
| * | National 4-H Council | ----- |
| | National Savings and Loan League | ----- |
| | Nature Conservancy | ----- |
| * | Pan American Development Foundation | ----- |
| * | Partnership for Productivity International, Inc. | ----- |
| * | Pathfinder Fund | 44,790 |
| | Rockefeller Foundation | 25,000 |
| * | Sister Cities International | ----- |
| * | Technoserve, Inc. | ----- |
| | Trickle Up Program | 4,200 |
| * | Unitarian Universalist Service Committee | ----- |
| | United Methodist Church | ----- |
| | United Methodist Committee on Relief | 51,000 |
| | United States Youth Council | ----- |
| * | Volunteer Development Corps | 30,053 |
| | Volunteer Optometric Services to Humanity (VOSH) | ----- |
| * | Volunteers in Technical Assistance, Inc. (VITA International) | ----- |

---

## CUBA

---

Of the 3 U.S. organizations listed in Cuba,
1 was able to provide TAICH with financial data
indicating program expenditures for FY 1982
totaling $284,000.

SALVA/CUB

**\*+ SALVATION ARMY**
Contact:  Major Jesus Santos
Calle 96, 5513
Marianao 14, Havana
Tel. 202171
Cuba

PROGRAM OF ASSISTANCE:  Community centers - Geriatric centers - Counseling.

PROGRAM INITIATION:  1918

..........

**CUBA - PROGRAM SUPPORT**

American Lung Association      -----
Ford Foundation               $284,000
United Methodist Church       -----

---

## DOMINICA

---

Of the 28 U.S. organizations listed in Dominica,
15 were able to provide TAICH with financial data
indicating program expenditures for FY 1982
totaling $422,265.

BEREAN/DMA

**BEREAN MISSION, INC.**
Contact:  Rev. Roy Hoover
P.O. Box 127
Roseau, Dominica

PROGRAM OF ASSISTANCE:  Elementary schools - Teacher training - Teaching
materials - Teachers

PERSONNEL:  4 U.S., 4 local.

PROGRAM INITIATION:  1971

TAICH Regional                93

**CHRISTIAN REFORMED WORLD RELIEF COMMITTEE**                    CRWRC/DMA
Contact:  Greg Geleynes
          St. Andrew's High School
          Wesley, Dominica
PROGRAM OF ASSISTANCE:  Agricultural training - Self-help programs

PERSONNEL:  1 U.S.

PROGRAM INITIATION:  1982          EXPENDITURES FOR FY 1982:  $30,000

COOPERATING ORGANIZATION:  St. Andrew's High School.


..........


\*  **PAN AMERICAN DEVELOPMENT FOUNDATION**                      PADF/DMA
Contact:  National Development Foundation of Dominica
          19-21 George Street
          Roseau, Dominica

PROGRAM OF ASSISTANCE:  Medical equipment - Medical supplies - Equipment -
Vocational education - Tools - Credit/loans - Income generation - Management
training - Small enterprises - Self-help programs - Institution building.

PROGRAM INITIATION:  1980

COOPERATING ORGANIZATIONS:  Hobart Brothers Company; National Development
Foundation of Dominica; Stanley Tools; U.S. Agency for International
Development; U.S. hospitals, health care institutions, and manufacturers of
medical equipment.


..........


\*  **PARTNERS OF THE AMERICAS**                                PARTNERS/DMA
Contact:  Charles Savarin, General Secretary
          Dominica Civil Service Association
          Kennedy Avenue
          Roseau, Dominica
          Tel:  (809) 445-2101

PROGRAM OF ASSISTANCE:  Income generation - Women - Medical education - Solar
energy - Food/food products - Reforestation.

PERSONNEL:  U.S. and local volunteers.

PROGRAM INITIATION:  1982


..........

\*   **PARTNERSHIP FOR PRODUCTIVITY INTERNATIONAL, INC.**
    Contacts: Philip Nassief, Chairman
              National Development Foundation of Dominica
              Roseau, Dominica
              Tel. (809) 445-3240
              Andrew Royer, Director
               Giraudel Farming Center
              Giraudel, Dominica
              Tel. (809) 445-3102

PROGRAM OF ASSISTANCE: Management training - Credit/loans - Small enterprises - Institution building - Economic research - Policy and planning - Information systems - Mass media - Marketing - Integrated rural development - Urban development.

PERSONNEL: 1 U.S., 6 local, 1 international.

PROGRAM INITIATION: 1980          EXPENDITURES FOR FY 1982: $10,000

COOPERATING ORGANIZATIONS: Banque Antillies (France), Barclay's Development Fund (U.K.), Government of Dominica, Inter-American Foundation, RoBo Bank Foundation (Netherlands), Rockefeller Brothers Fund, Royal Bank (Canada), U.S. Agency for International Development.

..........

**PLENTY**
Contact:  Norman Ayerst
          General Delivery
          Roseau, Dominica

PROGRAM OF ASSISTANCE: Vegetables - Vocational education - Material aid - Seeds - Crop improvement - Food preservation - Intensive farming - Gardens - Crop processing - Demonstration projects - Food/food products - Food preparation - Nutrition education.

PERSONNEL: 3 (Canadian).

PROGRAM INITIATION: 1983

COOPERATING ORGANIZATIONS: Canadian International Development Agency (CIDA);, Government of Dominica, Ministry of Education, Ministry of Agriculture; INTSOY (International Soybean Program, University of Illinois at Urbana-Champaign); Public Welfare Foundation.

..........

SCF/DMA

**\*+  SAVE THE CHILDREN FEDERATION, INC.**
Contact:  Allan Brown, Field Representative
Save the Children Federation
Hummingbird Drive
Weirs, Marigot
Dominica
P.O. Box 109
Roseau, Dominica
Tel.  (809) 445-7113

PROGRAM OF ASSISTANCE:  Community centers - Integrated rural development -
Leadership  training  -  Self-help  programs  -  Adult  education  -  Non-formal
education  -  Income-generation  -  Small  enterprises  -  Agricultural  experiment
centers  -  Agricultural  training  -  Demonstration  projects  -  Gardens  -
Vegetables - Food preparation - Nutrition education - Appropriate technology -
Youth.

PERSONNEL:  5 local, 1 international.

PROGRAM INITIATION:  1980          EXPENDITURES FOR FY 1982:  $39,000

COOPERATING  ORGANIZATIONS:    Government  of  Dominica,  U.S.  Agency  for
International Development.

. . . . . . . . . .

**DOMINICA - PROGRAM SUPPORT**

| | | |
|---|---|---:|
| | Center for Human Services | $155,875 |
| * | Centre for Development and Population Activities | ———— |
| * | Council of International Programs | |
| | for Youth Leaders and Social Workers, Inc. | 1,200 |
| | Darien Book Aid Plan, Inc. | ----- |
| * | Direct Relief International | 70,590 |
| | Freedom House, Inc. | 295 |
| *+ | Heifer Project International, Inc. | 9,086 |
| | International Book Project, Inc. | 928 |
| * | International Executive Service Corps | ----- |
| | Lions Clubs International | ----- |
| | Management Sciences for Health | ----- |
| * | National 4-H Council | ----- |
| | Nature Conservancy | ----- |
| | Operation Crossroads Africa | ----- |
| | Oxfam America | 47,314 |
| * | Pathfinder Fund | 991 |
| * | Population Council | 55,528 |
| | Stelios M. Stelson Foundation, Inc. | 138 |
| | Trickle Up Program | 1,100 |
| * | Volunteers in Technical Assistance, Inc. (VITA) | ----- |
| | United Methodist Committee on Relief | 220 |

---

## DOMINICAN REPUBLIC

---

Of the 76 U.S. organizations listed in Dominican Republic,
49 were able to provide TAICH with financial data
indicating program expenditures for FY 1982
totaling $8,417,059.


AITEC/DOM

* **ACCION INTERNATIONAL/AITEC**
   Contact:   Stephen H. Gross
              Fundacion Dominicana de Desarrollo
              Apartado Postal 857
              Santo Domingo, Dominican Republic

PROGRAM OF ASSISTANCE:   Accounting - Adult education - Conferences -
Cooperatives - Cottage industries - Courses - Crafts - Credit/loans - Income
generation - Management training - Marketing - Small enterprises.

PERSONNEL: 1 U.S.

PROGRAM INITIATION:   1980        EXPENDITURES FOR FY 1982:   $15,451

COOPERATING   ORGANIZATIONS:    A.T.   International,   Dominican   Development
Foundation,   Inter-American   Foundation,   U.S.   Agency   For   International
Development, local Dominican sources.


..........


AFL-CIO/DOM

* **AFL-CIO - American Institute for Free Labor Development**
   Contact:   Alva K. Moore
              Apartado Postal  1190
              Santo Domingo, Dominican Republic

PROGRAM OF ASSISTANCE:   Courses - Credit/loans - Seminars - Medical equipment
- Unions.

PERSONNEL:  1 U.S. and local personnel as necessary.

PROGRAM INITIATION:  1963

COOPERATING ORGANIZATIONS:  U.S. Agency for International Development.


..........

**AMERICAN BAPTIST CHURCHES IN THE USA**
Contact:  Rev. Jean Luc Phannord
lera Iglesia Bautista Misionera
Dr. Teofilo Hernandez #27
La Romana, Republica Dominicana

PROGRAM OF ASSISTANCE:  Medical services - Relief supplies.

PERSONNEL:  2 local.

PROGRAM INITIATION:  1980        EXPENDITURES FOR FY 1982:  $17,000

COOPERATING ORGANIZATION:  Haitian Baptist Convention.

. . . . . . . . . .

**\*+ AMERICAN ORT FEDERATION**
Contact:  Bernard Currat
Edificio Concordia 3er Piso - Apto. 316
Abraham Lincoln Ave., Calle 22 esq.
Apartado Postal 2609
Santo Domingo, Dominican Republic
Tel.  567-1051/52

PROGRAM OF ASSISTANCE:   On-the-job training - Management training -
Maintenance/repair - Equipment - Tools - Teaching materials.

PERSONNEL:  3 local, 1 international.

PROGRAM INITIATION:  1982        EXPENDITURES FOR FY 1982:  $99,086

COOPERATING ORGANIZATIONS:  Government of the Dominican Republic, Secretariat
of State of Public Works and Communications; U.S. Agency for International
Development.

. . . . . . . . . .

**BETHANY FELLOWSHIP, INC.**
Contact:  Bryan Holmes, Director
Distribuidora Betania
Apartado Postal 1925
Santo Domingo, Dominican Republic
Tel.  (809) 567-4630

PROGRAM OF ASSISTANCE:  Wells.

PERSONNEL:  2 U.S.

PROGRAM INITIATION:  1983

COOPERATING ORGANIZATIONS:   Lifewater, Inc.; Evangelicals for Action and Development (Dominican Republic).

. . . . . . . . . .

CARE/DOM

**\*+  CARE**
Contact:   Richard Steelman, Country Director
Almacenes CARE, Feria Ganadera
P.O. Box 1411
Santo Domingo, Dominican Republic
Tel.  533-1684, 2285, 2328

PROGRAM OF ASSISTANCE:   Agricultural economics - Agricultural training - Construction - Credit/loans - Immunizations - Income generation - Medical services - Medical education - PL 480 - Women - Mother/child health.

PERSONNEL:  3 U.S./Canada.

PROGRAM INITIATION:  1962      EXPENDITURES FOR FY 1982:  $2,966,874

COOPERATING ORGANIZATION:  FEDOCOOP (Dominican Federation of Savings and Loans and Multiple Services Cooperatives); Government of Dominican Republic, Secretariat of Public Health, Secretariat of Education.

. . . . . . . . . .

CRS/DOM

**\*+  CATHOLIC RELIEF SERVICES -- UNITED STATES CATHOLIC CONFERENCE**
Contact:   Carol Munroe, Program Director
CRS/Dominican Republic
Calle 51 esq., Calle 10 Ensanche la Fe
Apartado Postal 1457
Santo Domingo, Dominican Republic
Tel.  566-7776, 567-1271, 567-1272

Occasionally provides support through local groups in such areas as agricultural activities.

PROGRAM OF ASSISTANCE: Children - Clinics - Clothing - Construction - Dental clinics - Food supply programs - Health care teams - Information systems - Mass media - Medical supplies - Non-formal education - Nutrition education - PL 480 - Preventive medicine.

PERSONNEL:  2 U.S., 4 local.

PROGRAM INITIATION:  1961      EXPENDITURES FOR FY 1982:  $132,294

COOPERATING ORGANIZATIONS:  Caritas Dominicana, Caritas Denmark, Catholic Medical Mission Board, Center for Planning and Ecumenical Action (Dominican Republic), Danish International Development Authority, German Leprosy Relief Association, Government of the Dominican Republic, Oxfam (U.K.), U.S. Agency for International Development.

. . . . . . . . . .

**CHRISTIAN FOUNDATION FOR CHILDREN**
Contact:  Rev. Francisco Cordero, S.D.B.
          Parroguia Cristo Rey
          Barrio Cristo Rey
          Santo Dominigo, Dominican Republic
          Tel. (809) 565-1092

PROGRAM OF ASSISTANCE:  Books - Children - Clinics - Clothing - Elementary schools - Food/food products - Literacy education - Vocational education - Medical supplies - Mother/child programs - Nutrition education - Orphanges - Preschool programs - Preventive medicine - Sponsorships - Youth.

PERSONNEL:  4 local.

PROGRAM INITIATION:  1982        EXPENDITURES FOR FY 1982:  $4,000

COOPERATING ORGANIZATIONS:  Hogar y Escuela Santo Dominigo; Inspectoria Salesiana de las Antillas, Parro quia Cristo Rey.

. . . . . . . . . .

**CHRISTIAN MEDICAL SOCIETY**
Contact:  John W. Shannon, Director
          Apartado Postal 510
          Santo Domingo, Dominican Republic

PROGRAM OF ASSISTANCE:  Clinics - Health care teams - Medical services.

PERSONNEL:  3 U.S., 1 Canada.

COOPERATING ORGANIZATIONS:  Government of the Dominican Republic, local evangelical churches.

. . . . . . . . . .

**CHRISTIAN REFORMED WORLD MISSIONS**
Contact:  Rev. Raymond Brinks
          Apartado Postal 747-2
          Santo Domingo, Dominican Republic
          Tel. (809) 565-9601

PROGRAM OF ASSISTANCE:  Elementary schools - Income generation - Health care teams - Preventive medicine.

PERSONNEL:  11 U.S., 1 local.

PROGRAM INITIATION:  1980        EXPENDITURES FOR FY 1982:  $228,000

COOPERATING ORGANIZATIONS:  Christian Reformed World Relief Committee, The Luke Society.

. . . . . . . . . .

CRWRC/DOM

**+ CHRISTIAN REFORMED WORLD RELIEF COMMITTEE**
Contact:  Peter Vander Meulen
Apartado Postal 747-2
Santo Domingo, Dominican Republic

PROGRAM OF ASSISTANCE:  Integrated rural development - Self-help programs.

PERSONNEL:  4 U.S.

PROGRAM INITIATION:  1982          EXPENDITURES FOR FY 1982:  $250,000

COOPERATING ORGANIZATIONS:  Christian Reformed Church in the Dominican Republic, Christian Reformed World Missions.

. . . . . . . . . .

NAZ/DOM

**CHURCH OF THE NAZARENE**
Contact:  Rev. Marshall Griffith
Apartado Postal 1819
Santo Domingo, Dominican Republic

PROGRAM OF ASSISTANCE:  Elementary schools.

PERSONNEL:  40 local.

PROGRAM INITIATION:  1967

. . . . . . . . . . .

CWS/DOM

**\*+ CHURCH WORLD SERVICE**
Contact:  Rev. Juan Jose Feliz, Executive Director
Servicio Social de Iglesias Dominicanas, Inc.
Apartado Postal 659
Santo Domingo, Dominican Republic

Supports programs of Servicio Social de Iglesias Dominicanas (SSID) which are mentioned below.

PROGRAM OF ASSISTANCE:  Food supply programs - Fish farming - Goats - Integrated rural development - Medical services - Nutrition education.

PERSONNEL:  1 U.S., several local.

PROGRAM INITIATION:  1968          EXPENDITURES FOR FY 1982:  $202,262

COOPERATING ORGANIZATION:  Servicio Social de Iglesias Dominicanas Inc. (SSID).

. . . . . . . . . .

COMPASSION/DOM

**COMPASSION INTERNATIONAL,INC.**
\* **COMPASSION RELIEF AND DEVELOPMENT**
Contact: Wilbur Kent, Director
Apartado Postal 2829
Santo Domingo 1, Dominican Republic
Tel. (809) 567-8346

Works through existing missions and local organizations.

PROGRAM OF ASSISTANCE: Orphanages - Schools - Sponsorships - Community programs.

PERSONNEL: 3 U.S., 7 local.

PROGRAM INITIATION: 1976.     EXPENDITURES FOR FY 1982: $45,000.

COOPERATING ORGANIZATIONS: Compassion (Australia), Compassion (Canada), TEAR Fund (U.K.).

. . . . . . . . . .

CHF/DOM

\* **COOPERATIVE HOUSING FOUNDATION**
Contact: c/o USAID
Santo Domingo, Dominican Republic
APO
Miami, Florida 34041

PROGRAM OF ASSISTANCE: Housing - Construction - Cooperatives - Credit/loans - Consultants.

PROGRAM INITIATION: 1974

COOPERATING ORGANIZATION: U.S. Agency for International Development.

. . . . . . . . . .

EPISCO/DOM

\* **THE EPISCOPAL CHURCH IN THE U.S.A.**
**The Domestic and Foreign Missionary Society**
(including + **The Presiding Bishops Fund for World Relief)**
Contact: Rt. Rev. Telesforo Isaac, Bishop of the Dominican Republic
Apartado Postal 746
Santo Domingo, Dominican Republic

PROGRAM OF ASSISTANCE: Elementary schools - High schools - Clinics - Preventive medicine.

PROGRAM INITIATION: 1940

. . . . . . . . . .

EMC/DOM

**EVANGELICAL MENNONITE CHURCH, INC.**
Contact:  Harry Hyde, Missionary Coordinator
          Apartado Postal 603
          Santo Domingo, Dominican Republic

PROGRAM OF ASSISTANCE:  Cooperatives - Educational funding - Fish farming -
Gardens - Goats - Sponsorships.

PERSONNEL:  3 U.S.

PROGRAM INITIATION:  1962

COOPERATING ORGANIZATION:    Government of Dominican Republic, Agriculture
Extension Agency.

..........

FHI/DOM

\* **FOOD FOR THE HUNGRY INTERNATIONAL**
Contact:  Bernabe Manon Rossi, Field Projects Coordinator, Central
          America/Caribbean Coordinator
          Av. Pasteur #104
          Apartado Postal 2686
          Santo Domingo, Dominican Republic
          Tel. (809) 688-0875

PROGRAM OF ASSISTANCE:  Adult education - Agricultural training - Appropriate
technology - Community centers - Credit/loans - Dental clinics - Food
distribution centers - Gardens - Mother/child programs - Self-help programs -
Vocational education - Volunteers.

PERSONNEL: 3 U.S., 3 local.

PROGRAM INITIATION:  1976        EXPENDITURES FOR FY 1982:  $90,000

..........

FREE METH/DOM

**FREE METHODIST CHURCH OF NORTH AMERICA**
Contact:  Mrs. Ruth Bonney, Sponsorship Coordinator
          Apartado Postal 315
          Santiago, Dominican Republic

PROGRAM OF ASSISTANCE:  Sponsorships.

PERSONNEL:  3 U.S., 34 local.

PROGRAM INITIATION:  1982        EXPENDITURES FOR FY 1982:  $5,130

COOPERATING ORGANIZATION:  Compassion International, Inc.

..........

* **THE VICTORIA AND ALBERT GILDRED FOUNDATION FOR LATIN AMERICAN HEALTH AND EDUCATION**

PROGRAM OF ASSISTANCE: Medical services.

PERSONNEL: 15 U.S.

PROGRAM INITIATION: 1981          EXPENDITURES FOR FY 1982: $30,000

COOPERATING ORGANIZATION: Georgetown University.

. . . . . . . . . .

* **HOLY LAND CHRISTIAN MISSION INTERNATIONAL**
Contact:   Siervas de los Pobres
           Programa Amigos de los Ninos
           Sister Bertha Sanchez
           Apartado Postal 24
           Mao, Dominican Republic
           Tel.  (809) 572-3540

PROGRAM OF ASSISTANCE:  Animal husbandry -   Clothing - Education - Fish farming - Food/food products - Health care teams - Land tenure - Medical services - Orphanages - Refugees - Sponsorships.

PERSONNEL:  1 international.

PROGRAM INITIATION:  1981          EXPENDITURES FOR FY 1982:  $81,166

COOPERATING ORGANIZATION:  Siervas de los Pobres.

. . . . . . . . . .

* **INSTITUTE FOR INTERNATIONAL DEVELOPMENT, INC.**
Contact:   Rafael Contrenas
           ASPIRE
           Apartado 5, 1B
           Edificio, Aneitas
           Ensanche Tantin
           Santo Domingo, Dominican Republic
           Tel.  565-2863

PROGRAM OF ASSISTANCE:  Credit/loans - Income generation - Management training - Small enterprises.

PERSONNEL:  1 U.S., 3 local

PROGRAM INITIATION:  1982          EXPENDITURES FOR FY 1982:  $100,000

COOPERATING ORGANIZATION:  U.S. Agency for International Development.

. . . . . . . . . .

INTL EYE/DOM

**\* INTERNATIONAL EYE FOUNDATION**
Contact: Milagros Colon, R.N., C.O.M.T.
        I.E.F. Project Director
        c/o Rudy Fascell
        USAID
        APO Miami, Florida 34041

PROGRAM OF ASSISTANCE: Blindness prevention - Books - Medical education - Medical equipment - Medical supplies - Vehicles - Volunteers.

PERSONNEL: 1 U.S.

PROGRAM INITIATION: 1982      EXPENDITURES FOR FY 1982: $40,000

COOPERATING ORGANIZATIONS: Alcon; Chibret International; Department of Ophthalmology, Inc.; Ethicon, Inc.; Government of the Dominican Republic; Merck and Co., Inc.; U.S. Agency for International Development; University of Puerto Rico.

.........

SSJR/DOM

**SISTERS OF ST. JOSEPH (C.S.J.)**
**Rockville Center Diocese**
Contact: Sister Jane Reilly, C.S.J.
        Sisters of St. Joseph
        Hondovalle, Dominican Republic

PROGRAM OF ASSISTANCE: Clinics - Counseling - Dentistry - Medical auxiliaries - Medical supplies - Nutrition education - Self-help programs.

PERSONNEL: 2 U.S.

PROGRAM INITIATION: 1980

.........

MEDA/DOM

**MENNONITE ECONOMIC DEVELOPMENT ASSOCIATES, INC.**
Contact: Harry L. Hyde
        Apartado Postal 603
        Santo Domingo, Dominican Republic
        Tel. (809) 567-2063

PROGRAM OF ASSISTANCE: Credit/loans - Leadership training - Marketing.

PERSONNEL: 1 U.S., 2 local.

PROGRAM INITIATION: 1981      EXPENDITURES FOR FY 1982 $10.000

COOPERATING ORGANIZATIONS: Canadian International Development Agency (CIDA), Evangelical Mennonite Church.

.........

**MISSIONARY CHURCH, INC.**
Contact:   Rev. Mark Snider
           Asociacion de Iglesias Misioneras
           Apartado Postal 600
           Santo Domingo, Dominican Republic

PROGRAM OF ASSISTANCE:  Medical services.

PERSONNEL:  Number of U.S. personnel varies.

PROGRAM INITIATION:  1960        EXPENDITURES FOR FY 1982:  $300

. . . . . . . . . .

**MISSIONS HEALTH FOUNDATION, INC.**

PROGRAM OF ASSISTANCE:  Animal husbandry - Potable water - Swine.

PROGRAM INITIATION:  1982        EXPENDITURES FOR FY 1982:  $4,600

. . . . . . . . . .

\*   **PAN AMERICAN DEVELOPMENT FOUNDATION**
     Contact:   Fundacion Dominicana de Desarrollo
                Calle Mercedes
                Apartado Postal 857
                Santo Domingo, Dominican Republic

Primarily supports programs of the Fundacion Dominicana de Desarrollo
(FUNDADOM).

PROGRAM OF, ASSISTANCE:   Medical equipment - Vocational education -
Reforestation - Credit/loans - Courses.

PROGRAM INITIATION: 1966

COOPERATING ORGANIZATIONS:  Fundacion Dominicana de Desarrollo; U.S. Agency
for International Development; U.S. health care institutions, hospitals, and
manufacturers of medical equipment and supplies; U.S. manufacturers of
equipment for vocational training.

. . . . . . . . . .

\*   **PARTNERS OF THE AMERICAS**
     Contact:   c/o Dr. Emile A. de Boyrie
                Dominican Republic Partners
                Apartado Postal 236-9
                Los Jardines
                Santo Domingo, Dominican Republic
                Tel.  (809) 566-1131

PROGRAM OF ASSISTANCE: Educational exchange - Mass Media - Women - Seminars - Agricultural training - Nutrition education - Poultry - Medical training - Rehabilitation - Disabled.

PERSONNEL: Volunteer only.

PROGRAM INITIATION: 1970

COOPERATING ORGANIZATIONS: Fundacion Dominicana de Desarrollo; Government of the Dominican Republic, Ministry of Education; Save the Children Federation; University Madre y Maestra; U.S. Agency for International Development; the U.S. Embassy.

. . . . . . . . . .

REDEM FR/DOM

**REDEMPTORIST FATHERS (C.SS.R.)**
Contact:   Very Rev. Thomas Gavigan, C.SS.R., Superior
            Padres Redentoristas
            Apartado Postal 143
            San Juan de la Maguana, Dominican Republic

PROGRAM OF ASSISTANCE:   Construction - Elementary schools - Vocational education - Agricultural training.

PERSONNEL: 8 U.S., 6 local.

PROGRAM INITIATION:   1946

COOPERATING   ORGANIZATIONS:   Caritas,   U.S.   Agency   for   International Development.

. . . . . . . . . .

ROTARY/DOM

**ROTARY INTERNATIONAL**
Contact:   Dr. Pedro Ma. Perez R. (Rotary Club of Azua)
            Apartado Postal 28
            Azua, R.D. Dominican Republic

PROGRAM OF ASSISTANCE: Literacy education - Vocational education.

PROGRAM INITIATION:  1982          EXPENDITURES FOR FY 1982:  $61,500

COOPERATING ORGANIZATION:  Universidad Technologica del Sud (Azua).

. . . . . . . . . .

SALESIAN FR/DOM

* **SALESIAN SOCIETY, INC.**
**Salesians of St. John Bosco (S.D.B.)**
Contact:  Rev. Henry Mellano, S.D.B.
Calle San Juan Bosco 27-A, Zona 2
Apartado Postal 222
Santo Domingo, Dominican Republic

Supports programs of the International Salesian Society.

PROGRAM OF ASSISTANCE:  Agricultural training - Clinics - Elementary schools -
High schools - Orphanages - Vocational education.

PERSONNEL:  82 international and local.

PROGRAM INITIATION:  1934

..........

SCF/DOM

*+ **SAVE THE CHILDREN FEDERATION, INC.**
Contact:  Horacio Ornes Heded, Director
Fundacion para el Desarrollo
Comunitario, Inc. (FUDECO)
Avenida 27 de Febrero
Edificio Galerias Comerciales - Apartamento 301
Apartado Postal 366-2, Centro de los Heros
Santo Domingo, Dominican Republic
Tel. (809) 567-1175, 567-0618

PROGRAM OF ASSISTANCE:  Adult education - Agricultural experimental centers -
Agricultural training - Animal husbandry - Appropriate technology - Beekeeping
- Biogas/methane - Breastfeeding -  Children - Community centers -
Conservation - Credit/loans - Dairy animals - Demonstration projects -
Disaster relief - Elementary schools - Extension agents - Agriculturalists -
Fish - Food preparation - Food preservation - Gardens - Housing - Income-
generation - Integrated rural development - Intensive farming - Irrigation -
Leadership training - Medical education - Non-formal education - Nurseries -
Nutrition education - Pest control -  Potable water - Poultry - Preventive
medicine - Public heath education - Rabbits - Reforestation - Sanitation -
Self-help programs - Small enterprises - Sponsorships - Vegetables -
Vocational education - Women - Youth.

PERSONNEL:  33 local.

PROGRAM INITIATION:  1964      EXPENDITURES FOR FY 1982:  $845,000

COOPERATING  ORGANIZATIONS:      Canadian  Hunger  Foundation;  Deutsche
Welthungerhilfe; Government of the Dominican Republic, Ministry of Housing;
Inter-American Development Bank; Inter-American Foundation, U.S. Agency for
International Development.

..........

UFMI/DOM

**UFM INTERNATIONAL, INC.**
Contact: Rev. Larry Dawson, Field Leader
Apartado Postal 570
Santo Domingo, Dominican Republic

PROGRAM OF ASSISTANCE: Elementary schools - Teachers.

PERSONNEL: 16 U.S., 5 local.

PROGRAM INITIATION: 1961

..........

VIISA/DOM

**VOLUNTEERS IN INTERNATIONAL SERVICE**
**AND AWARENESS (VIISA)**
Contact: Agentina German, Coordinadora, Coordinator
Programe de Prevencion Antipoliomielitica
Associacion Dominicana de Rehabilitacion, Inc.
1054 J. F. Kennedy Ave.
Apartado de correos
Leopoldo Navarro
Santo Domingo, Dominican Republic
Tel. 689-7151/52

Roger Magloir Canstant
Operation Koumbite
62 Calle Guarocuya
Ensanche Quiqueya
Santo Domingo, Dominican Republic
Tel. 565-5245, 566-9345

PROGRAM OF ASSISTANCE: Self-help programs - Gardens - Intensive farming -
Reforestation - Vegetables - Immunizations - Public health education -
Nutrition education - Orphanages - Rehabilitation - Volunteers.

PERSONNEL: 8 U.S., 10 local.

PROGRAM INITIATION: 1982     EXPENDITURES FOR FY 1982: $125,000

COOPERATING ORGANIZATIONS: Asociacion Dominicana de Rehabilitacion, Inc.;
Government of the Dominican Republic; Operation Koumbite; U.S. Peace Corps.

..........

WRC/DOM

**\*+ WORLD RELIEF CORPORATION**

PROGRAM OF ASSISTANCE: Management training.

PROGRAM INITIATION: 1980     EXPENDITURES FOR FY 1982: $8,211

COOPERATING ORGANIZATIONS:   Accion Evangelica de Desarrollo, U.S. Agency for
International Development.

. . . . . . . . . .

**\*+ WORLD VISION RELIEF ORGANIZATION, INC.**
Contact:   Paul Petersen
          Associate Director, Field Projects
          World Vision International
          Curridabat Apartado 133
          San Jose, Costa Rica

PROGRAM OF ASSISTANCE:   Agricultural training - Literacy education - Medical
services - Nutrition education.

PROGRAM INITIATION:  1978       EXPENDITURES FOR FY 1982:  $66,000

. . . . . . . . . .

**\*+ YOUNG MEN'S CHRISTIAN ASSOCIATIONS OF THE UNITED STATES**
Contact:   D. Richard Domino, General Seceretary
          Asociaciones Cristianas de Jovenes
          Mercedes 501 (Altos)
          Apartado Postal 705
          Santo Domingo, Dominican Republic
          Tel.  688-7198/1507

PROGRAM OF ASSISTANCE:   Funding - Integrated rural development.

. . . . . . . . . .

**DOMINICAN REPUBLIC - PROGRAM SUPPORT**

|   | | |
|---|---|---:|
| | AFS International/Intercultural Programs | $   23,950 |
| | American Public Health International | 39,532 |
| \* | Amigos de las Americas | 20,000 |
| \* | Association for Voluntary Sterilization   (S) | 384,567 |
| \* | Brother's Brother Foundation | 2,000 |
| | Catholic Medical Mission Board, Inc. | 260,365 |
| | Center for Human Services | 73,133 |
| \* | Centre for Development and Population Activities | |
| | Children, Incorporated | 7,105 |
| \*+ | Coordination in Development, Inc. (CODEL) | 36,775 |
| \* | Council of International Programs | |
| | for Youth Leaders and Social Workers, Inc. | 1,200 |
| | Darien Book Aid Plan, Inc. | ----- |
| \* | Direct Relief International | 192,330 |
| | Education Development Center | ----- |
| \* | Family Planning International Assistance | 20,703 |

| | | |
|---|---|---|
| | Farallones Institute | ----- |
| | Ford Foundation | 4,000 |
| | Friends of SOS Children's Villages, Inc. | 1,500 |
| *+ | Heifer Project International, Inc. | 100,101 |
| | Interchurch Medical Assistance, Inc. | 19,867 |
| | International Adoptions, Inc. | 300 |
| | International Agricultural Development Service | 5,000 |
| * | International Executive Service Corps | ----- |
| | International Liaison, Inc. | ----- |
| | W.K. Kellogg Foundation | 1,431,587 |
| | Lions Clubs International | ----- |
| | Management Sciences for Health | ----- |
| *+ | MAP International | 2,637 |
| | Moravian Church in America, Inc. | ----- |
| | Orthopaedics Overseas, Inc. | ----- |
| | Outreach International | 13,400 |
| * | Pathfinder Fund | 134,455 |
| * | Population Council | 118,341 |
| * | Sister Cities International | ----- |
| | United Methodist Committee on Relief | 90,000 |
| * | Volunteers in Technical Assistance, Inc. (VITA) | ----- |
| *+ | World Concern | 7,337 |

---

## EL SALVADOR

---

Of the 41 U.S. organizations listed in El Salvador,
27 were able to provide TAICH with financial data
indicating program expenditures for FY 1982
totaling $5,443,488.

AFL-CIO/ELS

* **AFL-CIO --American Institute for Free Labor Development (AIFLO)**

PROGRAM OF ASSISTANCE: Unions - Courses - Basic education - Funding - Loans -
Community centers.

. . . . . . . . . .

ABC/SLV

**AMERICAN BAPTIST CHURCHES IN THE USA**
Contact:  Jose Rene Cedillos, Executive Secretary
          Asociacion Bautista de El Salvador
          Apartado Postal 347
          San Salvador, El Salvador

PROGRAM OF ASSISTANCE:  Integrated rural development - Elementary schools -
High schools - Cooperatives - Credit/loans - Housing - Clinics - Land tenure -
Refugees - Orphanages.

PERSONNEL:  86 local.

TAICH Regional                    111

PROGRAM INITIATION: 1920          EXPENDITURES FOR FY 1982: $45,000

COOPERATING ORGANIZATION: Baptist World Alliance.

. . . . . . . . . .

**CAM INTERNATIONAL**
Contact:  Gene Lambright, Field Committee President
          Apartado Postal CC-634
          San Salvador, El Salvador
          Tel.  25-3713

PROGRAM OF ASSISTANCE:  Food/food products - Clothing - Toilet facilities -
Orphanages - Refugees - Rehabilitation - Resettlement.

PERSONNEL: 2 local.

PROGRAM INITIATION:  1896          EXPENDITURES FOR FY 1982:          $85,500

COOPERATING ORGANIZATIONS:  Compassion International, Inc., TEAR Fund (U.K.),
World Relief.

. . . . . . . . . .

**\*+  CATHOLIC RELIEF SERVICES - UNITED STATES CATHOLIC CONFERENCE**
    Contact:  Thomas Kivlan, Program Director
              Edifico San Francisco
              40 Piso, No 7
              25 Avenida Norte #1198
              Apartado Postal 2047
              San Salvador, El Salvador
              Tel.  503-26-3998

PROGRAM OF ASSISTANCE:  Funding - Agricultural training - Crop improvement -
Food/food products - Clothing - Medical supplies - Medical equipment - Clinics
- Mother/child programs - Nutrition education - Disease treatment - Medical
education - Medical auxiliaries - Orphanages - Construction - Housing -
Displaced persons - Disaster relief - PL 480.

PERSONNEL: 2 U.S., 4 local.

PROGRAM INITIATION:  1961          EXPENDITURES FOR FY 1982:          $191,289

COOPERATING ORGANIZATIONS:  Brucke der Bruderhilfe, Caritas (Denmark), Caritas
(El Salvador), Caritas (Luxembourg), Catholic Medical Mission Board, European
Economic Community, Governments of Canada, El Salvador and the United States,
National Council of Catholic Women, Scottish Catholic International Aid Fund,

. . . . . . . . . .

CRWRC/SLV
+ **CHRISTIAN REFORMED WORLD RELIEF COMMITTEE**

PROGRAM OF ASSISTANCE: Disaster relief - Refugees - Resettlement.

EXPENDITURES FOR FY 1982: $135,000

COOPERATING ORGANIZATIONS: CESAD, local churches.

..........

EPISCO/SLV
* **THE EPISCOPAL CHURCH IN THE U.S.A.**
**(including + The Presiding Bishops Fund for World Relief)**
Contact:   The Rt. Rev. Edward Haynsworth
            815 Second Ave.
            New York, New York

PROGRAM OF ASSISTANCE:  Clinics - Agricultural training.

PERSONNEL:  2 U.S.

PROGRAM INITIATION:  1972        EXPENDITURES FOR FY 1982:  $1,700

COOPERATING ORGANIZATIONS:  Demographic Society of El Salvador; shipments of medicines are sent from U.S. through Interchurch Medical Assistance and Catholic Relief Services.

..........

FPP/SLV
* **FOSTER PARENTS PLAN**
Contact:   Larry Wolfe, Director
            Plan de Padrinos
            Apartado Postal 2233
            San Salvador, El Salvador

PROGRAM OF ASSISTANCE:  Construction - Community centers - Community programs - Housing - Bridges - Schools - Vocational education - Animal husbandry - Gardens - Clinics - Dentistry - Medical equipment - Potable water - Public health education - Sanitation - Toilet facilities - Medical services.

PERSONNEL:  124 local, 1 international.

PROGRAM INITIATION:  1976        EXPENDITURES FOR FY 1982:  $1,639,845

COOPERATING ORGANIZATIONS:  Canadian International Development Agency (CIDA) and the Provincial Government of Alberta (Canada), Government of El Salvador.

..........

OFM IMMAC/SLV
**FRANCISCAN FRIARS (O.F.M.)**
**Province of the Immaculate Conception**
Contact:  Rev. Custos, O.F.M.
          Iglesia Santissima Trinidad
          Casa Cural
          Sonsonate, El Salvador

PROGRAM OF ASSISTANCE:  Community programs - Construction - Housing - Education - Equipment - Nutrition education - Medical services - Social welfare.

PERSONNEL:  6 U.S., 39 local, 1 international.

PROGRAM INITIATION:  1946          EXPENDITURES FOR FY 1982:  $250,000

COOPERATING ORGANIZATIONS:  Franciscan Order of Friars Minor, SOS Children's Villages, Inc. (Austria).

..........

LECHE/SLV
* **LA LECHE LEAGUE INTERNATIONAL**
Contact:  Centro de Apoyo de Lactancia Materna (CALMA)
          Urbanizacion 1a Esperanza
          Diagonal 2, Poligono L-No. 226
          San Salvador, El Salvador
          Tel.  25-3063

PROGRAM OF ASSISTANCE:  Breast-feeding - Mother/child programs - Self-help programs - Women's education - Public health education.

PERSONNEL:  local only.

PROGRAM INITIATION:  1978

COOPERATING ORGANIZATION:  U.S. Agency for International Development.

..........

MCC/SLV
*+ **MENNONITE CENTRAL COMMITTEE**
Contact:  Blake Ortman
          Apartado Postal 1331
          #1124 8th Avenue N
          San Salvador, El Salvador
          Tel.  25-1741

PROGRAM OF ASSISTANCE:  Disaster relief - Displaced persons - Resettlement - Housing - Medical education - Clinics - Food distribution centers - Crafts - Gardens - Mother/child program - Self-help programs.

PERSONNEL:  3 U.S., 6 local.

TAICH Regional          114

PROGRAM INITIATION: 1980    EXPENDITURES FOR FY 1982: $130,000

COOPERATING ORGANIZATIONS: Catholic Relief Services, CRWRC, Government of El Salvador, Lutheran Church, Mennonite Voluntary Service.

..........

OEF/SLV

* **OVERSEAS EDUCATION FUND**
Contact:  Delmy Burgos, Project Director
          61A Avenida Norte #151
          San Salvador, El Salvador
          Tel. 24-68-25

PROGRAM OF ASSISTANCE:  Agricultural cooperatives - Food preservation - Community programs - Self-help programs - Literacy education - Credit/loans - Marketing - Tools - Vehicles - Institution building - Management training - Evaluation - Women.

PERSONNEL: 2 U.S., 3 local.

PROGRAM INITIATION: 1979    EXPENDITURES FOR FY 1982:    $26,893

COOPERATING ORGANIZATIONS: Calma-Centro Apoyo Lactancia Materna, Centa-Centro National of Tecndlosia Agropecuaria, Club Amas de Casa Campesinas, Government of El Salvador, Ministerio de Agricultura y Ganaderia, Technoserve, Inc., USAID/El Salvador.

..........

PARTNERS/SLV

* **PARTNERS OF THE AMERICAS**
Contact:  Clelia de Amaya
          Calle Arice No. 1280
          Edificio Alfaro Monge, 2 do Piso.
          Apt. 24
          San Salvador, El Salvador
          Tel. 21-3946

The Louisiana Partners cooperate with the El Salvador Partners in the following:

PROGRAM OF ASSISTANCE:  Agricultural education - Crop improvement - High schools - Seminars - Educational exchange - Medical supplies - Medical equipment - Rehabilitation - Evaluation - Disabled - Doctors - Cooperatives - Women's education - Leadership training.

PERSONNEL:  U.S. and local volunteers.

COOPERATING ORGANIZATIONS: Government of El Salvador, Ministries of Education and Health; Louisiana 4-H; Louisiana State University; TACA Airlines; Salvadorean Social Security Institute; Salvadorean Speech and Hearing Center.

..........

* **SALESIAN SOCIETY, INC.**
**Salesians of St. John Bosco (S.D.B.)**
Contact: Rev. Jose Carmen Di Pietro, S.D.B.
Institucion Salesiana
Apartado Postal 2324
San Salvador, El Salvador

Supports programs of the International Salesian Society.

PROGRAM OF ASSISTANCE: Elementary schools - High schools - Vocational education - Youth - Night schools.

PERSONNEL: 61 (approximately 60 percent local).

PROGRAM INITIATION: 1903

. . . . . . . . . .

*+ **SAVE THE CHILDREN FEDERATION, INC.**
Contact: David Rogers, Field Office Director
Desarrollo Juvenil Comunitario
Edificio Palomo, 40 Piso, Oficina No. 42
Calle Ruben Dario y 23 Av. Sur
Apartado 0595
San Salvador, El Salvador
Tel. 011-503-216677

PROGRAM OF ASSISTANCE: Community centers - Community programs - Leadership training - Seminars - Youth - Women - Construction - Roads - Schools - Teaching materials - Mother/child programs - Nutrition education - Breastfeeding - Immunizations - Medical services - Medical supplies - Public health education - Toilet facilities - Food/food products - Food preparation - Gardens - Agricultural training - Poultry - Credit/loans - Cottage industries - Income generation - Small enterprises - Displaced persons - Sponsorships.

PERSONNEL: 1 U.S., 41 local.

PROGRAM INITIATION: 1979          EXPENDITURES FOR FY 1982: $249,918

COOPERATING ORGANIZATIONS: Canadian International Development Agency (CIDA), Government of El Salvador , UNICEF, U.S. Agency for International Development.

. . . . . . . . .

* **TECHNOSERVE, INC.**
Contact: F. Lino Osegueda, Country Program Director
Apartado Postal (05) 38
San Salvador, El Salvador
Tel. 23-7043

PROGRAM OF ASSISTANCE: Management training - Cooperatives - Marketing - Small enterprises - Animal husbandry - Range animals - Dairies - Grains.

PERSONNEL: 25 local.

PROGRAM INITIATION: 1975          EXPENDITURES FOR FY 1982: $550,000

..........

WVRO/SLV
**\*+ WORLD VISION RELIEF ORGANIZATION, INC.**
Contact:  Paul Peterson
          Associate Director, Field Projects
          World Vision International
          Curridabat Apartado 133
          San Jose, Costa Rica

PROGRAM OF ASSISTANCE:  Sponsorships - Vocational education - Agricultural training - Water - Animal husbandry - Literacy education - Medical services - Disaster relief - Nutrition education.

PROGRAM INTIATION: 1975          EXPENDITURES FOR FY 1982: $1,716,070

COOPERATING ORGANIZATIONS: Local churches and municipal institutions.

..........

## EL SALVADOR - PROGRAM SUPPORT

| | | |
|---|---|--:|
| \* | Agua del Pueblo | ----- |
| | American Lung Association | ----- |
| + | Baptist World Aid | $ 21,000 |
| | Carr Foundation | ----- |
| \* | Centre for Development and Population Activities | |
| | Children, Incorporated | 48,679 |
| \* | Compassion Relief and Development | ----- |
| \* | Council of International Programs | |
| | for Youth Leaders and Social Workers, Inc. | 2,500 |
| | Darien Book Aid Plan, Inc. | ----- |
| \* | Direct Relief International | 29,690 |
| | Family Health International | ----- |
| | Friends of SOS Children's Villages, Inc. | 2,000 |
| | Inter-Aid, Inc. | 1,000 |
| | Interchurch Medical Assistance, Inc. | 43,981 |
| \* | International Executive Service Corps | ----- |
| | International Road Federation | 4,000 |
| | Lions Clubs International | ----- |
| | Lutheran Church - Missouri Synod | 3,380 |
| | National Council of Catholic Women | 5,000 |
| | National Savings and Loan League | ----- |
| | Oxfam America | 225,000 |
| \* | Pan American Development Foundation | ----- |
| \* | Pathfinder Fund | 1,755 |

```
     Rockefeller Foundation                        8,740
*+   Seventh-day Adventist World Service, Inc.     12,248
*    Sister Cities International                    -----
     United Methodist Committee on Relief          13,300
*    Volunteers in Technical Assistance, Inc.
     (VITA)                                         -----
```

---

## GRENADA

---

Of the 10 U.S. organizations listed in Grenada,
3 were able to provide TAICH with financial data
indicating program expenditures for FY 1982
totaling $44,695.

STPAT/GRD

**ST. PATRICK'S MISSIONARY SOCIETY (S.P.S.)**
Contact:  Rev. Oliver Leavy, S.P.S.
          Local Superior
          St. Peter's Presbytery
          Gouyave, St. John, Grenada
          Tel.  8255

PROGRAM OF ASSISTANCE:  Leadership training - Self-help programs - Women - Credit/loans - Demonstration projects - Management training - Preventive medicine - Community centers - Disabled.

PROGRAM INITIATION:  1970

. . . . . . . . . .

SALVA/GRD

**\*+   THE SALVATION ARMY**
Contact:  Salvation Army
          Grenville St.
          St. George's, Grenada

Assists programs operated by the international organization.

PROGRAM OF ASSISTANCE:  Counseling - Hostels - Community centers.

PROGRAM INITIATION:  1901

. . . . . . . . . .

## GRENADA - PROGRAM SUPPORT

| | | |
|---|---|---|
| * | Brother's Brother Foundation | $ 6,000 |
| | Carr Foundation | ----- |
| | Farallones Institute | ----- |
| | Lions Clubs International | ----- |
| * | National 4-H Council | ----- |
| | Oxfam America | 38,595 |
| * | Pan American Development Foundation | ----- |
| | Trickle Up Program | 100 |

---

## GUADELOUPE

---

There are 3 U.S. organizations listed in Guadeloupe.

## GUADELOUPE - PROGRAM SUPPORT

| | |
|---|---|
| Darien Book Aid Plan, Inc. | ----- |
| Lions Clubs International | ----- |
| Trickle Up Program | ----- |

---

## GUATEMALA

---

Of the 95 U.S. organizations listed in Guatemala,
55 were able to provide TAICH with financial data
indicating program expenditures for FY 1982
totaling $18,525,898.

AFL-CIO/GTM

* **AFL-CIO - American Institute for Free Labor Development**
  Contact:   J. Clemente Hernandez, Country Representative
              7+L Avenida
              1-20, Zona 4
              Edificio Torre-Cafe
              Guatemala City, Guatemala

Supports the program of the Instituto de Estudios Sindicales Centro-Americanos
(IESCA) which operates programs mentioned below.

PROGRAM OF ASSISTANCE:  Unions - Research/field studies - Educational funding.

PERSONNEL:  Only local.

PROGRAM INITIATION:  1974

TAICH Regional                    119

COOPERATING ORGANIZATIONS:  U.S. Agency for International Development.

. . . . . . . . . .

ACDI/GTM

**★ AGRICULTURAL COOPERATIVE DEVELOPMENT INTERNATIONAL**
Contact:  David C. Fledderjohn
Cooperative Advisor and Chief of Party, USAID/Guatemala
c/o American Embassy
APO New York  09891
Tel.  80881

PROGRAM OF ASSISTANCE:  Cooperatives - Integrated rural development - Resettlement.

PERSONNEL:  2 U.S.

PROGRAM INITIATION:  1977

COOPERATING ORGANIZATIONS:  Cooperative Federation (FECOAR); Government of Guatemala, Ministry of Agriculture; U.S. Agency for International Development.

. . . . . . . . . .

AGUA/GTM

**★ AGUA DEL PUEBLO**
Contact:  Carlos Gomez-Duarte, Executive Director
Associacion Pro-Agua Del Pueblo
41 Calle 5-01, Zona 8
Guatemala, Guatemala
Tel.  40913

PROGRAM OF ASSISTANCE:  Potable water - Sanitation - Toliet facilities - Public health education - Self-help programs - Vocational education - Appropriate technology.

PERSONNEL:  1 U.S., 12 local.

PROGRAM INITIATION:  1972          EXPENDITURES FOR FY 1982:  $147,000

COOPERATING ORGANIZATIONS:  Government of Guatemala, Ministry of Health; Norwegian Church; Private Agencies Collaborating Together (P.A.C.T.); Public Welfare Foundation, Save the Children Federation, World Bank.

. . . . . . . . . .

AFC/GTM

**AMERICAN FRIENDS OF CHILDREN, INC.**
Contact:  John H. Wetterer, Overseas Director
American Friends of Children, Inc.
6a Avenida 13-05, Zona 10
Guatemala City, Guatemala
Tel.  630321/682041

PROGRAM OF ASSISTANCE: Orphanages - Elementary schools - Vocational education.

PERSONNEL: 1 U.S., 20 local.

PROGRAM INITIATION: 1976

COOPERATING ORGANIZATIONS: Friends of Children; Government of Guatemala, Ministries of Education, Public Health and Social Welfare.

..........

AMGI/GTM

**AMG INTERNATIONAL**
Contact: Rev. Robert McRae
        AMG International
        Apartado Postal 2936
        Guatemala City, Guatemala

PROGRAM OF ASSISTANCE: Housing - Resettlement - Elementary schools - Clinics - Food distribution centers - Preschool programs - Vocational education.

PERSONNEL: 3 U.S.

PROGRAM INITIATION: 1974

COOPERATING ORGANIZATIONS: Kindernothilfe (Germany); Woord en Daad (Netherlands).

..........

BENBC/GTM

**BENEDICTINE FATHERS (O.S.B.)**
**Swiss-American Federation, Blue Cloud Abbey**
Contact: Monasterio Benedictino
        La Resurreccion
        Apartado Postal 19
        Coban, Guatemala

PROGRAM OF ASSISTANCE: Integrated rural development - Agricultural extension - Medical clinics - Elementary schools.

PERSONNEL: 6 U.S.

PROGRAM INITIATION: 1964        EXPENDITURES FOR FY 1982: $75,000

COOPERATING ORGANIZATIONS: Catholic Relief Services, Society for the Propagation of the Faith.

..........

CAM/GTM

**CAM INTERNATIONAL**
Contact:  Dr. Julian Lloret, Field Director
         Apartado 213
         Guatemala City, Guatemala
         Tel.  45160

PROGRAM OF ASSISTANCE:  Clothing - Food/food products - Children - Preschool programs.

PERSONNEL: 1 local.

PROGRAM INITIATION:  1899        EXPENDITURES FOR FY 1982:  $30,000

COOPERATING  ORGANIZATIONS:      AMG  International,  World  Vision  Relief Organization.

.........،؛؛

CARE/GTM

**\*+ CARE**
Contact:  Virginia Ubik, Country Director
         Edificio Amado, 5th floor
         6a Avenida 6-47, Zona 9
         Apartado Postal 1211
         Guatemala City, Guatemala
         Tel.  316192

PROGRAM OF ASSISTANCE:  Fish farming - Agricultural extension - Food supply programs - Land reclamation - Sanitation - Potable water - Nutrition education - National health programs - Reforestation - PL480 - Construction - Housing - Schools - Medical education.

PERSONNEL:  31 U.S./Canada.

PROGRAM INITIATION:  1958        EXPENDITURES FOR FY 1982:  $5,443,015

COOPERATING  ORGANIZATIONS:      Government  of  Guatemala,  National  Agrarian Transformation Institute (INTA), National Forestry Institute (INAFOR), Unidad Ejecutora del Programe de Acueductos Rurals (UNEPAR), U.S. Peace Corps.

..........

CRS/GTM

**\*+ CATHOLIC RELIEF SERVICES - UNITED STATES CATHOLIC CONFERENCE**
Contact:  Gustavo Carion, Program Director
         10 Avenida 10-57, Zona 10
         Guatemala City, Guatemala
         Tel.  (502) 2-310285

PROGRAM OF ASSISTANCE:  Construction - Nutrition education - Clothing - Potable water - Food distribution centers - Mass media - Disaster relief - Displaced persons - Community programs - Cottage industries - PL 480 - Agricultural extension.

PERSONNEL: 2 U.S., 6 local.

PROGRAM INITIATION: 1959        EXPENDITURES FOR FY 1982: $318,142

COOPERATING ORGANIZATIONS: Caritas (Denmark), Caritas (Guatemala), European Economic Community, Government of Guatemala, Help the Aged, U.S. Agency for International Development.

..........

CCF/GTM

**\*+ CHRISTIAN CHILDREN'S FUND, INC.**
Contact:  Lenore Powell
          Edificio Camara de Industria, Piso 6
          Calle Mariscal Cruz 9-21, Zona 4
          Apartado Postal 2542
          Guatemala City, Guatemala
          Tel.  65364, 310645

PROGRAM OF ASSISTANCE:  Integrated rural development - Elementary schools - Adult education - Clinics - Mental diseases - Sponsorships - Rehabilitation.

PERSONNEL: 1 U.S., 25 local.

PROGRAM INITIATION: 1969        EXPENDITURES FOR FY 1982: $2,362,591

COOPERATING ORGANIZATIONS:  Government of Guatemala, National Reconstruction Committee, National Social Welfare Council; Rural Resconstruction Committee.

..........

CFC/GTM

**CHRISTIAN FOUNDATION FOR CHILDREN**
Contact:  Rev. Gregory Schaffer
          Porroquia San Lucas
          San Lucas Toliman, Solola
          Guatemala

PROGRAM OF ASSISTANCE:  Clinics - Preventive medicine - Public health education - Vocational education - Preschool programs - Elementary schools - Literacy education - Mother/child programs - Children - Refugees - Sponsorships - Youth - Orphanages - Books - Clothing - Food/food products - Medical supplies.

PERSONNEL: 1 U.S., 2 local.

PROGRAM INITIATION: 1981        EXPENDITURES FOR FY 1982: $14,000

COOPERATING ORGANIZATIONS:  CENTRO Indigena, Parroquia San Lucas, Parroquia Santiago Atitlan.

..........

**CHRISTIAN NATIONALS' EVANGELISM COMMISSION, INC.**
Contact:  Rev Virgil Zapata
         Apartado 123
         Guatemala City, Guatemala

PROGRAM OF ASSISTANCE:  Elementary schools - High schools - Colleges/universities - Literacy education - Funding - Clinics.

PERSONNEL:  25 local.

PROGRAM INITIATION:  1965     EXPENDITURES FOR FY 1982:  $45,000

COOPERATING ORGANIZATION:  Instituto Evangelica America Latina.

. . . . . . . . . .

+   **CHRISTIAN REFORMED WORLD RELIEF COMMITTEE**

PROGRAM OF ASSISTANCE:  Integrated rural development - Self-help programs - Adult education - Translation programs.

PERSONNEL:  Numerous local.     EXPENDITURES FOR FY 1982:  $182,000

COOPERATING ORGANIZATIONS:  Local churches and Christian development organizations.

. . . . . . . . . .

**BROTHERS OF THE CHRISTIAN SCHOOLS (F.S.C.)**
Contact:  Brother Aurelian O'Dowd, F.S.C.
         Liceo LaSalle
         Apartado Postal 9
         Chiquimula, Guatemala

PROGRAM OF ASSISTANCE:  Vocational education - High schools - Elementary schools - Adult education - Training center for rural Indian youth.

PERSONNEL:  7 U.S., 5 local.

PROGRAM INITIATION:  1969

COOPERATING ORGANIZATIONS:  Coordination in Development, Inc. (CODEL), Council on the Overseas Apostolate (COSA); International LaSallian Cooperation Service (SECOLI).

. . . . . . . . . .

**\*+ CHURCH WORLD SERVICE**
Contact:  Vitalino Similox, Executive Director
          CONCAD
          Apartado Postal 2579
          Guatemala City, Guatemala

Supports the projects of CONCAD (Comite Nacional Cristiano de Agencias de Desarrollo).

PROGRAM OF ASSISTANCE:  Integrated rural development - Cooperatives - Funding - Nutrition education - Potable water - Vocational education - Legal services.

PERSONNEL:  Local.

PROGRAM INITIATION:  1974        EXPENDITURES FOR FY 1982:  $321,906

COOPERATING ORGANIZATIONS:  AGAPE (Program of the Presbyterian Church in Guatemala);  Behrhorst Clinic, Comite Evangelico Permanente de Ayuda (C.E.P.A.), Comite Nacional Cristiano de Agencias de Desarrollo) (CONCAD), Episcopal Church, Presbyterian Church of Guatemala.

..........

**CLARETIAN FATHERS (C.M.F.)**
Contact:  Rev. Edmund Andres, C.M.F.
          Parroquia Santo Tomas
          Santo Tomas, Izabal, Guatemala

PROGRAM OF ASSISTANCE:  Leadership training - Construction - Agricultural cooperatives - Credit/loans - Elementary schools - Teacher training - Literacy education - Non-formal education - Adult education - Animal husbandry - Poultry - Agricultural training - Improved seed - Fertilizers - Gardens - Reforestation - Mass media - Translation programs - Medical services - Public health education - Nutrition education - Clinics - Children.

PERSONNEL:  5 U.S., 8-10 local, several international.

PROGRAM INITIATION:  1971        EXPENDITURES FOR FY 1982:  $500,000

COOPERATING ORGANIZATION:  Claretian Fathers, Province of England.

..........

**\* COOPERATIVE HOUSING FOUNDATION**
Contact:  Carlos Giron
          National Federation of Housing Cooperatives
            (FEHCOVIL)
          3 Calle 4-09, Zona 1
          Guatemala City, Guatemala

PROGRAM OF ASSISTANCE: Housing - Construction - Cooperatives - Credit/loans - Consultants.

PERSONNEL: Short-term consultants.

PROGRAM INITIATION: 1977

COOPERATING ORGANIZATION: U.S. Agency for International Development.

. . . . . . . . . .

COVENANT/GTM

**COVENANT INTERNATIONAL FOUNDATION**
Contact: John Boyle
Apartado 400, Antigua
Guatemala
Tel. 502-320-285

PROGRAM OF ASSISTANCE: On-the-job training - Preschool programs - Elementary schools - Job placement - Vocational education - Language training - Agricultural training - Cash crops - Clothing - Food/food products - Disease prevention - Preventive medicine - Dental clinics - Family counseling - Disaster relief

PERSONNEL: 3 U.S.

PROGRAM INITIATION: 1981

. . . . . . . . . .

EASTMEN/GTM

**EASTERN MENNONITE BOARD OF MISSIONS AND CHARITIES**
Contact: Robert Brubaker, Field Director
Mision Evangelica Menonita
2a Avenida 6-35, Zona 2
Apartado Postal 1
San Pedro Carcha, Guatemala
Tel. 511360

PROGRAM OF ASSISTANCE: Literacy education.

PERSONNEL: 1 U.S., 2 local.

PROGRAM INITIATION: 1968        EXPENDITURES FOR FY 1982: $10,000

COOPERATING ORGANIZATIONS: Iglesia Evangelica Menonita Kekchi, Mennonite Central Committee.

. . . . . . . . . .

EPISCO/GTM

* **THE EPISCOPAL CHURCH IN THE U.S.A.**
(including + Presiding Bishops Fund for World Relief)
Contact: Armando R. Guerra
Apartado Postal 960
Guatemala City, Guatemala

PROGRAM OF ASSISTANCE: Integrated rural development - Clinics - Agricultural extension - Youth - High schools.

PERSONNEL: 2 U.S., 9 local.

PROGRAM INITIATION: 1981

COOPERATING ORGANIZATION: Interchurch Medical Assistance.

..........

FHI/GTM

* **FOOD FOR THE HUNGRY INTERNATIONAL**
Contact: Billy D. Yeats, EVERYCHILD Manager/Guatemala
24 Avenida 13-40, Zona 7
Kaminal Juyu II
Guatemala City, Guatemala
Tel. (502) 244416

PROGRAMS OF ASSISTANCE: Community centers - Food distribution centers - Self-help programs - Vocational education - Appropriate technology.

PERSONNEL: 1 U.S., 3 local.

PROGRAM INITIATION: 1975          EXPENDITURES FOR FY 1982: $80,000

..........

FPP/GTM

* **FOSTER PARENTS PLAN**
Contact: Henricus Dijsselbloem
11 Calle 1-23, Zona 9
Guatemala City, Guatemala

PROGRAM OF ASSISTANCE: Construction - Bridges - Roads - Housing - Credit/loans unions - Cooperatives - Schools - Literacy education - Libraries - Teaching materials - Vocational education - Agricultural training - Animal husbandry - Gardens - Reforestation - Health care teams - Potable water - Sanitation - Toilet facilities - Public health education - Nutrition education.

PERSONNEL: 1 international, 122 local.

PROGRAM INITIATION: 1978          EXPENDITURES FOR FY 1982: $1,395,910

TAICH Regional                    127

COOPERATING ORGANIZATIONS: Alberta (Canada) Agency for International Development, Canadian International Development Agency (CIDA), Government of Guatemala, local and international voluntary agencies.

.........

OFM IMMAC/GTM
**FRANCISCAN FRIARS (O.F.M.)**
**Province of the Immaculate Conception**
Contact: Rev. Custos
Iglesia San Agustin
5a Avenida, 10-38, Zona 1
Guatemala City, Guatemala

PROGRAM OF ASSISTANCE: Community programs - Construction - Housing - Educational funding - Equipment - Nutrition education - Medical services - Social welfare.

PERSONNEL: 5 U.S., 22 local, 2 international.

PROGRAM INITIATION: 1945      EXPENDITURES FOR FY 1982: $200,000

COOPERATING ORGANIZATIONS: Franciscan Order of Friars Minor, SOS Children's Villages, Inc. (Austria).

.........

FC/GTM
* **FRIENDS OF CHILDREN, INC.**

PROGRAM OF ASSISTANCE: Medical equipment - Nurses - Funding - Orphanages.

PERSONNEL: 1 U.S.

PROGRAM INITIATION: 1975      EXPENDITURES FOR FY 1982: $79,142

COOPERATING ORGANIZATION: American Friends of Children.

.........

HABITAT/GTM
**HABITAT FOR HUMANITY, INC.**
Contact: Pedro Castro Lopez
Aguacatan, Huehuetenango
Guatemala

Edgar Fuentes
Apartado Postal 2579
Guatemala City, Guatemala

PROGRAM OF ASSISTANCE: Construction - Housing - Credit/loans - Cooperatives - Toilet facilities - Fertilizers.

PERSONNEL:  Several volunteers.

PROGRAM INITIATION:  1979          EXPENDITURES FOR FY 1982:  $28,150

COOPERATING ORGANIZATIONS:  Government of Guatemala, National Committee on Reconstruction; Christian Council of Development Agencies (CONCAD), United Methodist Committee on Relief.

..........

HOLY LAND/GTM

\* **HOLY LAND CHRISTIAN MISSION INTERNATIONAL**
Contact:   Rev. Gregory Schaffer
           Parroquia San Lucas
           San Lucas Toliman, Dept. de Solola
           Guatemala

           Capt. Stanley Melton
           Ejercito de Salvacion
           8 a Ave. 21-13, Zona 11
           Apartado Postal 1881
           Guatemala, Guatemala
           Tel.  491072

PROGRAM OF ASSISTANCE:  Construction - Orphanages - Resettlement - Sponsorships - Community centers - Community programs - Food distribution centers - Self-help programs - Education - Cottage industries - Small enterprises - Animal husbandry.

PERSONNEL:  1 U.S., 4 local.

PROGRAM INITIATION:  1980          EXPENDITURES FOR FY 1982:  $148,416

COOPERATING ORGANIZATIONS:  The Salvation Army, Parroquia San Lucas.

..........

ICA/GTM

\* **INSTITUTE OF CULTURAL AFFAIRS**
Contact:   Mr. and Mrs. Walter Epley
           Institute of Cultural Affairs
           9 Calle, 5-34, Zone 4
           Guatemala City, Guatemala
           Tel.  502-2-85119

PROGRAM OF ASSISTANCE:  Community programs - Animals - Irrigation.

PERSONNEL:  2 U.S., 4 local, 3 international.

PROGRAM INITIATION:  1978

COOPERATING ORGANIZATIONS:  Government of Guatemala, National Committee on Reconstruction; Inter-American Development Bank; local cooperatives.

..........

\* **INTERNATIONAL INSTITUTE OF RURAL RECONSTRUCTION**
Contact:  Gustavo Herrera, Chairman
Juan E. Cordova, Executive Director
Guatemala Rural Reconstruction
Movement (GRRM)
Of. No. 201, Torre Profesional I
Gran Centro Comercial, Zona 4
Apartado Postal 1697
Guatemala City, Guatemala
Tel. 516819

Supports programs of the GRRM described below.

PROGRAM OF ASSISTANCE:  Cooperatives - Integrated rural development - Agricultural extension - Fertilizers - Seeds - Nutrition education - Sanitation - Preventive medicine - Immunizations - Potable water - Family planning - Leadership training - Self-help programs - Credit/loans - Libraries - Literacy education - Non-formal education - Vocational education - Women's education.

PERSONNEL:  21 local.

PROGRAM INITIATION:  1964          EXPENDITURES FOR FY 1982:  $25,000

COOPERATING ORGANIZATIONS:  BANDESA (Bank of Development); Caritas; Christian Children's Fund; Fundacion Centavo; Government of Guatemala, Ministries of Public Health, Education and Agriculture; Institute of Agricultural Commercialization (INDECA); National Association of Coffee Growers; National Union of Wheat Growers, U.S. Agency for International Development.

..........

\* **LA LECHE LEAGUE INTERNATIONAL**
Contact:  Dina Nathusius
La Leche League of Guatemala
Apartado Postal 149
Guatemala City, Guatemala
Tel. 65715

PROGRAM OF ASSISTANCE:  Breast-feeding - Mother/child programs - Self-help programs - Women's education.

PERSONNEL:  1 U.S., 1 local.

PROGRAM INITIATION:  1970

..........

**\*+ LUTHERAN WORLD RELIEF, INC.**
Contact: Vitalino Similox S.
Executive Director
Christian Council of Development
Agencies (CONCAD)
Apartado Postal 2579
Guatemala City, Guatemala
Tel. 81342

Marco Tulio
Executive Director
Association of Community
Health Services (ASECSA)
Apartado Postal 27
Chimaltenango, Guatemala
Tel. 391033

PROGRAM OF ASSISTANCE: Women - Nutrition education - Mother/child programs - Income generation - Literacy education - Youth - Preventive medicine - Medical supplies - Teaching materials - Libraries - Courses - Conferences - Agricultural cooperatives - Agricultural training - Animal husbandry - Crop improvement - Cash crops.

PROGRAM INITIATION: 1965      EXPENDITURES FOR FY 1982: $63,500

COOPERATING ORGANIZATION: Bread for the World, Catholic Relief Services, Christian Aid, Church World Service, Coordination in Development, Inc. (CODEL), Oxfam, United Presbyterian Church in the U.S.A.

..........

**MARYKNOLL FATHERS AND BROTHERS (M.M.)**
Contact: Rev. Ronald S. Michels, M.M.
Casa Parroquiai
Sayaxche, Peten
Guatemala

PROGRAM OF ASSISTANCE: Animateurs - Community programs - Leadership training - Self-help programs - Housing - Cooperatives - Adult education - Audio visual materials - Courses - Conferences - Educational funding - Elementary schools - Literacy education - Non-formal education - Seminars - Teaching materials - Women's education - Mass media - Blankets - Books - Clothing - Dental equipment - Medical supplies - Clinics - Disease treatment - Health care teams - Medical auxiliaries - Medical education - Medical supplies - Mother/child programs - Nurses - Potable water - Preventive medicine - Public health education - Sanitation - Toilet facilities - Traditional medicine - Nutrition education - Disaster relief - Refugees.

PERSONNEL: 29 U.S.

PROGRAM INITIATION: 1943

..........

TAICH Regional                131

**MARYKNOLL SISTERS OF ST. DOMINIC (M.M.)**
Contact:  Maryknoll Sisters
          Colegio Monte Maria
          Km. 8 1/2 Carretera
          Amatitlan, Zona 12

Mailing:  Apartado Postal 1121
          Guatemala City, Guatemala

PROGRAM OF ASSISTANCE:  Leadership training - Elementary schools - High schools - Adult education - Hospitals - Doctors - Clinics - Teacher training - Mother/child programs.

PERSONNEL:  16 U.S.

PROGRAM INITIATION:  1953

COOPERATING ORGANIZATIONS:  Catholic Medical Mission Board, Institute of Nutrition of Central America, University of San Carlos.

. . . . . . . . . .

**\*+ MENNONITE CENTRAL COMMITTEE**
Contact:  Rich Sider, MCC Guatemala Director
          Apartado Postal 1779
          42 Ave. 0-51, Zona 7
          Guatemala City, Guatemala
          Tel.  910858

PROGRAM OF ASSISTANCE:  Appropriate technology - Housing - Construction - Cooperatives - Medical auxiliaries - Sanitation - Nutrition education - Mother/child programs - Refugees - Literacy education - Agricultural extension - Agricultural training - Conservation - Women's education - Crafts - Income generation.

PERSONNEL:  9 U.S., 6 local, 2 international.

PROGRAM INITIATION:  1976      EXPENDITURES FOR FY 1982:  $130,000

COOPERATING ORGANIZATIONS:  Christian Council of Development Agencies (CONCAD); Government of Guatemala, National Reconstruction Committee; Habitat for Humanity.

. . . . . . . . . .

**MISSION AVIATION FELLOWSHIP**
Contact:  Carlos De Leon Campos
          13 Calle 7-20, Zona 9
          Guatemala City, Guatemala

PROGRAM OF ASSISTANCE:  Air transportation - Vehicles.

PERSONNEL: 4 U.S., 2 local, 2 international.

PROGRAM INITIATION: 1979

COOPERATING ORGANIZATIONS: Central American Mission, Mennonite groups, National Presbyterian Church, Southern Baptist Convention, World Vision.

..........

\* **PARTNERS OF THE AMERICAS**
Contact: Harris H. Whitbeck
Apartado Postal 50-A
Guatemala City, Guatemala
Tel. 460-552

PROGRAM OF ASSISTANCE: Educational exchange - Appropriate technology - Fishing - Energy - Animal husbandry - Swine - Medical equipment - Medical education - Teachers - Rehabilitation - Youth.

PERSONNEL: U.S. and local volunteers.

PROGRAM INITIATION: 1965

COOPERATING ORGANIZATIONS: Association of Business Managers; Carroll Behrhorst Foundation; Government of Guatemala, Ministry of Education, Ministry of Health, Red Cross.

..........

\* **THE PEOPLE-TO-PEOPLE HEALTH FOUNDATION, INC.**
**Project HOPE**
Contact: Dr. Alfonso Loarca
Apartado Postal 128
Zona 1
Quetzaltenango, Guatemala

PROGRAM OF ASSISTANCE: Integraged rural development - Medical services - Marketing - Crop improvement - Reforestation - Medical education - Mother/child programs - Potable water - Agricultural extension.

PERSONNEL: 1 U.S., several U.S. volunteers, several local.

EXPENDITURES FOR FY 1982: $1,000,000 (approximate).

COOPERATING ORGANIZATIONS: Government of Guatemala, Ministries of Agriculture and Health; USAID/Guatemala; U.S. Peace Corps.

..........

**PRIMITIVE METHODIST CHURCH IN THE U.S.A.**
International Mission Board
Contact:  Rev. Juan Par, Director
          Apartado Postal 1
          Santa Cruz del Quiche, Guatemala

PROGRAM OF ASSISTANCE:  Translation programs - Mass media - Books - Clinics -
Dental clinics - Hospitals - Preventive medicine - Accounting - Courses -
Elementary schools - High schools - Literacy education.

PERSONNEL:  7 U.S., 22 local.

PROGRAM INITIATION:  1925        EXPENDITURES FOR FY 1982:  $105,223

..........

PCI/GTM
\* **PROJECT CONCERN INTERNATIONAL**
  Contact:  Rudolfo Flores Meride
            Clinica Santiaguito
            Santiago Atitlan
            Department of Solola, Guatemala

PROGRAM OF ASSISTANCE:  Clinics - Disease treatment - Doctors - Health care
teams - Hospitals - Medical auxiliaries - Medical education - Potable water -
Preventive medicine - Public health education - Viral bacterial/diseases -
Mother/child programs - Nutrition education - Birth control methods - Family
planning.

PERSONNEL:  17 local.

PROGRAM INITIATION:  1974        EXPENDITURES FOR FY 1982:  $120,000

COOPERATING ORGANIZATIONS:  Government of Guatemala, Guatemalan National
Nutrition Program; Canadian Government, U.S. Agency for International
Development.

..........

ROTARY/GTM
**ROTARY INTERNATIONAL**
Contact:  Bernardo Neumann, Chairman
          Patronato Pro-Nutricion Infantil
          7a Avenida 6-26, Zona 9
          Guatemala City, Guatemala

PROGRAM OF ASSISTANCE:  Nutrition education - Food distribution centers.

PROGRAM INITIATION:  1981

COOPERATING ORGANIZATIONS:  Government of Guatemala, Guatemala City, INCAP,
local Boy Scouts.
..........

SALESIAN FR/GTM

**\* SALESIANS OF ST. JOHN BOSCO (S.D.B.)**
Contact:  Colegio Salesiano Don Bosco
26, Calle 2-46, Zona 1
Guatemala City, Guatemala

Supports programs of the International Salesian Society.

PROGRAM OF ASSISTANCE:  Funding - Fertilizers - Seeds - Elementary schools -
Clinics - Youth - High schools.

PERSONNEL: 1 U.S., 77 local.

PROGRAM INITIATION:  1929

COOPERATING ORGANIZATIONS:  Catholic Relief Services, Inter-American
Foundation, Misereor (Germany).

. . . . . . . . . .

SALVA/GTM

**\*+ THE SALVATION ARMY**
Contact:  Captain S. Melton, Regional Officer
Salvation Army Guatemala Region
Apartado 1881
15 Calle 8-39, Zona 1
Guatemala City, Guatemala
Tel.  763670

Assists programs operated by the international organization.

PROGRAM OF ASSISTANCE:  Housing - Resettlement - Vocational education -
Rehabilitation - Clinics - Mother/child programs - Family planning - Preschool
programs - Counseling - Community centers - Marketing.

PERSONNEL:  2 U.S., 15 local, 5 international.

PROGRAM INITIATION:  1976

COOPERATING ORGANIZATIONS:  Church World Service, Evangelical Alliance Relief
Fund, Government of Canada, Guatemalan National Reconstruction Committee, Holy
Land Christian Mission, INTECAP, Kindernothilfe (Germany), Tear Fund (U.K.),
U.S. Agency for International Development.

. . . . . . . . . .

SCF/GTM

**+ SAVE THE CHILDREN FEDERATION, INC.**
Contact:  Thomas B. Lent
ALIANZA
32 Calle 7-28, Zona 10
Apartado Postal 2903
Guatemala City, Guatemala

PROGRAM OF ASSISTANCE:   Integrated rural development - Animal husbandry - Gardens - Nutrition education - Small enterprises - Agricultural extension - Appropriate technology - Conservation - Fish farming - Orchards.

PERSONNEL:  1 U.S., 24 local.

PROGRAM INITIATION:  1976

COOPERATING ORGANIZATIONS:   Agua del Pueblo; Caritas; CEMAT (Centro Mesoamericano de Estudios sobre Tecnologia Apropiada) Guatemala; Central American Institute of Research and Industrial Technology; Government of Guatemala, General Administration for Agriculture, General Administration for Animal husbandry, National Institute for Training and Production; Private Agencies Collaborating Together (PACT); Regional Council on Health/Nutrition; Save the Children Alliance (Canada, Denmark, Norway, U.K.); Save the Children (Austria).

··········

SBC/GTM

**SOUTHERN BAPTIST CONVENTION**

Works through local national churches.

PROGRAM OF ASSISTANCE:  Disaster relief - Food-for-work - Housing.

EXPENDITURES FOR FY 1982:  $15,000

··········

SIL/GTM

*   **SUMMER INSTITUTE OF LINGUISTICS, INC.**
    Contact:   Glen Ager, Director
               Instituto Linguistico de Verano
               Apartado Postal 74
               12 Avenida "B" 10/65, Zona 2
               Guatemala City, Guatemala

PROGRAM OF ASSISTANCE:  Linguistic studies - Adult education.

PERSONNEL:  66 U.S., 22 international.

PROGRAM INITIATION:  1952

COOPERATING ORGANIZATIONS:   Government of Guatemala, Ministry of Education (through the National Indian Institute and the Office of Rural, Social and Education Development); MAP International.

··········

WN/GTM

**WORLD NEIGHBORS, INC.**
Contact:  Roland Bunch
          Apartado Postal 17
          Nochixtlan, Oaxaca
          Mexico  69600
          Tel.  952-20126

PROGRAM OF ASSISTANCE:  Housing - Cooperatives - Accounting - Adult education
- Income generation - Agricultural cooperatives - Fertilizers - Pest control -
Tools - Nutrition education - Birth control methods - Family planning.

PERSONNEL:  9 local.

PROGRAM INITIATION:  1964        EXPENDITURES FOR FY 1982:  $52,366

COOPERATING ORGANIZATIONS:  APROFAM (Asociacion Pro-Bienestar de la Familia de
Guatemala), Center for Development Resources, Federacion de Cooperativas de
Mercadeo "El Quetzal" (FECOMERQ).

..........

WVRO/GTM

**\*+ WORLD VISION RELIEF ORGANIZATION, INC.**
Contact:  Paul Peterson
          Associate Director, Field Projects
          World Vision International
          Curridabat Apartado 133
          San Jose, Costa Rica

PROGRAM OF ASSISTANCE:  Sponsorships - Literacy education - Integrated rural
development - Potable water - Irrigation - Vocational education - Construction
- Medical auxiliaries - Medical services - Disaster relief - Sanitation -
Nutrition education.

PROGRAM INITIATION:  1975        EXPENDITURES FOR FY 1982:  $2,817,642

COOPERATING ORGANIZATIONS:  Local churches and municipal institutions.

..........

YMCA/GTM

**\*+ YOUNG MEN'S CHRISTIAN ASSOCIATIONS OF THE UNITED STATES**
Contact:  Jorge Camors, General Secretary
          Asociaciones Christianes de Jovenes
          12 Calle A 3-75, Zona 1
          Apartado Postal 631
          Guatemala City, Guatemala
          Tel.  538113

PROGRAM OF ASSISTANCE:  Integrated rural development.

..........

## GUATEMALA - PROGRAM SUPPORT

|  |  |  |
|---|---|---|
|  | A.T. International | $100,000 |
| * | Accion International/AITEC | 7,821 |
|  | Aid to Artisans | 1,000 |
|  | American Lung Association | ----- |
|  | American Public Health Association | 7,227 |
|  | Americans for International Aid and Adoption | ----- |
|  | Aprovecho Institute | ----- |
| * | Association for Voluntary Sterilization, Inc. | 589,318 |
| * | Brother's Brother Foundation | 251,000 |
|  | Carr Foundation | ----- |
|  | Catholic Medical Mission Board, Inc. | 305,679 |
| * | Centre for Development and Population Activities | |
|  | Children, Incorporated | 90,430 |
|  | Claretian Fathers (C.M.F.) | ----- |
| * | Compassion Relief and Development | ----- |
| *+ | Coordination in Development, Inc. (CODEL) | 111,754 |
| * | Council of International Programs | |
|  | for Youth Leaders and Social Workers, Inc. | 2,500 |
|  | Darien Book Aid Plan, Inc. | ----- |
| * | Direct Relief International | 177,676 |
|  | Education Development Center | ----- |
|  | Family Health International | ----- |
| * | Family Planning International Assistance | 32,484 |
|  | Farallones Institute | ----- |
|  | Friends of SOS Children's Villages, Inc. | 1,500 |
|  | Friends of the Third World, Inc. | ----- |
| *+ | Heifer Project International, Inc. | 72,427 |
|  | Inter-Aid, Inc. | ----- |
|  | Interchurch Medical Assistance, Inc. | 54,491 |
|  | International Adoptions, Inc. | 1,600 |
| * | International Executive Service Corps | ----- |
|  | International Liaison, Inc. | ----- |
|  | W.K. Kellogg Foundation | 459,778 |
|  | Management Sciences for Health | ----- |
| *+ | MAP International | 483 |
|  | National Savings and Loan League | ----- |
|  | Oxfam America | 100,000 |
| * | Pan American Development Foundation | ----- |
| * | Pathfinder Fund | 53,211 |
| * | Population Council | 20,032 |
|  | Lions Clubs International | ----- |
| *+ | Private Agencies Collaborating Together, Inc. (PACT) | 185,071 |
|  | Public Welfare Foundation | 17,500 |
|  | Rockefeller Foundation | 23,747 |
| *+ | Seventh-day Adventist World Service, Inc. | 4,636 |
| * | Sister Cities International | ----- |
| * | Unitarian Universalist Service Committee | ----- |
|  | United Methodist Committee on Relief | 138,800 |
|  | Volunteer Optometric Services to Humanity | |
|  | (VOSH International) | ----- |
| *+ | World Concern | 2,214 |
| *+ | World Relief Corporation | 15,000 |

## GUYANA

Of the 16 U.S. organizations listed in Guyana,
9 were able to provide TAICH with financial data
indicating program expenditures for FY 1982
totaling $378,735.

ACDI/GUY

\* **AGRICULTURAL COOPERATIVE DEVELOPMENT INTERNATIONAL**
Contact:  GAIBANK
         Food Crop Production and Marketing Project
         Georgetown, Guyana

PROGRAM OF ASSISTANCE:  Management training - Marketing - Extension agents.

PERSONNEL:  2 U.S.

PROGRAM INITIATION:  1980          EXPENDITURES FOR FY 1982:  $172,000

COOPERATING ORGANIZATIONS:  Guyana Agricultural Extension Service, Guyana
Agricultural Industrial Development Bank (GAIBANK), Guyana Marketing
Corporation, Inter-American Development Bank.

. . . . . . . . . .

IRI/GUY

**IRI RESEARCH INSTITUTE, INC.**
Contact:  John Halick, Chief of Party
         Guyana Grains Board
         117 Cowan Street
         Georgetown, Guyana

PROGRAM OF ASSISTANCE:  Agricultural training - Crop improvement - Crop
processing - Demonstration projects - Extension agents - Fertilizers -
Irrigation - Storage.

PERSONNEL:  4 U.S.

PROGRAM INITIATION:  1980

COOPERATING ORGANIZATION:  U.S. Agency for International Development.

. . . . . . . . . .

**SISTERS OF MERCY OF THE UNION IN THE U.S.A.**
Contact:  Sister Theresa Marie Marques, R.S.M.
          Regional Coordinator
          264 Meadowbrook Gardens
          P.O. Box 10461
          Georgetown, Guyana
          Tel.  64856

The program is conducted by the Province of Scranton (Dallas, Pennsylvania).

PROGRAM OF ASSISTANCE:  High schools - Teachers - Elementary schools -
Hospitals - Clinics - Nursing schools - Medical education - Orphanages -
Hostels.

PERSONNEL:  3 U.S., 28 local.

PROGRAM INITIATION:  1935

. . . . . . . . . .

**\*+  THE SALVATION ARMY**
Contact:  Major Mortimer Jones, Divisional Commander
          The Salvation Army Headquarters
          5 Church Street
          P.O. Box 259
          Georgetown, Guyana
          Tel.  66638

Assists programs operated by the international organization:

PROGRAM OF ASSISTANCE:  High schools - Non-formal education - Preschool
programs - Food distribution centers - Counseling - Hostels - Youth -
Rehabilitation.

PERSONNEL:  28 international.

PROGRAM INITIATON:  1895

. . . . . . . . . .

**THE WESLEYAN CHURCH**
Contact:  Rev. Dean Phillips, Mission Coordinator
          P.O. Box 10920
          Georgetown, Guyana
          Tel.  61758

PROGRAM OF ASSISTANCE:  Clinics - Mother/child programs - Translation
programs.

PERSONNEL:  1 U.S.

PROGRAM INITIATION:  1913          EXPENDITURES FOR FY 1982:  $10,900

..........

YWCA/GUY

**\*+  YOUNG WOMEN'S CHRISTIAN ASSOCIATION OF THE U.S.A.**
Contact:  National General Secretary
          Young Women's Christian Association of Guyana
          106 Brickdam
          Georgetown, Guyana
          Tel.  02 65610/64295

Provides an assistance grant to the YMCA of Guyana.

PROGRAM OF ASSISTANCE:  Vocational education - Women's education - Youth.

PERSONNEL:  2 local.

PROGRAM INITIATION:  1914

COOPERATING ORGANIZATION:  World YWCA Cooperation for Development Program.

..........

**GUYANA - PROGRAM SUPPORT**

| | |
|---|---:|
| American Leprosy Missions, Inc. | $ 33,520 |
| \* Brother's Brother Foundation | 18,000 |
| Interchurch Medical Assistance, Inc. | 109,115 |
| Lions Clubs International | ----- |
| Lutheran Church in America | 4,200 |
| Moravian Church in America, Inc. | ----- |
| \* Population Council | 20,000 |
| \*+ Seventh-day Adventist World Service, Inc. | 10,000 |
| Trickle Up Program | 1,000 |

---

## HAITI

---

Of the 97 U.S. organizations listed in Haiti,
64 were able to provide TAICH with financial data
indicating program expenditures for FY 1982
totaling $31,140,534.

ABC/HTI

**AMERICAN BAPTIST CHURCHES IN THE USA**
Contact:  Rev. Philip J. Uhlinger
          B.P. 20
          Cap-Hatien, Haiti

PROGRAM OF ASSISTANCE:  Elementary schools - High schools - Educational
funding - Reforestation - Agriculturists - Cottage industries - Hospitals -
Clinics - Food supply programs - Family planning.

PERSONNEL:  19 U.S.

PROGRAM INITIATION:  1923          EXPENDITURES FOR FY 1982:  $42,000

COOPERATING ORGANIZATION:  Church World Service.

. . . . . . . . . .

AWHS/HTI

**AMERICAN WOMEN'S HOSPITALS SERVICE**
Contact:  Dr. William Hodges
          Hospital Le Bon Samaritan
          Limbe, Haiti

PROGRAM OF ASSISTANCE:  Nurses.

PERSONNEL:  6 local.

PROGRAM INITIATION:  1952          EXPENDITURES FOR FY 1982:  $3,600

COOPERATING ORGANIZATIONS:  Board of International Ministries of the American
Baptist Churches in the USA, Government of Haiti.

. . . . . . . . . .

AMGI/HTI

**AMG INTERNATIONAL**
Contact:  Rev. Cenofa Point du Jour
          B.P. 493
          Port-au-Prince, Haiti

PROGRAM OF ASSISTANCE:  Elementary schools - High schools - Vocational education - Clothing - Food supply programs.

PERSONNEL:  3 U.S., 107 local.

PROGRAM INITIATION:  1977

COOPERATING ORGANIZATIONS:  Second Baptist Church of Port-au-Prince, Walk Way Vocational and Bible Institute, Word en Daad (Netherlands).

..........

CARE/HTI
**\*+  CARE**
Contact:  Lawrence C. Holzman, Country Director
          B.P. 773
          Port-au-Prince, Haiti

PROGRAM OF ASSISTANCE:  Integrated rural development - Beekeeping - Seeds - Nurseries - Family planning - Nutrition education - Irrigation - Small enterprises - Women - Marketing - PL 480 - Food supply programs - Food-for-work - Medical services - Construction - Potable water - Gardening - Mother/child programs - Reforestation - Agricultural training - Crafts - Cooperatives - Schools.

PERSONNEL:  10 U.S., 127 local.

PROGRAM INITIATION:  1959          EXPENDITURES FOR FY 1982: $14,072,453

COOPERATING ORGANIZATIONS:  Government of Haiti, Ministries of Agriculture, Education, Finance and Health; Harmonisation de l'Action des Communautes Haitiennes Organisees; Operation Double Harvest; U.S. Agency for International Development; Voluntaires de Progres (France).

..........

CRS/HTI
**\*+  CATHOLIC RELIEF SERVICES - UNITED STATES CATHOLIC CONFERENCE**
Contact:  Jean Serge Picard
          Building Chatelain, 3 eme stage
          Place Dantes Destouches
          Angle Rue Pavee et Geffrard
          Port-au-Prince
          Tel.  20654

PROGRAM OF ASSISTANCE:  Food-for-work - Construction - Leadership training - Integrated rural development - Agricultural cooperatives - Preventive medicine - Sanitation - Appropriate technology - Non-formal education - Educational funding - Courses - Food supply programs - Vocational education - Gardens - Wells - Potable water - PL 480 - Credit/loans - Women.

PERSONNEL:  1 U.S., 7 local, 1 international.

PROGRAM INITIATION:  1955          EXPENDITURES FOR FY 1982: $645,091

TAICH Regional                    143

COOPERATING ORGANIZATIONS: Bishops Conference, Caritas, European Economic Community, Government of the United States, International Catholic Migration Commission, Misereor, Oxfam, Salesians, Secours Catholique, Sisters of Mother Teresa.

..........

CRWRC/HTI

+ **CHRISTIAN REFORMED WORLD RELIEF COMMITTEE**
Contact:  Jim Zylstra
          B.P. 1693
          Port-au-Prince, Haiti

PROGRAM OF ASSISTANCE:  Integrated rural development.

PERSONNEL:  6 U.S.

PROGRAM INITIATION:  1975          EXPENDITURES FOR FY 1982:  $230,000

COOPERATING ORGANIZATION:  Missionary Church.

..........

CBU/HTI

**CHURCH OF BIBLE UNDERSTANDING**
Contact:  Church of Bible Understanding
          B.P. 1551 F
          Petionville, Haiti

PROGRAM OF ASSISTANCE:  Medical services - Clinics - Food supply programs - Orphanages.

PERSONNEL:  10 volunteers U.S., 59 local.

..........

CG HOLI/HTI

**CHURCH OF GOD (HOLINESS)**
Contact:  Rev. Paul Michel, Assistant Director
          B.P. 59-W
          Port-au-Prince, Haiti

PROGRAM OF ASSISTANCE:  Elementary schools - Agricultural training - Gardens - Self-help programs.

PERSONNEL:  1 U.S., 6 local.

PROGRAM INITIATION:  1967          EXPENDITURES FOR FY 1982:  $14,000

..........

**CHURCH OF THE NAZARENE**
Contact:  Dr. Steve Weber
B.P. 1323
Port-au-Prince, Haiti

PROGRAM OF ASSISTANCE:  Elementary schools - Vocational education - Food supply programs - Disaster relief - Wells - Animal husbandry - Poultry - Marketing - Fuels - Clinics - Nutrition education - Medical services.

PERSONNEL:  4 U.S., 14 local.

PROGRAM INITIATION:  1960

COOPERATING ORGANIZATIONS:  Compassion International, Government of Canada, World Vision International.

..........

**\*+  CHURCH WORLD SERVICE**
Contact:  John Muilenberg, Representative
Service Chretien d'Haiti
B.P. 285
Port-au-Prince, Haiti

PROGRAM OF ASSISTANCE:  Water - Potable water - Wells - Nutrition education - Food supply programs - Mother/child programs - Children - Policy and planning - Storage.

PERSONNEL:  2 U.S., 50 local.

PROGRAM INITIATION:  1954          EXPENDITURES IN FY 1982:  $259,286

COOPERATING ORGANIZATIONS:  EZE (Protestant Central Agency for Development Aid, Germany); Government of Haiti; United Nations Development Programme; U.S. Agency for International Development.

..........

**CHURCHES OF GOD, GENERAL CONFERENCE**
Contact:  Rev. Mark Hosler, Director
Project Help
B.P. 2065
Port-au-Prince, Haiti

PROGRAM OF ASSISTANCE:  Elementary schools - High schools - Vocational education - Educational funding - Gardens - Animal husbandry - Rabbits - Poultry - Agricultural training - Agricultural clubs - Youth - Clinics - Medical services - Sanitation - Potable water - Nutrition education.

PERSONNEL:  14 U.S., 10 short-term volunteers; 1 Canada; 76 local.

PROGRAM INITIATION:  1967          EXPENDITURES FOR FY 1982:  $115,000

COOPERATING ORGANIZATIONS:  CARE, Church World Service, Crusade Against Viral Bacterial/Diseases, Government of Haiti, Ministries of Agriculture and Health; MAP International.

..........

COMPASSION/HTI

**COMPASSION INTERNATIONAL, INC.**
\* **COMPASSION RELIEF AND DEVELOPMENT**
Contact:  Danny Cook
          Compassion International
          c/o Missionary Flight International
          P.O. Box 15665
          West Palm Beach, Florida  33406
          Tel.  (509) 162-2781

Works through existing missions and local organizations.

PROGRAM OF ASSISTANCE:  Orphanages - Schools - Sponsorships - Water - Wells - Community programs.

PROGRAM INITIATION:  1975          EXPENDITURES FOR FY 1982:  $80,000

COOPERATING ORGANIZATIONS:  Australian Development Assistance Agency (ADAB), Canadian International Development Agency (CIDA), Compassion (Australia), Compassion (Canada), TEAR Fund (U.K.), U.S. Agency for International Development.

..........

CLUSA/HTI

\* **COOPERATIVE LEAGUE OF THE U.S.A.**
Contact:  Marcel Duret
          COOPEP
          B.P. 2129
          Port-au-Prince, Haiti

PROGRAM OF ASSISTANCE:  Management training - Marketing - Agricultural cooperatives - Extension agents - Poultry.

PERSONNEL:  2 U.S., 24 local.

PROGRAM INITIATION:  1983          EXPENDITURES FOR FY 1982:  $300,000

COOPERATING ORGANIZATIONS:  COOPEP, U.S. Agency for International Development.

..........

CSI/HTI

**CSI MINISTRIES, INC.**
Contact: CSI Headquarters
62 Delmas 5 Mesmin
Petionville, Haiti

PROGRAM OF ASSISTANCE: Health care teams - Medical programs - Medical supplies - Wells - Equipment - Construction.

PROGRAM INITIATION: 1963

COOPERATING ORGANIZATIONS: Grace Children's Hospital, UFM International, Wesleyan Church.

..........

DETELLIS/HTI

**GEORGE DETELLIS EVANGELISTIC ASSOCIATION, INC.**
Contact: Curt Smith, Director
New Missions
B. P. 11107
Carrefour Road
Port-au-Prince, Haiti
Tel: 28 102

PROGRAM OF ASSISTANCE: Construction - Schools - Clinics - Women - Fishing - Doctors - Potable water.

PERSONNEL: 7 U.S. volunteers.

PROGRAM INITIATION: 1971

..........

DOCARE/HTI

* **DOCARE INTERNATIONAL, INC.**
Contact: Jack Snyder, President
Mission Possible
No. 14, Delmas 75
B. P. 13473
Port-Au-Prince, Haiti

PROGRAM OF ASSISTANCE: Doctors - Dentists - Nurses - Medical supplies - Medical services - Disease treatment - Health care teams - Medical education - Preventive medicine.

PERSONNEL: 6 U.S., 2 local.

PROGRAM INITIATION: 1982          EXPENDITURES IN FY 1982: $5,000

COOPERATING ORGANIZATIONS: Florida Association of Voluntary Agencies for Caribbean Action, Government of Haiti, Mission Possible, U.S. Agency for International Development.

..........

* **THE EPISCOPAL CHURCH IN THE U.S.A.**
(including + The Presiding Bishops Fund for World Relief)
Contact:  Rt. Rev. Luc Garnier, S.T.D., Bishop of Haiti
B.P. 1309
Port-au-Prince, Haiti

Provides a yearly grant to the Episcopal Church of Haiti.

PROGRAM OF ASSISTANCE:  Elementary schools - High schools - Clinics - Hospitals - Geriatric centers - Schools for the disabled.

PERSONNEL:  3 U.S., approximately 285 local.

PROGRAM INITIATION:  1913          EXPENDITURES FOR FY 1982:  $22,231

..........

* **EYE CARE, INC.**
Contact:  Mireille Jolicoeur, Administrator
Ecole St. Vincent, B.P. 1319
Port-au-Prince, Haiti
Tel.  26095

PROGRAM OF ASSISTANCE:  Clinics - Blindness prevention - Disease treatment - Doctors - Health care teams - Medical auxiliaries - Medical education - Medical equipment - Medical services - Medical supplies - Ophthalmology - Rehabilitation - Evaluation - Sponsorships - Libraries - Small enterprises - Surveys.

PERSONNEL:  1 U.S., 51 local.

PROGRAM INITIATION:  1978          EXPENDITURES FOR FY 1982:  $400,000

..........

**FARMS INTERNATIONAL, INC.**
Contact:  Wally Turnbull, Jr.
Mountain Maid Self-Help Project
B.P. 1386
Port-au-Prince, Haiti

PROGRAM OF ASSISTANCE:  Poultry.

PROGRAM INITIATION:  1975          EXPENDITURES FOR FY 1982:  $5,000

COOPERATING ORGANIZATION:  Baptist Haiti Mission.

..........

* **FOSTER PARENTS PLAN**
  Contact:  Joy Greendige, Director
            Plan de Parrainage
            B.P. 2193
            Port-au-Prince, Haiti


PROGRAM OF ASSISTANCE:  Community centers - Community programs - Integrated rural development - Housing - Leadership training - Self-help programs - Educational funding - Schools - Construction - Libraries - Literacy education - Preschool programs - Teacher training - Crafts - Agricultural supplies - Irrigation - Animal husbandry - Vegetables - Clinics - Dentistry - Health care teams - Potable water - Sanitation - Toilet facilities - Nutrition education - Marketing.

PERSONNEL:  4 international, 296 local.

PROGRAM INITIATION:  1973          EXPENDITURES FOR FY 1982:  $3,046,603

COOPERATING ORGANIZATIONS:    Alberta  International  Assistance  Program, (Government of Alberta, Canada); Canadian International Development Agency (CIDA); Government of Haiti, Ministries of Public Health and Social Affairs; U.S. Agency for International Development.


. . . . . . . . .

**FREE METHODIST CHURCH OF NORTH AMERICA**
Contact:  Rev. Warren Land
          Free Methodist Mission
          Port-au-Prince, Haiti
          Tel.  60941


          c/o Missionary Flights International
          P.O. Box 15565
          West Palm Beach, Florida  33406

PROGRAM OF ASSISTANCE:  Construction - Elementary schools - Food supply programs - Animal husbandry - Goats - Range animals - Wells - Reforestation - Gardens - Self-help programs - Dentistry - Health care teams - Sponsorships.

PERSONNEL:  8 U.S., 28 local.

PROGRAM INITIATION:  1965          EXPENDITURES FOR FY 1982:  $116,724

COOPERATING ORGANIZATIONS:  Church World Service, Compassion International.


. . . . . . . . . .

* **FRIENDS OF CHILDREN, INC.**
Contact:  Etienne Prophete
          Eglise Chretienne des Rachettes d'Haiti
          4 Angle ruelles P. Baptiste et Melisse
          B.P. 1380
          Port-au-Prince, Haiti

PROGRAM OF ASSISTANCE:  Food supply programs - Medical supplies - Clinics - Hospitals - Orphanages.

PERSONNEL:  1 U.S., 1 local.

PROGRAM INITIATION:  1979          EXPENDITURES FOR FY 1982:  $99,029.


COOPERATING ORGANIZATIONS:  Amer-Haitian Bo-Zami, CARE, Eglise Chretienne des Rachetes.

..........

* **GLOBAL OUTREACH**
Contact:  Haitian Baptist Convention
          67 rue de L'enterement 67
          Cemetary Street
          B.P. 2101
          Annexe de Port-au-Prince, Haiti

PROGRAM OF ASSISTANCE:  Integrated rural development - Cooperatives - Marketing - Animals - Beekeeping - Rabbits - Reforestation - Nutrition education.

PROGRAM INTITATION:  1979          EXPENDITURES FOR FY 1982:  $34,580

COOPERATING ORGANIZATION:  Convention Batiste d'Haiti.

..........

**HABITAT FOR HUMANITY, INC.**
Contact:  Rev. Daniel Dieudonne
          Bethel Church of God
          B.P. 277
          Port-au-Prince, Haiti

PROGRAM OF ASSISTANCE:  Housing - Construction.

PERSONNEL:  3 U.S., several volunteers.

PROGRAM INITIATION:  1982          EXPENDITURES FOR FY 1982:  $28,743.

COOPERATING ORGANIZATION:  Bethel Church of God in Haiti.

..........

**\*+ HELEN KELLER INTERNATIONAL, INC.**
Contact: Serge Toureau, M.S. Project Coordinator
B.P. 707
Port-au-Prince, Haiti
Tel. 20650

PROGRAM OF ASSISTANCE: Disease treatment - Surveys - Food/food products - Children - Medical education - Nutrition education - Disaster relief - Vocational education.

PERSONNEL: 4 U.S., 4 local.

PROGRAM INITIATION: 1974

. . . . . . . . . .

**\* INSA (International Nursing Services Association, Inc.)**
Contact: Rev. Octave LaFontant
Grover C. Bolling Hospital
Darbonne, Haiti
P.O. Box 1213
Port-Au-Prince, Haiti
Tel. (Office) 5-1684

PROGRAM OF ASSISTANCE: Integrated rural development - Self-help programs - Non-formal education - Teaching materials - Books - Medical equipment - Medical supplies - Preventive medicine - Public health education - Nutrition education.

PERSONNEL: 4 U.S., 16 local, 1 international.

PROGRAM INITIATION: 1980          EXPENDITURES FOR FY 1982: $40,000

COOPERATING ORGANIZATION: Rural Outreach Opportunity to Serve (ROOTS).

. . . . . . . . . .

**INTERMEDIA**
Contact: Carrie Paultre, Executive Secretary
Comite Protestant d'Alphabetisation et de
Litterature (CPAL)
B.P. 154
Port-au-Prince, Haiti

Provides support for CPAL.

PROGRAM OF ASSISTANCE: Literacy education - Mass media - Adult education - Books - Teacher training - Seminars.

PROGRAM INITIATION: 1977          EXPENDITURES FOR FY 1982: $6,252

COOPERATING ORGANIZATIONS:   Bonne Nouvelle (Catholic nonformal education publication), Government of Haiti, Maison Haitienne de la Bible, commercial and missionary presses.

..........

**INTERNATIONAL CHILD CARE (USA), INC.**
Contact:   Harley Snyder, Field Administrator
           International Child Care/Haiti
           B.P. 1767
           Port-au-Prince, Haiti
           Tel.  60631

PROGRAM OF ASSISTANCE:  Viral/bacterial disease - Children - Clinics - Medical supplies - Medical services.

PERSONNEL:  8 U.S., 151 local, 3 international.

PROGRAM INITIATION:  1965          EXPENDITURES FOR FY 1982:  $1,298,188

COOPERATING ORGANIZATION:  International Child Care (Canada).

..........

**INTERNATIONAL LIFELINE, INC.**
Contact:   Esther Rocourt, Administrative Assistant
           International Lifeline
           B.P. 11320-Carrefour
           Port-au-Prince, Haiti
           Tel.  41619

PROGRAM OF ASSISTANCE:   Clinics - Health care teams - Medical education - Medical supplies - Sponsorships - Educational funding.

PERSONNEL:  15 volunteer; local.

PROGRAM INITIATION:  1979          EXPENDITURES FOR FY 1982:  $35,000

..........

*   **LA LECHE LEAGUE INTERNATIONAL**
    Contact:   Marilyn Needham
               La Leche League of Haiti
               c/o H.A.S.C.O.
               B.P. 1310
               Port-au-Prince, Haiti

PROGRAM OF ASSISTANCE:   Breast-feeding - Mother/child programs - Self-help programs - Women's education.

PERSONNEL: 1 international.

PROGRAM INITIATION: 1981

..........

**MANAGEMENT SCIENCES FOR HEALTH**
Contact: Jon E. Rohde, M.D.
MSH Representative and Chief of Party
Management Sciences for Health
B.P. 2560
Port-au-Prince, Haiti

PROGRAM OF ASSISTANCE: Medical services - Clinics - Disease treatment - Health care teams - Immunizations - Medical auxiliaries - Medical supplies - Consultants - Extension courses - Preventive medicine - Public health education - Nutrition education - Management training - Policy and planning - Evaluation - Animal husbandry - Food/food products - Teaching materials - Community programs.

PERSONNEL: 4 U.S., 7 local.

PROGRAM INITIATION: 1980          EXPENDITURES FOR FY 1982: $3,000,000

COOPERATING ORGANIZATIONS: Government of Haiti, Department of Public Health and Population; Inter-American Development Bank; Pan American Health Organization; U. S. Agency for International Development.

..........

**\*+ MENNONITE CENTRAL COMMITTEE**
Contact: Eldon & Rachel Stoltzfus
9 Impasse Herard
Sur Delmas 75
B.P. 2160
Port-au-Prince, Haiti
Tel. 61739

PROGRAM OF ASSISTANCE: Adult education - Educational funding - Teaching materials - Teachers - Food supply programs - Agricultural extension - Conservation - Agricultural training - Seeds - Animateurs - Agricultural clubs - Hospitals - Medical services - Cooperatives - Integrated rural development - Women - Reforestation.

PERSONNEL: 18 U.S., 12 local, 3 international volunteers, (Canada).

PROGRAM INITIATION: 1958          EXPENDITURES FOR FY 1982: $120,000

COOPERATING ORGANIZATIONS: Catholic Church of Haiti; Church World Service; Government of Haiti, Ministry of Agriculture, Ministry of Public Health and Population; Mennonite Medical Association; Missionary Church; World Neighbors; MAP International.

..........

MEDA/HTI

**MENNONITE ECONOMIC DEVELOPMENT ASSOCIATES, INC.**
Contact:  Theodule St. Fleur, President
          Co-op Jean Baptiste Chavannes
          Rue 21
          Cap Haitian, Haiti
          Tel.  20834

PROGRAM OF ASSISTANCE:  Agricultural cooperatives - Crop improvement - Cash
Crops - Crop processing - Nurseries - Marketing - Management training.

PERSONNEL:  1 U.S., 7 local.

PROGRAM INITIATION:  1982          EXPENDITURES FOR FY 1982:  $26,500

COOPERATING ORGANIZATIONS:  Canadian International Development Agency (CIDA),
Hershey Foods Corporation, U.S. Agency for International Development,
World Neighbors.

. . . . . . . . . .

MC/HTI

**MISSIONARY CHURCH, INC.**
Contact:  Rev. Steve Zurcher, Field Chairman
          Missionary Church Association
          B.P.  1096
          Port-au-Prince, Haiti

PROGRAM OF ASSISTANCE:  Community programs - Mass media - Roads - Teachers -
Elementary schools - Agriculturists - Fertilizers - Irrigation - Storage -
Hospitals - Clinics.

PERSONNEL:  6 U.S., 30 local.

PROGRAM INITIATION:  1962          EXPENDITURES FOR 1982:  $9,030

COOPERATING ORGANIZATIONS:  Christian Reformed World Relief Committee, World
Gospel Mission.

. . . . . . . . . .

MHF/HTI

**MISSIONS HEALTH FOUNDATION**
Contact:  Dr. Cidoine Jeannis
          DEZCOLAM Project
          B.P. 1566
          Port-Au-Prince, Haiti

PROGRAM OF ASSISTANCE:  Community programs - Integrated rural development -
Adult education - Educational funding - Elementary schools - High schools -
Literacy education - Crafts - Agricultural training -  Animal husbandry -
Conservation - Crop improvement  - Extension agents - Fish farming - Fruits -
Irrigation - Poultry - Rabbits - Reforestation - Tools - Vegetables - Clinics
- Medical services - Potable water - Preventive medicine - Toilet facilities -
Mother/child programs - Nutrition education.

PERSONNEL:  32 local.

PROGRAM INITIATION:  1979          EXPENDITURES FOR FY 1982:  $136,000

..........

**MONTFORT MISSIONARIES (S.M.M.)**
Contact:  Rev. John Breslin, S.M.M.
          Mole Saint Nicolas
          Port-de-Paix, Haiti

PROGRAM OF ASSISTANCE:  Clinics.

PERSONNEL:  1 U.S.

PROGRAM INITIATION:  1964

..........

**OBLATES OF MARY IMMACULATE (O.M.I.)**
**Province of St. John the Baptist**
Contact:  R.P. Hubert Constant, O.M.I.
          40 Avenue N
          B.P.  691
          Port-au-Prince, Haiti
          Tel.  55654

PROGRAM OF ASSISTANCE:  Leadership training - Construction - Cooperatives - Adult education - Agricultural cooperatives - Cash crops - Credit/loans - Crop improvement - Reforestation - Agricultural training - Irrigation - Animal husbandry - Clinics - Preventive medicine - Potable water - Food supply programs - Mother/child programs - Geriatric centers.

PERSONNEL:  16 U.S., 4 local, 6 international.

PROGRAM INITIATION:  1943          EXPENDITURES FOR FY 1982:  $125,000

COOPERATING ORGANIZATIONS:  ADVENIAT (Germany), CARE, Catholic Fund for Overseas Development (CAFOD), Catholic Relief Services, CEBEMO (Netherlands), Church World Service, Club 2/3 (Canada), Governments of Canada, Haiti, and the United States, Heifer Project International, Holy Childhood (France), Misereor (Germany), OXFAM (U.K.), VASTENAKTIE (Netherlands).

..........

**OMS INTERNATIONAL, INC.**
Contact:  Rev. Harold O. Brown, Haiti Field Director
          Ville Ormiso
          Rue Chaud Eau
          B.P.  1739
          Port-au-Prince, Haiti
          Tel.  40693

PROGRAM OF ASSISTANCE: Mass media - Roads - Elementary schools - Vocational education - Crafts - Reforestation - Clinics - Dental clinics - Sanitation - Toilet facilities - Potable water.

PERSONNEL: 12 U.S., 300 local, 2 international.

PROGRAM INITIATION: 1958

COOPERATING ORGANIZATIONS: CARE, Compassion International, TEAR Fund (U.K.), U.S. Agency for International Development, World Neighbors, World Vision International.

. . . . . . . . . .

PADF/HTI

\* **PAN AMERICAN DEVELOPMENT FOUNDATION**
Contact: Haitian Development Foundation
106 Ave. Christopher
Port-au-Prince, Haiti

PADF Agroforestry/Haiti
B.P. 15574
Petionville, Haiti

PROGRAM OF ASSISTANCE: Credit/loans - Grants - Small enterprises - Income generation - Management training - Self-help programs - Institution building - Reforestation - Dental equipment - Medical equipment - Vocational training - Boats - Tools.

PERSONNEL: 5 U.S., 15 local, 4 international.

PROGRAM INITITATION: 1978          EXPENDITURES FOR FY 1982: $1,300,000

COOPERATING ORGANIZATIONS: Canadian International Development Agency (CIDA); Government of Belgium; Government of Switzerland; Partnership for Productivity; Public Welfare Foundation; U.S. Agency for International Development; U.S. manufacturers of equipment for vocational training; U.S. hospitals, health care institutions, and manufacturers of medical and dental equipment.

. . . . . . . . . .

PARTNERS/HTI

\* **PARTNERS OF THE AMERICAS**
Contact: Dr. Toussaint Desvosiers
Rue Timmer No. 10
Port-au-Prince, Haiti
Tel. 4-2698

PROGRAM OF ASSISTANCE: Medical equipment - Doctors - Rehabilitation - Consultants - Educational exchange - Colleges/universities - Resettlement.

PERSONNEL: U.S. and local volunteers.

PROGRAM INITIATION: 1978

COOPERATING ORGANIZATIONS: Government of Haiti, Ministry of Education, Health and Social Welfare; Haitian Development Fund; Rutgers University; U.S. International Communications Agency.

..........

PFPI/HTI

\* **PARTNERSHIP FOR PRODUCTIVITY INTERNATIONAL, INC.**
Contact:  Jean Brisson, PfP Caribbean Representative
          #77 Rouxe de Freres
          B.P. 15059
          Petion-ville, Haiti
          Tel.  011-509-1  73004

PROGRAM OF ASSISTANCE: Animateurs - Management training - Small enterprises.

PERSONNEL: 1 local.

PROGRAM INITIATION:  1980          EXPENDITURES FOR FY 1982:  $18,860

COOPERATING ORGANIZATIONS:  Haitian Development Foundation, Pan American Development Foundation.

..........

RCLDS/HTI

**REORGANIZED CHURCH OF JESUS CHRIST OF LATTER DAY SAINTS**
Contact:  Sanon Jolivert
          B.P. 592
          Port-au-Prince, Haiti

PROGRAM OF ASSISTANCE:  Schools - Health care teams - Medical services - Dentistry - Medical supplies - Nutrition education - Women - Preventive medicine.

PERSONNEL:  200 U.S., 49 local.

PROGRAM INITIATION:  1970          EXPENDITURES FOR FY 1982:  $20,000

COOPERATING  ORGANIZATIONS:  Missions  Health  Foundation,  Outreach International.

..........

RHEMA/HTI

**RHEMA INTERNATIONAL, INC.**
Contact:  No. 4 Ludovie, Rllc.
          Port-au-Prince, Haiti

TAICH Regional          157

Haiti--**Part II**

PROGRAM OF ASSISTANCE: Self-help programs - Nutrition education - Agricultural training - Clinics - Medical services - Hospitals.

PERSONNEL: 7 U.S.

EXPENDITURES FOR FY 1982: $105,597

..........

ROTARY/HTI

**ROTARY INTERNATIONAL**
Contact:   Joe Anson
           Rotary Club of Port-au-Prince
           71 Rue du Quai
           B.P. 1364
           Port-au-Prince, Haiti

PROGRAM OF ASSISTANCE:  Immunizations.

PROGRAM INITIATION:  1982          EXPENDITURES FOR FY 1982:   $196,000
                                                        (five year grant)

COOPERATING ORGANIZATION:  Government of Haiti, Ministry of Health.

..........

SALESIAN FR/HTI

* **SALESIAN SOCIETY, INC.**
  **Salesians of St. John Bosco (S.D.B.)**
  Contact:  Rev. Sergius Lamaute, S.D.B.
            Ecole Nationale des Arts et Metiers
            Port-au-Prince, Haiti

Supports programs of the International Salesian Society.

PROGRAM OF ASSISTANCE:  Teachers - Elementary schools - High schools - Preschool programs - Food distribution centers.

PERSONNEL:  29 international and local.

PROGRAM INITIATION:  1935

COOPERATING ORGANIZATIONS:  Catholic Relief Services; Government of Haiti, Ministry of Education; Misereor (Germany); Netherlands Organization for International Development Cooperation (NOVIB).

..........

SALVA/HTI

*+ **THE SALVATION ARMY**
   Contact:   Major Alfred Pierre, Divisional Commander
              Armee du Salut
              P.O. Box 301
              Port-au-Prince, Haiti
              Tel.  24502

Assists programs operated by the international organization.

PROGRAM OF ASSISTANCE:  Elementary schools - Boarding schools - Non-formal education - Vocational education - Women - Medical services - Viral/bacterial diseases - Food distribution centers - Food supply programs - Disabled - Geriatric centers - Orphanages.

PERSONNEL:  2 U.S., 101 local including 36 Salvation Army officers.

PROGRAM INITIATION:  1950

COOPERATING ORGANIZATIONS:  Bread for Brethren, Canadian International Development Agency (CIDA), Canadian Save the Children (CANSAVE), Compassion International, Kindernotilfe (West Germany).

..........

SCF/HTI

**\*+  SAVE THE CHILDREN FEDERATION, INC.**
    Contact:  Claude Bouthillier, Field Office Director
              Alliance Pour l'Enfance et le Development Comunitaire
              3 Ruelle Duncombe
              Port-au-Prince, Haiti

PROGRAMS OF ASSISTANCE:  Community centers - Community programs - Seminars - Youth - Women - Nurseries - Agricultural training - Cash crops - Vegetable gardens - Food/food products - Grains - Land reclamation - Soil conservation - Rabbits - Poultry - Dairy animals - Fish farming - Nutrition education - Potable water - Toilet facilities - Sanitation - Teaching materials - Construction - Adult education - Preschool programs - Housing - Crafts - Small enterprises - Schools.

PERSONNEL:  5 local, 1 international.

PROGRAM INITIATION:  1979          EXPENDITURES FOR FY 1982:  $91,161

COOPERATING ORGANIZATIONS:  Canadian Save the Children (CANSAVE), U.S. Agency for International Development.

..........

SBC/HTI

**SOUTHERN BAPTIST CONVENTION**

Works through local national churches.

PROGRAM OF ASSISTANCE:  Wells - Potable water - Energy - Wind energy - Agricultural training - Cash crops - Farm machinery - Intensive farming - Reforestation - Gardens - Goats - Poultry - Rabbits - Beekeeping - Food distribution centers - Children - Nutrition education.

PROGRAM INITIATION:  1978          EXPENDITURES FOR FY 1982:  $195,990

..........

**UFM INTERNATIONAL, INC.**
Contact:  Rev. David Schmid, Field Leader
          B.P.  458
          Port-au-Prince, Haiti

PROGRAM OF ASSISTANCE:  Potable water - Hospitals - Disabled - Dental clinics
- Mother/child programs - Children - Orphanages.

PERSONNEL:  46 U.S., 8 Canada.

PROGRAM INITIATION:  1942

COOPERATING ORGANIZATIONS:  Albert Schweitzer Hospital, Christian Medical
Society, MAP International, Pan American Development Foundation, Public
Welfare Foundation.

..........

**THE WESLEYAN CHURCH**
Contact:  Rev. James Vermilya, Mission Coordinator
          B.P.  1764
          Port-au-Prince, Haiti
          Tel.  162274

PROGRAM OF ASSISTANCE:  Elementary schools - High schools - Vocational
education - Wells - Hospitals - Clinics - Dentistry.

PERSONNEL:  14 U.S.

PROGRAM INITIATION:  1948        EXPENDITURES FOR FY 1982:    $88,400

COOPERATING  ORGANIZATIONS:   Compassion  International  provides  financial
assistance for the elementary and secondary schools; West Indies Self Help.

..........

*  **WINROCK INTERNATIONAL**
Contact:  Montaigu Cantave
          DARNDR
          Damien, Port-au-Prince, Haiti

PROGRAM OF ASSISTANCE:  Goats - Food/food products - Income generation - Self-
help  programs  -  Agricultural  training  -  Appropriate  technology  -  Animal
husbandry - Crop improvement - Management training.

PERSONNEL:  2 U.S., 4 local.

PROGRAM INITIATION:  1982        EXPENDITURES FOR FY 1982:    $69,500

COOPERATING ORGANIZATION:   Government of Haiti, Departement de L'Agriculture des Ressources Naturelles et du Developpement Rural (DARNDR).

. . . . . . . . . .

WORLD CON/HTI

**\*+ WORLD CONCERN**
Contact:   Dr. Bill Baker
           c/o CODEPLA/CEEH
           B.P.   2475
           Port-au-Prince, Haiti
           Tel.   64-829

PROGRAM OF ASSISTANCE:   Animateurs - Community programs - Integrated rural development - Schools - Non-formal education - Agricultural training - Animal husbandry - Reforestation - Gardens - Goats - Poultry - Irrigation - Water - Veterinary services - Preventive medicine - Nutrition education - Immunizations.

PERSONNEL:   10 U.S., 8 local.

PROGRAM INITIATION:  1977        EXPENDITURES FOR FY 1982:  $127,693

COOPERATING ORGANIZATIONS:   Albert Schweitzer Hospital; Government of Haiti, Division of Public Health; International Child Care; M.E.B.S.H. (Organization of Baptist Churches), World Team.

. . . . . . . . . .

WGM/HTI

**WORLD GOSPEL MISSION**
Contact:   Rev. Dale Dorothy, Field Director
           MCA-MFI/Haiti
           P.O. Box 15665
           West Palm Beach, Florida  33406

PROGRAM OF ASSISTANCE:   Clinics - Mother/child programs - Health care teams - Nurses.

PERSONNEL:   2 U.S.

PROGRAM INITIATION:  1965        EXPENDITURES FOR FY 1982:  $10,000

COOPERATING ORGANIZATIONS:   Mennonite Central Committee, Missionary Church Association, Reformed Church.

. . . . . . . . . .

WN/HTI

**WORLD NEIGHBORS, INC.**

PROGRAM OF ASSISTANCE:   Animateurs - Integrated rural development - Leadership training - Cooperatives - Adult education - Audio visual materials - Non-formal education - Marketing - Agricultural cooperatives - Cash crops - Conservation - Crop improvement - Crop processing - Reforestation - Storage - Tools - Water - Mother/child programs - Nutrition education - Birth control methods - Family planning.

PERSONNEL: 3 U.S., 24 local.

PROGRAM INITIATION: 1966          EXPENDITURES FOR FY 1982: $14,261

COOPERATING ORGANIZATIONS:    B.C.A. Credit/loans; Bois de Laurence (local Catholic Church Parish); Canadian International Development Agency (CIDA); Christoffel-Blindenmission; Cooperative Jean-Baptiste Chavannes; Government of Haiti, Ministry of Agriculture; Grace Children's Hospital; Hershey Foods Corporation; International Child Care; Mennonite Central Committee; Mennonite Economic Development Associates; Oriental Missionary Society; TEAR Fund; World Vision.

..........

**WORLD RELIEF CORPORATION**                                    WRC/HTI
**\*+**   Contact:  Dr. Claude Noel, Secretary General
          Council of Evangelical Churches of Haiti
          B.P.  2475
          Port-au-Prince, Haiti

Cooperates with the Council of Evangelical Churches of Haiti; provides funding.

PROGRAM OF ASSISTANCE:   Seminars - Agricultural cooperatives - Vocational education - Educational funding - Marketing - Clinics - Medical services.

PERSONNEL: 35 local.

PROGRAM INITIATION: 1971          EXPENDITURES FOR FY 1982: $108,300

COOPERATING ORGANIZATION: Council of Evangelical Churches of Haiti (CEEH).

..........

**WORLD VISION RELIEF ORGANIZATION, INC.**                      WVRO/HTI
**\*+**   Contact:  Paul Peterson
          Associate Director, Field Projects
          World Vision International
          Curridabat Apartado 133
          San Jose, Costa Rica

PROGRAM OF ASSISTANCE:   Integrated rural development - Sponsorships - Animal husbandry - Reforestation - Agricultural training - Literacy education - Potable water - Storage - Nutrition education - Preventive medicine - Medical services - Vocational education.

PROGRAM INITIATION: 1973          EXPENDITURES FOR FY 1982: $2,075,282

..........

## HAITI - PROGRAM SUPPORT

|  |  |  |
|---|---|---|
|  | A.T. International | $ 37,000 |
|  | American Lung Association | ----- |
| * | Association for Voluntary Sterilization, Inc. | 61,538 |
| + | Baptist World Aid | 36,190 |
| * | Brother's Brother Foundation | 39,000 |
|  | Catholic Medical Mission Board, Inc. | 330,818 |
|  | Center for Human Services | 77,959 |
| * | Centre for Development and Population Activities | ----- |
|  | Church of the Brethren General Board | ----- |
| * | Council of International Programs for Youth Leaders and Social Workers, Inc. | 1,200 |
| * | Direct Relief International | 81,020 |
|  | Education Development Center | ----- |
|  | Family Health International | ----- |
| * | Family Planning International Assistance | 3,869 |
|  | Farallones Institute | ----- |
|  | Friends of SOS Children's Villages, Inc. | 6,000 |
|  | Friends of the Third World | ----- |
| *+ | Heifer Project International | 83,316 |
|  | Interchurch Medical Assistance, Inc. | 100,266 |
|  | International Book Project, Inc. | 75 |
| * | International Executive Service Corps | ----- |
|  | Lions Clubs International | ----- |
|  | International Liaison, Inc. | ----- |
|  | David Livingston Missionary Foundation, Inc. | ----- |
| *+ | MAP International | 781,880 |
|  | Medical Benevolence Foundation | 82,000 |
|  | Medical Relief of Haiti | $500 |
|  | Midwest Medical Mission | 55,090 |
|  | National Council of Catholic Women | 4,500 |
|  | Operation Crossroads Africa | ----- |
|  | Outreach International | 194,000 |
| * | Pathfinder Fund | 301 |
| *+ | Private Agencies Collaborating Together (PACT) | 94,316 |
|  | Public Welfare Foundation | 49,000 |
| *+ | Seventh-day Adventist World Service (SAWS) | 91,360 |
| * | Sister Cities International | ----- |
|  | Trickle Up Program | 3,600 |
| * | Unitarian Universalist Service Committee | ----- |
|  | United Methodist Committee on Relief | 845,800 |
| * | Volunteers in Technical Assistance, Inc. (VITA) | ----- |
|  | Volunteer Optometric Services to Humanity (VOSH International) | ----- |

---

## HONDURAS

---

Of the 108 U.S. organizations listed in Honduras,
71 were able to provide TAICH with financial data
indicating program expenditures for FY 1982
totaling $16,061,408.

AED/HDA

**ACADEMY FOR EDUCATIONAL DEVELOPMENT**
Contact:   Jose Mata
           Apartado Postal 140
           Tegucigalpa, Honduras

PROGRAM OF ASSISTANCE:   Health care teams - Mass media - Children - Health
education.

PROGRAM INITIATION:  1982          EXPENDITURES FOR FY 1982:  $34,000

COOPERATING ORGANIZATION:  Government of Honduras, Ministry of Health.

. . . . . . . . . .

AFL-CIO/HDA

\*    **AFL-CIO - American Institute for Free Labor Development**
     Contact:   Bernard Packer, Country Representative
                Apartado 209-C
                Tegucigalpa, Honduras

PROGRAM OF ASSISTANCE:  Cooperatives - Unions - Adult education - Educational
funding - Educational exchange.

PERSONNEL:  1 U.S.

PROGRAM INITIATION:  1964

COOPERATING ORGANIZATION:  U.S. Agency for International Development.

. . . . . . . . . .

ACDI/HDA

\*    **AGRICULTURAL COOPERATIVE DEVELOPMENT INTERNATIONAL**
     Contact:   Juan Alvarez, Chief of Party
                Edificio Plaza, 4 Piso
                5 Calle, 12 Ave.
                Tegucigalpa, Honduras
                Tel. 228048

PROGRAM OF ASSISTANCE:  Agribusiness - Cooperatives.

PERSONNEL:  2 U.S., 15 local, 1 international.

PROGRAM INITIATION:  1981          EXPENDITURES FOR FY 1982:  $400,000

COOPERATING ORGANIZATIONS:  Government of Honduras, Directorate of Cooperative Development (DIFOCOOP), National Agricultural Development Bank (BANDESA), National Agricultural Marketing Agency (IHMA); U.S. Agency for International Development.

..........

AMERICAS/HDA

## THE AMERICAS - HAND IN HAND

PROGRAM OF ASSISTANCE:  Appropriate technology - Self-help programs - Language training - Educational exchange - Vocational education - Clinics - Medical equipment - Mother/child programs, Nutrition education - Birth control methods - Family planning - Integrated rural development - Cottage industries - Small enterprises - Agricultural training - Animal husbandry - Beekeeping - Biogas/methane - Cash crops - Conservation - Crop improvement - Crop processing - Energy - Gardens - Grains - Vegetables - Hydroelectric energy - Irrigation - Pest control - Water.

PERSONNEL:  12 U.S., 4 local, 4 international.

PROGRAM INITIATION:  1965          EXPENDITURES FOR FY 1982:  $35,000

COOPERATING ORGANIZATION:  U.S. Agency for International Development.

..........

BMA/HDA

## BAPTIST MISSIONARY ASSOCIATION OF AMERICA
Contact:  Bob Bowman
          Apartado Postal 1212
          San Pedro Sula, Honduras

PROGRAM OF ASSISTANCE:  Clinics.

PERSONNEL:  2 U.S., 1 local.

PROGRAM INITIATION:  1976          EXPENDITURES FOR FY 1982:  $37,066.

..........

BUENA/HDA

## LA BUENA FE ASSOCIATION
Contact:  Lyle Leys, Project Director
          Apartado Postal 536
          San Pedro Sula, Honduras

PROGRAM OF ASSISTANCE:  Vocational education - Agricultural training - Clinics - Nutrition education.

TAICH Regional               165

PERSONNEL:  4 U.S., 15 local.

PROGRAM INITIATION:  1961          EXPENDITURES FOR FY 1982:  $60,000

COOPERATING ORGANIZATIONS:  CARE; Comite Evangelico de Desarrollo y Emergencia Nacional (CEDEN); Government of Honduras, Ministry of Public Health and Social Assistance.

..........

CAM/HDA

**CAM INTERNATIONAL**
Contact:  Harold Krause, Field Committee President
          Apartado Postal 7
          Siguatepeque, Honduras
          Tel. 73-2283

PROGRAM OF ASSISTANCE:  Elementary schools - High schools - Seeds - Food/food products.

PROGRAM INITIATION:  1896          EXPENDITURES FOR FY 1982:  $15,000

COOPERATING ORGANIZATIONS:  Tear Fund (U.K.), World Relief, World Vision.

..........

CARE/HDA

*+ **CARE**
Contact:  Jay Jackson, Country Director
          4a Avenida, 9 Calle, #810
          Colonia Alameda
          Apartado Postal 729
          Tegucigalpa, Honduras
          Tel. 32-8601, 32-8852

PROGRAM OF ASSISTANCE:  Housing - Credit/loans - Potable water - Sanitation - Construction - Mother/child health - Food distribution centers - PL 480 - Tools - Maintenance repair - Reforestation - Refugees - Agricultural training - Storage - Immunizations - Nutrition education.

PERSONNEL:  6 U.S. and/or Canada.

PROGRAM INITIATION:  1954          EXPENDITURES FOR FY 1982:  $3,070,794

COOPERATING ORGANIZATIONS:  Pan American Agricultural School (Guatemala), Servicio Autonomo Nacional de Acueductos y Alcantarillados (SANAA), United Nations High Commission for Refugees, U.S. Peace Corps.

..........

CRS/HDA

**\*+ CATHOLIC RELIEF SERVICES - UNITED STATES CATHOLIC CONFERENCE**
Contact:  John Contier, Program Director
Avenida Principal
Casa No 211, Comonia Reforma
Apartado Postal 257
Tegucigalpa, Honduras
Tel. 32-6421

PROGRAM OF ASSISTANCE:  Credit/loans - Funding - Educational funding - Women - Cooperatives - Storage - PL 480 - Small enterprises - Clothing - Agricultural training - Food/food products - Refugees - Self-help programs.

PERSONNEL:  2 U.S.  8 local.

PROGRAM INITIATION:  1961          EXPENDITURES FOR FY 1982:  $551,417

COOPERATING ORGANIZATIONS:  ASEPADE (Asesores para el Desarrollo), Bread for the World, Brucke der Bruderhilfe, CARE, Caritas, Catholic Medical Mission Board, Church World Service, European Economic Community, FEHMIC (Federacion de Mujeres Campesinas), Government of Honduras, IHDER (Instituto Hondureno de Desarrollo Rural), MASTA (Unidad de las Mosquitia), Meals for Millions/Freedom from Hunger Foundation, Medicines Sans Frontiers, Oxfam America, Scottish Catholic International Aid Fund, U.S. Agency for International Development.

..........

CCF/HDA

**\*+ CHRISTIAN CHILDREN'S FUND, INC.**
Contact:  Avenida La Paz y
Avenida Republica de Panama
Casa No. 109
Colonia Palmira
Apartado Postal 156-C
Tegucigalpa, Honduras
Tel. 32-5760, 32-5479

PROGRAM OF ASSISTANCE:  Community programs - Integrated rural development - Cooperatives - Elementary schools - Literacy education - Non-formal education - Mother/child programs - Children - Disabled - Orphanages - Rehabilitation - Sponsorships - Youth - Integrated rural development - Self-help programs.

PERSONNEL:  3 local

PROGRAM INITIATION:  1982          EXPENDITURES FOR FY 1982:  $10,000

..........

CFC/HDA

**CHRISTIAN FOUNDATION FOR CHILDREN**
Contact:  Sandra Zelaya, Coordinator
Caritas Vicariaz
Apartado 10
El Progreso, Yoro
Honduras
Tel. 504-56-4225

PROGRAM OF ASSISTANCE: Preschool programs - Elementary schools - Literacy education - Vocational education - Clinics - Preventive medicine - Public health education - Nutrition education - Mother/child programs - Food distribution centers - Children - Refugees - Sponsorships - Youth - Books - Clothing - Food/food products - Medical supplies.

PERSONNEL: 2 U.S., 4 local.

PROGRAM INITIATION: 1981          EXPENDITURES FOR FY 1982: $30,000

COOPERATING ORGANIZATIONS: Caritas Vicariaz de Yoro; Caritas Paraoquial de el Progreso; Clinica las Mealeoes, Programme de Nutricion; Comedor Infantil Olga de Romero; Caritas Sta. Rosa de Copan; Centro Amelissa.

..........

CRWRC/HDA
+ **CHRISTIAN REFORMED WORLD RELIEF COMMITTEE**
   Contact:  Betty Roldan
             c/o CEDEN
             Apartado Postal 1478
             Tegucigalpa, Honduras
             Tel 32-1719

PROGRAM OF ASSISTANCE:  Integrated rural development - Adult literacy - Refugees.

PERSONNEL: 2 U.S., 1 international.

EXPENDITURES FOR FY 1982: $280,000

COOPERATING ORGANIZATIONS:  Comite Evangelico de Desarrollo y Emergencia Nacional (CEDEN), Christian Reformed World Missions.

..........

CONCERN/HDA
**CONCERN America**
Contact:  Administered from U.S. headquarters office

PROGRAM OF ASSISTANCE:  Medical equipment - Medical supplies - Preventive medicine - Public health education - Sanitation - Breast-feeding - Food distribution centers - Food prepartion - Mother/child programs - Nutrition education.

PERSONNEL: 8 U.S., 100 local, 1 international.

PROGRAM INITIATION: 1981          EXPENDITURES FOR FY 1982: $40,000

COOPERATING ORGANIZATIONS:  Caritas, Catholic Relief Services, Medicine sans Frontiers (France).

..........

CONS BAPT/HDA
## CONSERVATIVE BAPTIST FOREIGN MISSION SOCIETY
Contact:  Darryl Davis
          Apartado Postal 115
          La Ceiba, Honduras
          Tel. 42-0320

PROGRAM OF ASSISTANCE:    Adult education - Gardens - Nurses - Medical education.

PERSONNEL: 2 U.S., 1 local.

PROGRAM INITIATION: 1965

COOPERATING ORGANIZATIONS:    Comite Evangelico de Desarrollo y Emergencia Nacional (CEDEN).

. . . . . . . . . .

CONV/HDA
## CONVENTUAL FRANCISCANS (O.F.M. CONV.)
Contact:  Fr. Mark Weaver (O.F.M CONV.)
          Noviciado Franciscano
          Apartado Postal 108
          Comayaguela, Honduras

PROGRAM OF ASSISTANCE:    Leadership training - Self-help programs - Adult education - High schools - Mass media - Medical supplies - Clothing.

PERSONNEL: 8 U.S., 6 local

. . . . . . . . . .

CHF/HDA
## * COOPERATIVE HOUSING FOUNDATION
Contact:  Federation of Housing Cooperatives
              (FEHCOVIL)
          Apartado Postal 853
          Tegucigalpa, Honduras

PROGRAM OF ASSISTANCE:  Housing - Construction - Cooperatives - Credit/loans - Consultants.

PERSONNEL:  Short-term consultants.

PROGRAM INITIATION: 1968

COOPERATING ORGANIZATION:  U.S. Agency for International Development.

. . . . . . . . . .

**EASTERN MENNONITE BOARD OF MISSIONS AND CHARITIES**
Contact:  Damian Rodriguez
          Honduras Mennonite Church
          Apartado Postal 77
          La Ceiba, Honduras

PROGRAM OF ASSISTANCE:  Children - Nutrition education - Rehabilitation.

PERSONNEL:  3 U.S., 3 local.

PROGRAM INITIATION:  1950          EXPENDITURES FOR FY 1982:  $48,000

COOPERATING ORGANIZATIONS:  Amor Viviente, Government of Honduras, Mennonite
Central Committee.

. . . . . . . . . .

\*  **THE EPISCOPAL CHURCH IN THE U.S.A.**
   **(including + The Presiding Bishop's Fund for World Relief)**
   Contact:  Missionary Diocese of Honduras
             Apartado Postal 1228
             San Pedro Sula, Honduras

PROGRAM OF ASSISTANCE:  Elementary schools - Orphanages - Clinics - Medical
equipment.

PERSONNEL:  12 U.S.

PROGRAM INITIATION:  1957

COOPERATING ORGANIZATIONS:  Interchurch Medical Assistance.

. . . . . . . . . .

\*  **FOSTER PARENTS PLAN**
   Contact:  Charles Winkler, Director
             PLAN en Honduras
             Apartado Postal 41-C
             Tegucigalpa, Honduras

PROGRAMS OF ASSISTANCE:  Construction - Community centers - Leadership
training - Self-help programs - Bridges - Housing - Credit/loans - Schools -
Educational funding - Teaching equipment - Small enterprises - Agricultural
cooperatives - Agricultural training - Animal husbandry - Fish farming -
Food/food products - Cooperatives - Equipment - Potable water - Sanitation -
Toilet facilities - Nutrition education.

PERSONNEL:  3 international, 191 local.

PROGRAM INITIATION:  1977          EXPENDITURES FOR FY 1982:  $2,302,515

COOPERATING ORGANIZATIONS: Government of Australia, Government of Canada and the Provincial Government of Albert (Canada); Government of Honduras, Ministry of Public Health.

. . . . . . . . . .

OSF SCHOOL/HDA

**SCHOOL SISTERS OF ST. FRANCIS (O.S.F.)**
Contact:  Sister Regina Ramos, (O.S.F.) Area Coordinator
          Casa Santa Teresita
          10 Avenida No. 502
          Tegucigalpa, Honduras
          Tel. 22-0758

PROGRAM OF ASSISTANCE:  Teachers - Nurses - Social welfare - Mother/child programs.

PERSONNEL: 3 U.S., 12 local.
PROGRAM INITIATION:  1951

COOPERATING ORGANIZATION:  Friends of Children.

. . . . . . . . . .

OSF PERP/HDA

**SISTERS OF ST. FRANCIS OF PERPETURAL ADORATION (O.S.F.)**
**Province of the Immaculate Heart of Mary**
Contact:  Sister M. Elizabeth Ann, O.S.F.
          Hermanas Franciscanas - St. Clare Convent
          Apartado Postal 262
          Comayaguela, Honduras

PROGRAM OF ASSISTANCE:  High schools - Clinics.

PERSONNEL:  3 U.S.

PROGRAM INTIATION:  1978

COOPERATING ORGANIZATIONS:  Conventual Franciscans, San Francisco Colonia (Honduras).

. . . . . . . . . .

OFM IMMAC/HDA

**FRANCISCAN FRIARS (O.F.M.)**
**Province of the Immaculate Conception**
Contact:  Rev. Custos, O.F.M.
          Instituto San Francisco
          Apartado Postal 554
          Tegucigalpa, Honduras

PROGRAM OF ASSISTANCE:   Community programs - Construction - Housing - Educational funding - Equipment - Medical services - Nutrition education - Social welfare.

PERSONNEL:   8 U.S., 4 local, 1 international.

PROGRAM INITIATION:   1944          EXPENDITURES FOR FY 1982:   $300,000

COOPERATING ORGANIZATION:   Franciscan Order of Friars Minor; SOS Villages (Austria).

.........

FC/HDA

* **FRIENDS OF CHILDREN, INC.**
  Contact:   Centro San Juan Bosco
             c/o Jay Boll, volunteer
             Apartado Postal 20
             Tela, Atlantida
             Honduras

PROGRAM OF ASSISTANCE:   Books - Clothing - Medical - Supplies - Tools - Orphanages - Youth.

PERSONNEL:   1 U.S., 1 international volunteer.

PROGRAM INITIATION:   1983          EXPENDITURES FOR FY 1982:   $10,000

..........

GLOBAL/HDA

* **GLOBAL OUTREACH**
  Contact:   Landon Wilkerson
             Mision Bautitista
             Puerto Lempira
             Gracias A Dios, Honduras

PROGRAM OF ASSISTANCE:   Mass media - Electrification - Credit/loans - Storage - Cooperatives - Agricultural training - Health care teams - Dentistry.

PERSONNEL:   2 U.S., 70 U.S. volunteers.

PROGRAM INITIATION:   1972          EXPENDITURES FOR FY 1982:   $103,669

COOPERATING ORGANIZATIONS:   Baptist Mission of Puerto Lempira; Govenment of Honduras, State and local governments.

..........

HERMAN/HDA

* **HERMANDAD, INC.**
  Contact:   Jose Carmen Fuentes
             Hermandad
             San Marcos, Ocotepeque
             Honduras

PROGRAM OF ASSISTANCE: Leadership training - Cooperatives - Vocational education - Medical services - Self-help programs - Women - Agricultural experiment centers - Fish farming - Appropriate technology.

PERSONNEL: 4 local, 1 international.

PROGRAM INITIATION: 1976          EXPENDITURES FOR FY 1982: $35,000

COOPERATING ORGANIZATIONS: Coordination in Development (CODEL), Church Women United.

. . . . . . . . . .

HOLY LAND/HDA

* **HOLY LAND CHRISTIAN MISSION INTERNATIONAL**
Contact:  Sister Lucy de Torres Lazo, Coordinadora
          Damas de la Caridad
          Programe Amigos de los Ninos
          Apartado Postal 874
          San Pedro Sula, Cortes
          Honduras
          Tel. 405-54-2139

PROGRAM OF ASSISTANCE: Sponsorships - Community centers - Food distribution centers - Refugees.

PERSONNEL: 2 local

PROGRAM INITIATION: 1981          EXPENDITURES FOR FY 1982: $158,138

COOPERATING ORGANIZATION: Damas de la Caridad.

. . . . . . . . . .

IIDI/HDA

* **INSTITUTE FOR INTERNATIONAL DEVELOPMENT, INC.**
Contact:  Sr. Oscare Chicas
          I.D.H.
          Apartado Postal 288
          Comayaguela, Honduras

PROGRAM OF ASSISTANCE: Credit/loans - Income generation - Management training - Small enterprises.

PERSONNEL: 10 local.

PROGRAM INITATION: 1978          EXPENDITURES FOR FY 1982: $35,000
COOPERATING ORGANIZATIONS: Inter-American Development Bank, U.S. Agency for International Development.

. . . . . . . . . .

INTL EYE/HDA
* **INTERNATIONAL EYE FOUNDATION**

PROGRAM OF ASSISTANCE:  Blindness prevention - Medical education - Medical supplies - Books - Ophthalmology - Vehicles - Consultants - Air transportation - Medical services - Doctors - Disease treatment - Evaluation.

PERSONNEL:  1 U.S.

PROGRAM INITIATION:  1979          EXPENDITURES FOR FY 1982:  $117,000

COOPERATING ORGANIZATIONS:  Chibret International, Government of Honduras, U.S. Agency for International Development.

. . . . . . . . . .

IVS/HDA
* **INTERNATIONAL VOLUNTARY SERVICES, INC.**
  Contact:  Chet Thomas, Field Director
            Apartado Postal 1149
            Tegucigalpa, Honduras
            Tel. 36-2241

PROGRAM OF ASSISTANCE:  Policy and planning - Medical education - Conservation - Small enterprises - Integrated rural development - Potable water - Sanitation - Water - Land reclamation.

PERSONNEL:  3 U.S.; 1 international.

PROGRAM INITIATION 1974          EXPENDITURES FOR FY 1982:  $237,100

COOPERATING ORGANIZATIONS:  Association of San Jose Obrero, Comite Evangelico de Desarrollo Emergencia Nacional (CEDEN), Coordination in Development (CODEL), Private Agencies Collaborating Together (PACT), United Methodist Committee on Relief.

. . . . . . . . . .

LECHE/HDA
* **LA LECHE LEAGUE INTERNATIONAL**
  Contact:  Judy de Canahuati
            La Leche League of Honduras
            Apartado Postal 512
            San Pedro Sula, Honduras
            Tel. 54-37-37

PROGRAM OF ASSISTANCE:  Breast-feeding - Mother/child programs - Self-help programs - Women's education - Public health education.
PERSONNEL:  1 U.S., 1 international.

PROGRAM INITIATION:  1970

. . . . . . . . . .

LWR/HDA

**\*+   LUTHERAN WORLD RELIEF, INC.**
Contacts: Dorcas Gonzalez, Executive Director
Evangelical Committee For National Development
and Emergency (CEDEN)
Apartado Postal 1478
Tegucigalpa, Honduras
Tel. 32-1719, 32-7938

Noemi Espinoza  Executive Director
Christian Commission For Development
and Emergency (CODE)
Apartado Postal 21
Colonia Kennedy
Tegucigalpa, Honduras
Tel. 32-8223

PROGRAM OF ASSISTANCE:   Leadership training - Literacy education - Public
health education - Nutrition education - Family planning - Dental clinics -
Integrated  rural  development  -  Agricultural  training  -  Agricultural
cooperatives - Demonstration projects - Immunizations - Animal husbandry -
Beekeeping - Toilet facilities - Potable water - Credit/loans - Gardens - Crop
improvement - Storage - Small enterprises.

PROGRAM INITIATION 1978          EXPENDITURES FOR FY 1982:  $40,000

COOPERATING  ORGANIZATIONS:    Church  World  Service,  EZE  (Germany),  ICCO
(Netherlands), Heifer Project International,Presbyterian Church, World Council
of Churches, United Church of Canada.

..........

MSH/HDA

**MANAGEMENT SCIENCES FOR HEALTH**
Contact:  Frederick Hartman, M.D., Chief of Party
Apartado Postal 7
Colonia Kennedy
Tegucigalpa, Honduras
Tel. (504) 22-7121

PROGRAM OF ASSISTANCE: Clinics - Health care teams - Immunizations - Medical
auxiliaries - Medical  services - Medical  supplies - Nurses - Preventive
medicine - Public health education - Breast-feeding - Mother/child programs -
Policy  and  planning  -  Evaluation  -  Integrated  rural  development  -
Maintenance/repair - Community programs - On-the-job training - Seminars -
Teaching equipments - Management training.

PERSONNEL:  4 U.S., 4 local, 2 international.

PROGRAM INITIATION:  1982          EXPENDITURES FOR FY 1982:  $407,000

COOPERATING ORGANIZATIONS:   Government of Honduras, Department of Public
Health and Development; Inter-American Development Bank; Pan American Health
Organization; U.S. Agency for International Development.

..........

MKNOLL FR /HDA

**MARYKNOLL FATHERS AND BROTHERS (M.M.)**
Contact:   Rev. Rudolph G. Kneuer, M.M.
           Casa Cural
           Choloma Cortes, Honduras

PROGRAM OF ASSISTANCE:  Animateurs - Community centers - Community programs - Food distribution centers - Food-for-work - Integrated rural development - Leadership training - Self-help programs - Housing - Roads - Adult education - Courses - Conferences - Literacy education - Agricultural training - Conservation - Crop improvement - Extension agents - Gardens - Food distribution centers - Food preparation - Food supply programs - Nutrition education - Counseling - Displaced persons - Resettlement - Women - Youth - Evaluation - Volunteers.

PERSONNEL:  6 U.S.

PROGRAM INITIATION:  1982

..........

MM/FFHF/HDA
**\*+ MEALS FOR MILLIONS/FREEDOM FROM HUNGER FOUNDATION**
Contact:   Zoila Alvarez, Program Coordinator
           Apartado Postal 1693
           Tegucigalpa, Honduras

PROGRAM OF ASSISTANCE:  Integrated rural development - Self-help programs - Environment - Management training - Public health education - Sanitation - Mother/child programs - Nutrition education - Income generation - Agricultural training - Fish farming - Gardens - Rabbits - Storage.

PERSONNEL:  7 local.

PROGRAM INITIATION:  1978

COOPERATING ORGANIZATIONS:  Government of Honduras, Ministries of Agriculture and Natural Resources, Education, Health, National Agrarian Institute, National Development Bank, National Forestry Corporation, National Nutrition Education Planning Council; Women's Peasant Federation.

..........

MCC/HDA
**\*+ MENNONITE CENTRAL COMMITTEE**
Contact:   Charles Geiser
           c/o CEDEN
           San Marcos de Ocotepeque
           Honduras

PROGRAM OF ASSISTANCE:  Refugees - Resettlement - Housing - Food distribution centers - Sanitation - Potable water - Agricultural extension.

PERSONNEL: 5 U.S., 10 local, 2 international.

PROGRAM INITIATION: 1980    EXPENDITURES FOR FY 1982: $50,000
                                    (and $300,000 UNHCR funds)

COOPERATING ORGANIZATIONS: Caritas; Honduras Mennonite Church; Comite Evangelico de Desarrollo y Emergencia Nacional (CEDEN); Doctors without Frontiers; Government of Honduras, Refugee Board; U.N. High Commission for Refugees.

. . . . . . . . . .

MERCY SR/HDA

**SISTERS OF MERCY OF THE UNION IN THE U.S.A.** (R.S.M.)
Contact:  Centro de Rehabilitacion
          Apartado Postal 2
          San Pedro Sula, Honduras
          Tel. 54-11-52

The program is conducted by the Province of Providence (Rhode Island).

PROGRAM OF ASSISTANCE: Crafts - Literacy education - Small enterprises - Clinics - Rehabilitation - Self-help programs.

PERSONNEL  1 U.S., 5 local.

PROGRAM INITIATION: 1980

. . . . . . . . . .

AVIATION/HDA

**MISSION AVIATION FELLOWSHIP**
Contact:  David Jones, Manager
          Alas de Socorro
          Apartado Postal T227
          Zona Toncontin
          Tegucigalpa, Honduras
          Tel. 33-7025

PROGRAM OF ASSISTANCE: Air transportation - Vehicles - Refugees.

PERSONNEL: 9 U.S.

PROGRAM INITIATION: 1952

COOPERATING ORGANIZATIONS: California Yearly Meeting of Friends; Central American Mission; Church of God; Conservative Baptist Foreign Mission Society; Eastern Mennonite Board of Missions and Charities; Government of Honduras, Department of Public Health; Moravian Church in America; Southern Baptist Convention; United Brethren in Christ; Wesleyan Methodist Church; World Gospel Mission; World Relief.

. . . . . . . . . .

MORAV/HDA

**MORAVIAN CHURCH IN AMERICA, INC.**
Contact: Rev. Walter Navarro Allen, Superintendent
Cocobila, Gracias a Dios, Honduras

PROGRAM OF ASSISTANCE: Cooperatives - Land tenure - Storage - Clinics - Research/field studies - Books - Clothing - Food/food products - Medical equipment - Medical supplies - Seeds - Tools - Disease treatment - Doctors - Health care teams - Immunization - Medical services - Nurses - Preventive medicine - Public health education - Sanitation - Disaster relief - Displaced persons - Refugees - Resettlement - Transportation - Self-help programs - Volunteers - Water transportation - Educational funding - High schools - Cottage industries - Crafts - Marketing - Agriculturalists - Crop improvement.

PROGRAM INITIATION: 1930          EXPENDITURES FOR FY 1982: $50,000

COOPERATING ORGANIZATIONS: Agriculture Missions; Brot fur die Welt (Germany); Comite Evangelico de Desarrollo y Emergencia National (CEDEN); Eastern Mennonite Board of Missions and Charities; Evangelica Hondurena; Government of Honduras; Heifer Project International; Interchurch Coordination Committee for Development Aid, Netherlands (ICCD); Missionary Aviation Fellowship; Presbyterian Church in the U.S.; United Church of Canada.

. . . . . . . . . .

SSND/HDA

**SCHOOL SISTERS OF NOTRE DAME (S.S.N.D.)**
**Southern Province**
Contact: Blanca Maria Cruz
Apartado Postal 26
El Progreso, Yoro, Honduras

PROGRAM OF ASSISTANCE: High Schools - Vocational education - Medical clinics - Nutrition education.

PERSONNEL: 4 U.S., 6 local.

PROGRAM INITIATION: 1944

COOPERATING ORGANIZATIONS: Jesuit Fathers and Brothers (S.J.).

. . . . . . . . . .

OEF/HDA

\* **OVERSEAS EDUCATION FUND**
Contact: Bonnie Birker, Technical Advisor
Centro de Desarrollo Industrial
Programa de Tecnologias Rurales
Avda, La Paz Casa no. 407 Frente a Tecni Motores
Apartado Postal 703
Tegucigalpa, Honduras
Tel. 32-4050

PROGRAM OF ASSISTANCE: Appropriate technology - Integrated rural development - Extension agents - Small enterprises - Income generation.

PERSONNEL:  2 U.S., 1 local.

PROGRAM INITIATION:  1980          EXPENDITURES FOR FY 1982:  $19,825

COOPERATING ORGANIZATIONS:  Centro de Desarrollo Industrial, Partnership for Productivity International, U.S. Agency for International Development.

. . . . . . . . . .

PADF/HDA

\* **PAN AMERICAN DEVELOPMENT FOUNDATION**
Contact:  Instituto para el Desarrollo Hondureno
          Apartado Postal 288
          Comayaguela, Honduras

PROGRAM OF ASSISTANCE:  Integrated rural development - Small enterprises - Income generation - Self help programs - Management training - Credit/loans - Appropriate technology - Health care training - Medical equipment - Vocational training - Boats - Institution building - Tools.

PROGRAM INITITATION:  1965

COOPERATING ORGANIZATIONS:  Instituto para el Desarrollo Hondureno; Organization of American States; U.S. Agency for International Development; U.S. manufacturers of equipment related to vocational training; U.S. hospitals, health care institutions, and manufacturers of medical equipment.

. . . . . . . . . .

PARTNERS/HDA

\* **PARTNERS OF THE AMERICAS**
Contact:  Jose Elias Sanchez, President Honduras Partners
          ACORDE
          Apartado Postal 163-C
          Tegucigalpa, Honduras
          Tel.  22-56-21

The Vermont Partners cooperate with the Honduras Partners in the following programs:

PROGRAM OF ASSISTANCE:  Educational exchange - Educational materials - Books - Medical supplies - Clinics - Potable water - Sanitation - Rehabilitation - Vocational education - Women - Integrated rural development.

PERSONNEL:  U.S. and local volunteers.

PROGRAM INITIATION:  1965

COOPERATING ORGANIZATIONS:  Government of Honduras, Honduras Development Foundation, Ministry of Natural Resources; Lions Clubs; National University of Honduras, National School of Agriculture (Catacamas), San Jose Obrero Health Clinic (Choluteca).

. . . . . . . . . .

PFPI/HDA

\* **PARTNERSHIP FOR PRODUCTIVITY INTERNATIONAL, INC.**
Contact:  Patnership for Productivity Foundation
& Overseas Education Fund
c/o Centro de Desarrollo Industrial
Programa de Tecnologias Rurales
Apartado Postal 703
Tegucigalpa, Honduras

PROGRAM OF ASSISTANCE:  Small enterprises - Marketing - Management training - Credit/loans - Appropriate technology - Maintenance/repair - Integrated rural development - Biogas methane - Solar energy - Crop processing - Farm machinery - Irrigation.

PERSONNEL:  5 U.S., 40 local.

PROGRAM INITIATION:  1980         EXPENDITURES FOR FY 1982:  $84,950

COOPERATING ORGANIZATIONS:  Honduran PVOs, Ministerio de Recursos Naturales, U.S. Agency for International Development.

··········

HOPE/HDA

\* **PEOPLE-TO-PEOPLE HEALTH FOUNDATION, INC.**
**Project HOPE**
Contact:  Dr. Donald Kaminsky
c/o Dr. Samuel Dickerman
Head of Medical Services Division
Instituto Hondureno de Seguridad Social
Apartado Postal 71
Tegucigalpa, Honduras

PROGRAM OF ASSISTANCE:  Medical education - Nurses - Doctors - Hospitals.

PERSONNEL:  14 U.S., 3 local.

PROGRAM INITIATION:  1983

COOPERATING ORGANIZATIONS:  Government of Honduras, Ministry of Health, Institute of Social Security.

··········

RCLDS/HDA

**REORGANIZED CHURCH OF JESUS CHRIST OF LATTER DAY SAINTS**
Contact:  Antonio Jimenez
Apartado Postal 636
San Pedro Sula, Honduras

PROGRAM OF ASSISTANCE:  Immunizations - Sanitation - Clinics - Nutrition education - Family planning.

PERSONNEL:  5 U.S., 2 local

TAICH Regional                    180

PROGRAM INITIATION: 1961

COOPERATING ORGANIZATIONS: ACORDE (Confederation of Honduran Cooperatives); Government of Honduras, Ministry of Public Health; La Buena Fe Foundation; RLDS Medical, Dental and Nurses Association.

. . . . . . . . . .

ROTARY/HDA

**ROTARY INTERNATIONAL**
Contact: Felipe Arguello Carazo
        Casa Matthews
        Apartado Postal 37
        San Pedro Sula, Honduras

PROGRAM OF ASSISTANCE: Agricultural extension - Nutrition education.

PROGRAM INITIATION: 1982        EXPENDITURES FOR FY 1982: $71,250

. . . . . . . . . .

SALESIAN FR/HDA

\*   **SALESIAN SOCIETY, INC.**
**Salesians of St. John Bosco (S.D.B.)**
Contact: Rev. Luis Alfonso Santos, S.D.B.
        Institute Salesiano San Miguel
        Apartado Postal 125
        Tegucigalpa, Honduras

PROGRAM OF ASSISTANCE: Youth - Elementary schools - High schools - Colleges/universities.

. . . . . . . . . .

SCF/HDA

\*+  **SAVE THE CHILDREN FEDERATION, INC.**
Contact: Antonio Ramirez
        Federacion Desarrollo Juvenil Comunitario
        Apartado Postal 333
        Tegucigalpa, Honduras

PROGRAM OF ASSISTANCE: Community centers - Integrated rural development - Leadership training - Self-help programs - Urban development - Dams - Cooperatives - Credit/loans - Adult education - Literacy education - Non-formal education - Seminars - Women's education - Cottage industries - Crafts - Income-generation - Management training - Marketing - Small enterprises - Agricultural training - Fertilizers - Fish farming - Food preservation - Fruits - Gardens - Intensive farming - Irrigation - Poultry - Reforestation - Water - Wind energy - Immunizations - Mother/child programs - Potable water - Preventive medicine - Nutrition education - Children - Sponsorships - Appropriate technology.

PERSONNEL: 23 local, 2 international.

PROGRAM INITIATION: 1968          EXPENDITURES FOR FY 1982: $267,184

COOPERATING ORGANIZATIONS: Government of Honduras, Ministry of Health; U.S. Agency for International Development.

. . . . . . . . . .

SBC/HDA

**SOUTHERN BAPTIST CONVENTION**

Works through local national churches.

PROGRAM OF ASSISTANCE: Disaster relief - Food-for-work - Roads - Seeds - Housing - Fertilizers.

PROGRAM INITIATION: 1954          EXPENDITURES FOR FY 1982: $48,129

. . . . . . . . . .

SIL/HDA

\* **SUMMER INSTITUTE OF LINGUISTICS, INC.**
    Contact: Glen Ager, Director
             Institute Linguistico de Verano
             Apartado Postal 74
             12 Avenida "B" 10/65, Zona 2
             Guatemala City, Guatemala

PROGRAM OF ASSISTANCE: Language training - Literacy education - Non-formal education - Teaching equipment.

PERSONNEL: 3 U.S.

PROGRAM INITIATION: 1968

COOPERATING ORGANIZATIONS: Government of Honduras, Ministry of Education; Institute of Anthropology and History.

. . . . . . . . . .

VITA/HDA

\* **VOLUNTEERS IN TECHNICAL ASSISTANCE, INC. (VITA)**
    Contact: Glenn Solomon
             Roatan Development Committee
             Roatan, Bay Islands, Honduras

PROGRAM OF ASSISTANCE: Wind energy - Potable water - Small enterprises - Consultants - Public administration - Management training - Maintenance/repair.

PROGRAM INITIATION 1981          EXPENDITURES FOR FY 1982: $65,000

COOPERATING ORGANIZATIONS: Private Agencies Collaborating Together (PACT), Pan American Development Foundation, Public Welfare Foundation, U.S. Agency for International Development.

..........

WINROCK/HDA

\* **WINROCK INTERNATIONAL**
Contact: Anthony Cauterucci, Director
USAID Mission
American Embassy
Tegucigalpa, Honduras

PROGRAM OF ASSISTANCE: Marketing - Food/food products - Consultants - Evaluation - Policy and planning - Agricultural economics.

PERSONNEL: 9 U.S., 2 local.

PROGRAM INITIATION: 1982          EXPENDITURES FOR FY 1982: $12,355

COOPERATING ORGANIZATIONS: Presidential Agricultural Mission, U.S. Agency for International Development.

..........

WGM/HDA

**WORLD GOSPEL MISSION**
Contact: Jim Hawk, Field Director
Apartado Postal 698
Tegucigalpa, Honduras

PROGRAM OF ASSISTANCE: Children - Elementary schools - High schools - Agricultural training - Vocational education - Hostels.

PERSONNEL: 8 U.S.

PROGRAM INITIATION: 1952          EXPENDITURES FOR FY 1982: $50,000

..........

WN/HDA

**WORLD NEIGHBORS, INC.**
Contact: Roland Bunch
Apartado Postal 17
Nochixtlan, Oaxaca
Mexico 69600
Tel. 952-20126

PROGRAM OF ASSISTANCE: Animateurs - Integrated rural development - Leadership training - Adult education - Audio visual equipments - Non-formal education - Income generation - Agricultural training - Conservation - Crop improvement - Gardens - Grains - Irrigation - Land reclamation - Pest control - Tools - Vegetables - Nutrition education - Birth control methods - Family planning.

PERSONNEL:  2 local, 8 international,

PROGRAM INITIATION:  1972          EXPENDITURES FOR FY 1982:  $87,867

COOPERATING ORGANIZATIONS:  ACORDE (Confederation of Honduran Cooperatives), Government of Honduras, Ministry of Natural Resources; ASHONPLAFA (Associacion Hondurena de Planificacion Familiar).

. . . . . . . . . .

WRC/HDA

**\*+ WORLD RELIEF CORPORATION**
Contact:  Tom Hawk, Country Director/Honduras
          Apartado Postal 196-C
          Tegucigalpa, Honduras
          Tel.  32-7667

PROGRAM OF ASSISTANCE:  Refugees - Rehabilitation - Resettlement - Clothing - Equipment - Food/food products - Medical supplies - Seeds - Tools - Sanitation - Food distribution centers.

PROGRAM INITIATION:  1974          EXPENDITURES FOR FY 1982:  $1,971,914

COOPERATING ORGANIZATION:  UN High Commission for Refugees.

. . . . . . . . . .

WVRO/HDA

**\*+ WORLD VISION RELIEF ORGANIZATION, INC.**
Contact:  Paul Petersen
          Associate Director, Field Projects
          World Vision International
          Curridabat Apartado 133
          San Jose, Costa Rica

PROGRAM OF ASSISTANCE:  Integrated rural development - Sponsorships - Agricultural training - Potable water - Vocational education - Medical services - Disaster relief - Irrigation - Sanitation.

PROGRAM INITIATION:  1974          EXPENDITURES FOR FY 1982:  $1,808,542

COOPERATING ORGANIZATIONS:  Local churches and municipal institutions.

. . . . . . . . . .

**HONDURAS - PROGRAM SUPPORT**

| | |
|---|---|
| AFS International/Intercultural Programs | $ 23,000 |
| \* Agua del Pueblo | ----- |
| Aid to Artisans, Inc. | 500 |
| American Friends Service Committee | (see regional listing) |

| | | |
|---|---|---|
| * | American Dentists for Foreign Service | 150,000 |
| | American Lung Association | ----- |
| | American Public Health Association | 7,227 |
| * | Amigos de las Americas | 33,500 |
| * | Association for Voluntary Sterilization, Inc. | 425,325 |
| * | Brother's Brother Foundation | 118,000 |
| | Carr Foundation | ----- |
| | Catholic Medical Mission Board, Inc. | 340,589 |
| | Center for Human Services | 91,511 |
| | Claretian Fathers (C.M.F.) | ----- |
| * | Centre for Development and Population Activities | |
| | Children, Incorporated | 21,987 |
| | Church of the Brethren General Board | ----- |
| * | Compassion Relief and Development | ----- |
| * | Cooperative League of the U.S.A. | ----- |
| *+ | Coordination in Development, Inc. (CODEL) | 48,000 |
| | Darien Book Aid Plan, Inc. | ----- |
| * | Direct Relief International | 354,690 |
| | Education Development Center | ----- |
| | Family Health International | ----- |
| | Farallones Institute | ----- |
| | Ford Foundation | 63,726 |
| | Friends of SOS Children's Villages | 48,000 |
| *+ | Heifer Project International, Inc. | 34,500 |
| | Help the Aged | 2,000 |
| | Inter-Aid, Inc. | 6,000 |
| | Interchurch Medical Assistance, Inc. | 100,388 |
| | International Agricultural Development Service | 7,400 |
| * | International Executive Service Corps | ----- |
| | International Projects Assistance Services | 5,285 |
| | Interplast, Inc. | 55,667 |
| | Lions Clubs International | ----- |
| *+ | MAP International | 153,578 |
| | National Council of Catholic Women | 4,000 |
| | National Savings and Loan League | ----- |
| | Operation California, Inc. | 236,500 |
| | Orthopaedics Overseas, Inc. | ----- |
| | Outreach International | 34,300 |
| | Oxfam America | 178,150 |
| * | Pathfinder Fund | 143,586 |
| * | Population Council | 9,421 |
| *+ | Private Agencies Collaborating Together, Inc. (PACT) | 69,145 |
| | Public Welfare Foundation | 10,000 |
| *+ | Seventh-day Adventist World Service (SAWS) | 52,049 |
| * | Sister Cities International | ----- |
| * | Unitarian Universalist Service Committee | ----- |
| | United Church Board for World Ministries (Service | |
| | Division | 10,000 |
| | United Methodist Committee on Relief | 189,000 |
| | Volunteer Optometric Services to Humanity | |
| | (VOSH International) | ----- |
| *+ | World Concern | 88,798 |
| | World Opportunities International | ----- |

---
**JAMAICA**

---

Of the 72 U.S. organizations listed in Jamaica,
36 were able to provide TAICH with financial data
indicating program expenditures for FY 1982
totaling $4,122,909.

ACDI/JAM

**\* AGRICULTURAL COOPERATIVE DEVELOPMENT INTERNATIONAL**
Contact:  Matthew Tokar
Christina Potato Growers Cooperative Association
Christina, Jamaica

PROGRAM OF ASSISTANCE:   Cooperatives - Marketing.

PERSONNEL: 1  U.S.

PROGRAM INITIATION: 1983

COOPERATING ORGANIZATIONS:  Christina Potato Growers Cooperative Association;
Government of Jamaica, Ministry of Agriculture; U.S. Agency for International
Developement.

· · · · · · · · · ·

CRS/JAM

**\*+ CATHOLIC RELIEF SERVICES -- UNITED STATES CATHOLIC CONFERENCE**
Contact:  Donald L. Carcieri, Program Director
CRS/Jamaica
10 Emerald Road
Kingston 4, Jamaica
Tel. (809) 922-4309

PROGRAM OF ASSISTANCE:   Food distribution centers - Medical supplies -
Clothing - Gardens - Integrated rural development - Agricultural extension -
Animal husbandry - Nutrition education - Children - Agricultural training -
Extension agents.

PERSONNEL:   1 U.S., 5 local.

PROGRAM INITIATION:  1956           EXPENDITURES FOR FY 1982:  $57, 862

COOPERATING ORGANIZATIONS:   Bishops of Jamaica, Catholic Medical Mission
Board, European Economic Community, Food For The Poor, Governments of Canada,
Jamaica and the United States, Help the Aged (Canada and U.K.),
St. Vincent de Paul Society (Jamaica), Servite Sisters (Italy).

· · · · · · · · · ·

**BROTHERS OF THE CHRISTIAN SCHOOLS (F.S.C.)**
Contact: Brother Alfred Marshall (F.S.C.)
        P.O. 598
        St. Vincent Island, Jamaica

PROGRAM OF ASSISTANCE: Elementary schools - High schools.

PERSONNEL: 4 U.S.

PROGRAM INITIATION: 1969

COOPERATING ORGANIZATION: Coordination in Development (CODEL).

. . . . . . . . . .

**CHURCH OF GOD (HOLINESS)**
Contact: Rev. Raymond W. Mauck, Headmaster
        Venture High School and Bible College
        Glenislay P.O.
        Westmoreland, Jamaica

PROGRAM OF ASSISTANCE: High schools - Agricultural extension.

PERSONNEL: 5 U.S.

PROGRAM INITIATION: 1933          EXPENDITURES FOR FY 1982: $26,000

COOPERATING ORGANIZATIONS: Government of Jamaica, Ministry of Education, Ministry of Agriculture.

. . . . . . . . . .

**CSI MINISTRIES, INC.**
Contact: Ivor Wilson
        P.O. Box 73
        Highgate, St. Mary
        Jamaica

PROGRAM OF ASSISTANCE: Health care teams - Medical programs - Medical supplies - Equipment - Construction.

PROGRAM INITIATION: 1970

COOPERATING ORGANIZATION: Jamaica Yearly Meeting of Friends.

. . . . . . . . . .

DOM SR/JAM

**DOMINICAN SISTERS, (O.P.)**
**Congregation of St. Dominic**
Contact: Sister Catherine Fitzmaurice, O.P.
St. Joseph Hospital
Deanery Road
Kingston, 3, Jamaica

PROGRAM OF ASSISTANCE: Elementary schools - Hospitals - High schools - Counseling.

PERSONNEL: 3 U.S., 2 local, 1 international.

PROGRAM INITIATION: 1953

COOPERATING ORGANIZATION: Catholic Diocese of Kingston.

. . . . . . . . . .

OSF ALLEGA/JAM

**FRANCISCAN SISTERS OF ALLEGANY, N.Y. (O.S.F.)**
Contact: Sister M. Avril Chin Fatt, O.S.F.
Alvernia Convent
16 Old Hope Road
Kingston 5, Jamaica
Tel. 809-926-2576

PROGRAM OF ASSISTANCE: Preschool programs - Elementary schools - High schools - Colleges/universities.

PERSONNEL: 23 U.S., 19 local.

PROGRAM INITIATION: 1879

COOPERATING ORGANIZATIONS: St. Elizabeth Mission Society, Franciscan Fathers Of Holy Name Province, Government of Jamaica.

. . . . . . . . . .

FUM/JAM

**FRIENDS UNITED MEETING**
Contact: Frank Davis
Jamaica Yearly Meeting of Friends
11 Caledonia Avenue
Kingston 5, Jamaica

PROGRAM OF ASSISTANCE: Youth - Leadership training.

PERSONNEL: 2 U.S.

PROGRAM INITIATION: 1981          EXPENDITURES FOR FY 1982: $18,000

COOPERATING ORGANIZATION: Jamaica Yearly Meeting of Friends.

. . . . . . . . .

GOODWILL/JAM

**\*+ GOODWILL INDUSTRIES OF AMERICA, INC.**
Contacts: Mr. Tony Wong, Executive Director
Combined Disabilities Association
P.O. Box 92
Kingston 7, Jamaica
Tel. 809-927-5770

PROGRAM OF ASSISTANCE: - Small enterprises - Management training - Disabled - Seminars - Rehabilitation.

PERSONNEL: 4 local.

PROGRAM INTIATION: 1983

COOPERATING ORGANIZATION: Disabled Peoples' International.

..........

ICA/JAM

**\* INSTITUTE OF CULTURAL AFFAIRS**
Contact: Robertson and Mary Work
Institute of Cultural Affairs
1B Goodwood Terrace
Kingston 10, Jamaica
Tel. 809-925-4089

PROGRAM OF ASSISTANCE: Community programs - Cooperatives - Leadership training.

PERSONNEL: 6 U.S., 6 local, 9 international.

PROGRAM INITIATION: 1978

COOPERATING ORGANIZATIONS: Council of Volunteer Social Services; Government of Jamaica, Ministry of Youth and Community Development; Rotary International; UNICEF, University of the West Indies, local cooperatives.

..........

ICROSS/JAM

**INTERNATIONAL COMMUNITY FOR THE RELIEF OF
STARVATION AND SUFFERING (ICROSS)**
Contact: Dr. William Gaynor
The Cornwallis Hospital
Jamaica

PROGRAM OF ASSISTANCE: Medical education - Doctors - Clinics - Medical equipment.

PERSONNEL: 1 U.S.

PROGRAM INITIATION: 1981          EXPENDITURES FOR FY 1982: $5,000

..........

TAICH Regional                    189

**JESUIT FATHERS AND BROTHERS (S.J.)**
Contacts: Rev. Louis L. Grenier, S.J.
            Director, Archidiocesan Secretariat
            3 Emerald Road
            Kingston 4, Jamaica
            Tel. 927-2335

Provides funding and personnel.

PROGRAM OF ASSISTANCE:  Counseling - High schools - Colleges/universities - Agricultural extension.

PERSONNEL:  Approximately 23 U.S., 102 local.

PROGRAM INITIATION:  1926

COOPERATING ORGANIZATIONS:  Government of Jamaica, Ministry of Education; Jesuit Missions (New England) and alumni associations provide supplies and/or gifts for the schools.

..........

**MARIST MISSIONARY SISTERS (MISSIONARY SISTERS OF THE SOCIETY OF MARY, INC.)**
   **(S.M.S.M.)**
Contact:  Sister Agnes Anne, S.M.S.M., Regional Superior
           P.O. Box 1415
           Montego Bay, Jamaica

PROGRAM OF ASSISTANCE:  High schools - Clinics - Counseling.

PERSONNEL:  10 U.S., 1 local, 4 international

PROGRAM INITIATION:  1978

..........

**\*+   MENNONITE CENTRAL COMMITTEE**
   Contact:  Peter and Jane Andres, Directors
              29 Windsor Avenue
              Kingston 5, Jamaica
              Tel.  927-0069

PROGRAM OF ASSISTANCE:  Ophthalmology - Mental diseases - Vocational education - High schools - Teacher training - Income generation - Credit/loans - Small enterprises - Disabled.

PERSONNEL:  13 U.S., 4 international.

PROGRAM INITIATION:  1970            EXPENDITURES FOR FY 1982:  $118,000

COOPERATING ORGANIZATIONS:  Government of Jamaica, Ministry of Education, Ministry of Health; Jamaica Association for the Deaf.

. . . . . . . . . .

MEDA/JAM

**MENNONITE ECONOMIC DEVELOPMENT ASSOCIATES, INC.**
Contact:  Barrington Shand, Chairman
          Jamaican Mennonite Economic Development Corporation (JAMEOEC)
          Retreat Post Office
          St. Mary, Jamaica

PROGRAM OF ASSISTANCE:  Small enterprises - Credit/loans - Poultry - Management training - Colleges/universities - Income generation.

PERSONNEL:  2 U.S./Canada, 5 local volunteers.

PROGRAM INITIATION:  1979          EXPENDITURES FOR FY 1982:  $26,000

COOPERATING ORGANIZATIONS:  Jamaica Mennonite Church, Mennonite Central Committee, Virginia Mennonite Mission Board, Retreat Enterprises, Ltd..

. . . . . . . . . .

SR MERCY/JAM

**SISTERS OF MERCY OF THE UNION IN THE U.S.A.**
Contact:  Sister Marie Chin (R.S.M.)
          Mt. Mercy Convent
          2 Widcombe Road
          Kingston 6, Jamaica

The program is conducted by the Province of Cincinnati (Ohio).

PROGRAM OF ASSISTANCE:  Preschool programs - Elementary schools - High schools - Vocational education - Agricultural training - Cottage industries - Clinics - Hospitals - Leprosariums - Doctors - Nurses - Disease treatment.

PERSONNEL:  15 U.S., 16 local, 13 international.

PROGRAM INITIATION:  1880

COOPERATING ORGANIZATION:  Sisters of Mercy (R.S.M.), Province of Kingston.

. . . . . . . . . .

PADF/JAM

* **PAN AMERICAN DEVELOPMENT FOUNDATION**
Contact:  National Development Foundation of Jamaica
          2 Trafalgar Road
          Kingston 5, Jamaica

PROGRAM OF ASSISTANCE:  Small enterprises - Institution building - Self-help programs - Income generation - Management training - Credit/loans - Medical equipment - Tools - Vocational training - Water transportation.

PROGRAM INITIATION:  1980

COOPERATING  ORGANIZATIONS:  Jamaica-America  Society;  Partnership  for Productivity International; U.S. Agency for International Development; U.S. manufacturers of equipment related to vocational training; U.S. hospitals, health care institutions, and manufacturers of medical equipment.

. . . . . . . . .

PARTNERS/JAM

* **PARTNERS OF THE AMERICAS**
  Contact:  Dr. Lloyd B. Hunter
            Jamaica-Western New York Partners of the Americas
            9A Montrose Road
            Kingston 10, Jamaica

The Western New York-Jamaica Partners works in the following areas:

PROGRAM OF ASSISTANCE:  Literacy education - Educational exchange - Small enterprises - Mother/child programs - Rehabilitation - Disabled.

PERSONNEL:  U.S. and local volunteers only.

PROGRAM INITIATION:  1970

COOPERATING ORGANIZATIONS:  Caribbean Institute on Mental Retardation and Developmental  Disabilities;  Combined  Disabilities  Association;  Early Stimulation Project; Government of Jamaica, Ministry of Education, Ministry of Culture; Insurance College of Jamaica; Jamaica Association for the Deaf; Jamaica Adult Literacy Program; Jamaica Association  for Mentally Handicapped Children; Jamaica Chamber of Commerce; Jamaica School of Art; Michael Teachers College; Mona Rehabilitation Centre; Rotary Club International; Salvation Army; Jamaica Tourism Board; University of the West Indies-Mona Campus; VOUCH (Voluntary Organization for the Uplift of Children).

. . . . . . . . . .

PFPI/JAM

* **PARTNERSHIP FOR PRODUCTIVITY INTERNATIONAL, INC.**
  Contact:  Gene McEvoy
            PfP/I
            c/o USAID/Jamaica
            Kingston, Jamaica

            Justin Vincent, Executive Director
            National Development Foundation of Jamaica
            2 Trafalgar Road
            Kingston, 5, Jamaica, W.I.
            (809) 927-7071

PROGRAM OF ASSISTANCE:   Management  training  -  Credit/loans  -  Cottage
industries - Income generation - Marketing - Small enterprises - On-the-job
training - Accounting - Urban development - Animateurs - Economic research -
Policy and planning - Information systems - Institution building - Vocational
education.

PERSONNEL:  1 U.S.

PROGRAM INITIATION:  1982          EXPENDITURES FOR FY 1982:  $4,423

COOPERATING ORGANIZATIONS:  Pan American Development Foundation, Government of
Jamaica, U.S. Agency for International Development.

. . . . . . . . . .

HOPE/JAM

* **THE PEOPLE-TO-PEOPLE HEALTH FOUNDATION, INC.**
**Project HOPE**
Contact:   David E. Edwards, Program Director
           Project HOPE
           P.O. Box 6000
           Kingston, Jamaica

PROGRAM OF ASSISTANCE:   Medical  education  -   Nurses  -  Doctors  - Medical
supplies.

PERSONNEL:  8 U.S. 7 local.

PROGRAM INITIATION:  1971

COOPERATING  ORGANIZATIONS:   College  of  Arts,  Science  and  Technology;
Government  of  Jamaica,  Ministry  of  Health  and  Environmental  Control;
University of the West Indies.

. . . . . . . . . .

PLENTY/JAM

**PLENTY**

PROGRAM OF ASSISTANCE:   Vegetables  -  Seeds  -  Crop  improvement  -  Food
preservation - Intensive farming - Gardens - Crop processing - Demonstration
projects - Food/food products - Food preparation - Nutrition education.
PERSONNEL:  4 U.S.

PROGRAM INITIATION:  1983

COOPERATING ORGANIZATIONS:  Canadian International Development Agency (CIDA),
INTSOY (International Soybean Program, University of Illinois at Urbana-
Champaign).

. . . . . . . . . .

ROTARY/JAM

**ROTARY INTERNATIONAL**
Contact:  Winston Hay
          Jamaica Public Service (Rotary Club of Kingston)
          6 Knutsford Blvd.
          Kingston 10, Jamaica

PROGRAM OF ASSISTANCE:  Integrated rural development.

PROGRAM INITIATION:  1983          EXPENDITURES FOR FY 1982:  $120,000

COOPERATING ORGANIZATION:  Institute of Cultural Affairs (Jamaica)

··········

SALVA/JAM

**\*+  THE SALVATION ARMY**
Contact:  Colonel Edward Read
          Territorial Commander
          P.O. Box 378
          Kingston 10, Jamaica
          Tel. 929-6910/12/13

Assists programs operated by the international organization:

PROGRAM OF ASSISTANCE:  Blindness prevention - Food supply programs -
Rehabilitation - Orphanages - Clinics - Hospitals - Agricultural extension -
Hostels - Preschool program.

PERSONNEL:  182 international.

PROGRAM INITIATION:  1887

COOPERATING ORGANIZATIONS:  Bread for the Brethren (Switzerland), British High
Commission, Canadian International Development Agency (CIDA), Christian
Children's Fund (Canada), Christopher Blinden Mission (West Germany), Gulf and
Western Foundation, Government of Jamaica, Rotary Clubs, Swiss Solidarity
World, World Vision Relief Organization.

··········

WINROCK/JAM

**\*  WINROCK INTERNATIONAL**
Contact:  Jack Muschutte
          Smallstock Specialist
          Agricultural Development Corporation
          46 Trinidad Terrace
          Kingston 5, Jamaica
          Tel. (809) 929-1290

PROGRAM OF ASSISTANCE:  Adult education - Extension courses - On-the-job
training - Vocational education - Audio-visual materials - Self-help programs
- Teaching materials.

PERSONNEL: 4 U.S., 2 local.

PROGRAM INITIATION: 1982          EXPENDITURES FOR FY 1982: $89,695

COOPERATING ORGANIZATION: Control Data Corporation.

..........

\*+ **YOUNG WOMEN'S CHRISTIAN ASSOCIATION OF THE U.S.A.**
   Contact: National General Secretary
            YWCA of Jamaica
            2H Camp Road
            Kingston 5, Jamaica
            Tel. 928-3023

Provides an assistance grant to the YWCA of Jamaica.

PROGRAM OF ASSISTANCE:  Youth - Leadership training - Women - Vocational education - Hostels.

PERSONNEL:  4 international; 414 local, including 400 volunteer.

PROGRAM INITIATION:  1930

COOPERATING ORGANIZATIONS:  Council for Voluntary Services (Kingston), Embassy of the Netherlands (Jamaica), Inter-Church Coordination Committee for Development (Netherlands), U.S. Agency for International Development, U.S. Peace Corps, World YWCA (Geneva), YWCA Cooperation for Development Program.

..........

**JAMAICA - PROGRAM SUPPORT**

| | |
|---|---:|
| A.T. International | $ 90,000 |
| AFS International/Intercultural Programs | 3,800 |
| American Public Health Association | 25,481 |
| \* Association for Voluntary Sterilization, Inc. | 211,358 |
| \* Brother's Brother Foundation | 1,871,000 |
| Catholic Medical Mission Board, Inc. | 210,822 |
| Center for Human Services | 162,858 |
| \* Centre for Development and Population Activities | ----- |
| \* Compassion Relief and Development | ----- |
| \* Cooperative League of the U.S.A. | ----- |
| \*+ Coordination in Development, Inc. (CODEL) | 69,000 |
| \* Council of International Programs for Youth Leaders and Social Workers, Inc. | 1,200 |
| Darien Book Aid Plan, Inc. | ----- |
| \* Direct Relief International | 12,920 |
| Education Development Center | ----- |
| Eisenhower Exchange Fellowships, Inc. | ----- |
| \* Family Planning International Assistance | 405 |
| Ford Foundation | 198,500 |
| Friends of SOS Children's Villages, Inc. | 6,000 |

TAICH Regional                195

Interchurch Medical Assistance, Inc.   24,659
International Agricultural Development Service   8,000
International Book Project, Inc.   475
  *   International Executive Service Corps   -----
International Liaison, Inc.   -----
International Road Federation   4,000
Interplast, Inc.   1,300
W.K. Kellogg Foundation   560,070
Lions Clubs International   -----
Lutheran Church - Missouri Synod   4,000
Management Sciences for Health   -----
*+   MAP International   54,062
*   National 4-H Council   -----
National Savings and Loan League   -----
Orthopaedics Overseas, Inc.   -----
Operation Crossroads Africa   -----
*   Pathfinder Fund   43,173
*   Population Council   24,446
Public Welfare Foundation   14,000
*   Margaret Sanger Center   25,000
*   Sister Cities International   -----
Surgical Eye Expeditions International   -----
Trickle Up Program   6,400
United Methodist Committee on Relief   25,000
United States Youth Council   -----
*   Volunteers in Technical Assistance, Inc. (VITA)   -----
Volunteer Optometric Services to Humanity
  (VOSH International)   -----

---

## MARTINIQUE

---

There are 4 U.S. organizations listed in Martinique.

## MARTINIQUE - PROGRAM SUPPORT

*   Council of International Programs for Youth
    Leaders and Social Workers, Inc.   -----
Darien Book Aid Plan, Inc.   -----
Lions Clubs International   -----
Trickle Up Program   -----

## MEXICO

Of the 112 U.S. organizations listed in Mexico,
73 were able to provide TAICH with financial data
indicating program expenditures for FY 1982
totaling $25,946,695.

AFL-CIO/MEX

* **AFL-CIO - American Institute for Free Labor Development**
Contact:  Paul Somodyi
          Organizacion Regional Interamericano de Trabajadores
          (ORIT) Liaison Representative
          Apartado 7039
          Mexico, D.F., Mexico

PROGRAM OF ASSISTANCE:  Unions - Seminars - Leadership training.

PERSONNEL:  1 U.S.

PROGRAM INITIATION:  1964

. . . . . . . . . .

AITEC/MEX

* **ACCION INTERNATIONAL/AITEC**
Contact:  Jose Benito Cabello Zul
          Asesoria Dinamica a Microempresas
          Vicente Ferrara 133-7
          Col. Obispado
          Monterrey, Nuevo Leon, Mexico

PROGRAM OF ASSISTANCE:  Accounting - Adult education - Courses - Conferences -
Cottage industries - Crafts - Credit/loans - Income generation - Management
training - Marketing - Small enterprises.

PERSONNEL:  1 local.

PROGRAM INITIATION:  1979          EXPENDITURES FOR FY 1982:  $136,397

COOPERATING ORGANIZATIONS:  Asesoria Dinamica a Microempresas, Inter-American
Development Bank, Inter-American Foundation, local banks, local and U.S.
private sector.

. . . . . . . . . .

**AMERICAN BAPTIST CHURCHES IN THE USA**
Contact:  AGAPE, ASEPP
c/o Dr. Daniel Rodriguez
San Jeronimo 111
Colonia San Angel
Del Alvaro Obregon
01000 Mexico, D.F. Mexico

PROGRAM OF ASSISTANCE:  Health education - Nutrition education - Refugees -
Housing - Construction - Appropriate technology.

PERSONNEL:  4 U.S., 5 local, 1 international.

PROGRAM INITIATION:  1975          EXPENDITURES FOR FY 1982:  $40,000

COOPERATING ORGANIZATIONS:  Church World Service, Reformed Church of
Switzerland.

..........

**AMERICAN FRIENDS SERVICE COMMITTEE**
Contacts: Ignacio Gozalez, Director
Commite de Servicio de los Amigos
Ignacio Mariscal 132
Mexico 1, D.F., Mexico
Tel. (905) 535-2752

Servicio Desarrollo y Paz
Roma 1, 3rd floor
Mexico, D.F.  07030

Supports the work of the Mexican Friends Service Committee.

PROGRAM OF ASSISTANCE:  Agricultural cooperatives - Solar energy - Refugees -
Equipment.

PERSONNEL:  2 U.S., 14 local, 1 international.

PROGRAM INITIATION:  1939

..........

+  **AMERICAN/MEXICAN MEDICAL FOUNDATION, INC.**
Contact:  Arturo Villagram, Secretary
Sierra de San Telmo, #316
Fracc. Las Sierras
Monterrey, N. L., Mexico C.P.  66350

PROGRAM OF ASSISTANCE:   Construction - Agricultural training - Animal husbandry - Gardens - Mass media - Clothing - Food/food products - Clinics - Medical supplies - Mother/child programs - Nutrition education - Family planning - Health care teams - Public health education - Sanitation - Toilet facilities.

PERSONNEL: 3 local, approximately 50 - 60 volunteer.

PROGRAM INITIATION: 1970          EXPENDITURES FOR FY 1982: $23,000

COOPERATING ORGANIZATIONS:   Lutheran Church - Missouri Synod; Government of Mexico, Department of Health.

· · · · · · · · · ·

ORT/MEX

**\*+  AMERICAN ORT FEDERATION**
Contract: Ricardo Nemirovsky
          Projecto ORT
          Colegio Israelita de Mexico
          Retorno del Recuerdo No. 44
          Lomas de Vista Hermosa
          05100 Mexico, D.F. Mexico
          Tel. 570-03-93

PROGRAM OF ASSISTANCE: Educational funding - Vocational education.

PROGRAM INITIATION: 1977          EXPENDITURES FOR FY 1982: $170,000

· · · · · · · · · ·

ARPC/MEX

**ASSOCIATE REFORMED PRESBYTERIAN CHURCH**
Contact:  Rev. P.G. Covone
          c/o Artes Y. Hospital
          Ciudad Valles, San Luis Potosi, Mexico
          Tel. 20394

PROGRAM OF ASSISTANCE:   Hospitals - Educational funding - Clinics - Medical services.

PERSONNEL: 6 U.S., 82 local.

PROGRAM INITIATION: 1878

· · · · · · · · · ·

BMA/MEX

**BAPTIST MISSIONARY ASSOCIATION OF AMERICA**
Contact:  Dr. John Ladd
          #5 de Febrero #14
          Tempoal, Veracruz, Mexico

PROGRAM OF ASSISTANCE: Clinics - Doctors.

PERSONNEL: 2 U.S.

PROGRAM INITIATION: 1977          EXPENDITURES FOR FY 1982: $30,511

..........

BENBA/MEX

**BENEDICTINE MONKS (O.S.B.)**
**St. Benedict's Abbey**
Contact:   Rev. Elias Cortes, O.S.B. Director
           Monasterio Benedictino
           Apartado 296
           Morelia, Michoacan, Mexico
           Tel.  42647

PROGRAM OF ASSISTANCE:   Construction - Housing - Cooperatives - Educational
funding - Animal husbandry - Crop improvement - Medical services - Nutrition
education - Potable water - Counseling - Community centers - Youth.

PERSONNEL:  4 U.S., 23 local.

PROGRAM INITIATION:  1959          EXPENDITURES FOR FY 1982:  $75,004

..........

BETH/MEX

**BETHANY FELLOWSHIP, INC.**
Contact:   Dennis Renich, Director
           Campers Bethania
           Apartado 27
           78700 Matehuala, San Luis Potosi, Mexico
           Tel.  52(488)2-05-82

PROGRAM OF ASSISTANCE:  Vocational education.

PERSONNEL:  3 U.S., 2 local, 1 international.

PROGRAM INITIATION:  1962          EXPENDITURES FOR FY 1982:  $31,949

..........

BUENA/MEX

**LA BUENA FE ASSOCIATION**
Contact:   Rosemary Fishburn
           Centro Estudiantil Restaumex
           Calle Antonio Narro 707 Sur
           Saltillo, Coahuila, Mexico

PROGRAM OF ASSISTANCE:  Hostels - Youth.

TAICH Regional                 200

PERSONNEL: 2 U.S., 5 local.

PROGRAM INITIATION: 1965          EXPENDITURES FOR FY 1982: $55,000

. . . . . . . . . .

**\*+ CATHOLIC RELIEF SERVICES - United States Catholic Conference**
Contact:  Harvey Leach, Program Director
          Mexico City 6, D.F.  06600 Mexico
          Tel. (905) 525-2007

PROGRAM OF ASSISTANCE:  Agricultural cooperatives - Animateurs - Evaluation -
Cooperatives - Disaster relief - Food/food products - Clothing - Tribal
peoples - Medical supplies - Beekeeping - Credit/loans - Refugees - Displaced
persons - Social services - Counseling - Community programs - Potable water -
Small enterprises - Farm machinery.

PERSONNEL: 1 U.S., 3 local.

PROGRAM INITIATION: 1958          EXPENDITURES FOR FY 1982: $200,732

COOPERATING ORGANIZATIONS:  Brucke der Bruderhilfe; Caritas; Caritas Denmark;
Cenami (National Center for Help to the Indigenous Mexican); CEPS (Mexico);
Civil Association for the Economic and Social Development of the Mexican
Indians (DESMI); Concern, America; Coordination in Development (CODEL); Danish
International Development Authority (DANIDA); Dioceses of Nayarit, Yucatan and
Tehuacan; European Economic Committee; GORTA/Ireland; Government of Canada;
HIVOS; Inter-Governmental Committee for Migration (ICEM); Mexican Development
Foundation; Murray MacDonald Foundation; OXFAM; Promocion del Desarrollo
Popular; U.N. High Commissioner for Refugees.

. . . . . . . . . .

**\*+ CHRISTIAN CHILDREN'S FUND**
Contact:  Lic. Cristina Casares, Field Representative
          CCF Ninos de Mexico
          03630 Mexico, D.F., Mexico

          Apartado 13-576
          03500 Mexico
          D.F., Mexico
          Tel. 672-7211

PROGRAM OF ASSISTANCE:  Sponsorships - Children - Schools - Hostels -
Community centers.

PERSONNEL: 30 local.

PROGRAM INITIATION: 1971          EXPENDITURES FOR FY 1982: $2,347,329

. . . . . . . . . .

TAICH Regional                    201

CC DISCIP/MEX

**CHRISTIAN CHURCH (DISCIPLES OF CHRIST), INC.**
Contact:  Courtney Swander
Apartado 147, Aguascalientes
Aguascalientes, Mexico  720000

PROGRAM OF ASSISTANCE:  Community centers - Libraries - Language training.

PERSONNEL:  2 U.S., 1 local.

PROGRAM INITIATION:  1895          EXPENDITURES FOR FY 1982:  $5,000

COOPERATING ORGANIZATIONS:  Asociacion de Iglesias Cristianas Evangelicas (CAICE).

........

CFC/MEX

**CHRISTIAN FOUNDATION FOR CHILDREN**
Contact:  Hogar de Ninas
Leon, Guanajuato, Mexico

Hna. Dolores Aguilar
Bachajon, Chiapas, Mexico

PROGRAM OF ASSISTANCE:  Nutrition education - Preventive medicine - Food/food products - Medical supplies.

PERSONNEL:  2 local.

PROGRAM INITIATION:  1982          EXPENDITURES FOR FY 1982:  $500

........

CNEC/MEX

**CHRISTIAN NATIONALS' EVANGELISM COMMISSION, INC.**
Contact:  Miqueas Bustos
Apartado M-8580
Mexico 1, D.F., Mexico

PROGRAM OF ASSISTANCE:  Courses - Social welfare - Youth - Literacy education.

PERSONNEL:  18 local

PROGRAM INITIATION:  1949          EXPENDITURES FOR FY 1982:  $34,000

........

CRWRC/MEX

**+  CHRISTIAN REFORMED WORLD RELIEF COMMITTEE**
Contact:  Tom Post
Apartado 16
70400 Tlacolula, Oaxaca, Mexico
Tel. 20148

PROGRAM OF ASSISTANCE:   Integrated rural development - Refugees - Disaster relief.

PERSONNEL:  3 U.S.

PROGRAM INITIATION:  1972          EXPENDITURES FOR FY 1982:  $153,000

COOPERATING ORGANIZATIONS:   Evangelical Committee For Rural Development, Independent Presbyterean Church of Mexico, National Presbyterean Church.

..........

CLARE/MEX

**CLARETIAN FATHERS (C.M.F.)**
Contact:    Rev. Redolfo Garcia Mireles, C.M.F.
            Provincial Superior
            Padres Claretianos
            Cuauhtemoc 939
            Mexico 12, D.F., Mexico

Claretian Fathers provide consulting for programs of the Mexican Claretian Fathers.

PROGRAM OF ASSISTANCE:   Adult education - Crafts - Vocational education - Beekeeping - Improved seed - Crop diversification - Reforestation - Hospitals - Potable water - Sanitation - Literacy education.

PERSONNEL:  8 local.

PROGRAM INITIATION:  1960

..........

COMBONI FR/MEX

**COMBONI MISSIONARIES OF THE HEART OF JESUS (M.C.C.J.)**
Contact:    Rev. Fr. Jaime Rodriguez (M.C.C.J.), Provincial Superior
            Misioneros Combonianos
            Apartado 9-207
            15500 Mexico, D.F., Mexico
            Tel.  (905) 571-6888

U.S. Comboni Missionaries cooperate with the International Missioneros Combonianos to support programs mentioned below.

PROGRAM OF ASSISTANCE:   High schools - Clinics - Orphanages - Geriatric centers.

PERSONNEL:  3 U.S., 53 local, 60 international.

PROGRAM INITIATION:  1948          EXPENDITURES FOR FY 1982:  $10,000

COOPERATING ORGANIZATION:  Comboni Missionary Sisters.

..........

**COMBONI MISSIONARY SISTERS (C.M.S.)**
Contact:  Sr. Carmen Mecdez Martin, C.M.S.
          Misioneras Combonianas
          Riobamba 919
          Colonia Lindavista
          Delegacion Gustavo A. Madero
          07300 Mexico

Provides some financial support to the following programs operated by the Mexican order.

PROGRAM OF ASSISTANCE:  Clinics - Preschool programs - Mother/child programs - Vocational education.

PROGRAM INITIATION:  1971

..........

**CONCERN AMERICA**
Contact:  Administered U.S. Headquarters Office

PROGRAM OF ASSISTANCE:  On-the-job training - Cottage Industries - Crafts - Income generation - Management Training - Marketing - Small Enterprises - Doctors - Breast Feeding - Food preparation - Mother/Child programs - Nutrition education.

PERSONNEL:  3 U.S., 50 local.

PROGRAM INITIATION:  1982      EXPENDITURES IN FY 1982:  $15,000

COOPERATING ORGANIZATIONS:  OXFAM, Pueblo to People.

..........

* **DOCARE INTERNATIONAL, INC.**

PROGRAM OF ASSISTANCE:  Doctors - Dentists - Nurses - Medical supplies - Medical services - Disease treatment - Health care teams - Medical education - Preventive medicine.

PERSONNEL:  20 U.S.

PROGRAM INITIATION:  1971      EXPENDITURES IN FY 1982:  $1500

COOPERATING ORGANIZATIONS:  U.S. Agency for International Development, Florida Association of Voluntary Agencies for Caribbean Action.

..........

**DOMINICAN FATHERS (O.P.), ORDER OF PREACHERS**
Contact: Rev. Vincent Foerstler, O.P.
         Regional Representative
         Asociacion Mexicana pro Cultura
         Parroquia de San Jacinto
         Ocosingo, Chiapas, Mexico

PROGRAM OF ASSISTANCE: Leadership training - Integrated rural development - Self-help programs - Consultants - Literacy education - Adult education - Hospitals - Dental clinics - Mother/child programs - Food supply programs.

PERSONNEL: 4 U.S.

PROGRAM INITIATION: 1963        EXPENDITURES FOR FY 1982: $46,000

..........

\* **THE EPISCOPAL CHURCH IN THE U.S.A.**
**(including + Presiding Bishops Fund for World Relief)**
Contact: The Rt. Rev. Jose G. Saucedo, D.D., Bishop
         Missionary Diocese of Central and South America
         San Jeronimo 117
         Mexico 20, D.F., Mexico

PROGRAM OF ASSISTANCE: Agricultural cooperatives - Cooperatives - Fish farming - Elementary schools - Clinics.

PERSONNEL: 3 U.S., 28 local.

PROGRAM INITIATION: 1904        EXPENDITURES FOR FY 1982: $77,122

COOPERATING ORGANIZATIONS: United Thank Offering of the Women of the Episcopal Church.

..........

**ERIE DIOCESAN MISSION OFFICE**
Contract: Sister Marilyn Randolph
          Calle 8 #127
          Col. Garcia Gineres
          Merida, Yucatan, Mexico

PROGRAM OF ASSISTANCE: Non-formal education - Clothing - Books - Equipment - Medical supplies - Medical equipment - Vehicles - Dispensaries - Doctors - Nurses - Health care teams - Family planning - Hostel - Libraries - Crafts.

PERSONNEL: 5 U.S., 1 local.

PROGRAM INITIATION: 1971        EXPENDITURES FOR FY 1982: $5,000

COOPERATING ORGANIZATIONS: Diocese of Merida, Yucatan, CODEL, Society for the Propagation of the Faith.

.........

FCI/MEX

**FARM CENTERS INTERNATIONAL**

PROGRAM OF ASSISTANCE: Agricultural training - Fertilizers - Pest control - Beekeeping - Fish farming - Gardens - Veterinary services.

PERSONNEL: 10 local.

PROGRAM INITIATION: 1965          EXPENDITURES FOR FY 1982: $73,239

COOPERATING ORGANIZATIONS: Charis Fund, CODEL, Skaggs Foundation, Syntex Corporation.

.........

OFM ST BARB/MEX

**FRANCISCAN FRIARS (O.F.M.)**
**Province of St. Barbara**
Contact:   Rev. Martin Gates, O.F.M.
           Apartado 551
           Guaymas, Sonora, Mexico
           Tel.  2-23-02

PROGRAM OF ASSISTANCE: Credit/loans - Language training - Blankets - Books - Clothing - Food/food products - Medical supplies - Clinics - Disease treatment - Medical services - Nurses - Preventive medicine - Food supply programs - Adoption services - Children - Orphanages - Medical equipment.

PERSONNEL:  4 U.S., 10 local.

PROGRAM INITIATION: 1970          EXPENDITURES FOR FY 1982: $150,000

COOPERATING ORGANIZATIONS: Alexian Brothers (Elk Grove Village), Lions International, Miserior (Germany), Rotary, St. Jude Express.

.........

FREE METH/MEX

**FREE METHODIST CHURCH OF NORTH AMERICA**
Contact:   Yvonne Roller
           Lot 68
           2428 Tucson Hwy.
           Nogales, Arizonia  85621
           Tel.  (602) 281-0836

PROGRAM OF ASSISTANCE: Construction - Sponsorships.

PERSONNEL: 6 U.S., 17 local.

PROGRAM INITIATION: 1978          EXPENDITURES FOR FY 1982: $4,725

COOPERATING ORGANIZATIONS: General Missionary Board and other Free Methodist Church groups.

. . . . . . . . . .

GCMC/MEX

**GENERAL CONFERENCE MENNONITE CHURCH**
Contact:  Aaron Epp, Coordinator
          Apartado 336
          Cuauhtemoc, Chihuahua, Mexico
          Tel.  158-21945

PROGRAM OF ASSISTANCE: Medical services - Medical education - Adult education - Elementary schools - High schools - Counseling.

PERSONNEL: 4 U.S., 15 local.

PROGRAM INITIATION: 1956          EXPENDITURES FOR FY 1982: $15,000

. . . . . . . . . .

HESPER/MEX

**THE HESPERIAN FOUNDATION**

PROGRAM OF ASSISTANCE: Agricultural cooperatives - Grains - Credit/loans - Educational funding - Crop improvement - Rehabilitation - Integrated rural development - Animal husbandry - Clinics - Preventive medicine - Sanitation - Medical auxiliaries - Community programs.

PERSONNEL: 15 local.

PROGRAM INITIATION: 1964

. . . . . . . . . .

HOGAR/MEX

**HOGAR INFANTIL (ILLINOIS), INC.**
Contact:  Mr. Edein Cruz, Director
          Apartado 371
          Tuxtla Gutierrez, Chiapas, Mexico

PROGRAM OF ASSISTANCE: Orphanages.

PERSONNEL: 4 local.

PROGRAM INITIATION: 1965          EXPENDITURES FOR FY 1982: $76,807

. . . . . . . . . .

* **INSTITUTE OF INTERNATIONAL EDUCATION**
  Contact:  IIE/Mexico
  Londres 16
  Mexico 6, D.F.
  Mexico
  Tel.  905-566-88-07

  Educational Counseling Center
  American Embassy
  P.O. Box 3087
  Laredo, Texas  78041

PROGRAM OF ASSISTANCE:  Educational Exchange.

PERSONNEL:  3 U.S., 3 local.

PROGRAM INITIATION:  1973

COOPERATING ORGANIZATIONS:  U.S. Information Agency provides grant support for counseling of Mexican students in regard to educational opportunities in U.S. higher education.

. . . . . . . . . .

**INTERMEDIA**
Contact:  Debora Quintero
Centro Audio Visual Educativo, A.C. (CAVE)
Liverpool 65-206
Mexico 6, D.F., Mexico
Tel.  514-83-52

PROGRAM OF ASSISTANCE:  Leadership training - Audio-visual materials - Mass media.

PERSONNEL:  1 U.S., 10 local.

EXPENDITURES FOR FY 1982:  $8,000

COOPERATING ORGANIZATIONS:  Churches of Mexico.

. . . . . . . . . .

**SISTERS OF ST JOSEPH (C.S.J.)**
**Salina Diocese**
Contact:   Sr. Carmel Garcia, C.S.J.
Nuevo Casas Grandes 31700
Chihuahua, Mexico
Tel.  011-52-168, 4-12-34

PROGRAM OF ASSISTANCE:  Family planning - Mother/child programs - Community programs - Clothing - Food/food products.

PERSONNEL: 2 U.S.

PROGRAM INITIATION: 1980        EXPENDITURES FOR FY 1982: $5,934

COOPERATING ORGANIZATION: Immaculate Heart of Mary Parish (New Mexico).

. . . . . . . . . .

JUDE/MEX

**ST. JUDE EXPRESS, INC.**
Contact: Leticia Castillo
        DESMI (Desarollo Economico y Social de los Mexicanos Indigenas)
        Apartado 268
        Chihuahua, Chihuahua, Mexico

PROGRAM OF ASSISTANCE: Medical supplies - Medical equipment - Health care
teams - Dental equipment - Dentistry - Air transportation.

PERSONNEL: 4 local.

PROGRAM INITIATION: 1968        EXPENDITURES FOR FY 1982: $17,000

COOPERATING ORGANIZATION: DESMI.

. . . . . . . . . .

LAUBACH/MEX

\* **LAUBACH LITERACY INTERNATIONAL**
Contact: Guillermina Lopez Bravo
        Coordinator, Proyecto Tinaja de Negrete
        M. Doblado 106
        C.P., Abasolo, Gto., Mexico

PROGRAM OF ASSISTANCE: Literacy education - Leadership training - Non-formal
education - Public health education - Nutrition education - Self-help programs
- Women - Youth.

PERSONNEL: 3 local, 1 international.

PROGRAM INITIATION: 1979        EXPENDITURES FOR FY 1982: $12,504

. . . . . . . . . .

LECHE/MEX

\* **LA LECHE LEAGUE INTERNATIONAL**
Contact: Eugenia D. de Anda
        La Liga de la Leche de Mexico
        Apartado 10-962

        Col. Lomas de Chapulteper
        Del. Miguel Hidalgo
        Mexico, D.F. 11000, Mexico
        Petrarca 223-402
        Col. Chapultepec Morales
        Del. Miguel Midalgo
        Mexico, D.F. 11570, Mexico
        Tel. 905-589-31-05

PROGRAM OF ASSISTANCE: Breast-feeding - Mother/child programs - Self-help programs - Women's education - Public health education.

PERSONNEL: 2 U.S., 8 local, 4 international.

PROGRAM INITIATION: 1970

COOPERATING ORGANIZATION: The Servije Foundation.

. . . . . . . . . .

SM/MEX

**SOCIETY OF MARY (S.M.)**
**(Marianists - Brothers of Mary)**
**Province of St. Louis**
Contact: Brother Robert Wood, S.M.
        Apartado 58
        Apaseo El Grande, GTO (Guanajuato)
        Mexico 38160

PROGRAM OF ASSISTANCE: Elementary schools - High schools.

PERSONNEL: 4 U.S., 20 local.

PROGRAM INITIATION: 1981        EXPENDITURES FOR FY 1982: $32,000

. . . . . . . . . .

MKNOL FR/MEX

**MARYKNOLL FATHERS AND BROTHERS (M.M.)**
Contact: Rev. Thomas C. Saunders, M.M.
        Calle 27, Numero 221
        Col. Garcia Gineres
        97070 Merida, Yucatan, Mexico
        Tel. (52) (992) 5-44-84

PROGRAM OF ASSISTANCE: Animateurs - Community centers - Community programs - Leadership training - Self-help programs - Cooperatives - Unions - Adult education - Audio visual materials - Courses - Educational funding - Language training - Libraries - Literacy education - Seminars - Teachers - Teaching materials - Vocational education - Women's education - Crafts - Agricultural training - Gardens - Poultry - Reforestation - Mass media - Medical equipment - Medical supplies - Clinics - Doctors - Medical services - Preventive medicine - Public health education - Nutrition education - Birth control methods - Counseling - Family planning - Disabled - Displaced persons - Refugees - Policy and planning - Conservation - Evaluation - Research/field studies.

PERSONNEL: 25

PROGRAM INITIATION: 1943

. . . . . . . . . .

**MARYKNOLL SISTERS OF ST. DOMINIC (M.M.)**
Contact:  Maryknoll Sisters
          Apartado 21-170
          Mexico 21, D.F.  04000, Mexico

PROGRAM OF ASSISTANCE:  Urban development - Teachers - Community programs.

PERSONNEL:  3 U.S.

PROGRAM INITIATION:  1950

. . . . . . . . . .

**MEXICAN MEDICAL INCORPORATED**
Contact:  Dr. Cesar A. Tamez Fuentes
          CENTROS
          Mejoramiento Familiar, A.C.
          Apartado 132
          San Quintin, Baja California Norte, Mexico

PROGRAM OF ASSISTANCE:  Blankets - Clothing - Food/food products - Medical equipment - Medical supplies - Clinics - Dental clinics - Dental equipment - Dentistry - Disease treatment - Doctors - Health care teams - Hospitals - Immunizations - Medical education - Medical services - Nurses - Ophthalmology - Preventive medicine - Traditional medicine - Viral bacterial/diseases - Volunteers - Youth.

PERSONNEL:  4 U.S., 50 local, 1 international.

PROGRAM INITIATION:  1959          EXPENDITURES FOR FY 1982:  $250,000

COOPERATING ORGANIZATION:  CENTROS.

. . . . . . . . . .

**MISSION AVIATION FELLOWSHIP**
Contact:  Lic. Pedro De Koster Fuentes
          Alas de Socorro, A.C.
          Apartado 12-323
          Mexico 12, D.F., Mexico
          Tel.  (905) 592-2250 (office)
                (905) 560-4841 (home)

PROGRAM OF ASSISTANCE:  Air transportation - Vehicles.

PERSONNEL:  4 U.S., 1 local.

PROGRAM INITIATION:  1946

COOPERATING ORGANIZATIONS:  Christian Reformed Mission, Iglesia Nacional Presbiteriana, Reformed Church in America, Wycliffe Bible Translators.

. . . . . . . . . .

TAICH Regional                211

NINOS/MEX

**LOS NINOS**

PROGRAM OF ASSISTANCE: Leadership training - Self-help programs - Cooperatives - Educational funding - Non-formal education - Food/food products - Volunteers - Youth.

PERSONNEL: 20 U.S., 1 local, 1 international.

PROGRAM INITIATION: 1974          EXPENDITURES FOR FY 1982: $993,000

. . . . . . . . . .

PARTNERS/MEX

\* **PARTNERS OF THE AMERICAS**

The Arizona, Iowa, Oklahoma, New Mexico, San Francisco and Texas Partners cooperate with the Mexican Partners on the programs mentioned below.

PROGRAM OF ASSISTANCE: Corn - Demonstration projects - Poultry - Irrigation - Potable water - Agricultural training - Animal husbandry - Medical auxiliaries - Tribal peoples - Medical equipment - Medical supplies - Educational exchange - Medical schools - Dentistry - Seminars - Rehabilitation - Community programs - Volunteers - Family planning.

PERSONNEL: All volunteers, local and U.S.

PROGRAM INITIATION: 1965

COOPERATING ORGANIZATIONS: Mexican Center for the Study of Drug Dependency (CEMEP); Mexican State and municipal governments; National Fund for Social Activities (FONAPAS); U.S. Agency for International Development.

. . . . . . . . . .

PIACT/MEX

\* **PROGRAM FOR THE INTRODUCTION AND ADAPTATION OF**
**CONTRACEPTIVE TECHNOLOGY (PIACT)**
Contact:  Dr. Alfredo Gallegos, Executive Director
          PIATA
          Shakespeare No. 27
          Mexico 5, D.F., Mexico
          Tel. (905) 533-52-28

PROGRAM OF ASSISTANCE: Family planning - Birth control methods - Non-formal education - Teaching materials.

PERSONNEL: 3 local.

PROGRAM INITIATION: 1977          EXPENDITURES FOR FY 1982: $80,000

. . . . . . . . . .

* **PROJECT CONCERN INTERNATIONAL**
  Contact:  Andrew Krefft (Project Concern Representative)
            Carlos Mora (Chairman of the Board)
            Patronato de Medicina Social Communitaria, A.C.
            Avenue Batopilis, No. 245
            Tijuana, Baja California Norte, Mexico
            Tel. 706-684-14-43

PROGRAM OF ASSISTANCE:  Clinics - Disease treatment - Medical auxiliaries -
Medical education - Medical services - Potable water - Preventive medicine -
Public health education - Viral bacterial/diseases - Birth control methods -
Family planning - Mother/child programs.

PERSONNEL:  1 U.S., 10 staff; 140 local, including 130 volunteer.

PROGRAM INITIATION:  1965          EXPENDITURES FOR FY 1982:  $230,000

COOPERATING ORGANIZATIONS:  Baja California, Department of Public Health; U.S.
Agency for International Development.

..........

**PROMISE, INC.**
Contact:  Jose Magana, President, Board of Directors Promesa
          Calle 31, #224
          Colonia, Aleman
          Merida, Yucatan, Mexico

PROGRAM OF ASSISTANCE:  Clinics - Medical equipment - Medical services -
Preventive medicine.

PERSONNEL:  13 local.

PROGRAM INITIATION:  1973          EXPENDITURES FOR FY 1982:  $23,000 (U.S.)

..........

**ROTARY INTERNATIONAL**
Contact:  Joan Velazquez
          Tecal 7
          Mexico City, CP 14610 Mexico 22

PROGRAM OF ASSISTANCE:  Health care teams - Tribal peoples.

PROGRAM INITIATION:  1981          EXPENDITURES FOR FY 1982:  $524,000
                                                             (3 year grant)

COOPERATING ORGANIZATIONS:  Rotary Club Ventura Easy (California), Rotary Club
Anahuac (Mexico), Rotary Club Huau Chinango (Mexico), Rotary International
District 524 (California), Rotary Club 417 (Mexico).

..........

TAICH Regional                    213

\* **SALESIAN SOCIETY, INC.**
**Salesians of St. John Bosco (S.D.B.)**
Contacts: Rev. Salvatore Nava, S.D.B., Provincial for Guadalahara
Centro Provincial Salesiano
Lopez Cotilla, 1278, Guadalahara
Apartado 1-1197
Guadalahahara 1, Jalisco, Mexico
Tel. 25-31-61

Rev. Raimondo Gurruchaga, S.D.B., Provincial for Mexico City
2 Calle Colegio Salesiano
35-Mexico 17, D.F., Mexico
Apartado 927
Mexico 1, D.F., Mexico
Tel. 905-531-31-80

Supports programs of the International Salesian Society.

PROGRAM OF ASSISTANCE: Elementary schools - High schools - Educational
funding - Vocational education - Colleges/universities - Clinics - Youth -
Counseling.

PERSONNEL: 313 local.

PROGRAM INITIATION: 1892

..........

\+ **THE SALVATION ARMY**
Contact: Col. George Marshall, Territorial Commander
Apartado 12-668
03020 Mexico, D.F., Mexico
San Borjia 1456
Colonia, Vertz Naruarte
Delegation Benito Juarez
03600 Mexico, D.F.

Assists programs operated by the international organization.

PROGRAM OF ASSISTANCE: Orphanages - Preschool programs - Hostels -
Rehabilitation.

PROGRAM INITIATION: 1937

..........

\*+ **SAVE THE CHILDREN FEDERATION, INC.**
Contact: Miguel Ugalde, Executive Director
Fundacion para el Desarrollo de la Comunidad y Ayuda Infantil,
A.C.
Sufragio Efectivo No. 240 Sur
Altos No. 4
Apartado No. 182
Ciudad Obregon, Sonora, Mexico
Tel. 52-641-314-88

PROGRAM OF ASSISTANCE: Community centers - Integrated rural development - Leadership training - Self-help programs - Cooperatives - Elementary schools - High schools - Non-formal education - Seminars - Cottage industries - Income-generation - Small enterprises - Agricultural training - Animal husbandry - Demonstration projects - Fertilizers - Food preservation - Gardens - Intensive farming - Poultry - Seeds - Vegetables - Water - Breast-feeding - Immunizations - Potable water - Preventive medicine - Toilet facilities - Food preparation - Nutrition education - Family planning - Children - Sponsorships - Youth - Appropriate technology.

PERSONNEL: 12 local.

PROGRAM INITIATION: 1967          EXPENDITURES FOR FY 1982: $193,000

COOPERATING ORGANIZATIONS: German Development Agency, Government of Mexico, Red Barnet (Denmark).

..........

SELF HELP/MEX

**SELF HELP FOUNDATION**
Contact:  Ing. Nester Esteves Herrera
          Director Centro de Aciestramiento de Maquinaria Agricola (CADMA)
          Instituto Tecnologio Agropecuaria de Oaxaca
          Apartado 1158
          Oaxaca, Oaxaca, Mexico
          Tel. 52-051-584-55

PROGRAM OF ASSISTANCE: Equipment - Appropriate technology - Consultants - Evaluation - Integrated rural development - Maintenance/repair - Self-help programs - On-the-job training - Farm machinery.

PERSONNEL: 2 U.S., 30 local.

PROGRAM INITIATION: 1982

COOPERATING ORGANIZATIONS: Centro de Aciestramiento de Maquinaria Agricola, Instituto Tecnologico Agropecuaria de Oaxaca.

..........

SSS/MEX

**SISTERS OF SOCIAL SERVICE OF LOS ANGELES, INC. (S.S.S.)**
Contact:  Sr. Maria Teresa Velasquez, S.S.S.
          Medical Education/Preventive Medicine
          Apartado 96
          Zacapu, Michoacan, Mexico

PROGRAM OF ASSISTANCE: Non-formal education - Community centers.

PERSONNEL: 2 U.S., 3 local.

PROGRAM INITIATION: 1964

..........

SBC/MEX
**SOUTHERN BAPTIST CONVENTION**

Works through local national churches.

PROGRAM OF ASSISTANCE:   Disaster relief - Refugees - Churches - Food distribution centers - Medical supplies.

PROGRAM INITIATION:  1980          EXPENDITURES FOR FY 1982:  $51,301

..........

SIL/MEX
* **SUMMER INSTITUTE OF LINGUISTICS, INC.**
   Contact:  John Daly, Director
             Apartado 22067
             14000 Mexico, D.F., Mexico

PROGRAM OF ASSISTANCE:   Language training - Linguistic studies - Literacy education - Non-formal education - Teaching materials - Translation programs.

PERSONNEL:  100 U.S., 2 local, 16 international.

PROGRAM INITIATION:  1936

..........

VITA/MEX
* **VOLUNTEERS IN TECHNICAL ASSISTANCE, INC. (VITA)**
   Contact:  Institute de Investigaciones Electricas
             Cuernavaca, Morelos, Mexico

PROGRAM OF ASSISTANCE:   Wind energy - Appropriate technology - Potable water.

PROGRAM INITIATION:  1976          EXPENDITURES FOR FY 1982:  $4,000

COOPERATING ORGANIZATION:   General Electric Corporation.

..........

WN/MEX
**WORLD NEIGHBORS, INC.**
   Contact:  Roland Bunch
             Area Representative for Central America
             Apartado 17
             Nochixtlan, Oaxaca, Mexico  69600
             Tel. (952) 201-25

PROGRAM OF ASSISTANCE:   Animateurs - Leadership training - Adult education - Audio visual materials - Non-formal education - Crop improvement - Fertilizers - Gardens - Grains - Intensive farming - Reforestation - Nutrition education.

PERSONNEL: 1 local, 6 international.
PROGRAM INITIATION: 1981          EXPENDITURES FOR FY 1982: $81,088

COOPERATING ORGANIZATIONS:   CETAMEX (Centro de Tecnologia Apropiada Para Mexico), Mexican Friends Service Committee.

. . . . . . . . . .

WVRO/MEX

**\*+ WORLD VISION RELIEF ORGANIZATION, INC.**
Contact:   Paul Petersen
           Associate Director, Field Projects
           World Vision International
           Curridabat Apartado 133
           San Jose, Costa Rica

PROGRAM OF ASSISTANCE:  Integrated rural development - Sponsorships - Medical services - Sanitation - Agricultural extension - Wind energy - Disaster relief.

PROGRAM INITIATION:  1963          EXPENDITURES FOR FY 1982:  $4,474,221

. . . . . . . . . .

XAV/MEX

**XAVERIAN MISSIONARY FATHERS (S.X.)**
Contact:  Father Adoph Menendez, S.X.
          Apartado 39
          Queratero, Mexico

PROGRAM OF ASSISTANCE:  Colleges/universities - Clinics - Nurses - Doctors.

PERSONNEL:  2 U.S., 91 local, 4 international.

PROGRAM INITIATION:  1960          EXPENDITURES FOR FY 1982:  $10,000

COOPERATING ORGANIZATION:  Missioneros Xaverianos (Provincia de Mexico).

. . . . . . . . . .

YMCA/MEX

**\*+ YOUNG MEN'S CHRISTIAN ASSOCIATIONS OF THE UNITED STATES**
Contact:  Roberto Hoyes, General Secretary
          Federation of YMCA'S of the Republic of Mexico
          Mazatian 83 - 302 Col. Condesa
          Mexico 11, D.F., Mexico

YMCA of the U.S. supports programs of the Mexican Federation of YMCA's.

PROGRAM OF ASSISTANCE:  Adult education - Colleges/universities - Non-formal education - Kindergartens - Medical services - Food supply programs - Community centers - Children - Disabled.

PERSONNEL:  1 - 4 U.S., 106 local.
PROGRAM INITIATION:  1902

COOPERATING ORGANIZATIONS:  Government of Mexico, Bureau of Education; Latin American Confederation of YMCA's; National University of Mexico; Springfield College (Springfield, Massachusetts).

. . . . . . . . . .

YWCA/MEX

**\*+  YOUNG WOMEN'S CHRISTIAN ASSOCIATION OF THE U.S.A.**
**World Relations Unit of the National Board**
135 West 50th Street, New York, New York  10022--(212) 621-5115

Contact:  National General Secretary
Asociacion Cristiana Femenina (ACF)
Humboldt 62
Mexico 1, D.F., Mexico

Provides an assistance grant to the Asociacion Cristiana Femenina.

PROGRAM OF ASSISTANCE:  Leadership training - Hostels - Women - Education - Community programs.

PROGRAM INITIATION:  1920.

COOPERATING ORGANIZATION:  World YWCA Cooperation for Development Program.

. . . . . . . . . .

**MEXICO - PROGRAM SUPPORT**

|   |   |   |
|---|---|---|
|   | AFS International/Intercultural Programs | $  88,800 |
| \* | American Dentists for Foreign Service | 10,000 |
|   | American Lung Association | ----- |
| \* | Amigos de las Americas | 39,000 |
|   | Aprovecho Institute | ----- |
| \* | Association for Voluntary Sterilization, Inc. | 703,281 |
|   | Carr Foundation | ----- |
|   | Catholic Medical Mission Board, Inc. | 7,674 |
|   | Center for Human Services | 5,000 |
| \* | Centre for Development and Population Activities | ----- |
|   | Children, Incorporated | 65,579 |
|   | Claretian Fathers (C.M.F.) | ----- |
| \* | Compassion Relief and Development | ----- |
| \*+ | Coordination in Development, Inc. (CODEL) | 75,000 |
| \* | Council of International Programs for Youth Leaders and Social Workers, Inc. | 1200 |
| \* | Direct Relief International | 171,940 |
|   | Family Health International | ----- |
| \* | Family Planning International Assistance | 6,298,981 |
|   | Ford Foundation | 722,904 |
|   | Foundation for His Ministry | 400,000 |
|   | Friends of SOS Children's Villages, Inc. | 2,000 |

|  | | |
|---|---|---:|
| | Friends of SOS Children's Villages, Inc. | 2,000 |
| | Friends of the Third World | ----- |
| *+ | Heifer Project International, Inc. | 36,787 |
| | International Book Project, Inc. | 336 |
| | International Community for the Relief of Starvation and Suffering (ICROSS) | ----- |
| * | International Executive Service Corps | ----- |
| | International Liaison, Inc. | |
| | International Projects Assistance Service (IPAS) | 36,700 |
| | International Road Federation | 4,000 |
| | Interplast, Inc. | 3,973 |
| | W.K. Kellogg Foundation | 3,446,988 |
| | Lions Clubs International | ----- |
| | David Livingston Missionary Foundation, Inc. | 1,500 |
| | Management Sciences for Health | ----- |
| *+ | MAP International | 170,111 |
| | Nature Conservancy | ----- |
| | Outreach International | 8,500 |
| * | Pan American Development Foundation | ----- |
| * | Pathfinder Fund | 67,924 |
| * | Population Council | 186,164 |
| | Population Crisis Committee/Draper Fund | ----- |
| | Population Institute | ----- |
| *+ | Private Agencies Collaborating Together, Inc. (PACT) | 22,104 |
| | Rockefeller Foundation | 816,029 |
| *+ | Seventh-day Adventist World Service, Inc. (SAWS) | 49,327 |
| * | Sister Cities International | ----- |
| | Surgical Eye Expeditions International | ----- |
| | United Church Board for World Ministries | 4,500 |
| | United Methodist Church | ----- |
| | United Methodist Committee on Relief | 24,500 |
| | Volunteer Optometric Services to Humanity (VOSH International) | ----- |
| *+ | World Concern | 22,608 |
| | World Medical Relief, Inc. | 1,738,723 |

---

### MONTSERRAT

---

Of the 9 U.S. organizations listed in Montserrat,
7 were able to provide TAICH with financial data
indicating program expenditures for FY 1982
totaling $238,170.

INTL EYE/MSR

* **INTERNATIONAL EYE FOUNDATION**

PROGRAM OF ASSISTANCE:   Surveys - Blindness prevention - Doctors - Disease
treatment - Medical services - Consultants - Air transportation - Volunteers.

PERSONNEL:  2 U.S.

PROGRAM INITIATION:  1982          EXPENDITURES FOR FY 1982:  $5,000

COOPERATING ORGANIZATIONS:   Inter-island Eye Services, Montserrat Government,
St. Lucia Government.

. . . . . . . . . .

PARTNERS/MSR

* **PARTNERS OF THE AMERICAS**
  Contact:   Howard A. Fergus, Resident Tutor for Montserrat
             University Centre
             P.O. Box 256
             Plymouth, Montserrat
             Tel.  491-2344

PROGRAM OF ASSISTANCE:  Educational exchange.

PERSONNEL:  U.S. and local volunteers.

PROGRAM INITIATION:  1982

. . . . . . . . . .

VITA/MSR

* **VOLUNTEERS IN TECHNICAL ASSISTANCE, INC. (VITA)**
  Contact:   Jeffrey Wartluft
             Manager, Charcoal/Cookstove Project
             c/o Ministry of Agriculture
             Box 272
             Plymouth, Montserrat, W.I.
             Tel. 491-2075

PROGRAM OF ASSISTANCE:   Fuels - Food preparation - Demonstration projects -
Appropriate technology

PERSONNEL: 1 U.S., 1 local.

PROGRAM INITIATION: 1982     EXPENDITURES FOR FY 1982: $10,000

COOPERATING ORGANIZATIONS: Caribbean Development Bank, Government of Montserrat.

..........

## MONTSERRAT - PROGRAM SUPPORT

| | |
|---|---|
| * American Dentists for Foreign Service | $ 3,000 |
| * Direct Relief International | 18,144 |
| International Book Project, Inc. | 201,000 |
| Operation Crossroads Africa | ----- |
| * Pathfinder Fund | 426 |
| Trickle Up Program | 600 |

---

## NETHERLANDS ANTILLES

---

Of the 6 U.S. organizations listed in Netherlands Antilles,
1 was able to provide TAICH with financial data
indicating program expenditures for FY 1982
totaling $2,500.

SALESIAN FR/NLD

* **SALESIAN SOCIETY, INC.**
**Salesians of St. John Bosco (S.D.B.)**
Contact:  Rev. Luis Secco, S.D.B.
          Pastorie Buena Vista
          Sto. Domingoweg, 158
          Curacao, Netherlands Antilles

PROGRAM OF ASSISTANCE: Youth.

PERSONNEL: 3 international.

PROGRAM INITIATION: 1979

..........

## NETHERLANDS ANTILLES - PROGRAM SUPPORT

| | |
|---|---|
| * Council of International Programs for Youth Leaders and Social Workers, Inc. | $2,500 |
| Darien Book Aid Plan, Inc. | ----- |

TAICH Regional                221

Lions Clubs International       -----
Nature Conservancy       -----
Operation Crossroads Africa       -----

---

## NICARAGUA

---

Of the 52 U.S. organizations listed in Nicaragua,
34 were able to provide TAICH with financial data
indicating program expenditures for FY 1982
totaling $4,711,480.

AGNES/NIC

### SISTERS OF THE CONGREGATION OF ST. AGNES (C.S.A.)
Contact:   Sister Raymond Grieble, C.S.A.
          Hermanas de Santa Ines
          Apartado Postal P-125
          Managua, Nicaraga
          Tel. 51277

PROGRAM OF ASSISTANCE: Elementary schools - High schools - Language training - Literacy education - Non-formal education - Libraries - Teacher training - Teaching materials - Leadership training - Wells - Sanitation - Agricultural training - Elementary schools - Clinics - Mother/child programs - Medical education - Preventive medicine - Youth - Vocational education - Preschools programs - Community programs - Books - Clothing - Medical supplies - Crafts.

PERSONNEL: 7 U.S.

PROGRAM INITIATION: 1945.

COOPERATING ORGANIZAITONS: ADVENIAT (Germany), Capuchin Fathers (Nicaragua and U.S.); Government of Nicaragua, Ministry of Education, Ministry of Health; SIMAVI (Netherlands).

. . . . . . . . . .

ABC/NIC

### AMERICAN BAPTIST CHURCHES IN THE USA
Contact:   Baptist Convention of Nicaragua
          Tomas Tellez
          Apartado Postal 2593
          Managua, Nicaragua

PROGRAM OF ASSISTANCE: Disaster relief - Nurses - Geriatric centers - Elementary schools - High schools - Hospitals - Clinics - Medical education - Vocational education - Colleges/universities.

PERSONNEL: 3 U.S.

PROGRAM INITIATION:  1917          EXPENDITURES FOR FY 1982:  $58,900

COOPERATING ORGANIZATIONS:  Church World Service and Comite Evangelica Pro Ayuda al Desarrollo (CEPAD).

. . . . . . . . . .

AMGI/NIC

**AMG INTERNATIONAL**
Contact:  Misael Lopez
          Apartado Postal 3362
          Managua, Nicaragua

PROGRAM OF ASSISTANCE:  Preschool programs - Food distribution centers.

PERSONNEL:  10 local.

PROGRAM INITIATION:  1979

COOPERATING ORGANIZATION:  Woord en Daad (Netherlands).

. . . . . . . . . .

BICM/NIC

**BRETHERN IN CHRIST MISSIONS**
Contact:  Marshall Poe, Country Representative
          Apartado Postal A-257
          Mamagua, Nicaragua

PROGRAM OF ASSISTANCE:  Leadership training.

PERSONNEL:  2 U.S.

PROGRAM INITIATION:  1965          EXPENDITURES FOR FY 1982:  $46,000

COOPERATING ORGANIZATION:  Comite Evangelico Pro Ayuda al Desarrollo (CEPAD).

. . . . . . . . . .

CARE/NIC

**\*+  CARE**
Contact:  Dale Harrison, Director
          Apartado Postal 3084
          Managua, Nicaragua
          Tel.  70482, 70386

PROGRAM OF ASSISTANCE:  Cooperatives - Women - Agricultural training - Loans - Potable water - Food distribution centers - PL 480 - Warehouses - Wells - Toilet facilities - Food-for-work - Sanitation - Seeds - Food/food products - Nutrition education - Beekeeping - Agricultural extension - Irrigation - Vocational education - Gardens - Animals - Integrated rural development - Appropriate technology.

TAICH Regional                   223

PERSONNEL:  2 U.S. or Canada, 10 local.

PROGRAM INITIATION:  1967          EXPENDITURES FOR FY 1982:  $1,301,532

· · · · · · · · · ·

                                                                CRS/NIC

**\*+ CATHOLIC RELIEF SERVICES - UNITED STATES CATHOLIC CONFERENCE**
Contact:  Miguel Mahfoud, Program Director
          De La Ferreteria
          Lang Carretera Sur
          1 Cuadro lago
          1/2 cuadro arriba
          Apartado Postal 2617
          Managua, Nicaragua
          Tel. 60404

PROGRAM OF ASSISTANCE:  Cooperatives - Small enterprises - Food distribution
centers - Medical equipment - Medical supplies - Credit/loans - Refugees -
Transportation - Medical education - Medical auxiliaries - Clinics - Potable
water - Mother/child programs - Disaster Assistance - Construction - Geriatric
Centers - Leadership training - Community Programs - Agricultural training.

PERSONNEL:  1 International, 3 Local.

PROGRAM INITIATION:  1966          EXPENDITURES FOR FY 1982:  $163,746.

COOPERATING ORGANIZATIONS:  Bishops Conference, Caritas; Conferencia Nacional
de Religiosos de Nicaragua (CONFER); GORTA/Ireland, Government of Nicaragua,
Ministries of Agriculture, Education, Labor and Welfare; Help the Aged; local
groups, such as community cooperatives and barrio committees.

· · · · · · · · · ·

                                                                CRWRC/NIC

**+  CHRISTIAN REFORMED WORLD RELIEF COMMITTEE**
Contact:  c/o CEPAD
          Apartado Postal 3091
          Managua, Nicaragua

PROGRAM OF ASSISTANCE:  Preventive Medicine - Agricultural training.

PROGRAM INITIATION:  1973          EXPENDITURES FOR FY 1982:  $131,000

COOPERATING ORGANIZATIONS:  Comite Evangelica Pro Ayuda al Desarrollo (CEPAD),
Provadenic.

· · · · · · · · · ·

**\*+ CHURCH WORLD SERVICE**
Contact:  Gilberto Aguirre, Executive Director
          Comite Evangelico Pro Ayuda al Desarrollo (CEPAD)
          Apartado Postal 3091
          Managua, Nicaragua
          Tel. 24330

Works through CEPAD which was organized following the 1972 earthquake and is composed of 32 denominations.

PROGRAM OF ASSISTANCE:  Appropriate technology - Community centers - Leadership training - Potable water - Literacy education - Cooperatives - Agricultural education - Disaster relief - Food-for-work.

PERSONNEL: Local only.

PROGRAM INITIATION:  1973          EXPENDITURES IN FY 1982:  $245,810

COOPERATING ORGANIZATIONS:  U.S. Agency for International Development.

.........

**\* THE EPISCOPAL CHURCH IN THE U.S.A.**
**(including + The Presiding Bishops Fund for World Relief)**
Contact:  The Rt. Rev. C.J. Wilson, Bishop in Charge
          Apartado Postal 1207
          Managua, Nicaragua

PROGRAM OF ASSISTANCE:  Elementary schools - Literacy education - Clinics - Counseling - Leadership training - Dental clinics.

PERSONNEL: 4 U.S., 35 local.

PROGRAM INITIATION:  1956

COOPERATING ORGANIZATIONS:  Interchurch Medical Assistance; Moravian Church in America provides medical supervision.

.........

**\* FOSTER PARENTS PLAN**
Contact:  Dr William Timothy Farrell, Director
          PLAN en Nicaragua
          Carretera Sur Km 9½
          Shangrila, Managua, Nicaragua

PROGRAM OF ASSISTANCE:  Housing - Construction - Schools - Equipment - Vocational education - Medical services - Dentistry - Potable water - Medical supplies.

PERSONNEL: 1 international; 35 local.

TAICH Regional                    225

PROGRAM INITIATION: 1977          EXPENDITURES FOR FY 1982: $316,067

COOPERATING ORGANIZATIONS:  Government of Nicaragua, Ministry of Social Welfare; Government of Australia.

. . . . . . . . . .

LWR/NIC

**\*+  LUTHERAN WORLD RELIEF, INC.**
Contact:  Gilberto Aguirre, Executive Director
          Comite Evangelico Pro-Ayuda al Desarrollo (CEPAD)
          Apartado Postal 3091
          Managua, Nicaragua
          Tel. 24330

PROGRAM OF ASSISTANCE:  Funding - Housing - Teacher training - Leadership training - Literacy education - Land tenure - Integrated rural development - Roads - Disaster relief - Food distribution centers - Sponsorship - Children - Orphanages - Adoption services - Hospitals - Medical auxiliaries - Family planning - Potable water - Toilet facilities - Urban development - Youth - Women - Adult education - Cooperatives - Credit/loans.

PROGRAM INITIATION: 1972          EXPENDITURES FOR FY 1982: $94,000

COOPERATING ORGANIZATIONS:  CEPAD; Church World Service; Government of Nicaragua, Ministries of Health and Social Welfare.

. . . . . . . . . .

MMS/NIC

**MEDICAL MISSION SISTERS (S.C.M.M.)**
Contact:  Sr. Nina Fritsch, S.C.M.M.
          Hermanas Misioneras Medicas
          Apartado Postal 60
          Esteli, Nicaragua

          Sr. Teresa Jaramillo, S.C.M.M.
          Esquipulas
          Matagalpa, Nicaragua

PROGRAM OF ASSISTANCE:  Leadership training - Literacy Education - Demonstration Projects Mother/Child programs.

PERSONNEL: 2 U.S.

PROGRAM INITIATION: 1979          EXPENDITURES FOR FY 1982: $5,000

COOPERATING ORGANIZATIONS:  Catholic Relief Services, Diocese of Esteli.

. . . . . . . . . .

MCC/NIC

**\*+ MENNONITE CENTRAL COMMITTEE**
Contact: Gerald and Joetta Schlabach
Apartado Postal 5594
Managua, Nicaragua
Tel: 61367

PROGRAM OF ASSISTANCE: Leadership training - Housing - Refugees - Disaster relief - Credit/loans - Food/food products - Literacy education - Health care teams - Educational exchange.

PERSONNEL: 2 U.S., 5 local, 2 international.

PROGRAM INITIATION 1979          EXPENDITURES FOR FY 1982:  $80,000

COOPERATING ORGANIZATION: Comite Evagelica Pro Ayuda al Desarrollo (CEPAD).

. . . . . . . . . .

MONTFORT/NIC

**MONTFORT MISSIONARIES (S.S.M.)**
Contact: Montfort Missionaries (S.S.M.)
Santo Tomas Chantales, Nicaragua

PROGRAM OF ASSISTANCE: Non-formal education.

PERSONNEL: 4 U.S.

PROGRAM INITIATION: 1979

. . . . . . . . . .

NBC/NIC

**NATIONAL BAPTIST CONVENTION, U.S.A., INC.**
Contact: Rev. Gilbert Bent
Zion Baptist Mission School
Bluefield, Nicaragua

PROGRAM OF ASSISTANCE: Elementary schools.

PERSONNEL: 2 U.S., 6 local.

PROGRAM INITIATION: 1958          EXPENDITURES FOR FY 1982:  $22,500

. . . . . . . . . .

PARTNERS/NIC

**\* PARTNERS OF THE AMERICAS**
Contact: Dr. Bayardo Garcia, President
Nicaragua Partners
Linda Vista Norte, No. 108
Managua, Nicaragua
Tel. 51-517 or 51-307

PROGRAM OF ASSISTANCE: Construction - Leadership training - Agricultural training - Vocational education - Educational supplies - Transportation - Mass media - Animal husbandry - Poultry - Agricultural extension - Medical services - Medical auxiliaries - Hospitals - Appropriate Technology - Seeds - Pest control - Veterinary services - Food preservation - Schools - Educational exchange - Pumps.

PERSONNEL: Volunteers, both local and U.S.

PROGRAM INITIATION: 1965

COOPERATING ORGANIZATIONS: Government of Nicaragua, Pan American Development Foundation, University of Wisconsin Medical School, U.S. Agency for International Development, U.S. Peace Corps, Wisconsin Extension Homemakers Council, Wisconsin Rural Electric Cooperatives.

..........

RSCJ/NIC

**SOCIETY OF THE SACRED HEART (R.S.C.J.)**
Contact: Sister Lisa Fitzgerald, R.S.C.J.
Casa Nazareth
Bolomia 1
C.P. 4291
Managua, Nicaragua

PROGRAM OF ASSISTANCE: Research/field studies - Adult education - Colleges/universities.

PERSONNEL: 2 U.S., 5 international.

PROGRAM INITIATION: 1979

COOPERATING ORGANIZATION: CIERA

..........

SALESIAN FR/NIC

* **SALESIAN SOCIETY, INC.**
**Salesians of St. John Bosco (S.D.B.)**
Contact: Rev. Mario Fiandri, S.D.B.
Centro Juvenil Don Bosco
Apartado Postal 1266
Managua, Nicaragua

PROGRAM OF ASSISTANCE: Youth - Elementary schools - High schools - Colleges/universities.

PERSONNEL: 20 local.

PROGRAM INITIATION: 1911

..........

**\*+ SAVE THE CHILDREN FEDERATION, INC.**
Contact: Mario Cerna Barquero, Director
Fundacion para el Desarrollo Juvenile Communitario Nicaraguense
"Fudejuconic"
Apartado Postal 4557
Managua, Nicaragua
Tel. (505) 2-23676

PROGRAM OF ASSISTANCE: Self-help programs - Cooperatives - Seminars - Vocational education - Agricultural cooperatives - Agricultural training - Animal power technology - Draft animals - Demonstration projects - Extension agents - Storage - Intensive farming - Fertilizers - Housing.

PERSONNEL: 8 local.

PROGRAM INITIATION: 1981       EXPENDITURES FOR FY 1982: $30,900

COOPERATING ORGANIZATIONS: Government of Nicaragua, Ministry of Housing; U.S. Agency for International Development.

..........

**SOUTHERN BAPTIST CONVENTION**

Works through local national churches.

PROGRAM OF ASSISTANCE: Food-for-work - Medical supplies - Food distribution centers - Disaster relief - Nutrition education - Children - Vocational education - Elementary schools.

PROGRAM INITIATION: 1976       EXPENDITURES FOR FY 1982: $30,000

..........

**\* TECHNOSERVE, INC.**
Contact: Silvia Baltodano, Country Program Director
Apartado Postal 1027
Managua, Nicaragua
Tel. 61985

PROGRAM OF ASSISTANCE: Agricultural training - Crop improvement - Cooperatives - Small enterprises - Vocational education - Consultants - Marketing.

PERSONNEL: 13 local.

PROGRAM INITIATION: 1976       EXPENDITURES FOR FY 1982: $350,000

COOPERATING ORGANIZATIONS: Catholic Relief Services; FUNDE (Fundacion Nicaraguense do Desarrollo); International Development Bank; Maryknoll Fathers; Private Agencies Collaborating Together (PACT); U.S. Agency for International Development.

..........

TAICH Regional                 229

**WORLD NEIGHBORS, INC.**
Contact:  Roland Bunch, Area Representative for Central America
          Apartado Postal 27
          Nochixtlan, Oaxaca
          Mexico 69600
          Tel. 962-20126

PROGRAM OF ASSISTANCE:  Animateurs - Leadership training - Adult education - Audio visual materials - Educational exchange - Research/field studies institutes.

PERSONNEL:  3 local.

PROGRAM INITIATION:  1982

COOPERATING ORGANIZATIONS:  John XXIII Institute of Central American University; Comite Evangelico Pro Ayuda al Desarrollo (CEPAD).

. . . . . . . . . .

*+  **WORLD VISION RELIEF ORGANIZATION, INC.**
Contact:  Paul Petersen
          Associate Director, Field Projects
          World Vision International
          Curridabat Apartado 133
          San Jose, Costa Rica

PROGRAM OF ASSISTANCE:  Counseling - Rehabilitation - Disaster relief.

PROGRAM INITIATION:  1972          EXPENDITURES FOR FY 1982:  $140,500

COOPERATING ORGANIZATIONS:  Local churches and municipal institutions.

. . . . . . . . . .

**NICARAGUA - PROGRAM SUPPORT**

|  |  |  |
|---|---|---|
|  | A.T. International | $ 95,500 |
|  | Aid to Artisans, Inc. | 750 |
| + | American Friends Service Committee | ----- |
|  | American Lung Association | ----- |
| * | Association for Voluntary Sterilization, Inc. | 37,776 |
| + | Baptist World Aid | 50,000 |
| * | Brother's Brother Foundation | 584,000 |
|  | Children, Incorporated | 5,763 |
| * | Compassion Relief and Development | ----- |
| *+ | Coordination in Development, Inc. (CODEL) | 30,000 |
|  | Darien Book Aid Plan, Inc. | ----- |
| * | Direct Relief International | 94,880 |
|  | Farallones Institute | ----- |
|  | Ford Foundation | 88,000 |
|  | Friends of SOS Children's Villages, Inc. | 4,000 |

| | | |
|---|---|---|
| Help the Aged | | 2,045 |
| Interchurch Medical Assistance, Inc. | | 31,817 |
| * International Executive Service Corps | | ----- |
| Lions Clubs International | | ----- |
| *+ MAP International | | 23,549 |
| Operation California, Inc. | | 40,000 |
| Oxfam America | | 380,181 |
| * Pathfinder Fund | | 60,261 |
| * Pan American Development Foundation | | ----- |
| *+ Seventh-day Adventist World Service, Inc. | | 11,903 |
| * Sister Cities International | | ----- |
| Trickle Up Program | | 100 |
| * Unitarian Universalist Service Committee | | ----- |
| United Church Board for World Ministries (Service Division) | | 10,000 |
| United Methodist Committee on Relief | | 175,000 |
| Volunteer Optometric Services to Humanity (VOSH International) | | ----- |
| * Volunteers in Technical Assistance, Inc. (VITA) | | ----- |

---

## PANAMA

---

Of the 54 U.S. organizations listed in Panama,
26 were able to provide TAICH with financial data
indicating program expenditures for FY 1982
totaling $5,143,333.

AFL-CIO/PAN

* **AFL-CIO - American Institute for Free Labor Development**
Contact: Richard V. Houlahan, Country Representative
Apartado Postal 8729
Panama City 5
Tel. 25-8749

PROGRAM OF ASSISTANCE: Unions - Courses - Education - Funding - Loans - Community centers.

PERSONNEL: 1 U.S., 3 local.

COOPERATING ORGANIZATIONS: U.S. Agency for International Development, American Federation of Labor and Congress of Industrial Organizations, Panamanian Labor Confederations's Training Institute (INEL).

..........

CARE/PAN

*+ **CARE**
Contact: Swaleh Karanja, Field Representative
Apartado 4257, Panama City 5, Panama
Tel. 25-1427, 25-1428

PROGRAM OF ASSISTANCE: Construction - Self-help programs - Food-for-work - PL 480 - Schools - Seeds - Food distribution centers - Mother/child programs - Women - Vocational education - Small enterprises.

PERSONNEL: 2 international.

PROGRAM INITIATION: 1953          EXPENDITURES FOR FY 1982: $3,628,071

COOPERATING ORGANIZATION: Institute for the Training and Development of Human Resources (IFARHU), Overseas Education Fund.

. . . . . . . . . .

CRS/PAN

**\*+ CATHOLIC RELIEF SERVICES - UNITED STATES CATHOLIC CONFERENCE**
Contact:  Mark D. Moriarty, Program Director
          Apartado 5483
          San Jose, Costa Rica
          Tel. 32-64-61

PROGRAMS OF ASSISTANCE: Food/food products - PL 480 - Mother/child programs - Food programs - Clothing - Vocational education - Medical supplies - Medical equipment - Nutrition education education - Food/food products - Crop improvement - Public health education - Food-for-work - Food/food products - Leadership training - Agricultural cooperatives.

PERSONNEL:  Short-term consultants.

PROGRAM INITIATION: 1962          EXPENDITURES FOR FY 1982: $72,325

COOPERATING ORGANIZATIONS:  Brucke der Bruderhilfe; Caritas/Panama; Government of Panama, Ministries of Public Health and Agricultural Development; Institute for the Training and Utilization of Human Resources (IFARHU); National Council of Catholic Women; Panamanian Red Cross; U.S. Government; USAID/Panama.

. . . . . . . . . .

CG ANDER/PAN

**CHURCH OF GOD, INC. (ANDERSON, INDIANA)**
Contact:  Rev. Keith Plank
          Apartado 6048
          San Jose, Costa Rica
          Tel. 24-02-57

PROGRAM OF ASSISTANCE:  Medical services - Tribal peoples.

. . . . . . . . . .

CLARE/PAN

**CLARETIAN FATHERS (C.M.F.)**
Contact:  Rev. Gonzalo Mateo, C.M.F., Superior of the Mission Catedral
          Apartado 243
          Colon, Panama

PROGRAM OF ASSISTANCE:    Leadership  training - Agricultural  cooperatives -
Credit/loans - Literacy education - Cash crops - Animal husbandry - Land
reclamation - Nutrition education - Public health education - Potable water -
Food supply programs - Children.

PERSONNEL:  9 international.

PROGRAM INITIATION:  1972

COOPERATING ORGANIZATIONS:  Fe y Alegria (Spain); Misereor (Germany); U.S.
Conference of Bishops, Latin American Bureau.

..........

EPISCO/PAN

* **THE EPISCOPAL CHURCH IN THE U.S.A.**
**(including + PRESIDING BISHOPS FUND FOR WORLD RELIEF)**
Contact:   The Rt. Rev. Lemuel Shirley, Bishop
           P.O. Box R, Balboa, Canal Zone
           Missionary Diocese of Panama

PROGRAM OF ASSISTANCE:  Kindergartens - Elementary schools - High school -
Orphanages.

PERSONNEL:  1 U.S.

PROGRAM INITIATION:   1906

..........

GOODWILL/PAN

*+ **GOODWILL INDUSTRIES OF AMERICA, INC.**
Contact:   Shelia Sanchez, Directora Ejecutiva
           Associacion Panamena de Industrias de Buena Voluntad
           Apartado Postal 8-248
           Urbanization Los Andes, No. 2
           Sector Industrial-Transistmica
           Panama 8
           Tel. 67-7692

PROGRAM OF ASSISTANCE: Vocational education - Small enterprise development -
Disabled - Rehabilitation.

PERSONNEL:  5 local.

PROGRAM INITIATION:  1983

COOPERATING ORGANIZATION:  U.S. Agency for International Development.

..........

**GOSPEL MISSIONARY UNION**
Contact:  David Fast, Field Director
          Apartado Postal 1115 W
          Colon, Panama
          Tel. 011-507-45-1854

PROGRAM OF ASSISTANCE:  Medical supplies - Medical services - Nutrition education - Cottage industries - Elementary schools - High schools - Educational funding - Extension courses.

PERSONNEL:  8 U.S., 1 local, 5 international.

PROGRAM INITIATION:  1953

. . . . . . . . . .

\*  **LAUBACH LITERACY INTERNATIONAL**
Contact:  Dr. Luis Oscar Londono
          Latin American Regional Director
          CLEBA, Apartado Aereo  2561
          Medelin, Colombia

PROGRAM OF ASSISTANCE:  Literacy education - Teaching materials - Evaluation - Leadership training - Non-formal education.

PERSONNEL:  local, and local volunteers

PROGRAM INITIATION:  1969          EXPENDITURES FOR FY 1982:  $43,584

. . . . . . . . . .

\*  **LA LECHE LEAGUE INTERNATIONAL**
Content:  Linda Linforo
          c/o Firestone
          La Leche League of Panama
          P.O. Box 511
          Panama 1, Oabana
          Tel.:  602086

PROGRAM OF ASSISTANCE:  Breast-feeding - Mother/child program - Self-help programss - Women's education.

PERSONNEL:  2 international

PROGRAM INITIATION:  1975

COOPERATING ORGANIZATION:  Prolacma

. . . . . . . . . .

MKNOL SR/PAN

**MARYKNOLL SISTERS OF ST. DOMINIC (M.M.)**
Contact:  Maryknoll Sisters
         P.O. Box 0
         Balbos, Panama

PROGRAM OF ASSISTANCE:  Teachers - Elementary schools.
PERSONNEL:  1 U.S.

PROGRAM INITIATION:  1943

. . . . . . . . . .

MBMS/PAN

**MENNNONITE BRETHREN MISSION/SERVICES**
Contact:  Harold Ens
         Apartado Postal 2478
         Panama 9-A, Panama
         Tel. 64-57-48

PROGRAM OF ASSISTANCE:  Integrated rural development - Marketing - Agricultural training - Preventive medicine - Public health education - Traditional medicine - Leadership training - Self-help programs - Sanitation - Vocational education - Potable water.

PERSONNEL:  2 U.S., 3 local.

PROGRAM INITIATION  1956          EXPENDITURES FOR FY 1982:  $114,300

COOPERATING ORGANIZATION:  Canadian International Development Agency (CIDA).

. . . . . . . . . .

OEF/PAN

\*  **OVERSEAS EDUCATION FUND**
Contact:  Carmen Nunez, Technical Advisor
         Apartado Postal 11291
         Panama 6, Panama
         Tel. 60-22-34, 23-75-92

PROGRAM OF ASSISTANCE  Women's education - Vocational education - Income generation - Job placement - Credit/loans - Small enterprises - Vehicles.

PERSONNEL:  2 U.A., 3 local.

PROGRAM INITIATION  1981          EXPENDITURES FOR FY 1982:  $23,977

COOPERATING ORGANIZATIONS:  Banco Nacional; CARE; FARHU (Institute para la Formacion y Recursos Humanos);  Government of El Salvador, Ministries of Planning and Commerce and Industry; USAID/Panama.

. . . . . . . . . .

\* **PARTNERS OF THE AMERICAS**
Contact: Oderay Perez de Valdes, Chairman, President
Apartado Postal 6-3056
Panama City
Panama
Tel. 22-0088

PROGRAM OF ASSISTANCE: Agriculturists - Crop improvement - Water transportation - Tribal peoples - Maintenance repair - Appropriate technology - Storage - Marketing - Vocational education - Nutrition education - Women - Income generation - Educational exchange - Medical training - Disabled.

PERSONNEL: Local and U.S. volunteers.

PROGRAM INITIATION: 1964

COOPERATING ORGANIZATIONS: CARITAS; Government of Panama, Ministry of Education, Ministry of Agriculture, Ministry of Health; U.S. Agency for International Development; University of Panama.

..........

\* **SALESIAN SOCIETY, INC.**
Contact: Rev. Isidro Gonzalez, S.D.B.
Apartado Postal 7244
Panama, Panama

Supports programs of the International Salesian Society.

PROGRAM OF ASSISTANCE: Elementary schools - Vocational education - Youth - Night schools - Counseling.

PERSONNEL: 16 local.

PROGRAM INITIATION: 1907          EXPENDITURES FOR FY 1982:

..........

\*+ **THE SALVATION ARMY**
Contact: Major Lester Anderson, Divisional Commander
P.O. Box N,
0792 LaBoca Rd.
Panama, Panama
Tel. 52-6693

Assists programs operated by the international organization.

PROGRAM OF ASSISTANCE: Schools for disabled - Day schools - Kindergartens - Food distribution centers - Orphanages - Geriatric centers - Community centers - Youth - Preschool programs - Rehabilitation.

PROGRAM INITIATION:   1904

. . . . . . . . . .

\* **TECHNOSERVE, INC.**
Contact:  Mario Ganuza
          Apartado Postal 6-2045
          Estafeta-El Dorado
          Panama City, Panama

PROGRAM OF ASSISTANCE:  Agricultural cooperatives - Swine - Vegetables.

PERSONNEL:  5 local, 1 international.

PROGRAM INITIATION:  1981          EXPENDITURES FOR FY 1982:  $206,952

COOPERATING ORGANIZATION:  A.T. International.

. . . . . . . . . .

**WORLD RADIO MISSIONARY FELLOWSHIP, INC.**
Contact:  Cliff Daffron
          Apartado Postal 3269
          Panama City, Panama
          Tel.  252-5471

PROGRAM OF ASSISTANCE:  Mass media.

PERSONNEL:  4 U.S.

PROGRAM INITIATION:  1963

. . . . . . . . . .

\*+ **WORLD VISION RELIEF ORGANIZATION, INC.**
Content:  Paul Peterson
          Associate Director, Field Projects
          World Vision International
          Curridabat Apartado 133
          San Juan, Costa Rica

PROGRAM OF ASSISTANCE:  Leadership training.

PROGRAM INITIATION:  1979          EXPENDITURES FOR FY 1982:  $33,000

COOPERATING ORGANIZATIONS:  Local churches.

. . . . . . . . . .

TAICH Regional                    237

## PANAMA - PROGRAM SUPPORT

|  | | |
|---|---|---|
| | AFS International/Intercultural Programs | $23,300 |
| | American Lung Association | ----- |
| | American Public Health Association | 58,532 |
| * | Amigos de las Americas | 15,500 |
| * | Association for Voluntary Sterilization, Inc. | 5,050 |
| | Association Internationale des Etudiants en Sciences Economiques et Commerciales | 1000 |
| | Carr Foundation | ----- |
| | Catholic Medical Mission Board, Inc. | 91,740 |
| * | Centre for Development and Population Activities | |
| * | Cooperative League of the U.S.A. | ----- |
| * | Council of International Programs for Youth Leaders and Social Workers, Inc. | 1,200 |
| | Darien Book Aid Plan, Inc. | ----- |
| | Education Development Center | ----- |
| | Family Health International | ----- |
| * | Family Planning International Assistance | 95,086 |
| | Friends of SOS Children's Villages, Inc. | ----- |
| *+ | Heifer Project International, Inc. | 4,035 |
| | Interchurch Medical Assistance, Inc. | 115 |
| | International Center for Research on Women | ----- |
| * | International Executive Service Corps | ----- |
| | W.K. Kellogg Foundation | 463,743 |
| | Lions Clubs International | ----- |
| *+ | MAP International | 32,138 |
| | National Council of Catholic Women | 3,000 |
| | National Savings and Loan League | ----- |
| | Nature Conservancy | ----- |
| * | Pan American Development Foundation | ----- |
| * | Pathfinder Fund | 32,669 |
| *+ | Private Agencies Collaborating Together, Inc. (PACT) | 93,000 |
| | Trickle Up Program | 200 |
| | United Methodist Church | ----- |
| | United Methodist Committee on Relief | 15,000 |
| * | Volunteer Development Corps | 80,046 |
| | Volunteer Optometric Services to Humanity (VOSH International) | ----- |
| * | Volunteers in Technical Assistance, Inc. (VITA) | ----- |
| *+ | World Concern | 5,770 |

## ST. KITTS - NEVIS

Of the 13 U.S. organizations listed in St. Kitts,
4 were able to provide TAICH with financial data
indicating program expenditures for FY 1982
totaling $250,953.

HIGH SCOPE/KNA

**\* HIGH/SCOPE EDUCATIONAL RESEARCH FOUNDATION**
Contact:  Leonne James, Chief, Early Childhood Unit
          Ministry of Health, Education & Social Affairs
          Bassterre, St. Kitts  2
          Tel. 2626

PROGRAM OF ASSISTANCE:  Preschool programs - Community programs - Mother/child
programs- Women.

PERSONNEL:  1 U.S., 41 local.

PROGRAM INITIATION:  1981          EXPENDITURES FOR FY 1982:  $250,000

COOPERATING ORGANIZATIONS:  U.S. Peace Corps, U.S. AID/Barbados.

. . . . . . . . . .

MEDA/KNA

**MENNONITE ECONOMIC DEVELOPMENT ASSOCIATES, INC.**
Contact:  Doug Robertson
          Ministry of Education, Health & Social Affairs
          P.O. Box 333, Newstead Bldg.
          Basseterre, St. Kitts
          Tel. 2365

PROGRAM OF ASSISTANCE:  Seminars - Management training.

PERSONNEL:  1 U.S., 2 local.

PROGRAM INITIATION:  1982

COOPERATING ORGANIZATIONS:  Canadian International Development Agency (CIDA),
Government of St. Kitts - Nevis, Ministry of Education, Health and Community
Development, U.S. Peace Corps.

. . . . . . . . . .

\* **PARTNERS OF THE AMERICAS**
Contact:  Constantine Richardson
          Extra-Mural Tutor
          University Centre
          P.O. Box 326
          Basseterre, St. Kitts, W.I.
          Tel. (809) 465-2190

PROGRAM OF ASSISTANCE:  Educational exchange - Libraries - Medical education.

PERSONNEL:  U.S. and local volunteers.

PROGRAM INITIATION:  1982.

. . . . . . . . . .

\*+  **THE SALVATION ARMY**
Contact:  Salvation Army
          P.O. Box 56
          Cayon Rd.
          Basseterre, St. Kitts
          Tel. 2106
Assists programs operated by the international organization:

PROGRAM OF ASSISTANCE:  Community centers - Counseling.

PROGRAM INITIATION:  1901

**ST. KITTS - NEVIS - PROGRAM SUPPORT**

|   |   |   |
|---|---|---|
|   | Freedom House, Inc. | $ 90 |
|   | Management Sciences for Health | ----- |
|   | Moravian Church in America, Inc. | ----- |
| \* | National 4-H Council | ----- |
|   | Operation Crossroads Africa, Inc. | ----- |
| \* | Pan American Development Foundation | ----- |
| \* | Pathfinder Fund | 463 |
|   | Trickle Up Program | 400 |
| \* | Unitarian Universalist Service Committee | ----- |

## ST. LUCIA

Of the 25 U.S. organizations listed in St. Lucia,
5 were able to provide TAICH with financial data
indicating program expenditures for FY 1982
totaling $886,502.

INTL EYE/LCA

**\* INTERNATIONAL EYE FOUNDATION**
Contact:  Dr. Bradford J. Shingleton
I.E.F. Project Director
Department of Ophthalmology
Queen Victoria Hospital
Castries, St. Lucia
Tel. (809) 462-2421

PROGRAM OF ASSISTANCE:  Blindness prevention - Clinics - Disease treatment - Doctors - Medical education - Medical equipment - Medical services - Medical supplies - Ophthalmology - Preventive medicine - Surveys - Volunteers - Books - Consultants - Vehicles.

PERSONNEL:  2 U.S., 3 local.

PROGRAM INITIATION:  1980        EXPENDITURES FOR FY 1982:  $120,000

COOPERATING ORGANIZATIONS:  Alcon, Inc., Chibret International, Ethicon, Inter-island Eye Sservices, St. Lucia Government, Masschusetts Eye & Ear, infirmary, Merck and Co. Inc., Pan American Health Organization, U.S. Agency for International Development.

. . . . . . . . . .

NOSR/LCA

**\* NATIONAL OFFICE FOR SOCIAL RESPONSIBILITY IN THE PRIVATE SECTOR**
Contact:  SRI/Gordon Kunde
c/o Ministry of Community Development
Corner of St. Louis & Peynier Streets
Castries, St. Lucia, West Indies
Tel (809) 452-4880

PROGRAM OF ASSISTANCE:  Youth - Cooperatives - Non-formal education - Food preservation - Crafts.

PERSONNEL:  3 U.S., 15 local.

PROGRAM INITIATION:  1980        EXPENDITURES OF FY 1982:  $183,000

COOPERATING ORGANIZATIONS:  Government of St. Lucia, Ministry of Education, Ministry of Community Affairs; U.S. Agency for International Development.

. . . . . . . . . .

* **PAN AMERICAN DEVELOPMENT FOUNDATION**
Contact:   St. Lucia National Development Corporation
           P.O. Box 495
           Castries, St. Lucia

PROGRAM OF ASSISTANCE:   Small enterprises - Self-help programs - Credit/loans
- Management training - Medical equipment - Vocational education - Institution
building - Tools.

PROGRAM INITITATION:  1980

COOPERATING ORGANIZATIONS:   U.S. Agency for International Development; U.S.
manufacturers of equipment related to vocational training; U.S. hospitals,
health care institutions, and manufactuers of medical equipment.

. . . . . . . . . .

* **PARTNERS OF THE AMERICAS**
Contact:  Mrs. Marilyn Floissac
          P.O. Box 45
          Castries, St. Lucia
          Tel. (809) 455-4761

PROGRAM OF ASSISTANCE:   Educational exchange - Rehabilitation - Teachers -
Vocational  education - Small  enterprises - Medical  education - Preventive
medicine - Medical auxiliaries.

PERSONNEL:   U.S. and local volunteers.

PROGRAM INITIATION:  1981

COOPERATING ORGANIZATIONS:   Government of St. Lucia, Ministry of Education,
Ministry of Health; St. Lucian National Development Corporation.

. . . . . . . . . .

* **THE PEOPLE-TO-PEOPLE HEALTH FOUNDATION, INC.**
**Project Hope**
Contact:   Philip Kneller, Head of Faculty
           Project Hope
           P.O. Box 1069
           Castries, St. Lucia
           Tel.  (809) 452-1283

PROGRAM OF ASSISTANCE:   Sanitation - Medical education.

PERSONNEL:   4 U.S., 5 local.

PROGRAM INITIATION:  1983

COOPERATING ORGANIZATIONS: Barbados Community College; CARICOM; USAID/Barbados; Government of St. Lucia, Ministries of Health and Education.

..........

PLENTY/LCA

**PLENTY**
Contact: Patrick O'Connor
General Delivery
Castries, St. Lucia
Tel. 2413

PROGRAM OF ASSISTANCE: Vegetables - Crop improvement - Food preservation - Intensive farming - Gardens - Seeds - Crop processing - Demonstration projects - Food/food products - Food preparation - Nutrition education.

PERSONNEL: 4 U.S., 3 local, 3 international (British).

PROGRAM INITIATION: 1983

COOPERATING ORGANIZATIONS: Canadian International Development Agency (CIDA); Government of St. Lucia, Ministry of Finance and Planning, Ministry of Agriculture; INTSOY (International Soybean Program, University of Illinois at Urbana-Champaign).

..........

SOROW SR/LCA

**SISTERS OF THE SORROWFUL MOTHER (THIRD ORDER OF ST. FRANCIS) (S.S.M.)**
Contact: Sister M. Shares Hurtgen, (S.S.M.), Administrator
St. Jude Hospital
Vieux Fort, St. Lucia

PROGRAM OF ASSISTANCE: Hospitals.

PERSONNEL: 2 U.S.

PROGRAM INITIATION: 1966          EXPENDITURES FOR FY 1982: $260,000

COOPERATING ORGANIZATIONS: Government of St. Lucia.

..........

WE/LCA

* **WORLD EDUCATION, INC**
Contact: Youth Development Program
National Office for Social Responsibility
Castries, St. Lucia

PROGRAM OF ASSISTANCE: Cooperatives - Vocational education - Income generation - Youth.

TAICH Regional               243

PERSONNEL: 1 U.S., 12 local.

PROGRAM INITIATION: 1981          EXPENDITURES FOR FY 1982: $3,000

COOPERATING ORGANIZATIONS: Government of St. Lucia, Ministry of Community
Development, USAID (Barbados).


. . . . . . . . . .


## ST. LUCIA - PROGRAM SUPPORT

|   |   |
|---|---|
| Aid for International Medicine, Inc. | ----- |
| * Brother's Brother Foundation | ----- |
| * Caribbeana Council | (see regional listing) |
| Carr Foundation | ----- |
| * Council of International Programs for Youth Leaders and Social Workers, Inc. | ----- |
| Darien Book Aid Plan, Inc. | ----- |
| * Direct Relief International | $320,502 |
| Environmental Research Projects | ----- |
| * International Executive Service Corps | ----- |
| W.K. Kellogg Foundation | ----- |
| Lions Clubs International | ----- |
| Management Sciences for Health | ----- |
| * National 4-H Council | ----- |
| Operation Crossroads Africa | ----- |
| * Population Council | ----- |
| *+ Seventh-day Adventist World Service, Inc. | ----- |
| * Volunteers in Technical Assistance, Inc. (VITA) | ----- |


---

## ST. MARTIN

---


There is 1 U.S. organization listed in St. Martin.

## ST. MARTIN - PROGRAM SUPPORT

Darien Book Aid Plan, Inc.                            -----

---

## ST. VINCENT AND THE GRENADINES

---

Of the 19 U.S. organizations listed in St. Vincent & the Grenadines,
8 were able to provide TAICH with financial data
indicating program expenditures for FY 1982
totaling $66,665.


PARTNERS/VCT

\* **PARTNERS OF THE AMERICAS**
Contact:   Col. Sydney A. Anderson
           Argyle Services, Ltd.
           P.O. Box 530
           Kingstown, St. Vincent
           Tel. (809) 457-1550 (O)

PROGRAM OF ASSISTANCE:   Women - Income generation - Educational exchange -
Livestock - Dairy animals - Poultry - Nutrition education - Rehabilitation.

PERSONNEL:   U.S. and local volunteers.

PROGRAM INITIATION:   1981


. . . . . . . . . . .


SALVA/VCT

\*+   **THE SALVATION ARMY**
Contact:   Salvation Army
           Middle Street
           Kingstown, St. Vincent
           Tel. 615-74

Assists programs operated by the international organization.

PROGRAM OF ASSISTANCE:   Counseling - Community centers - Food distribution
centers.


. . . . . . . . . .


WE/VCT

\* **WORLD EDUCATION, INC.**
Contact:   Peggy Antrobus
           Women and Development Unit
           University Of The West Indies
           Barbados

PROGRAM OF ASSISTANCE:   Non-formal education - Income generation - Evaluation.

PERSONNEL:   4 local.

PROGRAM INITIATION: 1980            EXPENDITURES FOR FY 1982: $9,000

COOPERATING ORGANIZATIONS:   Government  of  St.  Vincent,  Ministries  of
Agriculture  and  Education;  University  of  the  West  Indies;  U.S.  Agency  for
International Development.


. . . . . . . . . .


## ST. VINCENT AND THE GRENADINES - PROGRAM SUPPORT

| | | |
|---|---|---|
| * | Brother's Brother Foundation | $ 1,000 |
| *+ | Catholic Relief Services | ----- |
| * | Council of International Programs For Youth | |
| | Leaders and Social Workers, Inc. | 1,200 |
| | Darien Book Aid Plan, Inc. | ----- |
| | Freedom House, Inc. | 90 |
| *+ | Heifer Project International, Inc. | 27,816 |
| | Lions Clubs International | ----- |
| | Management Sciences for Health | ----- |
| | National Council of Catholic Women | 2,032 |
| * | National 4-H Council | ----- |
| | Operation Crossroads Africa, Inc. | ----- |
| | Oxfam America | 25,427 |
| * | Pan American Development Foundation | ----- |
| * | Sister Cities International | ----- |
| | Trickle Up Program | 100 |
| * | Volunteers in Technical Assistance, Inc. (VITA) | ----- |

---

## SURINAME

---

Of the 11 U.S. organizations listed in Suriname,
6 were able to provide TAICH with financial data
indicating program expenditures for FY 1982
totaling $25,022.


AVIATION/SUR

**MISSION AVIATION FELLOWSHIP**
Contact:   Terry Rezncser, Program Manager
            Stichting Missionary Aviation Fellowship Suriname
            P.O. Box 2031, Krakalaan 4
            Paramaribo, Suriname
            Tel. 97893

PROGRAM OF ASSISTANCE:  Air transportation - Vehicles.

PERSONNEL:  3 U.S.

PROGRAM INITIATION:  1963

COOPERATING ORGANIZATIONS:  Moravian Church, Suriname Gospel Center, Suriname Medical Society, West Indies Mission, Wycliffe Bible Translators.

..........

SALVA/SUR

**\*+  THE SALVATION ARMY**
Contact: Major Frank Sumter
        P.O. Box 317
        Gravenstraat 172,
        Paramaribo, Suriname
        Tel. 73310

The Salvation Army in the U.S.A. provides financial and personnel assistance to programs operated by the international organization.

PROGRAM OF ASSISTANCE:  Hostels - Geriatric centers - Food/food products - Children - Orphanages - Food distribution centers - Rehabilitation.

PROGRAM INITIATION:  1926

..........

SIL/SUR

**\*  SUMMER INSTITUTE OF LINGUISTICS**
Contact:  James Park, Director
        P.B. 1919
        Paramaribo, Suriname

PROGRAM OF ASSISTANCE:  Teaching materials - Linguistic studies - Literacy education.

PERSONNEL:  17 U.S., 7 international.

PROGRAM INITIATION:  1967

COOPERATING ORGANIZATION:  Government of Suriname, Ministry of Education.

..........

WESLEY/SUR

**THE WESLEYAN CHURCH**
Contact: Rev. C.T. Knupp
        Box 17, Moengo (Pelgrim Kondre) Suriname

PROGRAM OF ASSISTANCE:  Elementary schools.

PERSONNEL:  2 U.S., 5 local.

PROGRAM INITIATION:  1945        EXPENDITURES FOR FY 1982:  $19,020

**SURINAME - PROGRAM SUPPORT**

* Council of International Programs for Youth
  Leaders and Social Workers, Inc.                    $1,200
  Darien Book Aid Plan, Inc.                           -----
  Friends of SOS Children's Villages, Inc.               420
  Lions Clubs International                            -----
  David Livingston Missionary Foundation, Inc.         2,250
  National Council of Catholic Women                   2,032
  Trickle Up Program                                     100

---

## TRINIDAD AND TOBAGO

---

Of the 18 U.S. organizations listed in Trinidad & Tobago,
5 were able to provide TAICH with financial data
indicating program expenditures for FY 1982
totaling $109,360.

PARTNERS/TTO

* **PARTNERS OF THE AMERICAS**
  Contact:  David Sui-Sang Chin
            Trinidad & Tobago Partners President
            27 Scotland Terrace
            Andalusia, Maraval
            Trinidad
            Tel.  27-003 or 34-318

PROGRAM OF ASSISTANCE:    Rehabilitation  -  Educational  exchange  -  Medical
education - Mass media.

PERSONNEL:  U.S. and local volunteers.

PROGRAM INITIATION:  1978

COOPERATING ORGANIZATIONS:   Caribbean Agricultural Research and Development
Institute (CARDI), Caribbean Institute for Mental Retardation, University of
the West Indies, YMCA.

. . . . . . . . . .

SALVA/TTO

*+ **THE SALVATION ARMY**
   Contact:  Major Clifford Yearwood
             P.O. Box 248
             27 Edward Street
             Port Of Spain, Trinidad

PROGRAM OF ASSISTANCE:  Counseling - Hostels - Community centers - Preschool

programs.
PROGRAM INITIATION:  1901

. . . . . . . . . .

\* **WINROCK INTERNATIONAL**
Contact:  Dr. P. Alleyne, Permanent Secretary
Ministry of Agriculture Lands and Fisheries
St. Claixe Circle
Port Of Spain, Trinidad

PROGRAM OF ASSISTANCE:  Agricultural experiment centers - Range animals -
Veterinary services - Appropriate technology - On-the-job training -
Agricultural extension - Institution building - Animal husbandry - Animal feed
- Demonstration projects - Fertilizers - Management training - Pastureage -
Animal health - Animal breeding - Agricultural research - Evaluation.

PERSONNEL:  3 U.S., 1 local.

PROGRAM INITIATION:  1981          EXPENDITURES FOR FY 1982:  $67,521

COOPERATING ORGANIZATION:  Government of Trinidad and Tobago.

. . . . . . . . . .

**TRINIDAD AND TOBAGO - PROGRAM SUPPORT**

| | |
|---|---:|
| American Lung Association | ----- |
| American Public Health Association | $ 6,035 |
| Carr Foundation | ----- |
| \* Centre for Development and Population Activities | |
| \* Council of International Programs for Youth | |
| Leaders and Social Workers, Inc. | 1,200 |
| \* International Executive Service Corps | ----- |
| International Liaison, Inc. | ----- |
| Lions Clubs International | ----- |
| Moravian Church in America, Inc. | ----- |
| \* National 4-H Council | ----- |
| \* Pan American Development Foundation | ----- |
| \* Pathfinder Fund | 4,604 |
| United Methodist Committee on Relief | 30,000 |
| United States Youth Council | ----- |
| \* Volunteers in Technical Assistance, Inc. (VITA) | ----- |

---

## TURKS AND CAICOS ISLANDS

---

There are 4 U.S. organizations listed in Turks and Caicos Islands.

### TURKS AND CAICOS ISLANDS - PROGRAM SUPPORT

| | |
|---|---|
| Darien Book Aid Plan, Inc. | ----- |
| Freedom House, Inc. | ----- |
| Lions Clubs International | ----- |
| * Volunteers in Technical Assistance, Inc. (VITA) | ----- |

---

### REGIONAL

---

Of the 23 U.S. organizations listed as having regional programs,
16 were able to provide TAICH with financial data
indicating program expenditures for FY 1982
totaling $1,318,330.

AFSC/REG

+ **AMERICAN FRIENDS SERVICE COMMITTEE**
Contact:  American Friends Service Committee
Apartado 876-A
Tegucigalpa, Honduras

Through Honduran AFSC administers funding for projects in Costa Rica, El Salvador, Guatemala, Honduras, Nicaragua and Panama.

PROGRAM OF ASSISTANCE:  Refugees -Displaced persons - Equipment - Leadership training - Self-help programs - Medical auxiliaries - Public health education.

PERSONNEL:  1 U.S.

PROGRAM INITIATION:  1961

COOPERATING ORGANIZATIONS:  Government of Honduras, Ministry of Health.

. . . . . . . . . .

AFL-CIO/REG

* **AFL-CIO - American Institute for Free Labor Development**
Contact:  Michael Donovan, Regional Representative
P.O. Box 420
Bridgetown, Barbados

Through its regional office in Barbados, provides assistance in: Anguilla, Antigua, Bahamas, Barbados, Belize, Bermuda, Dominica, Grenada, Guyana, Haiti, Jamaica, Montserrat, Netherlands Antilles, St. Kitts-Nevis, St. Lucia, St. Vincent and the Grenadines, Suriname, Trinidad and Tobago, Turks and Caicos Islands.

Program is also active in several countries where AIFLD has regular offices including Dominican Republic, El Salvador, Guatemala, Honduras and Panama.

PROGRAM OF ASSISTANCE: Unions - Courses - Adult education - Funding - Credit/loans - Community centers.

..........

CARIB/REG

**\* THE CARIBBEANA COUNCIL**
Contact: Mrs. D. Gannum, Caribbeana Council Regional Office
Maxwell Gardens, Christ Church
Barbados

Lawson Calderon, General Manager
St. Lucia National Development Corporation
P.O. Box 495
Castries, St. Lucia

Assists projects in eastern Caribbean countries (Antigua, Barbados, Jamaica, Dominica, Dominican Republic, St. Lucia).

PROGRAM OF ASSISTANCE: Small enterprises - Animal husbandry - Cash Crops - Energy - Gardens - Vegetables - Mass media - Material aid - Nutrition education.

PERSONNEL: 10 U.S. (short-term)

PROGRAM INITIATION: 1977          EXPENDITURES FOR FY 1982: $233,478

COOPERATING ORGANIZATIONS: U.S. Agency for International Development, U.S. Department of State, U.S. Department of Commerce, private foundations and corporations, e.g. British American Insurance Corporation, C.S. Mott Foundation, Ford Foundation.

..........

CRS/REG

**\*+  CATHOLIC RELIEF SERVICES - United States Catholic Conference**
Contact: Donald Carcieri, Program Director
10 Emerald Road
Kingston 4, Jamaica

PROGRAM OF ASSISTANCE: Provides support to various socio-economic development projects in Dominica, St. Lucia and St. Vincent and the Grenadines.

PERSONNEL: 1 U.S.

PROGRAM INITIATION: 1972        EXPENDITURES FOR FY 1982: $6,293

COOPERATING ORGANIZATIONS: Local governments and churches.

..........

CWS/REG

**\*+ CHURCH WORLD SERVICE**
Contact:  Dr. Lawson Nurse
          Asst. General Secretary
          Caribbean Conference of Churches
          P.O. Box 616
          Bridgetown, Barbados

Provides funding to the Caribbean Conference of Churches for development work throughout the Caribbean including Belize.

PROGRAM OF ASSISTANCE:  Integrated rural development - Disaster relief.

PERSONNEL: Local only.

PROGRAM INITIATION: 1969        EXPENDITURES FOR FY 1982: $204,926

..........

INTL EYE/REG

**\* INTERNATIONAL EYE FOUNDATION**

Provides assistance in the Caribbean region.

PROGRAM OF ASSISTANCE:  Blindness prevention - Medical education - Books - Consultants - Air transportation.

PERSONNEL: 2 U.S., 2 local, 1 international.

PROGRAM INITIATION: 1978        EXPENDITURES FOR FY 1982: $55,000

COOPERATING ORGANIZATIONS:  Chibret International, St. Lucia Government, U.S. Agency for International Development, participating island governments.

..........

WINROCK/REG

**\* WINROCK INTERNATIONAL**
Contact:  Dr. Sam Parasram, Director
          Research and Development
          CARDI
          University Campus
          St. Augustine, Trinidad
          Tel. 809-662-5511

Provides assistance in Belize, Costa Rica, Grenada, Guyana, Jamaica, and Trinidad and Tobago.

PROGRAM OF ASSISTANCE: Agricultural research institutes - Agricultural training - Animal feed - Animal husbandry - Crop improvement - Dairy animals - Range animals - Cash crops.

PERSONNEL: 5 U.S.

PROGRAM INITIATION: 1981          EXPENDITURES FOR FY 1982: $26,686

COOPERATING ORGANIZATIONS: Caribbean Agricultural Research and Development Institute (CARDI), Agricultural Research and Training Center (CAITE), U.S. Agency for International Development.

. . . . . . . . . .

## REGIONAL - PROGRAM SUPPORT

|  |  |
|---|---:|
| A.T. International (Caribbean) | $ 36,000 |
| American Public Health Association (Caribbean) | ----- |
| Carnegie Corporation of New York (Caribbean) | 19,000 |
| *+ Coordination in Development, Inc. (CODEL) | 7,500 |
| Environmental Research Projects | 83,502 |
| Farallones Institute | ----- |
| * Inter-American Development Institute | 25,000 |
| Island Resources Foundation | ----- |
| League for International Food Education | ----- |
| * National Council for International Health (Caribbean) | 148,000 |
| * Pathfinder Fund (Caribbean) | 6,000 |
| Population Reference Bureau | ----- |
| *+ Private Agencies Collaborating Together, Inc. (PACT) (Caribbean) | 10,000 |
| United Methodist Church | ----- |
| United Methodist Committee on Relief (Caribbean) | 125,000 |
| *+ World Concern (Caribbean) | 6,910 |
| World Medical Relief, Inc. (Caribbean) | 325,035 |

COUNTRY INDEX

## ANGUILLA

OPERATION CROSSROADS AFRICA,
INC. (S)

## ANTIGUA

AMERICAN DENTISTS FOR FOREIGN
SERVICE (S)

CARR FOUNDATION (S)

DARIEN BOOK AID PLAN, INC. (S)

FREEDOM HOUSE, INC. (S)

INTERNATIONAL BOOK PROJECT,
INC. (S)

LIONS CLUB INTERNATIONAL (S)

MEALS FOR MILLIONS/FREEDOM FROM
HUNGER FOUNDATION

MORAVIAN CHURCH IN AMERICA,
INC. (S)

NATIONAL 4-H COUNCIL (S)

OPERATION CROSSROADS AFRICA,
INC. (S)

OXFAM AMERICA (S)

PAN AMERICAN DEVELOPMENT
FOUNDATION (S)

PARTNERS OF THE AMERICAS

PEOPLE-TO-PEOPLE HEALTH
FOUNDATION, INC.

SALVATION ARMY

TRICKLE UP PROGRAM (S)

UNITED METHODIST CHURCH (S)

UNITED METHODIST COMMITTEE ON
RELIEF (S)

VOLUNTEERS IN TECHNICAL
ASSISTANCE, INC. (VITA) (S)

## BAHAMAS

BROTHER'S BROTHER FOUNDATION (S)

CATHOLIC MEDICAL MISSION BOARD,
INC. (S)

COUNCIL OF INTERNATIONAL PROGRAMS
FOR YOUTH LEADERS AND SOCIAL
WORKERS, INC. (S)

DARIEN BOOK AID PLAN, INC. (S)

SISTERS OF ST. FRANCIS, CLINTON,
IOWA (O.S.F.)

FREEDOM HOUSE, INC. (S)

GOSPEL MISSIONARY UNION

INTERNATIONAL LIAISON, INC. (S)

LA LECHE LEAGUE INTERNATIONAL

LIONS CLUBS INTERNATIONAL (S)

PAN AMERICAN DEVELOPMENT FOUNDATION

SALESIAN SOCIETY, INC.

SALVATION ARMY

VOLUNTEERS IN TECHNICAL ASSISTANCE,
INC. (VITA) (S)

## BARBADOS

A.T. INTERNATIONAL (S)

AFL-CIO - American Institute for
Free Labor Development (see
regional listing)

AFS INTERNATIONAL/INTERCULTURAL
PROGRAMS

AMERICAN PUBLIC HEALTH
ASSOCIATION (S)

BEREAN MISSION, INC. (S)

CARIBBEANA COUNCIL (see regional
listing)

CARNEGIE CORPORATION OF NEW YORK
(S)

CHURCH WORLD SERVICE (see regional listing)

COUNCIL OF INTERNATIONAL PROGRAMS FOR YOUTH LEADERS AND SOCIAL WORKERS, INC. (S)

DARIEN BOOK AID PLAN, INC. (S)

FAMILY PLANNING INTERNATIONAL ASSISTANCE (S)

FORD FOUNDATION (S)

INTERNATIONAL EXECUTIVE SERVICE CORPS (S)

INTERNATIONAL EYE FOUNDATION

LA LECHE LEAGUE INTERNATIONAL

LIONS CLUBS INTERNATIONAL (S)

MANAGEMENT SCIENCES FOR HEALTH (S)

MORAVIAN CHURCH IN AMERICA, INC. (S)

NATIONAL 4-H COUNCIL (S)

NATIONAL SAVINGS AND LOAN LEAGUE (S)

PAN AMERICAN DEVELOPMENT FOUNDATION

PARTNERS OF THE AMERICAS

PARTNERSHIP FOR PRODUCTIVITY INTERNATIONAL, INC. (S)

POPULATION COUNCIL (S)

SALVATION ARMY

SISTERS OF THE SORROWFUL MOTHER (Third Order of St. Francis) (S.S.M.)

TRICKLE UP PROGRAM (S)

UNITED STATES YOUTH COUNCIL (S)

VOLUNTEERS IN TECHNICAL ASSISTANCE, INC. (VITA) (S)

## BELIZE

CARE

CARR FOUNDATION (S)

CHRISTIAN FOUNDATION FOR CHILDREN

COMPASSION INTERNATIONAL, INC.
COMPASSION RELIEF AND DEVELOPMENT (S)

CONSERVATIVE BAPTIST FOREIGN MISSION SOCIETY

COOPERATIVE HOUSING FOUNDATION

COUNCIL OF INTERNATIONAL PROGRAMS FOR YOUTH LEADERS AND SOCIAL WORKERS, INC. (S)

DARIEN BOOK AID PLAN, INC. (S)

EASTERN MENNONITE BOARD OF MISSIONS AND CHARITIES

FREEDOM HOUSE, INC. (S)

FRIENDS UNITED MEETING

GLOBAL OUTREACH

GOSPEL MISSIONARY UNION

HEIFER PROJECT INTERNATIONAL, INC. (S)

CONGREGATION OF THE SISTERS OF THE HOLY FAMILY (S.S.F.)

INTERCHURCH MEDICAL ASSISTANCE, INC. (S)

INTERNATIONAL AGRICULTURAL DEVELOPMENT SERVICE (S)

INTERNATIONAL BOOK PROJECT, INC. (S)

INTERNATIONAL EXECUTIVE SERVICE CORPS (S)

LIONS CLUBS INTERNATIONAL (S)

MAP INTERNATIONAL (S)

MENNONITE CENTRAL COMMITTEE

MENNONITE ECONOMIC DEVELOPMENT
ASSOCIATES, INC.

NATIONAL 4-H COUNCIL  (S)

OPERATION CROSSROADS AFRICA,
INC.  (S)

PAN AMERICAN DEVELOPMENT FOUNDATION

PARTNERS OF THE AMERICAS

PEOPLE-TO-PEOPLE HEALTH FOUNDATION,
INC.

PROJECT CONCERN INTERNATIONAL

ROTARY INTERNATIONAL

SALVATION ARMY

SISTER CITIES INTERNATIONAL  (S)

TRICKLE UP PROGRAM  (S)

UNITED CHURCH BOARD FOR WORLD
MINISTRIES  (S)

THE UNITED METHODIST CHURCH

UNITED METHODIST COMMITTEE ON
RELIEF  (S)

VOLUNTEER OPTOMETRIC SERVICES TO
HUMANITY (VOSH INTERNATIONAL)  (S)

WINROCK INTERNATIONAL

WORLD VISION RELIEF ORGANIZATION,
INC.


## BERMUDA

W. K. KELLOGG FOUNDATION  (S)

LIONS CLUBS INTERNATIONAL  (S)

SALVATION ARMY


## CAYMAN ISLANDS

DARIEN BOOK AID PLAN, INC.  (S)

LA LECHE LEAGUE INTERNATIONAL

LIONS CLUBS INTERNATIONAL  (S)

OPERATION CROSSROADS AFRICA, INC.
(S)


## COSTA RICA

ACCION INTERNATIONAL/AITEC

AFL-CIO - American Institute for
Free Labor Development

AFS INTERNATIONAL/INTERCULTURAL
PROGRAMS  (S)

AMERICAN LUNG ASSOCIATION  (S)

AMERICAN PUBLIC HEALTH ASSOCIATION
(S)

AMIGOS DE LAS AMERICAS  (S)

ASSOCIATION INTERNATIONALE DES
ETUDIANTS EN SCIENCES ECONOMIQUES
ET COMMERCIALES (AIESEC-UNITED
STATES)  (S)

BROTHER'S BROTHER FOUNDATION  (S)

CARE

CARR FOUNDATION  (S)

CATHOLIC MEDICAL MISSION BOARD,
INC.  (S)

CATHOLIC RELIEF SERVICES -- UNITED
STATES CATHOLIC CONFERENCE

CENTRE FOR DEVELOPMENT AND
POPULATION ACTIVITIES (S)

CHILDREN, INCORPORATED  (S)

CHRISTIAN REFORMED WORLD RELIEF
COMMITTEE

CHURCH OF GOD, INC. (ANDERSON,
INDIANA)

CHURCH WORLD SERVICE

COMBONI MISSIONARIES OF THE HEART OF
JESUS (M.C.C.J.)

CONSERVATIVE MENNONITE BOARD OF
MISSIONS AND CHARITIES, INC.

COOPERATIVE LEAGUE OF THE USA (S)

COUNCIL OF INTERNATIONAL PROGRAMS
FOR YOUTH LEADERS AND SOCIAL
WORKERS, INC. (S)

DARIEN BOOK AID PLAN, INC. (S)

EPISCOPAL CHURCH IN THE U.S.A.

FAMILY HEALTH INTERNATIONAL (S)

FORD FOUNDATION (S)

FREEDOM HOUSE, INC. (S)

FRIENDS OF SOS CHILDREN'S VILLAGES,
INC. (S)

GOODWILL INDUSTRIES OF AMERICA, INC.

HEIFER PROJECT INTERNATIONAL, INC.
(S)

INSTITUTE FOR INTERNATIONAL
DEVELOPMENT, INC.

INTERMEDIA

INTERNATIONAL BOOK PROJECT, INC.
(S)

INTERNATIONAL EXECUTIVE SERVICE
CORPS (S)

W. K. KELLOGG FOUNDATION (S)

LA LECHE LEAGUE INTERNATIONAL

LATIN AMERICAN MISSION

LIONS CLUBS INTERNATIONAL (S)

LUTHERAN WORLD RELIEF, INC.

MAP INTERNATIONAL (S)

MENNONITE ECONOMIC DEVELOPMENT
ASSOCIATES, INC. (S)

MORAVIAN CHURCH IN AMERICA,
INC. (S)

NATIONAL COUNCIL OF CATHOLIC WOMEN
(S)

NATIONAL 4-H COUNCIL (S)

NATIONAL SAVINGS AND LOAN
LEAGUE (S)

NATURE CONSERVANCY (S)

PAN AMERICAN DEVELOPMENT
FOUNDATION (S)

PARTNERS OF THE AMERICAS

PARTNERSHIP FOR PRODUCTIVITY
INTERNATIONAL, INC. (S)

THE PATHFINDER FUND (S)

THE ROCKEFELLER FOUNDATION (S)

SALESIAN SOCIETY, INC.

SALVATION ARMY

SISTER CITIES INTERNATIONAL (S)

TECHNOSERVE, INC. (S)

TRICKLE UP PROGRAM (S)

UNITARIAN UNIVERSALIST SERVICE
COMMITTEE (S)

UNITED METHODIST CHURCH (S)

UNITED METHODIST COMMITTEE ON
RELIEF (S)

UNITED STATES YOUTH COUNCIL (S)

VOLUNTEER DEVELOPMENT CORPS (S)

VOLUNTEER OPTOMETRIC SERVICES TO
HUMANITY (VOSH INTERNATIONAL) (S)

VOLUNTEERS IN TECHNICAL ASSISTANCE, INC. (VITA) (S)

WINROCK INTERNATIONAL

WORLD CONCERN

WORLD VISION RELIEF ORGANIZATION, INC.

YOUNG MEN'S CHRISTIAN ASSOCIATIONS OF THE UNITED STATES

## CUBA

AMERICAN LUNG ASSOCIATION (S)

FORD FOUNDATION (S)

SALVATION ARMY

UNITED METHODIST CHURCH (S)

## DOMINICA

BEREAN MISSION, INC.

CENTER FOR HUMAN SERVICES (S)

CENTRE FOR DEVELOPMENT AND POPULATION ACTIVITIES (S)

CHRISTIAN REFORMED WORLD RELIEF COMMITTEE

COUNCIL OF INTERNATIONAL PROGRAMS FOR YOUTH LEADERS AND SOCIAL WORKERS, INC. (S)

DARIEN BOOK AID PLAN, INC. (S)

DIRECT RELIEF INTERNATIONAL (S)

FREEDOM HOUSE, INC. (S)

HEIFER PROJECT INTERNATIONAL, INC. (S)

INTERNATIONAL BOOK PROJECT, INC. (S)

INTERNATIONAL EXECUTIVE SERVICE CORPS (S)

LIONS CLUBS INTERNATIONAL (S)

MANAGEMENT SCIENCES FOR HEALTH (S)

NATIONAL 4-H COUNCIL (S)

NATURE CONSERVANCY (S)

OPERATION CROSSROADS AFRICA, INC. (S)

OXFAM AMERICA (S)

PAN AMERICAN DEVELOPMENT FOUNDATION

PARTNERS OF THE AMERICAS

PARTNERSHIP FOR PRODUCTIVITY INTERNATIONAL, INC.

PATHFINDER FUND (S)

PLENTY

POPULATION COUNCIL (S)

SAVE THE CHILDREN FEDERATION, INC.

STELIOS M. STELSON FOUNDATION, INC. (S)

TRICKLE UP PROGRAM (S)

UNITED METHODIST COMMITTEE ON RELIEF (S)

VOLUNTEERS IN TECHNICAL ASSISTANCE, INC. (VITA) (S)

## DOMINICAN REPUBLIC

ACCION INTERNATIONAL/AITEC

AFL-CIO - American Institute for Free Labor Development'

AFS INTERNATIONAL/INTERCULTURAL
PROGRAMS (S)

AMERICAN BAPTIST CHURCHES IN THE USA

AMERICAN ORT FEDERATION

AMERICAN PUBLIC HEALTH
ASSOCIATION (S)

AMIGOS DE LAS AMERICAS (S)

ASSOCIATION FOR VOLUNTARY
STERILIZATION,INC. (S)

BETHANY FELLOWSHIP, INC.

BROTHER'S BROTHER FOUNDATION (S)

CARE

CATHOLIC MEDICAL MISSION BOARD,
INC. (S)

CATHOLIC RELIEF SERVICES -- UNITED
STATES CATHOLIC CONFERENCE

CENTER FOR HUMAN SERVICES (S)

CENTRE FOR DEVELOPMENT AND
POPULATION ACTIVITIES (S)

CHILDREN, INCORPORATED (S)

CHRISTIAN FOUNDATION FOR CHILDREN

CHRISTIAN MEDICAL SOCIETY

CHRISTIAN REFORMED WORLD MISSIONS

CHRISTIAN REFORMED WORLD RELIEF
COMMITTEE

CHURCH OF THE NAZARENE

CHURCH WORLD SERVICE

COMPASSION INTERNATIONAL, INC.
COMPASSION RELIEF AND DEVELOPMENT

COOPERATIVE HOUSING FOUNDATION

COORDINATION IN DEVELOPMENT, INC.
(CODEL) (S)

COUNCIL OF INTERNATIONAL PROGRAMS
FOR YOUTH LEADERS AND SOCIAL
WORKERS, INC. (S)

DARIEN BOOK AID PLAN, INC. (S)

DIRECT RELIEF INTERNATIONAL (S)

EDUCATION DEVELOPMENT CENTER (S)

EPISCOPAL CHURCH IN THE U.S.A.

EVANGELICAL MENNONITE CHURCH, INC.

FAMILY PLANNING INTERNATIONAL
ASSISTANCE (S)

FOOD FOR THE HUNGRY INTERNATIONAL

FORD FOUNDATION (S)

FREE METHODIST CHURCH OF NORTH
AMERICA

FRIENDS OF SOS CHILDREN'S VILLAGES,
INC. (S)

VICTORIA AND ALBERT GILDRED
FOUNDATION FOR LATIN AMERICAN
HEALTH AND EDUCATION

HEIFER PROJECT INTERNATIONAL,
INC. (S)

HOLY LAND CHRISTIAN MISSION
INTERNATIONAL

INSTITUTE FOR INTERNATIONAL
DEVELOPMENT, INC.

INTERCHURCH MEDICAL ASSISTANCE,
INC. (S)

INTERNATIONAL ADOPTIONS, INC. (S)

INTERNATIONAL AGRICULTURAL
DEVELOPMENT SERVICE (S)

INTERNATIONAL EXECUTIVE SERVICE
CORPS (S)

INTERNATIONAL EYE FOUNDATION

INTERNATIONAL LIAISON, INC. (S)

SISTERS OF ST. JOSEPH (C.S.J.)
  Rockville Centre Diocese

W. K. KELLOGG FOUNDATION (S)

LIONS CLUBS INTERNATIONAL (S)

MANAGEMENT SCIENCES FOR HEALTH (S)

MAP INTERNATIONAL (S)

MENNONITE ECONOMIC DEVELOPMENT
  ASSOCIATES, INC.

MISSIONARY CHURCH, INC.

MISSIONS HEALTH FOUNDATION, INC.

MORAVIAN CHURCH IN AMERICA,
  INC. (S)

ORTHOPAEDICS OVERSEAS, INC. (S)

OUTREACH INTERNATIONAL (S)

PAN AMERICAN DEVELOPMENT FOUNDATION

PARTNERS OF THE AMERICAS

PATHFINDER FUND (S)
POPULATION COUNCIL (S)

REDEMPTORIST FATHERS (C.SS.R.)

ROTARY INTERNATIONAL

SALESIAN SOCIETY, INC.

SAVE THE CHILDREN FEDERATION, INC.

SISTER CITIES INTERNATIONAL (S)

UFM INTERNATIONAL, INC.

UNITED METHODIST COMMITTEE ON
  RELIEF (S)

VOLUNTEERS IN INTERNATIONAL SERVICE
  AND AWARENESS (VIISA)

VOLUNTEERS IN TECHNICAL ASSISTANCE,
  INC. (VITA) (S)

WORLD CONCERN (S)

WORLD RELIEF CORPORATION

WORLD VISION RELIEF ORGANIZATION,
  INC.

YOUNG MEN'S CHRISTIAN ASSOCIATIONS
  OF THE UNITED STATES


## EL SALVADOR

AFL-CIO - American Institute for
  Free Labor Development

AGUA DEL PUEBLO (S)

AMERICAN BAPTIST CHURCHES IN THE USA

AMERICAN LUNG ASSOCIATION (S)

BAPTIST WORLD AID (S)

CAM INTERNATIONAL

CARR FOUNDATION (S)

CATHOLIC RELIEF SERVICES -- UNITED
  STATES CATHOLIC CONFERENCE

CENTRE FOR DEVELOPMENT AND
  POPULATION ACTIVITIES (S)

CHILDREN, INCORPORATED (S)

CHRISTIAN REFORMED WORLD RELIEF
  COMMITTEE

COMPASSION INTERNATIONAL, INC.
COMPASSION RELIEF AND DEVELOPMENT
  (S)

COUNCIL OF INTERNATIONAL PROGRAMS
  FOR YOUTH LEADERS AND SOCIAL
  WORKERS, INC. (S)

DARIEN BOOK AID PLAN, INC. (S)

DIRECT RELIEF INTERNATIONAL (S)

EPISCOPAL CHURCH IN THE U.S.A.

FAMILY HEALTH INTERNATIONAL  (S)

FOSTER PARENTS PLAN

FRANCISCAN FRIARS (O.F.M.)
Province of the Immaculate
Conception,

FRIENDS OF SOS CHILDREN'S VILLAGES,
INC.  (S)

INTER-AID, INC.  (S)

INTERCHURCH MEDICAL ASSISTANCE,
INC.  (S)

INTERNATIONAL EXECUTIVE SERVICE
CORPS  (S)

INTERNATIONAL ROAD FEDERATION  (S)

LA LECHE LEAGUE INTERNATIONAL

LIONS CLUBS INTERNATIONAL  (S)

LUTHERAN CHURCH-MISSOURI
SYNOD  (S)

MENNONITE CENTRAL COMMITTEE

NATIONAL COUNCIL OF CATHOLIC
WOMEN  (S)

NATIONAL SAVINGS AND LOAN
LEAGUE  (S)

OVERSEAS EDUCATION FUND

OXFAM AMERICA  (S)

PAN AMERICAN DEVELOPMENT FOUNDATION

PARTNERS OF THE AMERICAS

PATHFINDER FUND  (S)

ROCKEFELLER FOUNDATION  (S)

SALESIAN SOCIETY, INC.

SAVE THE CHILDREN FEDERATION, INC.

SEVENTH-DAY ADVENTIST WORLD SERVICE,
INC.  (S)

SISTER CITIES INTERNATIONAL  (S)

TECHNOSERVE, INC.

UNITED METHODIST COMMITTEE ON
RELIEF  (S)

VOLUNTEER OPTOMETRIC SERVICES TO
HUMANITY (VOSH INTERNATIONAL)  (S)

VOLUNTEERS IN TECHNICAL ASSISTANCE,
INC. (VITA)  (S)

WORLD VISION RELIEF ORGANIZATION,
INC.


## GRENADA

BROTHER'S BROTHER FOUNDATION  (S)

CARR FOUNDATION  (S)

DARIEN BOOK AID PLAN, INC.  (S)

LIONS CLUBS INTERNATIONAL  (S)

NATIONAL 4-H COUNCIL  (S)
OXFAM AMERICA  (S)

PAN AMERICAN DEVELOPMENT
FOUNDATION  (S)

ST. PATRICK'S MISSIONARY SOCIETY
(S.P.S.)

SALVATION ARMY

TRICKLE UP PROGRAM  (S)


## GUADELOUPE

DARIEN BOOK AID PLAN, INC.  (S)

LIONS CLUBS INTERNATIONAL  (S)

TRICKLE UP PROGRAM  (S)

## GUATEMALA

A.T. INTERNATIONAL (S)

ACCION INTERNATIONAL/AITEC (S)

AFL-CIO - American Institute for
Free Labor Development (S)

AGRICULTURAL COOPERATIVE DEVELOPMENT
INTERNATIONAL

AGUA DEL PUEBLO

AID TO ARTISANS, INC. (S).

AMERICAN FRIENDS OF CHILDREN, INC.

AMERICAN LUNG ASSOCIATION (S)

AMERICAN PUBLIC HEALTH
ASSOCIATION (S)

AMERICANS FOR INTERNATIONAL AID AND
ADOPTION (S)

AMG INTERNATIONAL

APROVECHO INSTITUTE (S)

ASSOCIATION FOR VOLUNTARY
STERILIZATION, INC. (S)

BENEDICTINE FATHERS (O.S.B.),
Blue Cloud Abbey

BROTHER'S BROTHER FOUNDATION (S)

CAM INTERNATIONAL

CARR FOUNDATION (S)

CATHOLIC MEDICAL MISSION BOARD,
INC. (S)

CATHOLIC RELIEF SERVICES -- UNITED
STATES CATHOLIC CONFERENCE

CENTRE FOR DEVELOPMENT AND
POPULATION ACTIVITIES (S)

CHILDREN, INCORPORATED (S)

CHRISTIAN CHILDREN'S FUND, INC.

CHRISTIAN FOUNDATION FOR CHILDREN

CHRISTIAN NATIONALS' EVANGELISM
COMMISSION, INC.

CHRISTIAN REFORMED WORLD RELIEF
COMMITTEE

BROTHERS OF THE CHRISTIAN SCHOOLS
(F.S.C.)

CHURCH WORLD SERVICE

CLARETIAN FATHERS (C.M.F.) (S)

COMPASSION INTERNATIONAL, INC.
COMPASSION RELIEF & DEVELOPMENT
(S)

COOPERATIVE HOUSING FOUNDATION

COORDINATION IN DEVELOPMENT, INC.
(CODEL) (S)

COUNCIL OF INTERNATIONAL PROGRAMS
FOR YOUTH LEADERS AND SOCIAL
WORKERS, INC. (S)

COVENANT INTERNATIONAL FOUNDATION

DARIEN BOOK AID PLAN, INC. (S)

DIRECT RELIEF INTERNATIONAL (S)

EASTERN MENNONITE BOARD OF MISSIONS
AND CHARITIES

EDUCATION DEVELOPMENT CENTER (S)

EPISCOPAL CHURCH IN THE U.S.A.

FAMILY HEALTH INTERNATIONAL (S)

FAMILY PLANNING INTERNATIONAL
ASSISTANCE (S)

FOOD FOR THE HUNGRY INTERNATIONAL

FOSTER PARENTS PLAN

FRANCISCAN FRIARS (O.F.M.),
Province of the Immaculate
Conception

FRIENDS OF CHILDREN, INC.

FRIENDS OF SOS CHILDREN'S VILLAGES,
INC. (S)

FRIENDS OF THE THIRD WORLD,
INC. (S)

HABITAT FOR HUMANITY, INC.

HEIFER PROJECT INTERNATIONAL,
INC. (S)

HOLY LAND CHRISTIAN MISSION
INTERNATIONAL

INSTITUTE OF CULTURAL AFFAIRS
INTER-AID, INC. (S)

INTERCHURCH MEDICAL ASSISTANCE,
INC. (S)

INTERNATIONAL ADOPTIONS, INC. (S)

INTERNATIONAL EXECUTIVE SERVICE
CORPS (S)

INTERNATIONAL INSTITUTE OF RURAL
RECONSTRUCTION

INTERNATIONAL LIAISON, INC. (S)

W. K. KELLOGG FOUNDATION (S)

LA LECHE LEAGUE INTERNATIONAL

LIONS CLUBS INTERNATIONAL (S)

LUTHERAN WORLD RELIEF, INC.

MANAGEMENT SCIENCES FOR HEALTH (S)

MAP INTERNATIONAL (S)

MARYKNOLL FATHERS AND BROTHERS
(M.M.)

MARYKNOLL SISTERS OF ST. DOMINIC
(M.M.)

MENNONITE CENTRAL COMMITTEE

MISSION AVIATION FELLOWSHIP

NATIONAL SAVINGS AND LOAN
LEAGUE (S)

OXFAM AMERICA (S)

PAN AMERICAN DEVELOPMENT
FOUNDATION (S)

PARTNERS OF THE AMERICAS

PATHFINDER FUND (S)

PEOPLE-TO-PEOPLE HEALTH FOUNDATION,
INC.

POPULATION COUNCIL (S)

PRIMITIVE METHODIST CHURCH IN THE
U.S.A.

PRIVATE AGENCIES COLLABORATING
TOGETHER, INC. (PACT) (S)

PROJECT CONCERN INTERNATIONAL
PUBLIC WELFARE FOUNDATION (S)

ROCKEFELLER FOUNDATION (S)

ROTARY INTERNATIONAL

SALESIAN SOCIETY, INC.

SALVATION ARMY

SAVE THE CHILDREN FEDERATION, INC.

SEVENTH-DAY ADVENTIST WORLD SERVICE,
INC. (S)

SISTER CITIES INTERNATIONAL (S)

SUMMER INSTITUTE OF LINGUISTICS,
INC.

UNITARIAN UNIVERSALIST SERVICE
COMMITTEE (S)

UNITED METHODIST COMMITTEE ON
RELIEF (S)

VOLUNTEER OPTOMETRIC SERVICES TO HUMANITY (VOSH INTERNATIONAL) (S)

WORLD CONCERN (S)

WORLD NEIGHBORS, INC.

WORLD RELIEF CORPORATION (S)

WORLD VISION RELIEF ORGANIZATION, INC.

YOUNG MEN'S CHRISTIAN ASSOCIATIONS OF THE UNITED STATES

## GUYANA

AGRICULTURAL COOPERATIVE DEVELOPMENT INTERNATIONAL

AMERICAN LEPROSY MISSIONS, INC. (S)

BROTHER'S BROTHER FOUNDATION (S)

DARIEN BOOK AID PLAN, INC. (S)

INTERCHURCH MEDICAL ASSISTANCE, INC. (S)

IRI RESEARCH INSTITUTE, INC.

LIONS CLUBS INTERNATIONAL (S)

LUTHERAN CHURCH IN AMERICA (S)

SISTERS OF MERCY OF THE UNION IN THE U.S.A. (R.S.M.)

MORAVIAN CHURCH IN AMERICA, INC.

POPULATION COUNCIL (S)

SALVATION ARMY

SEVENTH-DAY ADVENTIST WORLD SERVICE, INC. (S)

TRICKLE UP PROGRAM (S)

WESLEYAN CHURCH

YOUNG WOMEN'S CHRISTIAN ASSOCIATION OF THE U.S.A.

## HAITI

A.T. INTERNATIONAL (S)

AMERICAN BAPTIST CHURCHES IN THE USA

AMERICAN LUNG ASSOCIATION (S)

AMERICAN WOMEN'S HOSPITALS SERVICE

AMG INTERNATIONAL

ASSOCIATION FOR VOLUNTARY STERILIZATION, INC. (S)

BAPTIST WORLD AID (S)

BROTHER'S BROTHER FOUNDATION (S)

CARE

CATHOLIC MEDICAL MISSION BOARD, INC. (S)

CATHOLIC RELIEF SERVICES -- UNITED STATES CATHOLIC CONFERENCE

CENTER FOR HUMAN SERVICES (S)

CENTRE FOR DEVELOPMENT AND POPULATION ACTIVITIES (S)

CHRISTIAN REFORMED WORLD RELIEF COMMITTEE

CHURCH OF BIBLE UNDERSTANDING

CHURCH OF GOD (HOLINESS)

CHURCH OF THE BRETHREN GENERAL BOARD (S)

CHURCH OF THE NAZARENE

CHURCH WORLD SERVICE

CHURCHES OF GOD, GENERAL CONFERENCE

COMPASSION INTERNATIONAL, INC.
COMPASSION RELIEF AND DEVELOPMENT (S)

COOPERATIVE LEAGUE OF THE USA.

COUNCIL OF INTERNATIONAL PROGRAMS FOR YOUTH LEADERS AND SOCIAL WORKERS, INC. (S)

CSI MINISTRIES, INC.

GEORGE DETELLIS EVANGELISTIC ASSOCIATION, INC.

DIRECT RELIEF INTERNATIONAL (S)

DOCARE INTERNATIONAL, INC.

EDUCATION DEVELOPMENT CENTER (S)

EPISCOPAL CHURCH IN THE U.S.A.

EYE CARE, INC.

FAMILY HEALTH INTERNATIONAL (S)

FARMS INTERNATIONAL, INC.

FOSTER PARENTS PLAN
FREE METHODIST CHURCH OF NORTH AMERICA

FRIENDS OF CHILDREN, INC.

FRIENDS OF SOS CHILDREN'S VILLAGES, INC. (S)

FRIENDS OF THE THIRD WORLD, INC. (S)

GLOBAL OUTREACH

HABITAT FOR HUMANITY, INC.

HEIFER PROJECT INTERNATIONAL, INC. (S)

HELEN KELLER INTERNATIONAL, INC.

INSA

INTERCHURCH MEDICAL ASSISTANCE, INC. (S)

INTERMEDIA

INTERNATIONAL BOOK PROJECT, INC. (S)

INTERNATIONAL CHILD CARE (USA), INC.

INTERNATIONAL EXECUTIVE SERVICE CORPS (S)

INTERNATIONAL LIAISON, INC. (S)

INTERNATIONAL LIFELINE, INC.

LIONS CLUBS INTERNATIONAL (S)

LA LECHE LEAGUE INTERNATIONAL

DAVID LIVINGSTONE MISSIONARY FOUNDATION, INC. (S)

MANAGEMENT SCIENCES FOR HEALTH

MAP INTERNATIONAL (S)

MEDICAL BENEVOLENCE FOUNDATION (S)

MEDICAL RELIEF OF HAITI, INC. (S)

MENNONITE CENTRAL COMMITTEE

MENNONITE ECONOMIC DEVELOPMENT ASSOCIATES, INC.

MIDWEST MEDICAL MISSION, INC. (S)

MISSIONARY CHURCH, INC.

MISSIONS HEALTH FOUNDATION, INC.

MONTFORT MISSIONARIES (S.M.M.)

NATIONAL COUNCIL OF CATHOLIC WOMEN (S)

OBLATES OF MARY IMMACULATE (O.M.I.) Province of St. John the Baptist

OMS INTERNATIONAL, INC.

OPERATION CROSSROADS AFRICA, INC. (S)

OUTREACH INTERNATIONAL (S)

PAN AMERICAN DEVELOPMENT FOUNDATION

PARTNERS OF THE AMERICAS

PARTNERSHIP FOR PRODUCTIVITY
INTERNATIONAL, INC.

PATHFINDER FUND (S)

PRIVATE AGENCIES COLLABORATING
TOGETHER (PACT) (S)

PUBLIC WELFARE FOUNDATION (S)

REORGANIZED CHURCH OF JESUS CHRIST
OF LATTER DAY SAINTS

RHEMA INTERNATIONAL, INC.

ROTARY INTERNATIONAL

SALESIAN SOCIETY, INC.

SALVATION ARMY

SAVE THE CHILDREN FEDERATION, INC.

SEVENTH-DAY ADVENTIST WORLD SERVICE,
INC. (S)

SISTER CITIES INTERNATIONAL (S)

TRICKLE UP PROGRAM (S)

UFM INTERNATIONAL, INC.

UNITARIAN UNIVERSALIST SERVICE
COMMITTEE (S)

UNITED METHODIST COMMITTEE ON
RELIEF (S)

VOLUNTEER OPTOMETRIC SERVICES TO
HUMANITY (VOSH INTERNATIONAL) (S)

VOLUNTEERS IN TECHNICAL ASSISTANCE,
INC. (VITA)

WESLEYAN CHURCH

WINROCK INTERNATIONAL

WORLD CONCERN

WORLD GOSPEL MISSION

WORLD MEDICAL RELIEF, INC. (S)

WORLD NEIGHBORS, INC.

WORLD RELIEF CORPORATION

WORLD VISION RELIEF ORGANIZATION,
INC.

## HONDURAS

ACADEMY FOR EDUCATIONAL
DEVELOPMENT

AFL-CIO - American Institute for
Free Labor Development

AFS INTERNATIONAL/INTERCULTURAL
PROGRAMS (S)

AGRICULTURAL COOPERATIVE
DEVELOPMENT INTERNATIONAL

AGUA DEL PUEBLO (S)
AID TO ARTISANS, INC. (S)

AMERICAN DENTISTS FOR FOREIGN
SERVICE (S)

AMERICAN FRIENDS SERVICE COMMITTEE
(see regional listing)

AMERICAN LUNG ASSOCIATION (S)

AMERICAN PUBLIC HEALTH
ASSOCIATION (S)

AMERICAS--HAND IN HAND

AMIGOS DE LAS AMERICAS (S)

ASSOCIATION FOR VOLUNTARY
STERILIZATION, INC. (S)

BAPTIST MISSIONARY ASSOCIATION OF
AMERICA

BROTHER'S BROTHER FOUNDATION
(S)

LA BUENA FE ASSOCIATION

CAM INTERNATIONAL

CARE

CARR FOUNDATION  (S)

CATHOLIC MEDICAL MISSION BOARD,
   INC.  (S)

CATHOLIC RELIEF SERVICES -- UNITED
   STATES CATHOLIC CONFERENCE

CENTER FOR HUMAN SERVICES  (S)

CENTRE FOR DEVELOPMENT AND
   POPULATION ACTIVITIES  (S)

CHILDREN, INCORPORATED  (S)

CHRISTIAN CHILDREN'S FUND, INC.

CHRISTIAN FOUNDATION FOR CHILDREN

CHRISTIAN REFORMED WORLD RELIEF
   COMMITTEE

CHURCH OF THE BRETHREN GENERAL
   BOARD  (S)

CHURCH WORLD SERVICE

CLARETIAN FATHERS (C.M.F.) (S)

COMPASSION INTERNATIONAL, INC.
COMPASSION RELIEF AND DEVELOPMENT
   (S)

CONCERN America

CONSERVATIVE BAPTIST FOREIGN
   MISSION SOCIETY

CONVENTUAL FRANCISCANS
   (O.F.M. Conv.)

COOPERATIVE HOUSING FOUNDATION

COOPERATIVE LEAGUE OF
   THE USA  (S)

COORDINATION IN DEVELOPMENT, INC.
   (CODEL)  (S)

DARIEN BOOK AID PLAN, INC.  (S)

DIRECT RELIEF INTERNATIONAL  (S)

EASTERN MENNONITE BOARD OF
   MISSIONS AND CHARITIES

EDUCATION DEVELOPMENT CENTER
   (S)

EPISCOPAL CHURCH IN THE U.S.A.

FAMILY HEALTH
INTERNATIONAL  (S)

FORD FOUNDATION  (S)

FOSTER PARENTS PLAN

SCHOOL SISTERS OF ST. FRANCIS
   (O.S.F.)

SISTERS OF ST. FRANCIS OF THE
   PERPETUAL ADORATION (O.S.F.),
   Province of the Immaculate Heart
   of Mary

FRANCISCAN FRIARS (O.F.M.),
   Province of the Immaculate
   Conception

FRANCISCAN FRIARS (O.F.M.)

FRIENDS OF CHILDREN, INC.

FRIENDS OF SOS CHILDREN'S
VILLAGES, INC.  (S)

GLOBAL OUTREACH

HEIFER PROJECT INTERNATIONAL,
   INC.  (S)

HELP THE AGED  (S)

HERMANDAD, INC.

HOLY LAND CHRISTIAN MISSION
   INTERNATIONAL

INSTITUTE FOR INTERNATIONAL
   DEVELOPMENT, INC.

INTER-AID, INC.  (S)

INTERCHURCH MEDICAL ASSISTANCE,
INC. (S)

INTERNATIONAL AGRICULTURAL
DEVELOPMENT SERVICE (S)

INTERNATIONAL EXECUTIVE SERVICE
CORPS (S)

INTERNATIONAL EYE FOUNDATION

INTERNATIONAL PROJECTS ASSISTANCE
SERVICES (S)

INTERNATIONAL VOLUNTARY SERVICES,
INC.

INTERPLAST, INC. (S)

LA LECHE LEAGUE INTERNATIONAL

LIONS CLUBS INTERNATIONAL (S)

LUTHERAN WORLD RELIEF, INC.

MANAGEMENT SCIENCES FOR HEALTH
MAP INTERNATIONAL (S)

MARYKNOLL FATHERS AND BROTHERS
(M.M.)

MEALS FOR MILLIONS/FREEDOM FROM
HUNGER FOUNDATION

MENNONITE CENTRAL COMMITTEE

SISTERS OF MERCY OF THE UNION IN THE
U.S.A. (R.S.M.)

MISSION AVIATION FELLOWSHIP

MORAVIAN CHURCH IN AMERICA, INC.

NATIONAL COUNCIL OF CATHOLIC
WOMEN (S)

NATIONAL SAVINGS AND LOAN
LEAGUE (S)

SCHOOL SISTERS OF NOTRE DAME
(S.S.N.D.), Southern Province

OPERATION CALIFORNIA, INC. (S)

ORTHOPAEDICS OVERSEAS, INC. (S)

OUTREACH INTERNATIONAL (S)

OVERSEAS EDUCATION FUND

OXFAM AMERICA (S)

PAN AMERICAN DEVELOPMENT FOUNDATION

PARTNERS OF THE AMERICAS

PARTNERSHIP FOR PRODUCTIVITY
INTERNATIONAL, INC.

PATHFINDER FUND (S)

PEOPLE-TO-PEOPLE HEALTH
FOUNDATION, INC.

POPULATION COUNCIL (S)

PRIVATE AGENCIES COLLABORATING
TOGETHER, INC., (PACT) (S)

PUBLIC WELFARE FOUNDATION (S)

REORGANIZED CHURCH OF JESUS CHRIST
OF LATTER DAY SAINTS

ROTARY INTERNATIONAL

SALESIAN SOCIETY, INC.

SAVE THE CHILDREN FEDERATION, INC.

SEVENTH-DAY ADVENTIST WORLD SERVICE,
INC. (S)

SISTER CITIES INTERNATIONAL (S)

SUMMER INSTITUTE OF LINGUISTICS,
INC.

UNITARIAN UNIVERSALIST SERVICE
COMMITTEE(S)

UNITED CHURCH BOARD FOR WORLD
MINISTRIES (S)

UNITED METHODIST COMMITTEE ON
RELIEF (S)

VOLUNTEER OPTOMETRIC SERVICES TO
HUMANITY (VOSH INTERNATIONAL) (S)

VOLUNTEERS IN TECHNICAL ASSISTANCE,
INC. (VITA)

WINROCK INTERNATIONAL

WORLD CONCERN (S)

WORLD GOSPEL MISSION

WORLD NEIGHBORS, INC.

WORLD OPPORTUNITIES
INTERNATIONAL (S)

WORLD RELIEF CORPORATION

WORLD VISION RELIEF
ORGANIZATION, INC.

## JAMAICA

A.T. INTERNATIONAL (S)

AFS INTERNATIONAL/INTERCULTURAL
PROGRAMS (S)

AGRICULTURAL COOPERATIVE DEVELOPMENT
INTERNATIONAL

AMERICAN PUBLIC HEALTH ASSOCIATION

ASSOCIATION FOR VOLUNTARY
STERILIZATION, INC. (S)

BROTHER'S BROTHER FOUNDATION (S)

CATHOLIC MEDICAL MISSION BOARD,
INC. (S)

CATHOLIC RELIEF SERVICES -- UNITED
STATES CATHOLIC CONFERENCE

CENTER FOR HUMAN SERVICES

CENTRE FOR DEVELOPMENT AND
POPULATION ACTIVITIES (S)

BROTHERS OF THE CHRISTIAN SCHOOLS
(F.S.C.)

CHURCH OF GOD (HOLINESS)

COMPASSION INTERNATIONAL, INC.
COMPASSION RELIEF AND DEVELOPMENT
(S)

COOPERATIVE HOUSING FOUNDATION

COOPERATIVE LEAGUE OF THE USA

COORDINATION IN DEVELOPMENT, INC.
(CODEL) (S)

COUNCIL OF INTERNATIONAL PROGRAMS
FOR YOUTH LEADERS AND SOCIAL
WORKERS, INC. (S)

CSI MINISTRIES, INC.

DARIEN BOOK AID PLAN, INC. (S)

DIRECT RELIEF INTERNATIONAL (S)

DOMINICAN SISTERS (O.P.),
Congregation of St. Dominic

EDUCATION DEVELOPMENT CENTER (S)

EISENHOWER EXCHANGE FELLOWSHIPS,
INC. (S)

FAMILY PLANNING INTERNATIONAL
ASSISTANCE (S)

FORD FOUNDATION (S)

FRANCISCAN SISTERS OF ALLEGANY, N.Y.
(O.S.F.)

FRIENDS OF SOS CHILDREN'S VILLAGES,
INC. (S)

FRIENDS UNITED MEETING

GOODWILL INDUSTRIES OF AMERICA, INC.

INSTITUTE OF CULTURAL AFFAIRS

INTERCHURCH MEDICAL ASSISTANCE,
INC. (S)

INTERNATIONAL AGRICULTURAL
DEVELOPMENT SERVICE (S)

INTERNATIONAL BOOK PROJECT,
INC. (S)

INTERNATIONAL COMMUNITY FOR THE
RELIEF OF STARVATION AND SUFFERING
(ICROSS)

INTERNATIONAL EXECUTIVE SERVICE
CORPS (S)

INTERNATIONAL LIAISON, INC. (S)

INTERNATIONAL ROAD FEDERATION (S)

INTERPLAST, INC. (S)

JESUIT FATHERS AND BROTHERS (S.J.)

W. K. KELLOGG FOUNDATION (S)

LIONS CLUBS INTERNATIONAL (S)

LUTHERAN CHURCH-MISSOURI
SYNOD (S)

MANAGEMENT SCIENCES FOR HEALTH (S)

MAP INTERNATIONAL (S)

MARIST MISSIONARY SISTERS
(MISSIONARY SISTERS OF THE SOCIETY
OF MARY) (S.M.S.M.)

MENNONITE CENTRAL COMMITTEE

MENNONITE ECONOMIC DEVELOPMENT
ASSOCIATES, INC.

SISTERS OF MERCY OF THE UNION IN THE
U.S.A. (R.S.M.)

NATIONAL 4-H COUNCIL (S)

NATIONAL SAVINGS AND LOAN
LEAGUE (S)

OPERATION CROSSROADS AFRICA,
INC. (S)

PAN AMERICAN DEVELOPMENT FOUNDATION

PARTNERS OF THE AMERICAS

PARTNERSHIP FOR PRODUCTIVITY
INTERNATIONAL, INC.

PATHFINDER FUND (S)

PEOPLE-TO-PEOPLE HEALTH FOUNDATION,
INC., Project HOPE

PLENTY

POPULATION COUNCIL (S)

PUBLIC WELFARE FOUNDATION (S)

ROTARY INTERNATIONAL

SALVATION ARMY

MARGARET SANGER CENTER (S)

SISTER CITIES INTERNATIONAL (S)

SURGICAL EYE EXPEDITIONS
INTERNATIONAL (S)

TRICKLE UP PROGRAM (S)

UNITED METHODIST COMMITTEE ON
RELIEF (S)

UNITED STATES YOUTH COUNCIL (S)

VOLUNTEER OPTOMETRIC SERVICES TO
HUMANITY (VOSH INTERNATIONAL) (S)

VOLUNTEERS IN TECHNICAL ASSISTANCE,
INC. (VITA) (S)

WINROCK INTERNATIONAL

YOUNG WOMEN'S CHRISTIAN ASSOCIATION
OF THE U.S.A.


## MARTINIQUE

COUNCIL OF INTERNATIONAL PROGRAMS
FOR YOUTH LEADERS AND SOCIAL
WORKERS, INC. (S)

DARIEN BOOK AID PLAN, INC. (S)

LIONS CLUBS INTERNATIONAL (S)

TRICKLE UP PROGRAM (S)


## MEXICO

ACCION INTERNATIONAL/AITEC

AFL-CIO - American Institute for
Free Labor Development (S)

AFS INTERNATIONAL/INTERCULTURAL
PROGRAMS (S)

AMERICAN BAPTIST CHURCHES IN THE USA

AMERICAN DENTISTS FOR FOREIGN
SERVICE (S)

AMERICAN FRIENDS SERVICE COMMITTEE

AMERICAN LUNG ASSOCIATION (S)

AMERICAN/MEXICAN MEDICAL
FOUNDATION, INC.

AMERICAN ORT FEDERATION

AMIGOS DE LAS AMERICAS (S)

APROVECHO INSTITUTE (S)

ASSOCIATE REFORMED PRESBYTERIAN
CHURCH

ASSOCIATION FOR VOLUNTARY
STERILIZATION, INC. (S)

BAPTIST MISSIONARY ASSOCIATION OF
AMERICA

BENEDICTINE MONKS (O.S.B.),
St. Benedict's Abbey

BETHANY FELLOWSHIP, INC.

LA BUENA FE ASSOCIATION

CARR FOUNDATION (S)

CATHOLIC MEDICAL MISSION BOARD,
INC. (S)

CATHOLIC RELIEF SERVICES -- UNITED
STATES CATHOLIC CONFERENCE

CENTER FOR HUMAN SERVICES (S)

CENTRE FOR DEVELOPMENT AND
POPULATION ACTIVITIES (S)

CHILDREN, INCORPORATED (S)

CHRISTIAN CHILDREN'S FUND, INC.

CHRISTIAN CHURCH (DISCIPLES OF
CHRIST), INC.

CHRISTIAN FOUNDATION FOR CHILDREN

CHRISTIAN NATIONALS' EVANGELISM
COMMISSION, INC.

CHRISTIAN REFORMED WORLD RELIEF
COMMITTEE

CLARETIAN FATHERS (C.M.F.)

COMBONI MISSIONARIES OF THE HEART OF
JESUS (M.C.C.J.)

COMBONI MISSIONARY SISTERS (C.M.S.)

COMPASSION INTERNATIONAL, INC.
COMPASSION RELIEF AND DEVELOPMENT
(S)

CONCERN America

COORDINATION IN DEVELOPMENT, INC.
(CODEL) (S)

COUNCIL OF INTERNATIONAL PROGRAMS
FOR YOUTH LEADERS AND SOCIAL
WORKERS, INC. (S)

DIRECT RELIEF INTERNATIONAL (S)

DOCARE INTERNATIONAL, INC.

DOMINICAN FATHERS (O.P.), ORDER OF
PREACHERS

EPISCOPAL CHURCH IN THE U.S.A.

ERIE DIOCESAN MISSION OFFICE

FAMILY HEALTH INTERNATIONAL  (S)

FAMILY PLANNING INTERNATIONAL
  ASSISTANCE  (S)

FARM CENTERS INTERNATIONAL

FORD FOUNDATION  (S)

FOUNDATION FOR HIS MINISTRY  (S)

FRANCISCAN FRIARS (O.F.M.)
  Province of Santa Barbara

FREE METHODIST CHURCH OF NORTH
  AMERICA

FRIENDS OF SOS CHILDREN'S VILLAGES,
  INC. (S)

FRIENDS OF THE THIRD WORLD,
  INC. (S)

GENERAL CONFERENCE MENNONITE CHURCH

HEIFER PROJECT INTERNATIONAL,
  INC. (S)

HESPERIAN FOUNDATION

HOGAR INFANTIL (ILLINOIS), INC.

INSTITUTE OF INTERNATIONAL EDUCATION

INTERMEDIA

INTERNATIONAL BOOK PROJECT,
  INC. (S)

INTERNATIONAL EXECUTIVE SERVICE
  CORPS (S)

INTERNATIONAL PROJECTS ASSISTANCE
  SERVICES (S)

INTERNATIONAL ROAD FEDERATION  (S)

INTERPLAST, INC.  (S)

SISTERS OF ST. JOSEPH (C.S.J.)
  Salina Diocese

ST. JUDE EXPRESS, INC.

W. K. KELLOGG FOUNDATION  (S)

LAUBACH LITERACY INTERNATIONAL

LA LECHE LEAGUE INTERNATIONAL

LIONS CLUBS INTERNATIONAL  (S)

DAVID LIVINGSTONE MISSIONARY
  FOUNDATION, INC.  (S)

MANAGEMENT SCIENCES FOR HEALTH  (S)

MAP INTERNATIONAL  (S)

SOCIETY OF MARY (S.M.)
  Province of St. Louis

MARYKNOLL FATHERS AND BROTHERS
  (M.M.)

MARYKNOLL SISTERS OF ST. DOMINIC
  (M.M.)

MEDICAL BENEVOLENCE FOUNDATION  (S)

MEXICAN MEDICAL INCORPORATED

MISSION AVIATION FELLOWSHIP

NATURE CONSERVANCY  (S)

LOS NINOS

OUTREACH INTERNATIONAL  (S)

PAN AMERICAN DEVELOPMENT
  FOUNDATION  (S)

PARTNERS OF THE AMERICAS

PATHFINDER FUND  (S)

PLENTY

POPULATION COUNCIL  (S)

POPULATION CRISIS COMMITTEE/DRAPER
  FUND  (S)

POPULATION INSTITUTE (S)

PRIVATE AGENCIES COLLABORATING TOGETHER, INC. (PACT) (S)

PROGRAM FOR APPROPRIATE TECHNOLOGY IN HEALTH (PATH) (S)

PROGRAM FOR THE INTRODUCTION AND ADAPTATION OF CONTRACEPTIVE TECHNOLOGY (PIACT)

PROJECT CONCERN INTERNATIONAL

PROMISE, INC.

ROCKEFELLER FOUNDATION (S)

ROTARY INTERNATIONAL

SALESIAN SOCIETY, INC.

SALVATION ARMY

SAVE THE CHILDREN FEDERATION, INC.

SELF HELP FOUNDATION

SEVENTH-DAY ADVENTIST WORLD SERVICE, INC. (S)

SISTER CITIES INTERNATIONAL (S)

SISTERS OF SOCIAL SERVICE OF LOS ANGELES, INC. (S.S.S.)

SUMMER INSTITUTE OF LINGUISTICS, INC.

SURGICAL EYE EXPEDITIONS INTERNATIONAL (S)

UNITED CHURCH BOARD FOR WORLD MINISTRIES (S)

UNITED METHODIST CHURCH (S)

UNITED METHODIST COMMITTEE ON RELIEF (S)

VOLUNTEER OPTOMETRIC SERVICES TO HUMANITY (VOSH INTERNATIONAL) (S)

VOLUNTEERS IN TECHNICAL ASSISTANCE, INC. (VITA) (S)

WORLD CONCERN

WORLD MEDICAL RELIEF, INC. (S)

WORLD NEIGHBORS, INC.

WORLD VISION RELIEF ORGANIZATION, INC.

XAVERIAN MISSIONARY FATHERS (S.X.)

YOUNG MEN'S CHRISTIAN ASSOCIATIONS OF THE UNITED STATES

YOUNG WOMEN'S CHRISTIAN ASSOCIATION OF THE U.S.A.

## MONTSERRAT

AMERICAN DENTISTS FOR FOREIGN SERVICE (S)

DARIEN BOOK AID PLAN, INC. (S)

DIRECT RELIEF INTERNATIONAL (S)

INTERNATIONAL BOOK PROJECT, INC. (S)

INTERNATIONAL EYE FOUNDATION

OPERATION CROSSROADS AFRICA, INC. (S)

PARTNERS OF THE AMERICAS

PATHFINDER FUND (S)

TRICKLE UP PROGRAM (S)

VOLUNTEERS IN TECHNICAL ASSISTANCE, INC. (VITA)

## NETHERLANDS ANTILLES

COUNCIL OF INTERNATIONAL PROGRAMS FOR YOUTH LEADERS AND SOCIAL WORKERS, INC. (S)

DARIEN BOOK AID PLAN, INC.  (S)

LIONS CLUBS INTERNATIONAL  (S)

NATURE CONSERVANCY  (S)

OPERATION CROSSROADS AFRICA,
  INC.  (S)

SALESIAN SOCIETY, INC.


## NICARAGUA

A.T. INTERNATIONAL  (S)

SISTERS OF THE CONGREGATION OF ST.
  AGNES (C.S.A.)

AID TO ARTISANS, INC.  (S)

AMERICAN BAPTIST CHURCHES IN THE USA

AMERICAN LUNG ASSOCIATION  (S)

AMG INTERNATIONAL

ASSOCIATION FOR VOLUNTARY
  STERILIZATION, INC.  (S)

BAPTIST WORLD AID  (S)

BRETHREN IN CHRIST MISSIONS

BROTHER'S BROTHER FOUNDATION  (S)

CARE

CATHOLIC RELIEF SERVICES -- UNITED
  STATES CATHOLIC CONFERENCE

CHILDREN, INCORPORATED  (S)

CHRISTIAN REFORMED WORLD RELIEF
  COMMITTEE

CHURCH WORLD SERVICE

COMPASSION INTERNATIONAL, INC.
COMPASSION RELIEF AND DEVELOPMENT
  (S)

COORDINATION IN DEVELOPMENT, INC.
  (CODEL)  (S)

DARIEN BOOK AID PLAN, INC.  (S)

DIRECT RELIEF INTERNATIONAL  (S)

EPISCOPAL CHURCH IN THE U.S.A.

FORD FOUNDATION  (S)

FOSTER PARENTS PLAN

FRIENDS OF SOS CHILDREN'S VILLAGES,
  INC.  (S)

HELP THE AGED  (S)

INTERCHURCH MEDICAL ASSISTANCE,
  INC.  (S)

INTERNATIONAL EXECUTIVE SERVICE
  CORPS  (S)

LIONS CLUBS INTERNATIONAL  (S)

LUTHERAN WORLD RELIEF, INC.

MARYKNOLL FATHERS AND BROTHERS
  (M.M.)

MEDICAL MISSION SISTERS (S.C.M.M.)

MENNONITE CENTRAL COMMITTEE

MONTFORT MISSIONARIES (S.M.M.)

NATIONAL BAPTIST CONVENTION, U.S.A.,
  INC.

OPERATION CALIFORNIA, INC.  (S)

OXFAM AMERICA  (S)

PAN AMERICAN DEVELOPMENT
  FOUNDATION  (S)

PARTNERS OF THE AMERICAS

PATHFINDER FUND  (S)

SOCIETY OF THE SACRED HEART
  (R.S.C.J.)

SALESIAN SOCIETY, INC.

SAVE THE CHILDREN FEDERATION, INC.

SEVENTH-DAY ADVENTIST WORLD
  SERVICE, INC. (S)

SISTER CITIES INTERNATIONAL (S)

TECHNOSERVE, INC.

TRICKLE UP PROGRAM (S)

UNITARIAN UNIVERSALIST SERVICE
  COMMITTEE (S)

UNITED CHURCH BOARD FOR WORLD
  MINISTRIES (S)

UNITED METHODIST COMMITTEE ON
  RELIEF (S)

VOLUNTEER OPTOMETRIC SERVICES TO
  HUMANITY (VOSH INTERNATIONAL) (S)

VOLUNTEERS IN TECHNICAL ASSISTANCE,
  INC. (VITA) (S)

WORLD NEIGHBORS, INC.

WORLD VISION RELIEF ORGANIZATION,
  INC.


## PANAMA

AFL-CIO - American Institute for
  Free Labor Development (S)

AFS INTERNATIONAL/INTERCULTURAL
  PROGRAMS (S)

AMERICAN LUNG ASSOCIATION (S)

AMERICAN PUBLIC HEALTH ASSOCIATION

AMIGOS DE LAS AMERICAS (S)

ASSOCIATION FOR VOLUNTARY
  STERILIZATION, INC. (S)

ASSOCIATION INTERNATIONALE DES
  ETUDIANTS EN SCIENCES ECONOMIQUES
  ET COMMERCIALES (AIESEC-UNITED
  STATES) (S)

CARE

CARR FOUNDATION (S)

CATHOLIC MEDICAL MISSION BOARD,
  INC. (S)

CATHOLIC RELIEF SERVICES -- UNITED
  STATES CATHOLIC CONFERENCE

CENTRE FOR DEVELOPMENT AND
  POPULATION ACTIVITIES (S)

CHURCH OF GOD, INC. (ANDERSON,
  INDIANA)

CLARETIAN FATHERS (C.M.F.)

COOPERATIVE LEAGUE OF THE USA

COUNCIL OF INTERNATIONAL PROGRAMS
  FOR YOUTH LEADERS AND SOCIAL
  WORKERS, INC. (S)

DARIEN BOOK AID PLAN, INC. (S)

EDUCATION DEVELOPMENT CENTER (S)

EPISCOPAL CHURCH IN THE U.S.A.

FAMILY HEALTH INTERNATIONAL (S)

FAMILY PLANNING INTERNATIONAL
  ASSISTANCE (S)

FRIENDS OF SOS CHILDREN'S VILLAGES,
  INC. (S)

GOODWILL INDUSTRIES OF AMERICA, INC.

GOSPEL MISSIONARY UNION

HEIFER PROJECT INTERNATIONAL,
  INC. (S)

INTERCHURCH MEDICAL ASSISTANCE,
  INC. (S)

INTERNATIONAL CENTER FOR RESEARCH ON
   WOMEN  (S)

INTERNATIONAL EXECUTIVE SERVICE
   CORPS  (S)

W. K. KELLOGG FOUNDATION  (S)

LAUBACH LITERACY INTERNATIONAL

LA LECHE LEAGUE INTERNATIONAL

LIONS CLUBS INTERNATIONAL  (S)

MAP INTERNATIONAL

MARYKNOLL SISTERS OF ST. DOMINIC
   (M.M.)

MENNONITE BRETHREN MISSIONS/SERVICES

NATIONAL COUNCIL OF CATHOLIC
   WOMEN  (S)

NATIONAL SAVINGS AND LOAN
   LEAGUE  (S)

NATURE CONSERVANCY  (S)

OVERSEAS EDUCATION FUND

PAN AMERICAN DEVELOPMENT
   FOUNDATION  (S)

PARTNERS OF THE AMERICAS

PATHFINDER FUND  (S)

PRIVATE AGENCIES COLLABORATING
   TOGETHER, INC. (PACT)  (S)

SALESIAN SOCIETY, INC.

SALVATION ARMY

TECHNOSERVE, INC.

TRICKLE UP PROGRAM  (S)

UNITED METHODIST CHURCH

UNITED METHODIST COMMITTEE ON
   RELIEF  (S)

VOLUNTEER DEVELOPMENT CORPS  (S)

VOLUNTEER OPTOMETRIC SERVICES TO
   HUMANITY (VOSH INTERNATIONAL)  (S)

VOLUNTEERS IN TECHNICAL ASSISTANCE,
   INC. (VITA)

WORLD CONCERN  (S)

WORLD RADIO MISSIONARY
   FELLOWSHIP, INC.

WORLD VISION RELIEF
   ORGANIZATION, INC.


## ST KITTS - NEVIS


DARIEN BOOK AID PLAN, INC.  (S)

FREEDOM HOUSE, INC.  (S)

HIGH/SCOPE EDUCATIONAL RESEARCH
   FOUNDATION

MANAGEMENT SCIENCES FOR HEALTH  (S)

MENNONITE ECONOMIC DEVELOPMENT
   ASSOCIATES, INC.

MORAVIAN CHURCH IN AMERICA,
   INC.  (S)

NATIONAL 4-H COUNCIL  (S)

OPERATION CROSSROADS AFRICA,
   INC.  (S)

PAN AMERICAN DEVELOPMENT
   FOUNDATION  (S)

PARTNERS OF THE AMERICAS

PATHFINDER FUND  (S)

SALVATION ARMY

TRICKLE UP PROGRAM  (S)

UNITARIAN UNIVERSALIST SERVICE
   COMMITTEE  (S)

## ST. LUCIA

AID FOR INTERNATIONAL MEDICINE,
INC. (S)

BROTHER'S BROTHER FOUNDATION (S)

CARIBBEANA COUNCIL
(see regional listing)

CARR FOUNDATION (S)

COUNCIL OF INTERNATIONAL PROGRAMS
FOR YOUTH LEADERS AND SOCIAL
WORKERS, INC. (S)

DARIEN BOOK AID PLAN, INC. (S)

DIRECT RELIEF INTERNATIONAL (S)

INTERNATIONAL EXECUTIVE SERVICE
CORPS (S)

INTERNATIONAL EYE FOUNDATION

W. K. KELLOGG FOUNDATION (S)

LIONS CLUBS INTERNATIONAL (S)

MANAGEMENT SCIENCES FOR HEALTH

NATIONAL 4-H COUNCIL (S)

NATIONAL OFFICE FOR SOCIAL
RESPONSIBILITY IN THE PRIVATE
SECTOR, INC.

OPERATION CROSSROADS AFRICA,
INC. (S)

PAN AMERICAN DEVELOPMENT FOUNDATION

PARTNERS OF THE AMERICAS

PEOPLE-TO-PEOPLE HEALTH
FOUNDATION, INC.

PLENTY

POPULATION COUNCIL (S)

SEVENTH-DAY ADVENTIST WORLD SERVICE,
INC. (S)

SISTERS OF THE SORROWFUL MOTHER
(Third Order of St. Francis)
(S.S.M.)

TRICKLE UP PROGRAM (S)

VOLUNTEERS IN TECHNICAL ASSISTANCE,
INC. (VITA) (S)

WORLD EDUCATION, INC.

## ST. MARTIN

DARIEN BOOK AID PLAN, INC. (S)

## ST. VINCENT AND THE GRENADINES

BROTHER'S BROTHER FOUNDATION (S)

COUNCIL OF INTERNATIONAL PROGRAMS
FOR YOUTH LEADERS AND SOCIAL
WORKERS, INC. (S)

DARIEN BOOK AID PLAN, INC. (S)

FREEDOM HOUSE, INC. (S)

HEIFER PROJECT INTERNATIONAL,
INC. (S)

LIONS CLUBS INTERNATIONAL (S)

MANAGEMENT SCIENCES FOR HEALTH (S)

NATIONAL COUNCIL OF CATHOLIC
WOMEN (S)

NATIONAL 4-H COUNCIL (S)

OPERATION CROSSROADS AFRICA,
INC. (S)

OXFAM AMERICA (S)

PAN AMERICAN DEVELOPMENT
FOUNDATION (S)

PARTNERS OF THE AMERICAS

SALVATION ARMY

SISTER CITIES INTERNATIONAL  (S)

TRICKLE UP PROGRAM  (S)

VOLUNTEERS IN TECHNICAL ASSISTANCE, INC. (VITA)  (S)

WORLD EDUCATION, INC.


## SURINAME

COUNCIL OF INTERNATIONAL PROGRAMS FOR YOUTH LEADERS AND SOCIAL WORKERS, INC.  (S)

DARIEN BOOK AID PLAN, INC.  (S)

FRIENDS OF SOS CHILDREN'S VILLAGES, INC.  (S)

LIONS CLUBS INTERNATIONAL  (S)

DAVID LIVINGSTONE MISSIONARY FOUNDATION, INC.  (S)

MISSION AVIATION FELLOWSHIP

NATIONAL COUNCIL OF CATHOLIC WOMEN (S)

SALVATION ARMY

SUMMER INSTITUTE OF LINGUISTICS, INC.

TRICKLE UP PROGRAM  (S)

WESLEYAN CHURCH


## TRINIDAD AND TOBAGO

AMERICAN LUNG ASSOCIATION  (S)

AMERICAN PUBLIC HEALTH ASSOCIATION

CARR FOUNDATION  (S)

CENTRE FOR DEVELOPMENT AND POPULATION ACTIVITIES  (S)

COUNCIL OF INTERNATIONAL PROGRAMS FOR YOUTH LEADERS AND SOCIAL WORKERS, INC.  (S)

INTERNATIONAL EXECUTIVE SERVICE CORPS  (S)

INTERNATIONAL LIAISON, INC.  (S)

LIONS CLUBS INTERNATIONAL  (S)

MORAVIAN CHURCH IN AMERICA, INC.  (S)

NATIONAL 4-H COUNCIL  (S)

PARTNERS OF THE AMERICAS

PAN AMERICAN DEVELOPMENT FOUNDATION  (S)

PATHFINDER FUND  (S)

SALVATION ARMY

UNITED METHODIST COMMITTEE ON RELIEF  (S)

UNITED STATES YOUTH COUNCIL  (S)

VOLUNTEERS IN TECHNICAL ASSISTANCE, INC. (VITA)  (S)

WINROCK INTERNATIONAL


## TURKS AND CAICOS ISLANDS

DARIEN BOOK AID PLAN, INC.  (S)

FREEDOM HOUSE, INC.  (S)

LIONS CLUBS INTERNATIONAL  (S)

VOLUNTEERS IN TECHNICAL ASSISTANCE, INC. (VITA)  (S)

## REGIONAL

A.T. INTERNATIONAL (S)

AFL-CIO - American Institute for
Free Labor Development

AMERICAN FRIENDS SERVICE COMMITTEE

AMERICAN PUBLIC HEALTH
ASSOCIATION (S)

CARIBBEANA COUNCIL

CARNEGIE CORPORATION OF NEW YORK
(Caribbean) (S)

CATHOLIC RELIEF SERVICES - UNITED
STATES CATHOLIC CONFERENCE

CHURCH WORLD SERVICE

COORDINATION IN DEVELOPMENT, INC.
(CODEL) (S)

ENVIRONMENTAL RESEARCH PROJECTS
(Caribbean) (S)

FARALLONES INSTITUTE (S)

INTER-AMERICAN DEVELOPMENT
INSTITUTE (S)

INTERNATIONAL EYE FOUNDATION
(Caribbean)

ISLAND RESOURCES FOUNDATION (S)

LEAGUE FOR INTERNATIONAL FOOD
EDUCATION (S)

NATIONAL COUNCIL FOR INTERNATIONAL
HEALTH, INC. (S)

PATHFINDER FUND (S)

POPULATION REFERENCE BUREAU (S)

PRIVATE AGENCIES COLLABORATING
TOGETHER, INC. (PACT) (S)

UNITED METHODIST CHURCH (S)

UNITED METHODIST COMMITTEE ON
RELIEF (S)

WINROCK INTERNATIONAL

WORLD CONCERN (S)

WORLD MEDICAL RELIEF, INC. (S)

# PROGRAM ACTIVITY INDEX

## PROGRAM ACTIVITY INDEX

This index serves as a quick reference for identifying which agencies are involved in a given activity in individual countries. It contains terms (descriptors) which have been used to describe the program activities of organizations listed in Part II. Each organization is indexed by its code name and the country under which it appears (e.g. Winrock International in Haiti is listed as WINROCK/HTI). A complete alphabetical listing of organizations with their codes names is found in the organization index. A listing of country code names is found in the appendix.

The program activities of the support organizations (S) are indexed under the broad category headings (in boldface) and appear at the end of this index. A fuller description of their overall activities appears in Part I.

It should be noted that this index provides reference only to those activities which are specifically mentioned under programs of assistance and, therefore, is not inclusive of all areas of agency support or operation in this region.

Below is a listing by category of the terms found in this index.


### COMMUNICATIONS

mass media


### COMMUNITY DEVELOPMENT

animateurs
community centers
community programs
food-for-work
integrated rural development
leadership training
self-help programs


### CONSTRUCTION & HOUSING

bridges
construction
dams
housing
roads


### COOPERATIVES & CREDIT/LOANS

cooperatives
credit/loans


### ECONOMIC POLICY & PLANNING

economic research
policy and planning


### EDUCATION

accounting
adult education
audio visual materials
boarding schools
books
colleges/universities
conferences
courses
education
educational exchange
educational funding
elementary schools
high schools
job placement
language training
linguistic studies
literacy education
night schools
non-formal education
on-the-job training
preschool programs
schools
seminars
teacher training
teachers

teaching materials
translation programs
vocational education
women's education


## ENTERPRISE DEVELOPMENT & MANAGEMENT

cottage industries
crafts
management training
marketing
small enterprises


## FOOD PRODUCTION & AGRICULTURE

agribusiness
agricultural clubs
agricultural cooperatives
agricultural economics
agricultural experiment
  centers
agricultural extension
agricultural research
  institutes
agricultural supplies
agricultural training
agriculturists
animal feed
animal husbandry
animal power technology
animals
appropriate technology
beekeeping
biogas/methane
cash crops
crop improvement
crop processing
dairies
dairy animals
demonstration projects
draft animals
energy
environment
equipment
evaluation
extension agents
extension courses
farm machinery
fertilizers
fish
fish farming
food/food products
food preservation

fruits
fuels
gardens
goats
grains
hydroelectric energy
improved seed
integrated rural developmen
intensive farming
irrigation
land reclamation
land tenure
maintenance/repair
nurseries
orchards
pest control
poultry
rabbits
reforestation
research/field studies
seeds
solar energy
storage
surveys
swine
vegetables
veterinary services
water
wells
wind energy


## MATERIAL AID

blankets
clothing
equipment
PL 480
tools


## MEDICINE & PUBLIC HEALTH

blindness prevention
breastfeeding
clinics
dental clinics
dental equipment
dentistry
dentists
disease treatment
doctors
health care teams
hospitals
immunizations

leprosariums
medical auxiliaries
medical education
medical equipment
medical services
medical supplies
mental diseases
nurses
ophthalmology
potable water
preventive medicine
public health education
sanitation
toilet facilities
traditional medicine

## NUTRITION

breastfeeding
food distribution centers
food preparation
food supply programs
mother/child programs
nutrition education

## POPULATION &
## FAMILY SERVICES

birth control methods
breastfeeding
family planning

## PUBLIC ADMINISTRATION

institution building
legal services
public administration

## SOCIAL WELFARE

adoption services
aged
children
counseling
disabled
disaster relief
displaced persons
geriatric centers
hostels
orphanages

refugees
rehabilitation
resettlement
social services
social welfare
sponsorships

## GENERAL

conservation
consultants
funding
integrated rural development
research/field studies
self-help programs
surveys
transportation
tribal peoples
vehicles
volunteers
water transportation
women
youth

## accounting

AITEC/DOM; PMCUS/GTM, WN/GTM;
PFPI/JAM

## adoption services

FFSB/MEX; LWR/NIC

## adult education

GMU/BHS; CRS/CRI, CRWRC/CRI,
YMCA/CRI; SCF/DMA; AITEC/DOM,
FHI/DOM, SCF/DOM; CCF/GTM,
CRWRC/GTM, MKNOL FR/GTM, MKNOL
SR/GTM, WN/GTM, SIL/GTM; AFL-
CIO/HDA, CLARE/HDA, CONS BAPT/HDA,
CONF/HDA, CONV/HDA, CRWC/HDA,
SCF/HDA, WN/HDA; MEDIA/HTI, MCC/HTI,
MHF/HTI, OMI/HTI, WN/HTI;
WINROCK/JAM; MEDIA/MEX, CLARE/MEX,
DOM FR/MEX, GCMC/MEX, MKNOL FR/MEX,
WN/MEX, YMCA/MEX; LWR/NIC, WN/NIC;
AFL-CIO/REG

## aged

AGED/NIC

## agribusiness

ACDI/HDA

## agricultural clubs

MCC/HTI, CGGC/HTI

## agricultural cooperatives

EAST MEN/BLZ; AITEC/CRI, LWR/CRI;
CLARE/GTM, LWR/GTM, WN/GTM; FPP/HDA,
LWR/HDA; CRS/HTI, CUSA/HTI,
MEDA/HTI, OMI/HTI, WN/HTI, WRC/HTI;
PFPI/JAM; AFSC/MEX, CRS/MEX,
EPISCO/MEX, HESPER/MEX, SDW/MEX;
SCF/NIC; CLARE/PAN, CRS/PAN; OEF/SLV

## agricultural economics

CLARE/DOM; WINROCK/HDA

## agricultural experiment centers

WINROCK/CRI; SCF/DMA; SCF/DOM;
HERMAN/HDA; WINROCK/TTO

## agricultural extension

MCC/BLZ, ROTARY/BLZ; BENBC/GTM,
CRS/GTM, EPISCO/GTM, IIRR/GTM,
MCC/GTM, HOPE/GTM; MCC/HDA,
ROTARY/HDA; WVRO/MEX; MCC/HTI;
AGED/NIC, CARE/NIC; CG HOLT/JAM,
CRS/JAM, SALVA/JAM, SOJ/JAM;
WINROCK/TTO

## agricultural research institutes

WINROCK/CRI; WN/NIC; WINROCK/REG

## agricultural supplies

FPP/HTI

## agricultural training

MFM/ATG; SBC/BLZ; AITEC/CRI,
CARE/CRI, CRS/CRI, CRWRC/CRI,
LWR/CRI, WINROCK/CRI, WORLD CON/CRI;
CRWRC/DMA, SCF/DMA; CARE/DOM,
FHI/DOM, PARTNERS/DOM, REDEM FR/DOM,
SALESIAN FR/DOM, WVRO/DOM, SCF/DOM;
CLARE/GTM, COVENANT/GTM, FPP/GTM,
LWR/GTM, MCC/GTM; IRI/GUY;

AMERICAS/HDA, CARE/HDA, CRS/HDA,
GLOBAL/HDA, LWR/HDA, MFM/HDA,
FFHF/HDA, SCF/HDA, WGM/HDA, WN/HDA,
WRVO/HDA; CARE/HTI, CGH/HTI,
CGGC/HTI, MCC/HTI, MHF/HTI, OMI/HTI,
WINROCK/HTI, WORLD CON/HTI,
WVRO/HTI; RHEMA/HTI, CRS/JAM, SR
MERCY/JAM, PFPI/JAM; FCI/MEX, MKNOL
FR/MEX; AGNES/NIC, CRWRC/NIC,
CRS/NIC, CWS/NIC, SCF/NIC,
TECHNO/NIC; MBMS/PAN; WINROCK/REG;
CRS/SLV, EPISCO/SLV, SCF/SLV,
WVRO/SLV

## agriculturists

SCF/DOM; MORAV/HDA; ABC/HTI, MC/HTI

## air transportation

INTL EYE/BRB; INTL EYE/DMA; MAF/GTM;
INTL EYE/HDA, MAF/HDA; JUDE/MEX,
MAF/MEX; INTL EYE/MSR; INTL
EYE/REG; MAF/SUR

## animal feed

WINROCK/BLZ; AITEC/CRI, WINROCK/CRI;
WINROCK/REG; WINROCK/TTO

## animal husbandry

LWR/CRI, WORLD CON/CRI,
WINROCK/CRI; HOLY LAND/DOM, MHF/DOM,
SCF/DOM; CLARE/GTM, FPP/GTM, HOLY
LAND/GTM, LWR/GTM; AMERICAS/HDA,
FPP/HDA, LWR/HDA; CGGC/HTI, FPP/HTI,
FREE METH/HTI, OMI/HTI, MHF/HTI,
NAZ/HTI, MSH/HTI, WORLD CON/HTI,
WE/HTI, WVRO/HTI; CRS/JAM; AMFM/MEX,
BENBA/MEX, HESPER/MEX, SCF/MEX;
CLARE/PAN; CARIB/REG, WINROCK/REG;
FPP/SLV, TECHNO/SLV, WVRO/SLV;
WINROCK/TTO

## animal power technology

SCF/NIC

## animals

OFM IMMAC/GTM; GLOBAL/HTI; CARE/NIC

## animateurs

MKNOL FR/GTM; MKNOL FR/HDA,
WN/HDA; MCC/HTI, PPF/HTI, WORLD
CON/HTI, WN/HTI; PFPI/JAM; CRS/MEX,
MKNOL FR/MEX, WN/MEX; WN/NIC

## appropriate technology

SBC/BLZ, SBC/BLZ, MCC/BLZ,
ROTARY/BLZ, WINROCK/BLZ; SCF/DMA;
FHI/DOM, SCF/DOM; BENBC/GTM,
CRS/GTM, FHI/GTM, HOPE/GTM,
IIRR/GTM, MCC/GTM; AMERICAS/HDA,
DEF/HDA, MCC/HDA, OEF/HDA, PPF/HDA,
ROTARY/HDA, SCF/HDA; CRS/HTI,
MCC/HTI; CRS/JAM, SALVA/JAM,
SOJ/JAM; WVRO/MEX; VITA/MSR;
AGED/NIC, CARE/NIC; WINROCK/TTO

## audio visual materials

YMCA/CRI; MKNOL FR/GTM; WN/HDA;
WN/HTI; WINROCK/JAM; CAVE/MEX, MKNOL
FR/MEX, WN/MEX; VITA/MSR

## aviation

MAF/HDA; MAF/VCT

## beekeeping

MFM/ATG; CARE/BLZ; AITEC/CRI;
SCF/DOM; AMERICAS/HDA, LWR/HDA;

CARE/HTI, GLOBAL/HTI, SBC/HTI;
CRS/MEX, CLARE/MEX, FCI/MEX;
CARE/NIC

## biogas/methane

AITEC/CRI; SCF/DOM; AMERICAS/HDA,
PPF/HDA

## birth control methods

PCI/GTM, WN/GTM; AMERICAS/HDA,
WN/HDA; WN/HTI; MKNOL FR/MEX,
PIACT/MEX, PCI/MEX

## blankets

FFSB/MEX, MMI/MEX

## blindness prevention

INTL EYE/DOM; INTL EYE/HDA; INTL
EYE/HTI; SALVA/JAM; INTL EYE/LCA;
INTL EYE/MISR; INTL EYE/REG

## boarding schools

SALVA/HTI

## books

CFC/BLZ; CFC/DOM, INTL EYE/DOM;
CFC/GTM, PMCUS/GTM; CFC/HDA, FC/HDA,
INTL EYE/HDA, MORAV/HDA; MEDIA/HTI,
INSA/HTI; INTL EYE/LCA; FFSB/MEX;
AGNES/NIC; INTL EYE/REG

## breastfeeding

LECHE/BHS; LECHE/BRB; LECHE/CRI;
LECHE/CYM; SCF/DOM; LECHE/DMA;

LECHE/GTM; LECHE/HDA, CONCERN/HDA;
LECHE/HTI; CONCERN/MEX, LECHE/MEX,
SCF/MEX; LECHE/PAN; LECHE/SLV,
SCF/SLV

## bridges

FPP/GTM; FPP/HDA; FPP/SLV

## cash crops

AITEC/CRI; COVENANT/GTM, LWR/GTM;
MEDA/HTI, SBC/HTI, WN/HTI;
AMERICAS/HDA; PFPI/JAM; CLARE/PAN;
CARIB/REG, WINROCK/REG

## children

CFC/BLZ; CFC/DOM, CRS/DOM, SCF/DOM;
CAM/GTM, CFC/GTM, CLARE/GTM;
CFC/HDA, CCF/HDA, EASTERN MEN/HDA,
SCF/HDA, WGM/HDA; CWS/HTI, ICC/HTI,
KELLER/HTI, SBC/HTI, UFMI/HTI;
CRS/JAM; FFSB/MEX, SCF/MEX,
YMCA/MEX; LWR/NIC, SBC/NIC;
CLARE/PAN; SALVA/SUR

## clinics

MCC/BLZ; CRS/CRI; CRS/DOM, CFC/DOM,
CMS/DOM, EPISCO/DOM, SALESIAN
FR/DOM, SSJR/DOM; AMGI/GTM,
BENBC/GTM, CCF/GTM, CFC/GTM,
CLARE/GTM, CNEC/GTM, EPISCO/GTM,
MKNOL SR/GTM, PMCUS/GTM, PCI/GTM,
SALVA/GTM, SALESIAN FR/GTM;
WESLEY/GUY; AMERICAS/HDA, BAM/HDA,
LBF/HDA, CFC/HDA, EPISCO/HDA, OSF
PERP/HDA, MVP/HDA, MORAV/HDA, OSF
PERP/HDA, RCLDS/HDA, SSND/HDA;
ABC/HTI, CBV/HTI, DETELLIS/HTI,
CGGC/HTI, EPISCO/HTI, FPP/HTI,
FC/HTI, DETELLIS/HTI, ICC/HTI, INTL
EYE/HTI, LIFELINE/HTI, MC/HTI,
MHF/HTI, MRH/HTI, MSH/HTI, NAZ/HTI,

OMI/HTI, OMS/HTI, RHEMA/HTI,
WESLEY/HTI, WGM/HTI, WRC/HTI;
ICROS/JAM, MFMS/JAM, SR MERCY/JAM,
SALVA/JAM; PADF/LCA; AMFM/MEX,
BMA/MEX, CMHJ/MEX, EPISCO/MEX,
FFSB/MEX, HESPER/MEX, MKNOL FR/MEX,
PCI/MEX, SALESIAN FR/MEX, XAV/MEX;
ABC/NIC, EPISCO/NIC; ABC/SLV,
CRS/SLV, EPISCO/SLV, FPP/SLV,
MCC/SLV

## clothing

CRS/CRI; CFC/DOM, CRS/DOM, HOLY
LAND/DOM; CAM/GTM, CFC/GTM,
COVENANT/GTM, CRS/GTM; CRS/HDA,
CFC/HDA, CONF/HDA, CONV/HDA,
CWS/HDA, FC/HDA, MORAV/HDA, WRC/HDA;
AMGI/HTI; CRS/JAM; AMFM/MEX,
CRS/MEX, FFSB/MEX, SSJ/MEX, MMI/MEX;
AGNES/NIC; CRS/PAN; CAM/SLV,
CRS/SLV, WORLD CON/SLV

## colleges/universities

CNEC/GTM; SALESIAN FR/HDA; OSF
ALLEGA/JAM, MEDA/JAM, SOJ/JAM;
SALESIAN FR/MEX, XAV/MEX; SALESIAN
FR/NIC

## community centers

SALVA/ATG; SALVA/BER; SALVA/BHS;
SALVA/BRB; SALVA/BLZ; CARE/CRI,
EPISCO/CRI, LWR/CRI; SALVA/CUB;
SALVA/DMA, SCF/DMA; FHI/DOM,
SCF/DOM; ST PAT/GRD, SALVA/GRD;
FHI/GTM, HOLY LAND/GTM, SALVA/GTM;
FPP/HDA, HOLY LAND/HDA, MKNOL
FR/HDA, SCF/HDA; FPP/HTI; SALVA/KNA;
BENBA/MEX, CC/MEX, CCF/MEX, MKNOL
FR/MEX, SCF/MEX, SS/MEX, YMCA/MEX;
CWS/NIC; SALVA/PAN; AFL-CIO/REG;
FPP/SLV, SCF/SLV; SALVA/TTO;
SALVA/VCT

## community programs

EPISCO/CRI; COMPASSION/DOM; CRS/GTM,
FMV/GTM, HOLY LAND/GTM, ICA/GTM,
MKNOL FR/GTM, OFM IMMAC/GTM;
CCF/HDA, FF/HDA, OFM IMMAC/HDA;
COMPASSION/HTI, FPP/HTI, MC/HTI,
MHF/HTI, MSH/HTI, WORLD CON/HTI;
ROTARY/JAM; MSH/KNA; CC/MEX,
CRS/MEX, HESPER/MEX, MKNOL FR/MEX,
SSJ/MEX, MKNOL/MEX, YWCA/MEX;
AGNES/NIC, CRS/NIC, MKN/NIC;
FPP/SLV, FMU/SLV, OEF/SLV, OFM
IMMAC/SLV, SCF/SLV

## conferences

BEREAN/BRB; AITEC/DOM; LWR/GTM;
AITEC/MEX

## conservation

AITEC/CRI; AMERICAS/DMA; SCF/DOM;
MCC/GTM; IVA/HDA, WN/HDA; MCC/HTI,
MHF/HTI, WN/HTI; MKNOL FR/MEX

## construction

CHF/BLZ; CARE/CRI, LWR/CRI;
CARE/DOM, CHF/DOM, CRS/DOM, REDEM
FR/DOM; CHF/GTM, CLARE/GTM, CRS/GTM,
FPP/GTM, FMV/GTM, HFH/GTM, HOLY
LAND/GTM, MCC/GTM, OFM IMMAC/GTM,
WVRO/GTM; CARE/HDA, CHF/HDA,
FPP/HDA, FF/HDA, OFM IMMAC/HDA;
CARE/HTI, CRS/HTI, FPP/HTI, FREE
METH/HTI, DETELLIS/HTI, HFH/HTI,
OMI/HTI; ABC/MEX, AMFM/MEX,
BENBA/MEX, FREE METH/MEX; CRS/NIC,
FPP/NIC; CARE/PAN, CLARE/PAN;
CRS/SLV, FPP/SLV, FMU/SLV, OFM
IMMAC/SLV, SCF/SLV

## consultants

CARE/BLZ, CHF/BLZ, WINROCK/BLZ; INTL
EYE/BRB; CRWRC/CRI; INTL EYE/DMA;
CHF/DOM; CHF/GTM; CHF/HDA, INTL
EYE/HDA, VITA/HDA, WINROCK/HDA;
MSH/HTI; INTL EYE/LCA, SOROW/LCA;
DOM FR/MEX, SELF/MEX; INTL EYE/MISR;
TECHNO/NIC; INTL EYE/REG

## cooperatives

MFM/ATG; CARE/BLZ, CHF/BLZ,
MEDA/BLZ; CRS/CRI; AITEC/DOM,
CHF/DOM, EMC/DOM; CWS/GTM, FPP/GTM,
HFH/GTM, IIRR/GTM, MCC/GTM, MKNOL
FR/GTM, WN/GTM; ACDI/HDA, AFL-
CIO/HDA, CRS/HDA, CCF/HDA, CHF/HDA,
FPP/HDA, GLOBAL/HDA, HERMAN/HDA,
MORAV/HDA, SCF/HDA; CARE/HTI,
GLOBAL/HTI, MCC/HTI, OMI/HTI,
WN/HTI; ACDI/JAM; SOROW/LCA,
NOSR/LCA; BENBA/MEX, CCF/MEX,
CRS/MEX, EPISCO/MEX, MKNOL FR/MEX,
NINOS/MEX, SCF/MEX; CRS/NIC,
CWS/NIC, LWR/NIC, SCF/NIC,
TECHNO/NIC; NOSR/PAN; ABC/SLV,
TECHNO/SLV

## cottage industries

CRS/CRI; AITEC/DOM; CRS/GTM, HOLY
LAND/GTM; AMERICAS/HDA, MORAV/HDA,
SCF/HDA; ABC/HTI; SR MERCY/JAM,
PFPI/JAM; AITEC/MEX, CONCERN/MEX,
SCF/MEX; GMU/PAN

## counseling

SALVA/ATG; SALVA/BER; SALVA/BHS;
EPISCO/CRI, SALESIAN FR/CRI,
SALVA/CRI; SALVA/CUB; SSJR/DOM;
SALVA/GRD; SALVA/GTM; SALVA/GUY; DOM
SR/JAM, MFMS/JAM, SOJ/JAM;
SALVA/KNA; BENBA/MEX, CRS/MEX,

GCMC/MEX, MKNOL FR/MEX, SALESIAN
FR/MEX; EPISCO/NIC, WVRO/NIC;
SVB/PAN; SALVA/TTO; SALVA/VCT

## courses

BEREAN/BRB; AITEC/DOM, AFL-CIO/DOM;
PMCUS/GTM, LWR/GTM; CRS/HTI;
AITEC/MEX; AFL-CIO/PAN; AFL-CIO/REG

## crafts

PARTNERS/ATG; SALVA/CRI; AITEC/DOM;
MCC/GTM; MVP/HDA, MORAV/HDA,
SCF/HDA; CARE/HTI, FPP/HTI, MHF/HTI,
OMS/HTI; NOSR/LCA; ALA/MEX,
CLARE/MEX, CONCERN/MEX; AGNES/NIC;
NOSR/PAN; MCC/SLV

## credit/loans

MFM/ATG; MCC/BLZ, PADF/BLZ;
PADF/BRB; CARE/CRI, IIDI/CRI,
PADF/CRI; PADF/DMA, PFPI/DMA;
AITEC/DOM, CARE/DOM, CHF/DOM,
FHI/DOM, IIDI/DOM, MEDA/DOM,
PADF/DOM, PFPI/DOM, SCF/DOM;
ST PAT/GRD; CHF/GTM, CLARE/GTM,
FPP/GTM, HFH/GTM, IIRR/GTM;
CARE/HDA, CHF/HDA, CRS/HDA,
GLOBAL/HDA, FPP/HDA, IIDI/HDA,
LWR/HDA, PPF/HDA, SCF/HDA; CRS/HTI,
OMI/HTI; MCC/JAM, MEDA/JAM,
PADF/JAM, PFPI/JAM; PADF/LCA;
AITEC/MEX, CRS/MEX, FFSB/MEX,
HESPER/MEX; CRS/NIC, LWR/NIC,
MCC/NIC; CLARE/PAN, OEF/PAN; AFL-
CIO/REG; ABC/SLV, OEF/SLV, SCF/SLV

## crop improvement

MEDA/BLZ, WINROCK/BLZ; AITEC/CRI,
CARE/CRI, LWR/CRI; PLENTY/DOM;
HOPE/GTM, LWR/GTM; IRI/GUY,
AMERICAS/HDA, LWR/HDA, MORAV/HDA,
WN/HDA; MEDA/HTI, MHF/HTI, OMI/HTI,
WINROCK/HTI, WN/HTI; PLENTY/LCA;

BENBA/MEX, CLARE/MEX, HESPER/MEX,
WN/MEX; TECHNO/NIC; WINROCK/REG;
CRS/PAN; CRS/SLV

## crop processing

AITEC/CRI; PLENTY/DOM; IRI/GUY;
AMERICAS/HDA, PPF/HDA; MEDA/HTI,
WN/HTI; PLENTY/LCA

## dairies

AITEC/CRI; TECHNO/SLV

## dairy animals

WINROCK/CRI; SCF/DOM; WINROCK/REG

## dams

SCF/HDA

## demonstration projects

AITEC/CRI, CRS/CRI; SCF/DMA;
PLENTY/DOM; ST PAT/GRD; IRI/GUY;
LWR/HDA; PLENTY/LCA; SCF/MEX;
VITA/MSR; MFMS/NIC, SCF/NIC;
WINROCK/TTO

## dental clinics

CRS/DOM, FHI/DOM; COVENANT/GTM,
PMCUS/GTM; LWR/HDA; OMS/HTI,
UFMI/HTI; DOM FR/MEX, MMI/MEX;
EPISCO/NIC; AMIGOS/PAN

## dental equipment

PADF/CRI; MKNOL FR/GTM; JUDE/MEX,
MMI/MEX

## dentistry

PARTNERS/CRI; SSJR/DOM; GLOBAL/HDA;
FPP/HTI, FREE METH/HTI, RCLDS/HTI,
WESLEY/HTI; JUDE/MEX, MMI/MEX;
FPP/NIC; FPP/SLV

## dentists

DOCARE/HTI; DOCARE/MEX

## disabled

EPISCO/CRI, PARTNERS/CRI;
PARTNERS/DOM, ST PAT/GRD; CCF/HDA;
EPISCO/HTI, SALVA/HTI, UFMI/HTI;
GIA/JAM, MCC/JAM; CCF/MEX, MKNOL
FR/MEX, YMCA/MEX; GIA/PAN,
SALVA/PAN; PARTNERS/SLV

## disaster relief

CWS/BRB; WVRO/CRI; SCF/DOM;
COVENANT/GTM, CRS/GTM, MKNOL FR/GTM,
SBC/GTM, WVRO/GTM; MORAV/HDA,
SBC/HDA, WVRO/HDA; KELLER/HTI,
NAZ/HTI; CRS/MEX, CTWRC/MEX,
SBC/MEX, WVRO/MEX; ABC/NIC,
AGED/NIC, CRS/NIC, CWS/NIC, LWR/NIC,
MCC/NIC, SBC/NIC, WVRO/NIC; CWS/REG;
CRS/SLV, CRWRC/SLV, MCC/SLV,
WVRO/SLV

## disease treatment

HOPE/BLZ, PCI/BLZ; COVENANT/GTM,
MKNOL FR/GTM, PCI/GTM; INTL EYE/HDA,
MORAV/HDA; INTL EYE/HTI, DOCARE/HTI,
KELLER/HTI, MSH/HTI; SR MERCY/JAM;

INTL EYE/LCA; DOCARE/MEX, FFSB/MEX,
MMI/MEX, PCI/MEX; INTL EYE/MISR;
CRS/SLV


## displaced persons

CRS/GTM; MORAV/HDA; CRS/MEX, MKNOL
FR/MEX; AFSC/REG; CRS/SLV, MCC/SLV,
SCF/SLV


## doctors

MKNOL SR/GTM, PCI/GTM; INTL EYE/HDA,
HOPE/HDA, MORAV/HDA; DOCARE/HTI,
INTL EYE/HTI, DETELLIS/HTI;
HOPE/JAM, ICROS/JAM, SR MERCY/JAM;
INTL EYE/LCA; BMA/MEX, CONCERN/MEX,
DOCARE/MEX, MKNOL FR/MEX, MMI/MEX,
XAV/MEX; INTL EYE/MISR; PARTNERS/SLV


## draft animals

SCF/NIC


## economic research

MEDA/BLZ; PFBI/DMA, PPF/DMA;
PEPI/JAM


## education

BEREAN/BRB; BEREA/DMA; HOLY
LAND/DOM; HOLY LAND/GTM; WORLD
CON/HTI; YWCA/MEX; SBC/NIC; FMU/SLV,
OFM IMMAC/SLV


## educational exchange

PARTNERS/ATG; PARTNERS/CRI;
PARTNERS/DOM; AFL-CIO/HDA,
AMERICAS/HDA; PARTNERS/JAM; MCC/NIC,
WN/NIC; PARTNERS/SLV


## educational funding

CONS BAPT/BLZ, CONS BAPT/BLZ;
COMBO/CRI; EMC/DOM; FMU/GTM, MKNOL
FR/GTM, OFM IMMAC/GTM; AFL-CIO/HDA,
CRS/HDA, FP/HDA, FPP/HDA, MORAV/HDA,
OFM IMMAC/HDA; ABC/HTI, CGGC/HTI,
CRS/HTI, FPP/HTI, LIFELINE/HTI,
MCC/HTI, MHF/HTI, WRC/HTI;
BENBA/MEX, MKNOL FR/ MEX, NINOS/MEX,
ORT/MEX, SALESIAN FR/MEX; GMU/PAN


## electrification

GLOBAL/HDA


## elementary schools

OSF CLINTON/BHS, SALESIAN FR/BHS;
CONS BAPT/BLZ, CONS BAPT/BLZ,
CFC/BLZ, CFC/BLZ, GMU/BLZ, SHF/BLZ;
SALESIAN FR/CRI; BEREAN/DMA;
CFC/DOM, CRWM/DOM, EPISCO/DOM,
NAZ/DOM, REDEM FR/DOM, SCF/DOM,
SALESIAN FR/DOM; AMGO/GTM,
BENBC/GTM, CCF/GTM, CFC/GTM,
CNEC/GTM, COVENANT/GTM, CLARE/GTM,
MKNOL FR/GTM, MKNOL SR/GTM,
PMCUS/GTM, SALESIAN FR/GTM; CAM/HDA,
CCF/HDA, CFC/HDA, EPISCO/HDA,
SALESIAN FR/HDA, WGM/HDA; ABC/HTI,
AMGI/HTI, CGGC/HTI, CGH/HTI,
EPISCO/HTI, FREE METH/HTI, MC/HTI,
MHF/HTI, NAZ/HTI, OMS/HTI,
SALVA/HTI, SALESIAN FR/HTI,
WESLEY/HTI; BCS/JAM, DOM SR/JAM, OSF
ALLEGA/JAM, SR MERCY/JAM; CCF/MEX,
EPISCO/MEX, GCMC/MEX, SCF/MEX,
SALESIAN FR/MEX, SMSL/MEX; ABC/NIC,
AGNES/NIC, EPISCO/NIC, NBC/NIC,
SALESIAN FR/NIC,SBC/NIC; AMIGOS/PAN,
GMU/PAN, MSSD/PAN, SALVA/PAN,
SVB/PAN; ABC/SLV, SALESIAN FR/SLV,
WESLEY/SUR


## energy

AMERICAS/HDA; SBC/HTI; CARIB/REG

## environment

MFM/HDA, FFHF/HDA

## equipment

COMBO/CRI; ORT/DOM, PLENTY/DOM;
PADF/DMA; FUM/GTM, OFM IMMAC/GTM;
FF/HDA, FPP/HDA, OFM IMMAC/HDA,
WRC/HDA; SELF/MEX; FPP/NIC;
AFSC/REG, CARIB/REG; FMU/SLV, OFM
IMMAC/SLV

## evaluation

HOPE/BLZ, WINROCK/BLZ; INTL EYE/HDA,
WINROCK/HDA; INTL EYE/HTI, MSH/HTI;
CRS/MEX, CRS/MEX, MKNOL FR/MEX,
SELF/MEX; LAUBACH/PAN; OEF/SLV,
PARTNERS/SLV; WINROCK/TTO; WE/VCT

## extension agents

SCF/DOM; ACDI/GUY, IRI/GUY;
DGF/HDA,OEF/HDA; CUSA/HTI, MHF/HTI,
MSH/HTI; CRS/JAM; SCF/NIC

## extension courses

CONS BAPT/BLZ, CONS BAPT/BLZ;
WINROCK/JAM; GMU/PAN

## family planning

PCI/BLZ; EPISCO/CRI, LWR/CRI;
COVENANT/GTM, IIRR/GTM, PCI/GTM,
SALVA/GTM, WN/GTM; AMERICAS/HDA,
LWR/HDA, RCLDS/HDA, WN/HDA; ABC/HTI,
CARE/HTI, WN/HTI; AMFM/MEX, MKNOL
FR/MEX, PCI/MEX, PIACT/MEX, SCF/MEX,
SSJ/MEX; LWR/NIC

## farm machinery

MEDA/BLZ; AITEC/CRI; PPF/HDA;
SBC/HTI; CRS/MEX, SELF/MEX

## fertilizers

CARE/CRI; CLARE/GTA, HFH/GTM,
HOPE/GTM, IIRR/GTM, SALESIAN FR/GTM,
WN/GTM; IRI/GUY; SBC/HDA, SCF/HDA;
MC/HTI; FCI/MEX, SCF/MEX, WN/MEX;
SCF/NIC; WINROCK/TTO

## fish

CARE/BLZ; YMCA/CRI; SCF/DOM;
DETELLIS/HTI

## fish farming

CWS/DOM, EMC/DOM, HOLY LAND/DOM;
SCF/GTM, FPP/HDA; HGRMA/HDA;
MFM/FFHF/HDA; SCF/HDA; MHF/HTI;
EPISCO/MEX, FCI/MEX

## food/food products

PARTNERS/ATG; WINROCK/BLZ; CARE/CRI,
CWS/CRI; CPC/DOM, HOLY LAND/DOM,
PLENTY/DOM; WINROCK/HTI; CAM/GTM,
CFC/GTM; CAM/HDA, CFC/HDA, CRS/HDA,
CWS/HDA, FPP/HDA, MORAV/HDA,
WINROCK/HDA, WRC/HDA; DLMF/HTI,
KELLER/HTI, PLENTY/LCA; MSH/HTI;
AMFM/MEX, CFC/MEX, CRS/MEX,
FFSB/MEX, MMI/MEX, NINOS/MEX,
SSJ/MEX; CARE/NIC, MCC/NIC; CRS/PAN;
CAM/SLV, CRS/SLV, SCF/SLV; SALVA/SUR

## food distribution centers

SALVA/BRB; CRS/CRI, SBC/CRI;
SALVA/DMA; FHI/DOM; AMGI/GTM,
CRS/GTM, CRS/GTM, FHI/GTM, HOLY

LAND/GTM, ROTARY/GTM; SALVA/GUY;
CONCERN/HDA, CARE/HDA, CFC/HDA, HOLY
LAND/HDA, MCC/HDA, WRC/HDA;
SALVA/HTI, SALESIAN FR/HTI, SBC/HTI;
CRS/JAM, SALVA/JAM; CCF/MEX,
SBC/MEX; AMGI/NIC, CTS/NIC, LWR/NIC,
SBC/NIC; SALVA/PAN; MCC/SLV,
SBC/SLV; SALVA/SUR; SALVA/VCT

### food-for-work

CARE/CRI; SBC/GTM; SBC/HDA;
CARE/HTI, CRS/HTI; PLENTY/LCA;
CWS/NIC, SBC/NIC; CARE/PAN, CRS/PAN

### food preparation

SCF/DMA; PLENTY/DOM, SCF/DOM;
CONCERN/HDA; PLENTY/LCA;
CONCERN/MEX, SCF/MEX; VITA/MSR;
SCF/SLV

### food preservation

PLENTY/DOM, SCF/DOM; SCF/HDA;
PLENTY/LCA, NOSR/LCA; SCF/MEX;
CRS/PAN, NOSR/PAN; OEF/SLV

### food supply programs

CARE/CRI; CRS/DOM, CWS/DOM; ABC/HTI,
AMGI/HTI, CARE/HTI, CBV/HTI,
CRS/HTI, CWS/HTI, FREE METH/HTI,
FC/HTI, MCC/HTI, NAZ/HTI, OMI/HTI,
SALVA/HTI; SALVA/JAM; DOM FR/MEX,
FFSB/MEX, YMCA/MEX, CLARE/PAN,
CRS/PAN

### fruits

AITEC/CRI; SCF/HDA; MHF/HTI

### fuels

NAZ/HTI; VITA/MSR

### funding

PADF/BLZ; CRS/CRI, MEDIA/CRI;
YMCA/DOM; CNEC/GTM, CWS/GTM, FC/GTM,
SALESIAN FR/GTM; CRS/HDA, CWS/HDA;
AGED/NIC, LWR/NIC; AFL-CIO/REG;
CRS/SLV

### gardens

MFM/ATG; SCF/DMA; FHI/DOM, GMC/DOM,
PLENTY/DOM, SCF/DOM, VIISA/DOM;
CLARE/GTA; CARE/HTI, CGH/HTI;
FPP/GTM; AHIHH/HDA, CONS BAPT/HDA,
LWR/HDA, MFM/FFHF/HDA, SCF/HDA,
WN/HDA; CGGC/HTI, CRS/HTI, FREE
METH/HTI, SBC/HTI, WORLD CON/HTI;
CRS/JAM; PLENTY/LCA; AMFM/MEX,
FCI/MEX, MKNOL FR/MEX, SCF/MEX,
WN/MEX; AGED/NIC, CARE/NIC;
CARIB/REG; FPP/SLV, MCC/SLV,
SCF/SLV; FPP/SW

### geriatric centers

SALVA/CUB; AGED/HDA; EPISCO/HTI,
OMI/HTI, SALVA/HTI; CMHJ/MEX;
ABC/NIC, AGED/NIC, ABC/NIC, CRS/NIC;
SALVA/PAN; SALVA/SUR

### goats

CWS/DOM, EMC/DOM; FREE METH/HTI,
SBC/HTI, WORLD CON/HTI, WINROCK/HTI

### grains

AITEC/CRI; AMERICAS/HDA, WN/HDA;
HESPER/MEX, WN/MEX; TECHNO/SLV

## health care teams

CMS/DOM, CRS/DOM, CRWM/DOM, HOLY
LAND/DOM; FPP/GTM; HOPE/GTM, MKNOL
FR/GTM, PCI/GTM; GLOBAL/HDA,
MORAV/HDA; DOCARE/HTI, INTL EYE/HTI,
FREE METH/HTI, FPP/HTI,
LIFELINE/HTI, MSH/HTI, RCLDS/HTI,
WGM/HTI, WHM/HTI; AMFM/MEX, DL/MEX,
JUDE/MEX, MMI/MEX, ROTARY/MEX;
MCC/NIC

## health education

MCC/BLZ; ABC/MEX

## high schools

GMU/BHS, SALESIAN FR/BHS; GMU/BLZ,
SHF/BLZ; SALESIAN FR/CRI;
EPISCO/DOM, SALESIAN FR/DOM;
CNEC/GTM, EPISCO/GTM, MKNOL SR/GTM,
PMCUS/GTM, SALESIAN FR/GTM;
SALVA/GUY; CAM/HDA, CONF/HDA,
CONV/HDA, OSF PERP/HDA, MORAV/HDA,
OSF PERP/HDA, SALESIAN FR/HDA,
SSND/HDA, WGM/HDA; ABC/HTI,
AMGI/HTI, CGGC/HTI, EPISCO/HTI,
MHF/HTI, SALESIAN FR/HTI,
WESLEY/HTI; BCS/JAM, CG HOLI/JAM,
DOM SR/JAM, OSF ALLEGA/JAM, MCC/JAM,
MFMS/JAM, SR MERCY/JAM, SOJ/JAM;
CMHJ/MEX, GGMC/MEX, LMHJ/MEX,
SCF/MEX, SALESIAN FR/MEX, SMSL/MEX;
ABC/NIC, AGNES/NIC, SALESIAN FR/NIC;
GMU/PAN; ABC/SLV, PARTNERS/SLV,
SALESIAN FR/SLV

## hospitals

SOROW/BRB; PADF/CRI; SOROW/DMA;
MKNOL SR/GTM, PCI/GTM, PMCUS/GTM;
HOPE/HDA; ABC/HTI, EPISCO/HTI,
FC/HTI, MC/HTI, MCC/HTI, RHEMA/HTI,
UFMI/HTI, WGS/HTI; DOM SR/JAM,

SALVA/JAM, SR MERCY/JAM; SOROW/LCA;
CLARE/MEX, DOM FR/MEX, MMI/MEX;
ABC/NIC, LWR/NIC

## hostels

SALVA/BLZ; SALVA/BRB; EPISCO/CRI;
SALVA/DMA, SALVA/DMA; SALVA/GRD;
SALVA/GUY; WGM/HDA; SALVA/JAM;
BUENA/MEX, SALVA/MEX, YWCA/MEX;
SALVA/SUR; SALVA/TTO

## housing

CHF/BLZ; CHF/DOM, SCF/DOM; AMGI/GTM,
CHF/GTM, FMU/GTM, FPP/GTM, HFH/GTM,
MCC/GTM, MKNOL FR/GTM, OFM
IMMAC/GTM, SALVA/GTM, WN/GTM;
CARE/HDA, CHF/HDA, FF/HDA, FPP/HDA,
MCC/HDA, OFM IMMAC/HDA, SBC/HDA;
FPP/HTI, HFH/HTI; ABC/MEX,
BENBA/MEX; FPP/NIC, LWR/NIC,
MCC/NIC, SCF/NIC; ABC/SLV, CRS/SLV,
FMU/SLV, FPP/SLV, MCC/SLV, OFM
IMMAC/SLV

## hydroelectric energy

AMERICAS/HDA

## immunizations

AMIGO/DOM, CARE/DOM, VIISA/DOM;
IIRR/GTM; CARE/HDA, LWR/HDA,
MORAV/HDA, RCLOS/HDA,
SCF/HDA; MSH/HTI, ROTARY/HTI, WORLD
CON/HTI; MMI/MEX, SCF/MEX; SCF/SLV

## improved seed

CLARE/GTA; CLARE/MEX

## Income generation

MFM/ATG; PADF/BLZ, WINROCK/BLZ;
PADF/BRB; CRS/CRI, IIDI/CRI;
SCF/DMA; AITEC/DOM, CARE/DOM,
CRWM/DOM, IIDI/DOM, SCF/DOM;
LWR/GTM, MCC/GTM, WN/GTM; OEF/HDA,
DEF/HDA, IIDI/HDA, MFM/FFHE/HDA,
SCF/HDA, WN/HDA; WINROCK/HTI;
MCC/JAM, MEDA/JAM, PADF/JAM,
PEPI/JAM; SOROW/LCA; AITEC/MEX,
CONCERN/MEX, SCF/MEX; OEF/PAN;
SCF/SLV; WE/VCT

## Information systems

CRS/DOM; PFPI/DMA; PFPI/JAM

## Institution building

PADF/BLZ; PADF/BRB; YMCA/CRI,
WINROCK/CRI; PADF/DMA, PPF/DMA,
PFPI/DMA, PFPI/DMA; PADF/JAM,
PEPI/JAM; PADF/LCA; OEF/SLV;
WINROCK/TTO

## Integrated rural development

GLOBAL/BLZ, WINROCK/BLZ; CWS/BRB;
CRWRC/CRI, YMCA/CRI; PFPI/DMA,
PPF/DMA, PFPI/DMA, SCF/DMA;
CRWRC/DOM, CWS/DOM, SCF/DOM,
YMCA/DOM; BENBC/GTM, CCF/GTM,
CWS/GTM, EPISCO/GTM, CRWRC/GTM,
HOPE/GTM, IIRR/GTM, YMCA/GTM,
WVRO/GTM; AMERICAS/HDA, CCF/HDA,
CCF/HDA, CRWRC/HDA, DEP/HDA,
IVS/HDA, LWR/HDA, MFM/FFHF/HDA,
OEF/HDA, PPF/HDA, SCF/HDA, WN/HDA,
WVRO/HDA; CARE/HTI, CRS/HTI,
CRWRC/HTI, FPP/HTI, GLOBAL/HTI,
INSA/HTI, MCC/HTI, MHF/HTI, WORLD
CON/HTI, WN/HTI, VRO/HTI; CRS/JAM,
ROTARY/JAM; CCF/MEX, CTWRC/MEX, DOM
FR/MEX, HESPER/MEX, SCF/MEX,
SELF/MEX, WVRO/MEX; CARE/NIC,
LWR/NIC; MBMS/PAN; CWS/REG; ABC/SLV

## Intensive farming

AITEC/CRI; PLENTY/DOM, SCF/DOM,
VIISA/DOM; SCF/HDA; SBC/HTI;
PLENTY/LCA; SCF/MEX, WN/MEX; SCF/NIC

## Irrigation

AITEC/CRI; SCF/DOM; HOPE/GTM,
ICA/GTM, WVRO/GTM; IRI/GUY,
AMERICAS/HDA, PPF/HDA, SCF/HDA,
WN/HDA, WVRO/HDA; CARE/HTI, FPP/HTI,
MC/HTI, MHF/HTI, OMI/HTI, WORLD
CON/HTI; CARE/NIC

## Job placement

COVENANT/GTM; OEF/PAN

## Land reclamation

SBC/BLZ; IVS/HDA, WN/HDA; CLARE/PAN

## Land tenure

MCC/BLZ; HOLY LAND/DOM; MORAV/HDA;
LWR/NIC

## Language training

COVENANT/GTM; AMERICAS/HDA, SIL/HDA;
CC/MEX, FFSB/MEX, SIL/MEX, MKNOL
FR/MEX; AGNES/NIC

## Leadership training

SCF/DMA; MEDA/DOM, SCF/DOM; ST
PAT/GRD; CLARE/GTM, IIRR/GTM, MKNOL
FR/GTM, MKNOL SR/GTM; CONF/HDA,
CONV/HDA, FPP/HDA, HERMAN/HDA,
LWR/HDA, SCF/HDA, WN/HDA; CRS/HTI,

DMI/HTI, FPP/HTI, WN/HTI; FUM/JAM;
AFL-CIO/MEX, DOM FR/MEX,
LAUBACH/MEX, MKNOL FR/MEX,
NINOS/MEX, SCF/MEX, YWCA/MEX,
WN/MEX; AGNES/NIC, BICM/NIC,
CRS/NIC, CWS/NIC, EPISCO/NIC,
LWR/NIC, MCC/NIC, MFMS/NIC, WN/NIC;
CLARE/PAN, CRS/PAN, LLIC/PAN,
MBMS/PAN, WVRO/PAN; AFSC/REG

## legal services

CRS/CRI; CWS/GTM

## leprosariums

SR MERCY/JAM

## libraries

MEDIA/CRI; LWR/GTA; FPP/GTM,
IIRR/GTM; FPP/HTI, INTL EYE/HTI;
CC/MEX, MKNOL FR/MEX; AGNES/NIC

## linguistic studies

SIL/GTM; SIL/MEX; SIL/SUR

## literacy education

BEREAN/BRB; LWR/CRI, MEDIA/CRI;
CFC/DOM, ROTARY/DOM, WVRO/DOM;
PADF/DMA; CLARE/GTA, LWR/GTA;
CFC/GTM, CNEC/GTM, EASTMEN/GTM,
FPP/GTM, IIRR/GTM, MCC/GTM, MKNOL
FR/GTM, PMCUS/GTM, WVRO/GTM;
CCF/HDA, CEC/HDA, LWR/HDA, MVP/HDA,
SCF/HDA, SIL/HDA; FPP/HTI,
MEDIA/HTI, MHF/HTI, WVRO/HTI;
PARTNERS/JAM; CCF/MEX, CLARE/MEX,
CNEC/MEX, DOM FR/MEX, LAUBACH/MEX,
MKNOL FR/MEX, SIL/MEX; AGNES/NIC,
CWS/NIC, EPISCO/NIC, LWR/NIC,
MCC/NIC, MFMS/NIC, MKN/NIC;

CLARE/PAN, LLIC/PAN; OFEF/SLV,
WVRO/SLV; SIL/SUR

## maintenance/repair

ORT/DOM; CARE/HDA, PFPI/HDA,
VITA/HDA; SELF/MEX

## management training

PADF/BLZ; PADF/BRB; CARE/CRI,
CRWRC/CRI, IIDI/CRI; PFPI/DMA;
AITEC/DOM, IIDI/DOM, ORT/DOM,
WRC/DOM; MFM/FFHF/HDA, IIDI/HDA,
PPF/HDA, SCF/HDA, VITA/HDA;
CUSA/HTI, MEDA/HTI, MSH/HTI,
PPF/HTI, WINROCK/HTI; ST PAT/GRD;
ACDI/GUY; GIA/JAM, MEDA/JAM,
PADF/JAM, PFPI/JAM; PADF/LCA;
AITEC/MEX, CONCERN/MEX; OEF/SLV,
TECHNO/SLV; WINROCK/TTO

## marketing

WINROCK/BLZ; SALVA/CRI; PFPI/DMA,
PFPI/DMA; MEDA/DOM, PFPI/DOM;
PFPI/DMA; HOPE/GTM, SALVA/GTM;
ACDI/GUY; MORAV/HDA, PPF/HDA,
SCF/HDA, WINROCK/HDA; CARE/HTI,
CUSA/HTI, FPP/HTI, GLOBAL/HTI,
MEDA/HTI, NAZ/HTI, WN/HTI, WRC/HTI;
ACDI/JAM, PFPI/JAM; AITEC/MEX,
CONCERN/MEX; TECHNO/NIC; MBMS/PAN;
OEF/SLV, TECHNO/SLV

## mass media

BMU/BLZ; MEDIA/CRI; PPF/DMA,
PFPI/DMA; CRS/DOM, PARTNERS/DOM,
PFPI/DOM; CLARE/GTA; CRS/GTM,
PMCUS/GTM; CONF/HDA, CONV/HDA,
GLOBAL/HDA; MC/HTI, MEDIA/HTI,
OMS/HTI; AMFM/MEX, CAVE/MEX, MKNOL
FR/MEX; WRMF/PAN; CARIB/REG

## medical auxiliaries

PCI/BLZ; SSJR/DOM; MCC/GTM, MKNOL
FR/GTM, PCI/GTM, WVRO/GTM; INTL
EYE/HTI, MSH/HTI; HESPER/MEX,
PCI/MEX; CRS/NIC, LWR/NIC; AFSC/REG;
CRS/SLV

## medical education

HOPE/ATG, PARTNERS/ATG; HOPE/BLZ,
PCI/BLZ; INTL EYE/BRB; PADF/CRI;
INTL EYE/DMA; CARE/DOM, INTL
EYE/DOM, PARTNERS/DOM, SCF/DOM;
HOPE/GTM, MKNOL FR/GTM, PCI/GTM;
CONS BAPT/HDA, INTL EYE/HDA,
HOPE/HDA, IVS/HDA; DOCARE/HTI, INTL
EYE/HTI, LIFELINE/HTI, KELLER/HTI;
HOPE/JAM, ICROSS/JAM; HOPE/LCA, INTL
EYE/LCA; DOCARE/MEX, GCMC/MEX,
MMI/MEX, PCI/MEX; AGNES/NIC,
CRS/NIC; INTL EYE/REG; CRS/SLV,
MCC/SLV

## medical equipment

PADF/BLZ; INTL EYE/BRB; INTL
EYE/DMA, PADF/DMA; AFL-CIO/DOM, INTL
EYE/DOM, PADF/DOM; FC/GTM;
AMERICAS/HDA, CONCERN/HDA,
EPISCO/HDA, MORAV/HDA; INSA/HTI,
INTL EYE/HTI; ICROSS/JAM, PADF/JAM;
INTL EYE/LCA, PADF/LCA; FFSB/MEX,
JUDE/MEX, MMI/MEX, MKNOL FR/MEX;
CRS/NIC; CRS/PAN; CRS/SLV, FPP/SLV,
PARTNERS/SLV

## medical services

CARE/DOM, CMS/DOM, CWS/DOM,
GILDRED/DOM, HOLY LAND/DOM, MC/DOM,
WVRO/DOM; CLARE/GTA; FMV/GTM,
HOPE/GTM, OFM IMMAC/GTM, WVRO/GTM;
FF/HDA, HERMAN/HDA, INTL EYE/HDA,
MORAV/HDA, OFM IMMAC/HDA, WVRO/HDA;
CARE/HTI, CBV/HTI, CGGC/HTI,
DOCARE/HTI, INTL EYE/HTI, ICC/HTI,
MCC/HTI, MHF/HTI, MSH/HTI, NAZ/HTI,
RCLDS/HTI, SALVA/HTI, WVRO/HTI,
WRC/HTI; INTL EYE/LCA; BENBA/MEX,
CCF/MEX, DOCARE/MEX, FFSB/MEX,
GCMC/MEX, MMI/MEX, MKNOL FR/MEX,
PCI/MEX, WVRO/MEX, YMCA/MEX; INTL
EYE/MISR; CRS/NIC, FPP/NIC, MKN/NIC;
CG ANDER/PAN, GMU/PAN; FMU/SLV,
FPP/SLV, OFM IMMAC/SLV, SCF/SLV,
WVRO/SLV

## medical supplies

INTL EYE/BRB; CWS/CRI; INTL EYE/DMA,
PADF/DMA; AMIGO/DOM, CFC/DOM,
CRS/DOM, INTL EYE/DOM, SSJR/DOM;
LWR/GTA; CFC/GTM, HOPE/GTM, MKNOL
FR/GTM; CONCERN/HDA, CFC/HDA,
CONF/HDA, CONV/HDA, INTL EYE/HDA,
FC/HDA, MORAV/HDA, WRC/HDA;
DOCARE/HTI, DLMF/HTI, INTL EYE/HTI,
FC/HTI, ICC/HTI, LIFELINE/HTI,
INSA/HTI, MRH/HTI, MSH/HTI,
RCLDS/HTI; CRS/JAM, HOPE/JAM; INTL
EYE/LCA; AMFM/MEX, CFC/MEX, CRS/MEX,
DOCARE/MEX, FFSB/MEX, JUDE/MEX,
MMI/MEX, MKNOL FR/MEX, SBC/MEX;
AGNES/NIC, FPP/NIC, SBC/NIC;
CRS/PAN, GMU/PAN; CRS/SLV,
PARTNERS/SLV, SCF/SLV

## mental diseases

CCF/GTM; MCC/JAM

## mother/child programs

MFM/ATG; LECHE/BHS; PCI/BLZ;
LECHE/BRB; CARE/CRI, LECHE/CRI;
LECHE/CYM; LECHE/DMA; CFC/DOM,
FHI/DOM; LWR/GTA; CFC/GTM, HOPE/GTM,
LECHE/GTM, MCC/GTM, MKNOL FR/GTM,
MKNOL SR/GTM, PCI/GTM, SALVA/GTM;
WESLEY/GUY; AMERICAS/HDA,

CONCERN/HDA, CARE/HDA, CCF/HDA,
CFC/HDA, LECHE/HDA, MFM/FFHF/HDA,
SCF/HDA, SSF/HDA; CARE/HTI, CWS/HTI,
LECHE/HTI, MHF/HTI, OMI/HTI,
RHEMA/HTI, UFMI/HTI, WGM/HTI,
WN/HTI; PARTNERS/JAM; HSF/KNA;
AMFM/MEX, CONCERN/MEX, DOM FR/MEX,
LECHE/MEX, PCI/MEX, SSJ/MEX;
AGNES/NIC, CRS/NIC, MKN/NIC,
MFMS/NIC; CARE/PAN, CRS/PAN,
LECHE/PAN; CRS/SLV, LECHE/SLV,
MCC/SLV, SCF/SLV

## night schools

SVB/PAN; SALESIAN FR/SLV

## non-formal education

SCF/DMA;CRS/DOM, SCF/DOM; CLARE/GTA;
IIRR/GTM, MKNOL FR/GTM; SALVA/GUY;
CCF/HDA, SCF/HDA, SIL/HDA, WN/HDA;
CRS/HTI, INSA/HTI, SALVA/HTI,
WC/HTI, WN/HTI; NOSR/LCA; CCF/MEX,
LLI/MEX, NINOS/MEX, PIACT/MEX,
SCF/MEX, SIL/MEX, SSS/MEX, WN/MEX,
YMCA/MEX; AGNES/NIC, MONTFORT/NIC;
LLIC/PAN, NOSR/PAN; WE/VCT

## nurseries

AITEC/CRI; SCF/DOM; CARE/HTI,
MEDA/HTI

## nurses

HOPE/ATG; FOC/GTM; CONS BAPT/HDA,
HOPE/HDA, MORAV/HDA, SSF/HDA;
AWHS/HTI, DOCARE/HTI, WGM/HTI;
HOPE/JAM, SMUC/JAM; DOCARE/MEX,
FFSB/MEX, MMI/MEX, XAV/MEX;
ABCF/NIC, MKN/NIC

## nutrition education

MFM/ATG; CARE/BLZ, GMU/BLZ; CRS/CRI,
LWR/CRI; SCF/DMA; CFC/DOM, CRS/
DOM, CWS/DOM, PARTNERS/DOM,
PLENTY/DOM, SCF/DOM, SSJR/DOM,
VIISA/DOM, WVRO/DOM; CLARE/GTA,
CWS/GTA, LWR/GTA; CRS/GTM,
FMV/GTM, FPP/GTM, IIRR/GTM,
MCC/GTM, MKNOL FR/GTM, OFM
IMMAC/GTM, PCI/GTM, ROTAR/GTM,
SCF/GTM, WVRO/GTM, WN/GTM; AMERICAS/
HDA, CONCERN/HDA, CARE/HDA, CFC/HDA,
EASTERN MEN/HDA, FF/HDA, FPP/HDA,
LBF/HDA, LWR/HDA, MFM/FFHF/HDA,
OFM IMMAC/HDA, RCLDS/HDA,
ROTARY/HDA, SCF/HDA, SSND/HDA, WN/
HDA; CARE/HTI, CGGC/HTI, CWS/HTI,
FPP/HTI, GLO/HTI, GLOBAL/HTI, INSA/
HTI, KELLER/HTI, MHF/HTI, MSH/HTI,
NAZ/HTI, RCLDS/HTI, RHEMA/HTI,
SBC/HTI, WORLD CON/HTI, WN/HTI,
WVRO/HTI; CRS/JAM; PLENTY/LCA;
ABC/MEX, AMFM/MEX, BENSA/MEX,
CONCERN/MEX, CFC/MEX, LAUBACH/MEX,
SCF/MEX, WN/MEX; CARE/NIC,
SBC/NIC; CLARE/PAN, CRS/PAN, GMU/
PAN; CARIB/REG; CRS/SLV, FMU/SLV,
OFM IMMAC/SLV, SCF/SLV, WVRO/SLV

## on-the-job training

ORT/DOM; COVENANT/GTM; PFPI/JAM,
WINROCK/JAM; CONCERN/MEX, SELF/MEX;
WINROCK/TTO

## ophthalmology

INTL EYE/HDA; INTL EYE/HTI; MCC/JAM;
INTL EYE/LCA; MMI/MEX

## orphanages

SALVA/BER; CFC/DOM,
COMPASSION/DOM, HLCM/DOM, SALESIAN
FR/DOM, VIISA/DOM; CFC/GTM,
FC/GTM, HOLY LAND/GTM; CCF/HDA,

EPISCO/HDA, FC/HDA; CBV/HTI,
COMPASSION/HTI, FC/HTI, SALVA/HTI,
UFMI/HTI; SALVA/JAM; CCF/MEX,
CMHJ/MEX, FFSB/MEX, HOGAR/MEX,
SALVA/MEX; LWR/NIC; SALA/PAN;
CAM/SLV, ABC/SLV, CRS/SLV,
SALVA/SUR

CRS/MEX, PCI/MEX, SCF/MEX, VITA/
MEX; CRS/NIC, CWS/NIC, FPP/NIC,
LWR/NIC; CLARE/PAN, MBMS/PAN;
FPP/SLV

## orchards

AITEC/CRI, LWR/CRI; SCF/GTM

## pest control

SCF/DOM; WN/GTM; AMERICAS/HDA,
WN/HDA; FCI/MEX

## pl 480

CARE/CRI; CARE/DOM, CRS/DOM;
CRS/GTM; CARE/HDA, CRS/HDA;
CARE/HTI, CRS/HTI; CARE/PAN,
CRS/PAN; CRS/SLV

## policy and planning

HOPE/BLZ; PFPI/DMA, PPF/DMA;
PFPI/DOM; CWS/HDA, IVS/HDA,
WINROCK/HDA; CWS/HTI, MSH/HTI;
PFPI/JAM; MKNOL FR/MEX

## potable water

HOPE/BLZ, PCI/BLZ; CARE/CRI, LWR/
CRI; MHF/DOM, SCF/DOM; CWS/GTA;
CRS/GTM, FPP/GTM, HOPE/GTM, IIRR/
GTM, MKNOL FR/GTM, PCI/GTM, WVRO/
GTM; AMIGO/HDA, CARE/HDA, FPP/HDA,
IVS/HDA, LWR/HDA, MCC/HDA, SCF/
HDA, VITA/HDA, WVRO/HDA; CARE/HTI,
CGGC/HTI, CRS/HTI, FPP/HTI,
DETELLIS/HTI, MHF/HTI, OMI/HTI,
OMS/HTI, SBC/HTI, UFMI/HTI,
WVRO/HTI; BENBA/MEX, CLARE/MEX,

## poultry

WINROCK/CRI; PARTNERS/DOM, SCF/DOM;
CLARE/GTA; SCF/HDA; CGGC/HTI,
CUSA/HTI, FARMS/HTI, MHF/HTI,
NAZ/HTI, SBC/HTI, WORLD CON/HTI;
MEDA/JAM; MKNOL FR/MEX, SCF/MEX;
SCF/SLV

## preschool programs

SALVA/ATG; SALVA/BLZ; SALVA/BRB;
EPISCO/CRI, SALVA/CRI; SALVA/DMA;
CFC/DOM; AMGI/GTM, CAM/GTM, CFC/
GTM, COVENANT/GTM, SALVA/GTM;
SALVA/GUY; CFC/HDA; FPP/HTI,
SALESIAN FR/HTI; OSF ALLEGA/JAM,
SALVA/JAM, SR MERCY/JAM; HSF/KNA;
SALVA/MEX, YMCA/MEX; AGNES/NIC,
AMGI/NIC; SALVA/PAN; SALVA/TTO

## preventive medicine

PCI/BLZ; LWR/CRI; CFC/DOM, CFC/
DOM, CRS/DOM, CRWM/DOM, EPISCO/
DOM, SCF/DOM; ST PAT/GRD; LWR/
GTA; CFC/GTM, COVENANT/GTM, IIRR/
GTM, MKNOL FR/GTM, PCI/GTM, PMCUS/
GTM; CONCERN/HDA, CFC/HDA, MORAV/
HDA, SCF/HDA; CRS/HTI, DOCARE/HTI,
INSA/HTI, MHF/HTI, MSH/HTI,
OMI/HTI, RCLDS/HTI, WORLD CON/HTI,
WVRO/HTI; INTL EYE/LCA; CFC/MEX,
DOCARE/MEX, FFSB/MEX, HESPER/MEX,
MMI/MEX, MKNOL FR/MEX, PCI/MEX,
SALVA/MEX; AGNES/NIC, CRWRC/NIC;
MBMS/PAN

## public administration

VITA/HDA

## public health education

PCI/BLZ; CRS/CRI; SCF/DOM,
VIISA/DOM; CLARE/GTA; CFC/GTM,
FPP/GTM, PCI/GTM; CONCERN/HDA,
CFC/HDA, LECHE/HDA, LWR/HDA,
MFM/FFHF/HDA, MORAV/HDA; INSA/
HTI, MSH/HTI; AMFM/MEX, LECHE/MEX,
LAUBACH/MEX, MKNOL FR/MEX, PCI/MEX;
CLARE/PAN, CRS/PAN, MBMS/PAN;
AFSC/REG; FPP/SLV, LECHE/SLV,
SCF/SLV

## rabbits

PARTNERS/CRI; SCF/DOM; HOPE/GTM;
MFM/FFHF/HDA; CGGC/HTI, GLOBAL/HTI,
MHF/HTI, SBC/HTI

## range animals

WINROCK/BLZ; FREE METH/HTI;
WINROCK/REG; TECHNO/SLV; WINROCK/TTO

## reforestation

AITEC/CRI, AMIGO/CRI; PADF/DOM,
SCF/DOM, VIISA/DOM; CLARE/GTA;
FPP/GTM, HOPE/GTM; CARE/HDA,
SCF/HDA; ABC/HTI, CARE/HTI, FREE
METH/HTI, GLOBAL/HTI, MCC/HTI, MHF/
HTI, OMI/HTI, OMS/HTI, SBC/HTI,
WORLD CON/HTI, WN/HTI, WVRO/HTI;
CLARE/MEX, MKNOL FR/MEX, WN/MEX

## refugees

CFC/BLZ; CRS/CRI; HOLY LAND/DOM;
CFC/GTM, MCC/GTM, MKNOL FR/GTM;
CARE/HDA, CFC/HDA, CRS/HDA,

CRWRC/HDA, HOLY LAND/HDA, MAF/HDA,
MCC/HDA, MORAV/HDA, WRC/HDA;
ABC/MEX, AFSC/MEX, CRS/MEX,
CRWRC/MEX, MKNOL FR/MEX, SBC/MEX;
CRS/NIC, MCC/NIC; AFSC/REG;
ABC/SLV, CAM/SLV, CRWRC/SLV,
SBC/SLV

## rehabilitation

SALVA/BHS; SALVA/CRF; EPISCO/CRI,
PARTNERS/CRI, WVRO/CRI;
PARTNERS/DOM, VIISA/DOM; CCF/GTM,
SALVA/GTM; SALVA/GUY; CCF/HDA,
EASTERN MEN/HDA, MVP/HDA, WRC/
HDA; INTL EYE/HTI; GIA/JAM, SALVA/
JAM; HESPER/MEX, SALVA/MEX; WVRO/
NIC; GIA/PAN, SALVA/PAN; CAM/SLV,
PARTNERS/SLV; SALVA/SUR

## research/field studies

HOPE/BLZ, WINROCK/BLZ; CRS/CRI,
YMCA/CRI, WINROCK/CRI; HOPE/GTM;
MORAV/HDA; WINROCK/TTO

## resettlement

EAST MEN/BLZ, MCC/BLZ; SALVA/CRE;
AMGI/GTM, HOLY LAND/GTM, SALVA/
GTM; MCC/HDA, MORAV/HDA, WRC/HDA;
CAM/SLV, CRWRC/SLV, MCC/SLV

## roads

FPP/GTM; MC/HTI, OMS/HTI; SBC/HDA;
LWR/NIC

## sanitation

HOPE/ATG, PARTNERS/ATG; HOPE/BLZ,
PCI/BLZ; LWR/CRI; AMIGO/DOM, SCF/
DOM; FPP/GTM, IIRR/GTM, MCC/GTM,
MKNOL FR/GTM, WVRO/GTM; AMIGO/HDA,
CONCERN/HDA, CARE/HDA, FPP/HDA,

IVS/HDA, MCC/HDA, MFM/FFHF/HDA, MORAV/HDA, RCLDS/HDA, WRC/HDA, WVRO/HDA; CGGC/HTI, CRS/HTI, FPP/HTI, OMS/HTI; HOPE/LCA; AMIGO/MEX, AMFM/MEX, CLARE/MEX, HESPER/MEX, WVRO/MEX; AGNES/NIC; MBMS/PAN; FPP/SLV

PADF/JAM, WINROCK/JAM; PADF/LCA; CCF/MEX, DOM FR/MEX, LECHE/MEX, LAUBACH/MEX, MKNOL FR/MEX, NINOS/MEX, SCF/MEX, SELF HELP/MEX; AGED/NIC, SCF/NIC; CARE/PAN, LECHE/PAN, MBMS/PAN; AFSC/REG; LECHE/SLV, MCC/SLV, OEF/SLV

## savings

AFL-CIO/DOM

## seminars

GMU/BLZ; BEREAN/BRB; AFL-CIO/DOM, PARTNERS/DOM; SCF/HDA; MEDIA/HTI, WRC/HTI; GIA/JAM; AFL-CIO/MEX, MKNOL FR/MEX, SCF/MEX; SCF/NIC; PARTNERS/SLV

## schools

CARE/BLZ, HOPE/BLZ; COMPASSION/DOM; FPP/GTM; FPP/HDA; CARE/HTI, COMPASSION/HTI, FPP/HTI, DETELLIS/HTI; RCLDS/HTI, WORLD CON/HTI; SDW/MEX; FPP/NIC; CARE/PAN; FPP/SLV, SCF/SLV

## small enterprises

PADF/BLZ; CRS/CRI, IIDI/CRI; PFPI/DMA, PPF/DMA, PFPI/DMA, SCF/DMA; AITEC/DOM, IIDI/DOM, PFPI/DOM, SCF/DOM; PADF/DMA; HOLY LAND/GTM; AMERICAS/HDA, AMERICAS/HDA, CRS/HDA, DEF/HDA, FPP/HDA, IIDI/HDA, IVS/HDA, LWR/HDA, MORAV/HDA, MVP/HDA, OEF/HDA, PPF/HDA, SCF/HDA, VITA/HDA; CARE/HTI, INTL EYE/HTI; PPF/HTI; GIA/JAM, MCC/JAM, MEDA/JAM, PADF/JAM, PARTNERS/JAM, PFPI/JAM; PADF/LCA; AITEC/MEX, CONCERN/MEX, CRS/MEX, SCF/MEX; CRS/NIC, TECHNO/NIC; GIA/PAN, OEF/PAN; CARIB/REG; SCF/SLV, TECHNO/SLV

## seeds

CARE/CRI, CWS/CRI, WORLD CON/CRI; PLENTY/DOM; HOPE/GTM, IIRR/GTM, SALESIAN FR/GTM; CAM/HDA, CWS/HDA, MORAV/HDA, SBC/HDA, WRC/HDA; CARE/HTI, MCC/HTI; PLENTY/LCA; SCF/MEX; CARE/PAN

## self-help programs

LECHE/BHS; PADF/BLZ; LECHE/BRB; CARE/CRI, CRWRC/CRI, LECHE/CRI, YMCA/CRI; LECHE/CYM; CRWRC/DMA, LECHE/DMA, SCF/DMA; CRWRC/DOM, FHI/DOM, SCF/DOM, SSJR/DOM, VIISA/DOM; ST PAT/GRD; CRWRC/GTM, FHI/GTM, HOLY LAND/GTM, IIRR/GTM, LECHE/GTM; AMERICAS/HDA, CCF/HDA, CONF/HDA, CONV/HDA, CRS/HDA, FPP/HDA, HERMAN/HDA, LECHE/HDA, MFM/FFHF/HDA, MORAV/HDA, MVP/HDA, SCF/HDA, SR MERCY/HDA; CGH/HTI, FREE METH/HTI, FPP/HTI, INSA/HTI, LECHE/HTI, RHEMA/HTI, WINROCK/HTI;

## social services

CRS/MEX

## social welfare

FUM/BLZ; CMBMC/CRI; FMV/GTM, OFM IMMAC/GTM; OFM IMMAC/HDA, SSF/HDA; CNEC/MEX; OFM IMMAC/SLV

## solar energy

MFM/ATG; AITEC/CRI; PPF/HDA;
AFSC/MEX

## sponsorships

WVRO/BLZ; WVRO/CRI;
COMPASSION/DOM, CFC/DOM, EMC/DOM,
FREE METH/DOM, HOLY LAND/DOM,
SCF/DOM; CCF/GTM, CFC/GTM, HLCM/GTM,
WVRO/GTM; CCF/HDA, CFC/HDA,
HOLY LAND/HDA, SCF/HDA, WVRO/HDA;
COMPASSION/HTI, INTL EYE/HTI, FREE
METH/HTI, LIFELINE/HTI, WVRO/HTI;
CCF/MEX, FREE METH/MEX, SCF/MEX,
WVRO/MEX; LWR/NIC; SCF/SLV, WVRO/SLV

## storage

MEDA/BLZ; IRI/GUY; CARE/HDA,
CRS/HDA, GLOBAL/HDA, LWR/HDA,
MFM/FFHF/HDA, MORAV/HDA; CWS/HTI,
MC/HTI, WN/HTI, WVRO/HTI; SCF/NIC

## surveys

INTL EYE/HTI, KELLER/HTI; INTL
EYE/LCA; INTL EYE/MSR

## swine

WINROCK/CRI; MHF/DOM; TECHNO/PAN

## teacher training

CARE/BLZ; MEDIA/CRI; BEREAN/DMA;
CLARE/GTA; MKNOL SR/GTM; FPP/HTI,
MEDIA/HTI; MCC/JAM; AGNES/NIC,
LWR/NIC

## teachers

BEREAN/DMA; UFMI/DOM; SSF/HDA;
MC/HTI, MCC/HTI, SALESIAN FR/HTI;
MKNOL FR/MEX, MKNOL SR/MEX; MSSD/PAN

## teaching materials

CONS BAPT/BLZ; MEDIA/CRI, PADF/CRI;
BEREAN/DMA; LWR/GTA; FPP/GTM;
FPP/HDA, SIL/HDA; INSA/HTI, MCC/
HTI, MSH/HTI; WINROCK/JAM;
MKNOL FR/MEX, PIACT/MEX, SIL/MEX;
VITA/MSR; AGNES/NIC; LLIC/PAN;
SCF/SLV; SIL/SUR

## toilet facilities

LWR/CRI; FPP/GTM, HFH/GTM, MKNOL
FR/GTM; FPPHDA, LWR/HDA; FPP/HTI,
MHF/HTI, OMS/HTI; AMFM/MEX,
SCF/MEX; LWR/NIC; CAM/SLV, FPP/
SLV, SCF/SLV

## tools

CARE/BLZ; PADF/BRB; PADF/CRI;
PADF/DMA; ORT/DOM; WN/GTM; CARE/HDA,
FC/HDA, MORAV/HDA, WN/HDA, WRC/HDA;
MHF/HTI, WN/HTI; PADF/JAM; PADF/LCA;
OEF/SLV

## traditional medicine

MKNOL FR/GTM; MMI/MEX; MBMS/PAN

## translation programs

CRWRC/CRI; CLARE/GTA; CRWRC/GTM,
PMCUS/GTM; WESLEY/GUY; SIL/MEX

## transportation

MORAV/HDA; CRS/NIC

## tribal peoples

CRS/MEX, ROTARY/MEX; CG ANDER/PAN

## unions

AFL-CIO/DOM; AFL-CIO/HDA; AFL-CIO/MEX; AFL-CIO/PAN; AFL-CIO/REG

## urban development

PPF/DMA, PFPI/DMA; PFPI/DOM;
SCF/HDA; PFPI/JAM; CCF/MEX,
MKNOL/MEX; LWR/NIC

## vegetables

AITEC/CRI; SCF/DMA; PARTNERS/DOM,
SCF/DOM; VIISA/DOM; AMERICAS/HDA;
WN/HDA; FPP/HTI, MHF/HTI;
PLENTY/LCA; SCF/MEX; TECHNO/PAN;
CARIB/REG

## vehicles

INTL EYE/DOM; MAF/GTM; INTL EYE/HDA;
MAF/HDA; INTL EYE/LCA; MAF/MEX;
OEF/PAN; OEF/SLV/; MAF/SUR

## veterinary services

AMIGO/CRI, WORLD CON/CRI; HOPE/GTM;
AMIGO/HDA; W/HTI; FCI/MEX;
WINROCK/TTO

## viral/bacterial diseases

PCI/BLZ; HOPE/GTM, PCI/GTM; ICC/HTI,
SALVA/HTI; MMI/MEX, PCI/MEX

## vocational education

CARE/BLZ, GLOBAL/BLZ; PADF/BRB;
CRS/CRI, PADF/CRI, PARTNERS/CRI,
SALESIAN FR/CRI; CFC/DOM, FHI/
DOM, PADF/DOM, PLENTY/DOM, REDEM
FR/DOM, ROTARY/DOM, SALESIAN FR/DOM,
SCF/DOM; CWS/GTA; AMGI/GTM,
CFC/GTM, COVENANT/GTM, FHI/GTM,
FPP/GTM, IIRR/GTM, SALVA/GTM,
WVRO/GTM; AMERICAS/HDA, CFC/HDA,
HERMAN/HDA, LBF/HDA, SSND/HDA,
WGM/HDA, WVRO/HDA; AMGI/HTI,
CGGC/HTI, CRS/HTI, KELLER/HTI,
NAZ/HTI, OMS/HTI, SALVA/HTI,
WESLEY/HTI, WRC/HTI, WVRO/HTI;
MCC/JAM, PFPI/JAM, SR MERCY/JAM,
WINROCK/JAM; PADF/LCA, SOROW/LCA;
BETH/MEX, CCF/MEX, CLARE/MEX,
MKNOL FR/MEX, ORT/MEX, SALESIAN FR/
MEX; ABC/NIC, AGNES/NIC, CARE/NIC,
FPP/NIC, SCF/NIC, TECHNO/NIC;
CRS/PAN, GIA/PAN, MBMS/PAN,
OEF/PAN, SVB/PAN; FPP/SLV,
SALESIAN FR/SLV, WVRO/SLV

## volunteers

AMIGO/CRI; INTL EYE/DOM, FHI/DOM,
VIISA/DOM; AMIGO/HDA, MORAV/HDA;
INTL EYE/LCA; AMIGO/MEX, MMI/MEX,
NINOS/MEX; INTL EYE/MSR; AMIGOS/PAN

## water

CARE/CRI; AMERICAS/HDA, IVS/HDA,
SCF/HDA; COMPASSION/HTI, CWS/HTI,
WN/HTI, WORLD CON/HTI; SCF/MEX;
WVRO/SLV

## water transportation

MORAV/HDA; PADF/JAM

## wells

CMBMC/CRI; BETH/DOM; COMPASSION/HTI,
CRS/HTI, CWS/HTI, FREE METH/HTI,
NAZ/HTI, SBC/HTI, WESLEY/HTI;
AGNES/NIC

## wind energy

SCF/HDA, VITA/HDA; SBC/HTI;
VITA/MEX, WVRO/MEX

## women

PARTNERS/ATG; CARE/DOM,
PARTNERS/DOM, SCF/DOM; ST PAT/GRD;
LWR/GTA; CRS/HDA, HERMAN/HDA;
CARE/HTI, CRS/HTI, DETELLIS/HTI,
MCC/HTI, RCLDS/HTI, SALVA/HTI;
HSF/KNA; LAUBACH/MEX, YWCA/MEX;
LWR/NIC; DEF/SLV, SCF/SLV

## women's education

LECHE/BHS; LECHE/BRB; CMBMC/CRI,
LECHE/CRI; LECHE/CYM; LECHE/DMA;
IIRR/GTM, LECHE/GTM, MCC/GTM;
LECHE/HDA, SCF/HDA; LECHE/HTI;
LECHE/MEX, MKNOL FR/MEX, OEF/PAN,
LECHE/PAN; LECHE/SLV

## youth

GMU/BHS, SALESIAN FR/BHS; FUM/BLZ,
GMU/BLZ; EPISCO/CRI, SALESIAN FR/
CRI; SCF/DMA; CFC/DOM, SCF/DOM;
EPISCO/GTA, LWR/GTA; CFC/GTM,
SALESIAN FR/GTM; SALVA/GUY; CCF/

HDA, CFC/HDA, FC/HDA, SALESIAN FR/
HDA; CGGC/HTI; FUM/JAM; SOROW/LCA,
NOSR/LCA; BENBA/MEX, CCF/MEX,
BUENA/MEX, LAUBACH/MEX, MMI/MEX,
NINOS/MEX, SCF/MEX, SALESIAN FR/
MEX; AGNES/NIC, LWR/NIC, SALESIAN
FR/NIC; NOSR/PAN, SALVA/PAN, SVB/
PAN, SALESIAN FR/SLV, SCF/SLV

## COMMUNICATIONS

CARR; CMMB; OXFAM; PCC/DF; PRB

## COMMUNITY DEVELOPMENT

APHA; CODEL; COMPASSION;
CROSSROADS; EDC; ENVIRN;
FARALL; FORD; 4-H; FTW;
HEIFER; IADS; IRF; LCA; LCMS;
LIAISON; MAP; MORAV; OUTREACH;
OXFAM; PACT; POP COUNCIL; SBC;
SISTER CITIES; UCBWM; UMCOR;
UNITARIAN; UMC; VDC; WORLD CON

## CONSTRUCTION & HOUSING

ADVENTIST; BWA; CROSSROADS;
FARALL; LCMS; LOAN; ROAD; SBC;
SISTER CITIES; SOS; UNIT METH

## COOPERATIVE & CREDIT/LOANS

ADVENTIST; IPAS; LOAN; OXFAM;
PACT; UMC; VDC

## EDUCATION

ADVENTIST; AFS; BROTHER; BWA;
CARNEGIE; CHILD; CIPYLSW;
CODEL; COMPASSION; DARIEN;
EISEN; ENVIRN; FARALL; FFHM;
FORD; 4-H; FPIA; FREE; ICRW;
INTER-AMERICAN; ITL BOOK;
KELLOG; LCA; LIONS; MORAV;
MRH; NATURE; NCCW; ORTHO;
OXFAM; PACT; PRB; PWF; ROAD;
SBC; SISTER CITIES; STELSON;
UCBWM; UMC; US YC

## ENTERPRISE DEVELOPMENT & MANAGEMENT

ATI; ARTISAN; CARNEGIE; FORD;
FPIA; FTW; IESC; LIONS; MSH;
PACT; ROAD; SBC; TRICKLE UP;
UCBWM; UMC; WORLD CON

## FOOD PRODUCTION & AGRICULTURE

APROVECHO; BWA; BROTHER;
CHILD; CODEL; CRS; DLMF;
ENVIRN; FARALL; FORD; HEIFER;
IADS; KELLOG; LCA; LIFE;
LIONS; MORAV; MRH; OXFAM;
PACT; ROCKEFELLER; SBC; UCBWM;
UMCOR; UMC; VITA; WORLD CON

## MATERIAL AID

ADFS; ADVENTIST; AIAA;
BROTHER; CALIF; CARR; CHILD;
CMMB; DARIEN; DLMF; DRI; FFHM;
FPIA; HEIFER; IMA; IPAS; ITL
ADOP; INTER-AID; ITL BOOK;
LEPROSY; LCMS; MAP; MBF;
MIDWEST; MRH; NCCW; PCC/DF;
RED CROSS; SANGER; SBC; SEE;
STELSON; UMC; WMR; WOI

## MEDICINE & PUBLIC HEALTH

ADFS; ADVENTIST; ALA; AMIGOS;
AMRC; APHA; AVS; BROTHER; BWA;
CARR; CDPA; CHILD; CHS; CMMB;
CODEL; COMPASSION; CROSSROADS;
DLMF; DRI; FARALL; FFHM; FAM
HEALTH; IMA; INTPLAST; IPAS;
ITL ADOP; INTER-AID; KELLOG;
LCA; LEPROSY; LIONS; MAP; MBF;
MIDWEST; MRH; MSH; NCIH;
ORTHO; OXFAM; PATHFINDER; PWF;
RED CROSS; ROCKEFELLER;
SANGER; SBC; SEE; SISTER
CITIES; STELSON; UCBWM;
UNITARIAN; UNIT MEHT; VOSH;
WMR

## NUTRITION

APHA; BROTHER; CODEL; EDC;
FARALL; LIFE; SBC; WORLD CON


## POPULATION & FAMILY SERVICES

AIAA; APHA; AVS; CBGB; CDPA;
EDC; FAM HEALTH; FORD; FPIA;
IPAS; NCCW; PATHFINDER;
PCC/DF; POP COUNCIL; POP INST;
PRB; ROCKEFELLER; SANGER; SBC;
UNITARIAN; UNIT METH


## SOCIAL WELFARE

ADVENTIST; AGED; AMRC;
CIPYLSW; COMPASSION; FFHM;
CULTUR; DLMF; FORD; ITL ADOP;
INTER-AID; NCCW; OXFAM; PWF;
RED CROSS; SBC; SOS; UMCOR;
UMC; WORLD CON

ORGANIZATION INDEX

# APPENDIX

## CENTRAL AMERICA/CARIBBEAN
## -- COUNTRY CODES --

ANGUILLA..............ANA

ANTIGUA...............ATG

BAHAMAS...............BHS

BARBADOS..............BRB

BELIZE................BLZ

BERMUDA...............BER

CAYMAN ISLANDS........CYM

COSTA RICA............CRS

CUBA..................CUB

DOMINICA..............DMA

DOMINICAN REPUBLIC....DOM

EL SALVADOR...........SLV

GRENADA...............GRD

GUADELOUPE............GUD

GUATEMALA.............GTM

GUYANA................GUY

HAITI.................HTI

HONDURAS..............HDA

JAMAICA...............JAM

MARTINIQUE............MTQ

MEXICO................MEX

MONTSERRAT............MSR

NETHERLANDS ANTILLES...ANT

NICARAGUA.............NIC

PANAMA................PAN

ST. KITTS - NEVIS......KNA

ST. LUCIA.............LCA

ST. MARTIN............MAR

ST. VINCENT AND THE
GRENADINES.......VCT/GRD

SURINAME..............SUR

TRINIDAD AND TOBAGO....TTO

TURKS AND CAICOS
ISLANDS..............TCA

REGIONAL .............REG